Functionalism

Theory and Practice in International Relations

Edited by A J R Groom and Paul Taylor

CRANE, RUSSAK & COMPANY, INC.
NEW YORK

Published in the United States by
Crane, Russak & Company, Inc.
347 Madison Avenue,
New York, N.Y. 10017

ISBN 0-8448-0305-7
Library of Congress Catalog Number 73-93664

First published 1975

Printed and bound in Great Britain

Contents

Preface

The idea of this book sprang out of the concern of the editors as teachers of international relations with a special interest in international organisation. Its purpose is two-fold—to provide students with a comprehensive survey of an important approach to the problems and organisation of world society and to provide an assessment of the current state of the theory, both conceptually and empirically. We have succeeded in bringing together a team of contributors with a common interest in functionalism but with a variety of viewpoints regarding its merits as a description and a prescription for world society.

In planning this volume we had the great advantage of frequent consultation with Professor David Mitrany to whom we owe a considerable debt. We also had the benefit of a seminar with contributors to discuss the framework of the volume and paper summaries. The contributions to the volume are all original (or substantially revised) articles. We wish to thank all our contributors—our team is a mixture of senior scholars, some with experience as practitioners, and younger research workers and teachers in institutes and universities in several countries; and we would also like to thank Miss Michèle Bole for her invaluable secretarial assistance.

Introduction: Functionalism and International Relations
Paul Taylor and A J Groom

This volume is about a particular approach to the understanding and treatment of the central problems of international relations. Functionalism is concerned with the ways of creating, in the words of Professor David Mitrany, its chief architect, a working peace system. It involves a diagnosis of the problems of disorder in international society, and a prescription for ways of shaping a better world. The following essays are intended to summarise the present status of the theory.

The editors have not attempted to advertise functionalism as the way which should be preferred above all others. This would have been a presumptuous undertaking. They have rather started with the observation that functionalism is studied wherever the work of international organisation and problems of international order are considered in universities and institutes of higher learning throughout the world, and it is frequently reflected in the speeches and writings of those who work in international organisations. It is, in other words, an established feature of the literature and practice of international relations and a force to be reckoned with. The essays in this volume reflect this strength in that they constitute a comprehensive theoretical and empirical examination: they are intended to constitute an assessment of the theory, rather than merely a flattering portrayal.

It would also be inappropriate for the editors to take upon themselves in this introduction the task of saying exactly what functionalism is, since such definitions are, in essence, nominal. In any case, functionalism is an approach rather than a tightly-knit theory. Each of the contributors has given a summary of those aspects of the theory with which he, or she, is particularly concerned. There is agreement about, though not necessarily support for, the central principles which are involved in the theory: the nation-state, while still successfully fulfilling some functions, is thought to promote values in high politics and national prestige at the expense of public welfare; international or cross-national organisations which are created to satisfy felt needs without regard for national frontiers could produce greater welfare benefits for individuals; and their work could eventually undermine popular loyalties to the state through the creation of a working peace system and the satisfaction of felt needs on a non-national basis; the central axiom is that form should follow function. Beyond this core of description and prescription, however, there are inconsistencies in the interpretations of functionalism given by different students of the theory. There are variations in stress and interpretation.

Of contemporary international relations theories functionalism is perhaps the main alternative to theories of power politics. Writings of international relations theorists often reflect an intellectual bi-polarity: conflict and cooperation, discord and collaboration, swords and ploughshares, war and peace, are the pervasive oppositions of the field. These oppositions are manifest in the literature in three major kinds of writing. One treats conflict as inherent and competition between states (and other social groupings) as inevitable; the literature in this case focuses upon the proffering of advice to governments on how to win in the competition which dominates international society. A second accepts similar assumptions, that the interests of governments are dominant, and the state unavoidable, but concentrates upon making it easier and safer for states to coexist: there are to be appropriate methods for coping with the undesirable aspects of power politics in the general interest. A third kind of literature begins by questioning the assumption that the state is irreduceable and that the interests of governments prevail, and proceeds to the active consideration of schemes for cooperation; it is peace oriented and seeks to avoid a win-lose-stalemate framework.

Functionalist writings are of the latter kind: they are about cooperation, collaboration, ploughshares, peace. But, more than this, the theory begins by rejecting the so-called realistic position that all cooperation must begin with the positive acceptance of the primacy of the exclusive and competing interests of governments. Functionalism stresses the plenitude of relationships of a legitimised character between all manner of diverse actors which forms the very fabric of world society: a working peace system exists and functionalism seeks to remove impediments to its further growth. The assumptions of functionalism, as reflected, for instance, in policy advice to governments, are different from those of strategic studies, or crisis management or foreign policy analysis. The billiard ball analogy of international society is rejected; greater significance is attached to the emergence of an increasing range of inter-, cross- and trans-national systems of inter-dependence; the term 'world politics' or 'world society' is preferred to 'international politics'; the role of governments is to be progressively reduced by indirect methods, and integration is to be encouraged by a variety of functionally based, cross-national ties; peace and security are to be guaranteed by the efficient provision of essential services to fulfill commonly-felt needs rather than 'non-war' being induced by fear of threat systems and sanctions.

This is not to decry the study of strategy or the analysis of foreign policy, but rather to locate the theory of functionalism in its intellectual context in the literature of international relations in the 1970s. Functionalism has a particular stress: it is also a meeting point between several other theories and approaches which are either explicitly or implicitly opposed to power politics. In covering such a wide territory it would indeed be surprising if there were no unexplored areas and no disagreements about the route towards the agreed goals. It is, however, not to the discredit of functionalism that this is so. It merely indicates a wide range of intellectual concern. It reflects the quality of functionalism as a focus of discussion, or a tendency in thinking, rather than as a determinate body of propositions. The problems which revolve around the alternative pole in the literature of international relations, power politics, are themselves liable to similar difficulties; yet these difficulties are frequently minimised in a cushion of conventional cynicism about human capacities and in a gloomy confidence in the inevitable attraction of the values of high politics.

It is also appropriate in this introduction to place functionalism in its historical context in the development of thinking about political, social and economic structures. The editors are very glad that Professor David Mitrany, who is the leading theorist of functionalism, is also a contributor to this volume. His development of the theory is indicated in his writings first in *The Progress of*

International Government, published in 1933[1]*; the classic statement, however, appears in his *A Working Peace System,* which was first published in 1943, and reprinted with other essays in 1966[2]. Since the Second World War Professor Mitrany has contributed regularly to journals such as *International Affairs* and the *Journal of Common Market Studies.*[3]

It is a commonly held view that new or revolutionary ideas about social, political or economic life are usually the product of a gifted mind which recognises and relates tendencies which are there for all to see. Professor Mitrany has said that he did not 'invent a doctrine' but that he 'learned a lesson'[4]. It is the case that his writings represent the clearest expression of ideas which had been clarified towards the end of the First World War and that they cannot be fully understood except in the context of various works on international organisation and domestic politics, particularly those of the early Fabians. It is an indication of the quality of Professor Mitrany's achievement that he was able to develop this thinking and relate it to the changing conditions of political life in the thirties and forties in a dynamic theory of peace-building at the world level.

Yet the tendency towards this fulfillment may be detected in such writings as Leonard Woolf's *The Framework of a Lasting Peace* (London: Allen and Unwin 1917), and *The Intelligent Man's Way to Prevent War* (London: Gollancz 1933), and in the work of Norman Angell, Robert Cecil and G.D.H. Cole. This is not the place for an exercise in literary criticism designed to show how these writers influenced each other, but anyone who cares to consult the original works may readily discover how strong the links are and how clearly they form a single inter-related body of ideas. The antecedents of these ideas include the works of several anarchist writers of whom perhaps the most relevant is Peter Kropotkin who, like later functionalist writers, was impressed by the implications of the new international organisations in the second half of the nineteenth century[5]. The reader will not need reminding that functionalist thinking has also found a more recent expression in the work of a number of contemporary scholars in the United States such as Professors Ernst B. Haas, J. Patrick Sewell and Leon N. Lindberg. These recent developments are discussed at several points in this book.

Three themes recur in the political and social writings which culminated in functionalism. These may now be recognised as reflections of actual developments in the structure of political, social and economic life in the first half of the twentieth century. The first theme is that of economic development; the second is that of the growth of concern with the state's role in the provision of welfare for the individual; the third is the growing uncertainty about the role of traditional democratic institutions in the modern state, and about what Professor Mitrany himself has called the crisis of 'democratic individualism'[6]. Functionalism is built upon a recognition of these changes and adapts them to a theory of international integration.

The theory assumes that there are values which can be understood and appreciated by most people, such as those which are the product of economic development, which might be increased by greater efficiencies resulting from international cooperation. It is thus firmly grounded in nineteenth century rationalism and radicalism with its background of growing material prosperity and eradication of social evils.

---

* Superior figures are for the notes and references, listed at the end of each individual paper.

Functionalism is also rooted in those changing structures and attitudes which culminated in the welfare state. It assumes, with the Fabians, that it is proper for organisations larger than the family to provide the essential welfare requirements of the individual. It assumes further that the provision of welfare is likely to remove one of the major causes of discontent in the modern world, one which easily leads to violence within states and between them. As Professor Mitrany wrote, in 1944, 'Give people a moderate sufficiency of what they need and ought to have and they will keep the peace: this has been proved time and time again nationally, but it has not yet been tried internationally'[7]. Professor Mitrany stressed that the League had failed because it had not concerned itself enough with these fundamental problems, and, making the same point about the United Nations, he wrote: 'if its outside activities and agencies do not multiply and prosper it will remain a mere shell'[8]. Functionalism marks a significant adjustment in the size of the units which are appropriate to the provision of welfare. The extended family gave way to the state because of the inadequacies of the former in terms of economic efficiency if not in participation: the state must now give way to inter- and cross-national organisations which in any case are more closely related to changing economic conditions and welfare needs.

It is here that one of the central dynamic elements of functionalism as a theory of international integration is encountered. Deficiencies are to be remedied, but it is not just a question of satisfying a need: there is to be a positive use made of the mechanisms of welfare provision to undermine loyalties to the state and to build an international socio-psychological community which transcends the frontiers of the state. It is not that man is necessarily naturally good; but he is sufficiently reasonable and clear about his true interests to respond to the experience of better welfare from international cooperation. Man goes to war because his social environment encourages him ('that we should fight is perhaps part of our nature; what we fight about is part of our nurture' as Angell put it[9]), and his social environment can equally restrain him from going to war. Man's sense of nationality can be separated from his conceptions of welfare needs so that he is increasingly tempted to seek welfare through international cooperation rather than national prestige through competition and possibly war. Welfare has a positive value in re-directing and diffusing loyalties and building a working peace system. Nationalism thus loses its sting and its association with power politics. In this respect, too, functionalism seems to reflect Fabian ideas, and, more generally, thinking in liberal socialism.

The third development which is reflected in functionalism is the growing doubt about some of the traditional forms of democratic government. In particular functionalism is critical of traditional-style popularly elected assemblies which are increasingly incapable of exercising detailed control over legislation in developed societies or of being responsive to changing needs[10]. The economic problems are too difficult; the range of technical difficulties within countries as in relations between them demands more the knowledge of experts than the judgements of politicians. Functionalists are willing to accept a phase of technocratic organisation of social and economic affairs as a tactical expedient in obtaining integration. But at the same time they stress the need to discover new ways for obtaining the representation of general interests in modern institutions. Professor Mitrany has agreed with the suggestion that there is a syndicalist influence in his thinking. This has led him to put forward the idea that there should be more specialist assemblies which could act as the link between institutions and the general public. They could act as a two-way transmission belt between the general public and the specialist where the felt needs of the one and the technical knowledge of the other could be intertwined in such a way as to maximise responsiveness, efficiency, knowledge, and participation in a democratic framework.

Professor Mitrany is accordingly sympathetic towards some of the new kinds of assembly which are attached to international organisations. The Assembly of the International Labour Organisation, and the Consultative Committee of the European Coal and Steel Community, and the special advisory groups linked with UNESCO depart from the traditional form of assemblies; their example could be followed within the state. Functionalists accept the prospective role of experts in the integration process, and are prepared to consider new forms of representation in democratic systems.

International functional organisations were set up in the nineteenth century in response to one-world problems such as posts and telegraph or to circumvent the impact of national frontiers, as in the case of river commissions. Parts of the Allied war effort in the First World War, such as shipping, were successfully organised along functional lines and the League of Nations set up several functional agencies. In the interwar period numerous national or a-national functional agencies achieved prominence. Perhaps the best known of these was the Tennessee Valley Authority in the USA. But there were examples in several countries of functions being organised in ways designed to minimise political intervention: boards or national corporations such as the British Broadcasting Company, are examples of these. These trends continued after the Second World War which had once again seen a vindication of functional forms of organisation in the Allied War effort.[11]

After the Second World War the debate on the relationship between the United Nations and the Specialised Agencies was resolved in a Mitranian fashion with a substantial degree of autonomy being given to the Agencies. The Agencies have multiplied and, on the whole, prospered, as have other forms of functional organisation: it is conventional wisdom to regard as desirable a functional solution to many of the world's most pressing problems be it development, pollution, or the deep sea bed. Functional forms of organisation have also developed on a regional basis, in some cases in response to growing integration, as in Europe, and in others to preserve integrated services after the break-up of colonial empires as in East Africa.

However, the greatest growth of functional organisation, and perhaps its most dramatic vindication as both a description and a prescription, lies not at the level of international governmental organisation (IGO) nor at the national level but at the level of international non-governmental organisation (INGO). For more than a century INGOs have been building the fabric of world society and reintegrating where the disintegrating effects of national frontiers had threatened. Without a knowledge of the purposes, functions and effects of such organisations our understanding of world society is substantially deficient. That such deficiencies exist is a serious reproach to the academic community. Happily this deficiency is now being realised and made good not least by the work of Judge, Skjelsbaek, Harrod and others[12]. We do not know the extent to which the INGO framework constitutes a working peace system, still less how and why it does or might do so. The study of INGOs is therefore an important new area of endeavour and functionalism provides an intellectual framework with which to approach it.

The essays contained in this volume reflect the range of current views on functionalism and its contribution to the problems of international order. They place the theory in the context of other theories in international relations in the 1970s and they reflect the present stage in the evolution of a style of thinking about international organisation, and the problems of international order. The theoretical essays are complemented by empirical studies: functionalism is meaningless if it has no relationship to the real everyday world; its claim is to be involved in building a *working* peace system—in part description, in part prescription. Our aim is to give an assessment of an approach to world society which seeks to confront contemporary problems both responsively and responsibly. That functionalism has flourished as an aspect of contemporary thinking about international organisation and world society in general is itself adequate justification for undertaking this task.

Notes and References

1   Allen and Unwin, London. This book is the text of the William Dodge Lectures delivered at Yale University in 1932.
2   Quadrangle Books, Chicago, 1966. This edition has an introduction by Professor Hans Morgenthau.
3   See *inter alia*, 'The functional approach in historical perspective', in *International Affairs*, **47** (3), London, July 1971; 'The prospect of integration: federal or functional', in *Journal of Common Market Studies*, 4, Oxford, December 1965; and 'The functional approach to world organisation', in *International Affairs*, **24** (3), July 1948.
4   In an unpublished note, 'The making of functional theory'.
5   For examples of links between Kropotkin and functionalist ideas see Peter Kropotkin, *The Conquest of Bread* (London: Allen Lane the Penguin Press 1972, pp. 9-10) for a quotation by the editor Peter Avrich, from Kropotkin's pamphlet 'Modern science and anarchism', and p. 69, as well as an apposite quotation from Kropotkin by a contemporary Dutch anarchist-cum-Provo, Roel van Duyn in his *Message of a Wise Kabouter* (London: Duckworth 1972, p. 21).
6   See Professor Mitrany's comments in Carnegie Endowment for International Peace, *Functionalism: Report of the Conference at Bellagio*, New York 1970.
7   David Mitrany, 'The road to security', in *Peace News Pamphlet No. 29*, London: National Press Council 1944, p. 14.
8   *Ibid.*, p. 9.
9   Norman Angell, 'Educational and psychological factors', in Leonard Woolf (ed.) *The Intelligent Man's Way to Prevent War*, London: Gollancz 1933, p. 465.
10 See David Mitrany, 'An advance in democratic representation', in *A Working Peace System*, Chicago: Quadrangle Books 1966, pp. 121-130.
11 See chapter by John Burton.
12 See chapter by Anthony Judge and Kjell Skjelsbaek.

Part One
A Theoretical Perspective

Functionalism and Theories of International Political Integration

Charles Pentland

To many students of international relations, the observation that there is, or should be, a natural, useful affinity between functionalism and integration theory will seem reasonable enough. That in fact there is considerable debate on this point perhaps serves as a commentary on the current state of integration theory and of international studies generally. Those who concern themselves with the building of empirical theories of international political integration tend to see the functionalists as belonging to a distant pre-scientific age. The functionalists, in turn, see much of integration theory as a misguided enterprise based on faulty, indeed dangerous, assumptions. To suggest that there can be a fruitful relationship between the two is therefore often to risk offending each.

Integration theorists, busy developing process-models and empirical measures of integration, do, of course, do the functionalists the dubious honour of considering them precursors, whose work is useful for the occasional hypothesis that can be teased out of it and trimmed into testable form, as well as for its inspirational reformist spirit. On the whole, however, functionalism is treated as a rather imprecise and outmoded mixture of empirical and prescriptive assertions about international cooperation. While functionalists' hearts are in the right place, it is argued, their theory is too deeply rooted in questionable assumptions about the mutability of men and institutions, the inevitability of socio-economic gradualism and the supremacy of welfare and technology over power politics, to be of much guidance to social scientists or policy-makers today.[1]

According to many functionalists, however, the integration theorists have taken a fundamentally wrong turn—toward a narrow pre-occupation with the building of massively bureaucratised regional super-states—which has led them away from the central issues of world order. These issues, the functionalists argue, are the same ones to which their predecessors were pointing early in this century. They derive from the economically irrational, socially unrealistic and politically dangerous discrepancy between the growing globalism of technology and welfare, and the continuing parochialism of political structures. To the extent that integration theory continues to employ traditional political models of regionalism and federalism, it is congenitally incapable of coming to grips with these problems.[2]

This functionalist critique of integration theory has had some impact in recent years. The criticism, however, is based on an unduly restricted picture of the current field of integration theory and on a surprisingly short historical perspective on its development. These misconceptions are not the fault of the functionalists alone: they can to a great extent be traced to the writings of the integration theorists themselves who, impressed with the early political and economic returns from the Western European experiment, narrowed their vision and extended their

9

claims rather too hastily. The aim of this paper is to show that growing awareness of the weaknesses in this orthodox version of integration theory should direct us back to a broader concept of political integration in which functionalist ideas can play a productive part.

General Principles

It has been aptly remarked that the field of integration studies has not yet passed its 'Hundred Flowers' period.[3] There is little agreement among scholars who claim to be studying political integration or unification as to the purposes or goals of integration, the structure of the integrated community which is to serve these purposes, the conditions likely to aid or hinder the growth of that community, or the appropriate methods for studying this process of growth. To some this is clearly a deplorable situation: there exists none of that consensus on the central problems or on operational concepts out of which a rigorous theory of integration might emerge. From this stance it is tempting to reach for one of two kinds of solution. Either we seek to legislate consensus, by imposing over the field a broad conceptual framework such as a systems model, in which many different approaches can be accommodated with relatively few adjustments[4]; or we engage in recurrent bouts of semantic imperialism or isolationism, in which by feats of definition we incorporate other approaches in some niche of our own, or exclude them as not being 'politically relevant' or really 'about integration'.[5]

However stimulating such exercises might be, they cannot be said to have advanced us much toward any set of systematic, verifiable general statements which are widely accepted as aiding our understanding of political integration. Indeed, it may well be that if such a goal is attainable at all, it will be reached by a much more difficult and circuitous route. Taking this route will require us first to return to a set of very general first principles on which consensus is reasonably likely, and then to identify the major cleavages which emerge among theorists as they render their conceptions of integration increasingly specific and operational.

Political integration can be defined very generally as 'the process whereby two or more actors form a new actor',[6] provided that we make two important qualifications in applying this definition on the international level. The first is that we take the original actors to be nation-states according to the formal criteria generally accepted in international society. This points us to the central concern of all integration theorists with the adequacy of such political units and of the system they collectively comprise, in meeting basic human needs for physical security, economic and social well-being and cultural identity. It suggests, too, that however important other types of actors might have become in the current international system, the entities in whose possible integration we are interested are the *dominant* units of the system, the sovereign nation-states.

The second qualification is that the emergent 'new actor' need not be a state in this same sense. Here, perhaps, there will be less ready agreement than on the first point. Traditionally, after all, integration has been closely associated in many minds with the idea of world government or of some type of regional federation such as a United States of Europe—ideas which represent state-building on the international level. As we shall see, however, not all integration theorists have accepted these models. Moreover, many of those who have done so in the past are now beginning to explore radically different possibilities which might meet the desired ends without necessarily reproducing on the international level some form with which we are familiar on the national level.

International political integration, then, is the process whereby two or more states form a new entity which can in some sense be described as a political community. On this much (or this little) it seems reasonable to assume most writers on integration would agree. The cleavages begin to emerge when we attempt to go beyond this, by asking two basic questions which arise from our general definition: (a) what kind of political community is, or should be, the result of a process of integration? (b) What conditions and strategies cause the process of integration to proceed, to stagnate or to break down?

As regards the first question the major distinction to be drawn is between those—still in the majority—who take integration to be directed toward the formation of a supranational political authority and those who look for the emergence of forms of international community which lack state-like institutions, and who emphasise instead the propensity of peoples to interact and cooperate across state boundaries. This distinction, between what might be described crudely as the 'state-model' and the 'community-model', emerges very sharply in the debates over postwar European integration. In the early years the 'state-model' of the federalists was countered by the 'community-model' of the functionalists; in the 'sixties a similar debate took place between the supranationalists of Brussels and the Gaullists.

The cleavage over the second question also runs through the ranks of academic theorists and policy-makers alike. For the academics, the debate concerns the independent variables which best account for the progress of integration among a group of states. For the policy-makers it concerns tactics and strategy in relation to this process of political change: where, in the whole complex of political, social and economic issues and institutions which make up modern international relations, are the levers that will best move the system toward a more integrated condition, and in what sequence ought they to be pulled? On one side are those who look to technology, the economy and society as the source of the drive to integration and the parameters in which it occurs. It is not so much that the political outcome is determined by these elements, but more that they give rise to demands on existing political structures and provide opportunities for the kinds of creative administration and political bargaining out of which an integrated community can gradually emerge. On the other side of the debate are those who stress the primacy of politics. The success of integration depends foremost, in this view, on the power, responsiveness and political will of the elites, and their ability to strike bargains within the limits of acceptability demarcated by the political attitudes and habits of the general public. The difference between the two sides is not merely one of emphasis. It derives from deep philosophical roots, and has important consequences both for analytical methods and for political tactics.[7]

Different Conceptions of Integration

On the basis of these two cross-cutting sets of distinctions it is possible to discern four major traditions of thought about international political integration, around which crystallise the ideas of most major postwar academics and political leaders. It would perhaps be useful very briefly to outline each of these traditions.

Federalism is the oldest and best-known tradition of thought about international integration. As suggested earlier, the federalist vision of the goal of integration—partly because of its simplicity, partly because of the familiarity of the analogy from which it derives—continues to dominate the field.[8] This goal is a supranational state which possesses sufficient political authority and coercive and material power to satisfy the member-states' needs for collective defence, internal security and economies of scale, while still permitting them to maintain their individual identities and to exercise local autonomy in appropriate fields of policy. While the imprint of Hobbes is unmistakable in much federalist writing, it is usually a limited form of Leviathan that is called for, with only as much centralisation and supranationality as consensus and common needs will bear. If the diagnosis points to extremity, then the proposed cure will be a strong central power; in other cases, the analyst will be hard pressed to discover what the federal government is supposed to do. In general, however, the federalist vision is one of a controlled and rational distribution of power and jurisdiction among two or more levels of government, in what was formerly an ungoverned international system.

In explaining the process of integration, federalists tend to rely heavily on the purely political elements of power and bargaining. The compellingness of the situation is assumed or asserted rather than analysed, but whether and how the necessary integration actually occurs is held to depend primarily on the will, ability and relative power of the elites involved in bringing it about. The image of the integrative process is thus a dramatic, revolutionary one: for any number of reasons the time becomes ripe for change; a constituent assembly of national governments or popular representatives is formed; bargains are struck at the top, against a backdrop of rising popular sentiment; and eventually a new set of common institutions emerge which embody the powers of which the states have agreed to divest themselves. In essence, then, federalists see integration as a rapid process of change from an international system to a supranational one—the primary evidence of change being the distribution of formal, constitutional authority in the new federal state.

The federalist approach to international integration draws on two major intellectual traditions, the one concerned with institutional designs for pacifying the relations among states, and the other related to the actual practice of federal government. As far back as the ancient Greeks, of course, men have looked to some form of government as the solution to international anarchy and war.[9] Frequently, however, what was advocated was not the voluntary creation of a common supranational authority, but either legitimisation of the rule of the most powerful state (empire or hegemony) or some form of agreement among the major states to keep order collectively (collective security or a concert of great powers). But with the development of the concept of sovereignty, the spread of contract theories of government and, above all, the emergence of federal systems in North America and Switzerland, the problem of international government became increasingly identified as that of designing a federal constitution for Europe or for the whole world. Nineteenth-century pacifist writings are full of such schemes, and their descendants are found today among the advocates of 'world peace through world law'.[10] In Europe, federalist aspirations and influence led to, and ultimately foundered in, the Council of Europe and the proposal for a European Political Community.

The accumulated knowledge of the practice of federal government has had both a sobering and an inspirational effect on this concept of world order. On the one hand, the practitioners of federalism in the United States, Switzerland, Canada and elsewhere have usually had a firm sense of the social, economic and political forces operating beneath the formal institutional surface of federal states and thus have not been slow to point out that federalising any system—whether by integrating separate states or decentralizing a unitary one—often creates as many problems as it solves. That the problems are of a different order, such as the continual readjustment of the constitutional division of responsibilities or the allocation of economic resources, does not make them more soluble or less dangerous than international problems. On the other hand, many of these same practitioners have made clear their belief that federalism combines the political virtues (and not the vices) of both unity and diversity and that it is thus not merely a superior form of government in itself but also a method of achieving world order at minimal cost to national identities. They have thus not been averse to proselytism themselves, nor at all reluctant to offer advice based on their own national experience.[11]

Pluralism, the second major approach to international political integration, also represents a venerable tradition of thought about international order, but one which differs fundamentally from federalism. According to pluralists, the integrated political community is a system of independent states which, while not governed by any supranational authority, is characterised by such an intensity of amity, communication and interaction between its members that war is quite inconceivable to them as a method of conflict resolution. The crudest measure of integration among a group of states is thus the frequency or general expectation of armed conflict.[12] More sophisticated measures are sought—for predictive purposes—in the numerous patterns of exchange between the states: trade, mobility of persons, communications of all kinds, and elite interaction both formal and informal. To the extent that such exchanges are intense, enduring and perceived as mutually rewarding, they represent the structural bonds of an integrated system which, it is argued, can be as stable and efficacious as one which is formally governed by a common authority.[13]

Pluralists, then, choose the community-model over the state-model preferred by the federalists. In explaining the emergence of this 'community of states', however, they share the federalists' emphasis on political rather than socio-economic forces. For the pluralists, the key to the integrative process is in the attitudes and behaviour of the political elites of the states concerned, and the manner in which these influence and reflect the attitudes and behaviour of the general public. Exchanges among societies may arise initially out of perceived mutual advantage and, perhaps, minimal compatibility of cultural values, regimes and social systems. Elites may encourage or attempt to hinder or channel these exchanges which, in a successfully integrating system, take on a self-reinforcing character. At the very least, then, pluralists take the frequency of elite interactions and the flow of exchanges between states as evidence of integration; more often, they see the exchanges themselves as essential factors in transforming the perceptions and behaviour of the political elites toward greater support of integration and greater formal cooperation at the top.[14]

The pluralist conception of integration as a dynamic process thus stresses the relationship between patterns of social communication and the predispositions of political elites in a system of sovereign states. It assumes, in opposition to most schools of thought on integration, that states can learn to govern their mutual relations—in particular to solve the problems without recourse to war—without giving up their sovereignty to a higher power. In the history of thought on international organisation this view is evident from earliest times. Most of the proposed leagues, confederacies or unions of sovereigns that flowed from the pens of European publicists and policy-makers like Dubois, Sully and St Pierre from the middle ages on, took a pluralist form. The same pattern is found in Cobden's picture of a free-trading world of peaceful liberal democracies or, more recently, in writings on peace which, in effect, advocate a world of nonaligned and mutually responsive states.[15]

For the very good reason that it appears to combine international order and stability with the continuation of national independence, the pluralist view has always been popular with policy-makers themselves. In Europe its strongest advocates have been the British—who saw it realised in the Council of Europe and OEEC against the wishes of the federalists—and the French, whose greatest postwar leader enshrined it in the phrase '*l'Europe des parties*'. The announcement, in May 1971, that Prime Minister Heath and President Pompidou had arrived at a common view of the political future of the European Community, clearly indicates that pluralism is now the established governmental doctrine of European integration.

The policy-makers, however, have implied rather than clearly developed a view of how the 'community of states' might emerge. Analysis of this process has been taken farthest in the work of Karl Deutsch and other political scientists who have adopted the communications approach to integration. While communications theorists acknowledge the possibility of supranationalism, most seem to agree with Deutsch's conclusion that the pluralistic security community is a more likely, more viable and perhaps even more desirable form of integrated system.[16] In general, however, they have been concerned more with describing and explaining the process than with positing various goals of integration. In measuring the flows of exchanges between states these theorists are attempting to express in a systematic, empirical manner a concept of the integrative process which is often intuitively understood and acted upon by political leaders.

If federalists and pluralists differ over the goal of integration, they at least agree that the process itself is directly political—that it is the capabilities, attitudes and behaviour of those holding political power which determines the success or failure of integration. These elites, moreover, decide about integration with their eyes open; they make their calculations about federation or cooperation in the clear understanding that they are creating new political forms, rather than in the belief that they are merely pursuing an economic interest or solving a common technical problem. It is the primacy of such political elements that most clearly distinguishes federalism and pluralism from the other two main approaches to integration, functionalism and neofunctionalism.

In discussing these two approaches we arrive at the crux of the debate referred to at the beginning of this chapter. Functionalism, as suggested there, is an underrated and often misunderstood body of ideas which, its critics notwithstanding, deals directly with important issues of integration. Neofunctionalism, on the other hand, has achieved such prominence in the field that it almost has the status of a theoretical and methodological orthodoxy. The debate between functionalism and integration theory thus becomes, in effect, the debate between functionalism and its intellectual descendant, neofunctionalism.

The two approaches share many characteristics which serve to distinguish them from federalism and pluralism. Among these are the stress on economic welfare and technical cooperation, the focus on utilitarian rather than symbolic factors in community building, the prerequisite of a liberal, pluralistic social setting in the integrating states, the emphasis on the role of technocrats[17] and, more generally and perhaps most important, a sense of the compelling nature of the economic, social and technological environment in its impact on political structures and actors. Where the two approaches differ, however, is over the dynamics of the integrative process itself and over the nature of the end-product—functionalists accepting a community model while the neofunctionalists have usually looked to some form of supranational authority.

Functionalism embodies a temperamental reluctance to designate, in an *a priori* manner, structural goals for social and political change—a practice so often identified with integration theory. This temperament is in fact the starting point for much of the functionalist critique. The whole point of functionalism, it is argued, is in the flexible creation and adaptation of institutions to social and economic needs as these arise, change and die out. Given the speed and continuity of this process of social evolution, it is futile, restrictive and unimaginative to try and specify a desirable future end-point in the sort of institutional blueprint commonly found in federalist writings.[18]

The fact that functionalists dislike blueprints for the structure of the integrated community does not, however, mean that a concept of this community is not to be found in their work. In essence this community is a network of organisations each of which has been designed to meet a specific set of social, economic or technical needs. The structure and jurisdiction of each organisation is determined by the nature and scope (demographic and geographic) of the needs themselves. As the functional needs arise, change or decline, so, ideally, do the organisations--'form' following 'function'. At the same time, of course, as these organisations proliferate in direct reflection of the growing complexity of modern global society, there will be considerable need for a coordinating level of organisation above them, and ultimately for some form of political control of the planning activities which inevitably arise from this task.[19] The functionalist hope is that these organisations will constitute a 'working peace system', a warless global community, by tying up the states in a complex web of interdependence and by solving economic and social problems so efficiently and humanely that they erode the material and psychological bases of conflict.[20] Structurally, the minimal result might be something like a pluralistic community of states whose sovereign power is reduced and controlled by international functional linkages. A more extreme and less likely possibility is the eventual disappearance of the nation-states as political units, and their replacement by a global administrative system whose organisational pattern is determined by criteria of functional rationality.

The process of integration, according to functionalist thinking, may be initiated at the intergovernmental or at the transnational levels. Governments which cannot separately cope with problems, or natural communities of interest that lie across national boundaries, may both create functional organisations. In either case, the central principle of organisational growth is 'technical self-determination'.[21] Functional needs, whether these are expressed as demands from social groups or formulated as problems by experts, are assumed to contain directions as to the scope, level and structure of the organisation needed to meet them. To the extent that these directions are followed, and governments and experts pay attention to the 'common index of need' rather than the 'individual index of power',[22] the attitudes and behaviour of both participants and beneficiaries begin to show greater support for new rounds of cooperation and integration. Functionalism thus embodies a theory of community-building through collective learning and techno-cratic management. Underlying this theory is the assumption—widely held today—that there is a steadily increasing tension between the continuing partic-ularism of political structures and the growing ecumenism of non-political needs and pressures, and that this tension, if it is not to lead to catastrophe, must be resolved in the direction of greater global political integration.

A number of intellectual archaeologists have traced the origins of functionalism in such progressive traditions as guild socialism, Marxism, pragmatism and utilitarian liberalism.[23] In particular, functionalism draws on the organic, socio-economic reformist ethos represented by British Fabianism and on ideas about the reconstruction of international society found in the writings of continental thinkers such as St Simon.[24] But the major source of functionalist thought has been in the experience of men who created, worked in or observed the numerous international organisations that began to emerge in the late nineteenth century. Functionalism emerged early in this century as an interpretation of such new forms of international cooperation as the Universal Postal Union and the Danube Com-mission; it fed on the experience of Allied cooperation during World War I and of the technical and economic activities of the League.[25] Since 1945, the Specialised Agencies of the United Nations and innumerable regional or bilateral organisations for economic and technical cooperation, socio-economic development, and other non-political purposes, have embodied explicitly functionalist aims and have provided opportunities to test functionalist hypotheses.[26]

Neofunctionalism was a direct product of the confrontation of functionalist ideas with the experience of one such regional organisation in western Europe. In the European Coal and Steel Community, proposed by Robert Schuman in 1950, those favouring integration had turned from the disappointments of broad and ambitious pan-European federalist schemes to the functionalist strategy of placing a sector of the economies of six countries under a common supranational authority. At the very least, it was hoped, this would remove those states' material capacity to make war again; more positively, it was expected that the conditions would speedily be created for the spread of such arrangements to other sectors (such as health, agriculture, transport), so that 'de facto solidarity'[27] would evolve gradually and almost automatically into a supranational, European government. Such a process would be a clear vindication and confirmation of functionalist theory.

From the experience of the Coal and Steel Community, however, and from that of its companions formed in 1957, Euratom and the European Economic Community,[28] came not the vindication but the reformulation of functionalism, both as practice and as theory. From their observations of the workings of these organisations, both the 'Eurocrats' and the academics concluded that while certain functionalist dynamics were clearly at work, the progress of integration could not be explained simply in terms of 'technical self-determination' and the learning of habits of cooperation. From this realisation emerged the set of ideas which became known as neofunctionalism.

In its early form, neofunctionalism embodied an acceptance of supranationalism as the goal of integration. Ernst Haas, in whose writings the theory was first developed, describes the emergent Europe as 'a new centre, whose institutions possess or demand jurisdiction over the pre-existing ones'.[29] The European policy-makers, such as Hallstein, Spaak and Monnet, who were working for integration through the ECSC and the EEC, were often described as 'functional federalists'—openly working toward a United States of Europe by functionalist rather than federalist tactics.

While the federalist model has been widely accepted, however, neofunctionalists have not always been entirely happy with it, particularly since it seemed to foreclose a number of possible options and to deny the uniqueness of the European experiment. Latterly these doubts have been reinforced by evidence of the stagnation of what had earlier seemed an inexorable process, and by the consequent need to consider different possible outcomes of integration. More recently Haas has described integration as leading to common decision-making among a group of states, whatever the formal institutional arrangements might be. Haas now conceives of several possibilities, under the master rubric of 'authority-legitimacy transfer',[30] while Lindberg sees the essence of political integration as 'the emergence or creation over time of collective decision-making processes, i.e., political institutions to which governments delegate decision-making authority and/or through which they decide jointly via more familiar intergovernmental negotiation'.[31] Supranationality remains important, then, but from being the touchstone it has become but one feature in an increasingly modified picture of the goal of integration.

If the federalist element in neofunctionalism lies in the assumed goal, the functionalist element is found in the explanation of the integrative process itself. But here too the original ingredient has become radically modified. The starting point is the observation that because the sectors of an international economy are so inter-related, integrating one or a few of them under a supranational authority will create economic incentives, psychological willingness and, above all, political pressures and capabilities, to integrate more sectors until, in effect, a single economy has emerged governed by a single authority. This 'spillover' occurs in a setting of interdependent economic and social needs, much as the functionalists might expect. But neofunctionalists add the important argument that such needs and pressures from the environment can only be said to cause integration to the degree that they lead to and constrain the international bargaining process among interest groups, parties, government officials and international organisations—all of whom are attempting to exploit these pressures in their own interests.[32] The outcome of bargaining which best advances integration is one which gives each major actor an acceptable payoff, brings a new sector into the system, and also results in an increase of the capacity of the supranational authority, which is thus in a better position to intervene decisively in the next round of bargaining. The 'spillover' process by which these kinds of advances occur once had an aura of automaticity about it—derived from a belief in the natural interdependence of functional sectors, the brokerage skills of the supranational elite and the non-ideological rationality of the other actors involved. It is now generally held that spillover (or 'forward linkage') is a matter of probability and only one of several possible paths.[33] Its likelihood depends on, among other things, the nature of the issue at hand, the degree of elite consensus and the immediate resources of the

17

supranational authority to bring about settlements which 'upgrade the common interest'.[34]

Neofunctionalism—Emergence and Decline

It should be evident to the reader by now that the field of integration studies as conceived here is considerably broader than its critics and many of its devotees admit. It embraces four major schools of thought, each of which derives from different values and traditions, advocates a different goal, explains the process of integration differently, embodies different prescriptions for policy-makers, and has different adherents both in the heat of the political kitchens and in the relative cool of academic groves. In part, this might answer the criticisms of the functionalists that all integration theorists are obsessed with regional state-building; it ought also to give perspective to some of the more restrictive views of other theorists about the actual or proper scope of the field.

Functionalism, it has been argued, stands in its own right as a major approach to the conception and explanation of political integration. More than this, indeed, the current difficulties of neofunctionalism as the dominant approach in both theory and practice, point to several areas where functionalist insights can be of particular aid. Before discussing these areas, it might be useful to ask why neofunctionalism emerged as the dominant approach, and why it is now undergoing something of a reassessment in many quarters.

In the first place, neofunctionalism was undoubtedly a theoretical breakthrough. It served both to define the field of integration in terms of a systematic and manageable scheme, advancing a limited and ordered set of variables, and to put forward hypotheses—such as 'spillover'—which explained the integrative process in a plausible and testable way. While other theoretical schools either became strongly policy-oriented or, like the Deutschians, turned to exhaustive numerical empiricism,[35] neofunctionalism embodied a drive toward middle-range theory, which enabled it to come forth rather early with a convincing and useful—if not always verified—analysis of the European situation. In great measure, then, neofunctionalism triumphed simply because it seemed to work.

As the European situation changed in the nineteen-sixties, however, it soon became clear that the attraction of neofunctionalism was based on a decreasingly certain set of expectations. The goal and purpose of European integration could not be taken as matters of consensus once de Gaulle had begun to exercise his will, nor could the process of integration be seen as automatic. The variables to be considered turned out to be less clearly delimited, particularly as the external political environment—which neofunctionalists had tended to hold constant—changed dramatically.[36] And the promise of more precise measures, unambiguous hypotheses and reasoned predictive or prescriptive power for the theory did not materialise as swiftly as expected.

Secondly, neofunctionalism, like the work of Deutsch and his colleagues, reflected the style, values and methods of the new American political science of the nineteen-fifties. The impact of behaviourism on the study of integration was powerful indeed, and led to changes not only of emphasis but of direction. In striving for 'value-free' theories of integration political scientists simply forgot about purposes, or assumed them to be unimportant or uncontroversial. In focussing on the integrative process, neofunctionalists paid little attention to the quality of policy consequences.[37] In drawing implicit or explicit analogies from American political life (pluralism, liberal group theory, incremental decision-making) or from development theory (inter-sectoral linkages) neofunctionalists tended to overlook the unique qualities of single cases such as Western Europe or East Africa.

In its post-behavioural period, however, American political science has turned against many of these tendencies. More stress is now placed on values and purposes in political life and less is heard of the 'end of ideology'. Policy studies now focus much more on the 'outcome' side of policy-making than on 'inputs' or processes. American political scientists are perhaps more circumspect about the importance and beneficence of interest-group pluralism and incremental decision-making, in their own country as well as in the political systems they study abroad. To these changes in mood, style and method, neofunctionalism has begun painfully to adjust.

A further reason for the early success of neofunctionalism was that it bore a close relation to the precepts of leading policy-makers in Europe and reflected to them convincingly their own view of what they were doing. The academic study and the political practice of integration grew for a time in a kind of symbiotic relationship. A Hallstein and a Haas, each in his different style, expressed the same kinds of assumptions and analyses.[38] Academics moved easily in the corridors of Brussels, interviewing Eurocrats and absorbing the Community ethos. Eurocrats, in turn, read the resulting publications and found their behaviour described, rationalised and even prescribed in a persuasive manner. The relation became so close that one neofunctionalist recently remarked on 'the unnerving experience of hearing our special jargon spouted back at us by those whom we are studying.'[39]

Since the early 'sixties, however, the locus of integration has been shifting, and, with it, the cast of leading characters. Other observers, from the vantage point of national governments, have been putting quite different meaning to the activities of the Eurocrats and of the Community, seeing the latter as an international bureaucracy rather than as a supranational government growing with its own momentum. National governments, it is clear, are still, and perhaps increasingly, the source of power and decision in the Community, and the traditional neofunctionalist focus on, and affinity with, the Brussels institutions risks considerable distortion of the overall picture of integration.

Another source of strength and support for neofunctionalism lay in its felicitous combination of the pragmatic, low-key, incremental style of functionalist methods with the compelling and comprehensible federalist goal of a supranational Europe. In adopting this goal, neofunctionalism assumed the mantle of legitimacy in the European movement and gained the support of many erstwhile federalists. The combination of the state-model with an explicitly regional focus gave neo-functionalism some of the characteristics and power of a nationalist movement on a European level. At the same time, the adoption of functionalist tactics reflected the disillusionment of many Europeans with the dramatic rhetoric and negligible impact of much of the early federalist movement.

In recent years, however, support for the goal of regional federation in Europe has declined, both in European capitals and in the international milieu. As suggested earlier, the pluralist model of a 'community of states' is now widely accepted, and even the Community's officials now use the term 'political union' in the French sense—meaning intergovernmental cooperation on defence and foreign policy rather than supranational government. Externally, the idea of a regional European federation has raised fears of economic exclusiveness and countervailing power not only in the Soviet Union and many developing countries—where this might be predicted—but also in the United States, once an uncritical supporter of European union. Paradoxically, the incrementalist method also has come under fire, not only from those who resent the political aspirations of the Eurocrats but also from those federalists who see neofunctionalist gradualism as procrastination in the face of the inevitable problems of national sovereignty. 'Federalism by stealth' is thus attacked both as a threat and as an illusion.

The Contributions of Functionalism

For a variety of reasons, then, neofunctionalism is experiencing a somewhat critical period in its existence. Many of its problems have arisen from the political stalemate which the European Community—as the neofunctionalist showpiece—experienced after the spectacular successes of its first five years. Others have arisen from changes in the discipline of political science. Whatever the source of these doubts and difficulties, however, it remains to ask if functionalism can contribute anything to their resolution.

In the first place, as a route to theory functionalism is less ambitious than neofunctionalism, and perhaps more likely to lead to concrete and immediate advances in our knowledge of the integrative process. What functionalism lacks in the way of comprehensive and systematic models, it makes up in the empirical immediacy of many of its propositions about cause and effect. For example, the central argument about the learning processes which occur in the context of international cooperation is easily formulated as a set of testable hypotheses.[40] Functionalism, then, represents a promising middle way between the high road of model-building and the low road of pure induction.

Secondly, functionalism is the only approach which measures the success of integration, not by changes in some quantifiable pattern of behaviour or by some institutional criterion such as supranationalism, but by the quality of policy which results. It is an approach which stresses concrete needs and problem-solving, and makes its judgements of success and failure in terms of policy outputs rather than assessments of processes or structures. In this respect, functionalism is very much in tune with much of post-behavioural political analysis, and provides a healthy corrective for many neofunctionalist assumptions.

Thirdly, functionalism need not assume the 'end of ideology' or a benign political environment as the precondition for integration. Because its focus is deliberately on the non-controversial, with no scenario of gradual politicisation built in, functionalism need assume no more than a set of specific, common instrumental interests as the precondition of cooperation. Whereas neo-functionalists posit the existence of a 'low' (or 'apolitical' to some) species of politics as the medium of integration, functionalists tailor their ambitions to the sphere of agreed common interest.

Nevertheless, it is true that, as a gradualist approach, functionalism must logically envisage a confrontation with the political at some point in the process. In this respect, what distinguishes it from neofunctionalism is the element of time. In the latter approach, as integration progresses 'spillover' leads the participants into increasingly political sectors, where the stakes of bargaining and the resources of each side are considerable. Crises, then, are an inevitable, indeed essential, part of the integrative process. Functionalism, however, sees the political effect of cooperation as occurring in the attitudes of participants and beneficiaries, slowly eroding the vestiges of particularism from within rather than attacking them directly in increasingly long and bitter bargaining sessions. A tactical corollary of this is that policy-makers with the customary disposition to view integration favourably in the long run but to resist it when it implies political concessions in the present, can feel that functional cooperation will benefit them now at the possible expense of future leaders. The functionalist hopes that the latter possibility is indeed high, and that present leaders do not much mind.

Fourthly, functionalism can contribute to the growing debate over the goals of integration. Because, in their view, form depends on function, and functional needs are shifting, growing and increasingly complex, functionalists are led logically to reject both the state-model and the regional focus as hopelessly rigid and inadequate. Instead of the standard vision of integration as a process of growth leading to a specified goal like this, functionalism points us to the concept of a process which not only operates in many social sectors at different speeds but also might result in one of a number of institutional forms, each of which remains subject to rapid change. This is a view to which many neofunctionalists appear to be coming around.[41]

Finally, functionalism can serve to point those disillusioned with such organisations as the European Community as agents of integration, towards other, more hopeful vehicles. Many long-standing intergovernmental organisations generally overlooked by neofunctionalists—such as the Council of Europe—are undertaking a wide range of functional activities whose effects may be underestimated. Moreover, the emergence, on an international scale, of such problems as pollution, might give heart to those who argue that governments are likely to cooperate, not for common economic incentives but out of common fears. Certainly the therapeutic element in functional cooperation is likely to be increasingly important in coming years. Lastly, the phenomenon of transnational relations is beginning to attract some attention among political scientists. The study of 'contacts, coalitions, and interactions across state boundaries that are not controlled by the central foreign policy organs of governments', it is stated in a recent volume, 'treats the reciprocal effects between transnational relations and the interstate system as centrally important to the understanding of contemporary world politics.'[42] Such organisations as multinational corporations, it is argued, are the heroes of a new species of functionalism in world politics.[43]

As a theoretical approach to integration, functionalism has lacked the appeal of a systematic set of explanations and prescriptions about relatively rapid political change. Nevertheless, it seems clear enough that functionalists have had hold of something which, in the excitement over the new methods of other theorists and over the growth of the European Community, was rather too easily overlooked. That the study of political integration has now reached the point where functionalism can once more contribute a fresh perspective, perhaps shows that both its critics and many of its friends have some rethinking to do.

Notes and references

1   For such arguments, see E. Haas, *Beyond the Nation-State*, Stanford University

Press, 1964, chs. 1 and 2; E. Haas 'The Study of Regional Integration', *International Organisation* **24** (4), 1970, where functionalism is conspicuously omitted from the list of 'pretheories' of integration (pp. 622-30); see also the one brief reference in K. Deutsch *et al., Political Community and the North Atlantic Area,* Princeton University Press, 1957, pp. 79-82.

2 D. Mitrany, 'The Prospects of European Integration: Federal or Functional?', *Journal of Common Market Studies,* 4 (2), 1965, pp. 119-49

3 L. Lindberg and S. Scheingold, 'Preface' to *International Organisation*, **24** (4), 1970, p. vii.

4 See, for example, the early attempt in L. Lindberg, 'The European Community as a Political System', *Journal of Common Market Studies,* **5** (4), 1967, pp. 344-87.

5 See Lindberg's critique of Deutsch, *ibid*, p. 345.

6 J. Galtung, 'A Structural Theory of Integration', *Journal of Peace Research* **5** (4), 1968, p. 377.

7 For a similar distinction between 'political' and 'economic' approaches to integration, see L. Lindberg and S. Scheingold, *Europe's Would-Be Polity,* Englewood Cliffs, New Jersey: Prentice-Hall, 1970, ch. 1.

8 A recent statement of federalist views is J. Pinder and R. Pryce, *Europe After de Gaulle,* Harmondsworth, Middlesex: Penguin, 1969.

9 Useful historical surveys of thought on international organisation are A. Bozeman, *Politics and Culture in International History,* Princeton University Press, 1960; and F. Hinsley, *Power and the Pursuit of Peace,* Cambridge University Press, 1963.

10 G. Clark and L. Sohn, *World Peace Through World Law,* rev. ed., Harvard University Press, 1960.

11 Note, for example, the role of American political scientists in advising the designers of European federalist schemes in the early postwar period. For a sample of their work, see C. Friedrich and R. Bowie, eds., *Studies in Federalism,* Boston: Little, Brown, 1954.

12 Deutsch *et al., op. cit.,* p. 5.

13 *Ibid.,* pp. 29-31, 65-69; see H. Alker and D. Puchala, 'Trends in Economic Partnership: the North Atlantic Area, 1928-1963', in J. Singer (ed.), *Quantitative International Politics,* New York: Free Press, 1968, pp. 287-90.

14 The germ of this theory of community-building is in K. Deutsch, *Nationalism and Social Communication,* Cambridge, Mass.: M.I.T. Press, 1953, especially chs. 4 and 5. P. Jacob and H. Teune, 'The Integrative Process' and K. Deutsch, 'Communication Theory and Political Integration' in P. Jacob and J. Toscano (eds.), *The Integration of Political Communities,* Philadelphia: Lippincott, 1964.

15 On the development of these ideas, see Hinsley, *op. cit.,* ch. 1-7. For a recent example of the nonalignment argument, see J. W. Burton, *International Relations: A General Theory,* Cambridge University Presss, 1965.

16 Deutsch *et al., Political Community and the North Atlantic Area,* ch. 6, especially p. 200.

17 J. Nye, *Peace in Parts,* Boston, Mass: Little Brown, 1971, p. 53.

18 D. Mitrany in *A Working Peace System,* Chicago, Quadrangle, 1966, refers to the 'grander federal designs' as 'offering prefabricated Cities of God for the Atlantic world or even for the world at large' (pp. 16-17). Cf. C. W. Jenks'

comment that 'world order will never be attained by a blueprint' in *The International Labour Organisation in the U.N. Family*, New York, UNITAR lecture series #3, 1971, p. 24. See also P. Taylor, 'The Functionalist Approach to the Problem of International Order: A Defence', *Political Studies*, **16** (3), 1968, pp. 400 and 405.

19 Mitrany, *A Working Peace System*, pp. 73-81.
20 *Ibid.*, pp. 96-99. See Taylor, *op. cit., passim.*
21 Mitrany, *A Working Peace System*, pp. 72-73. For a critique of this concept, see J. Sewell, *Functionalism and World Politics*, Princeton University Press, 1966, pp. 250-2.
22 D. Mitrany, 'The Functional Approach to World Organisation' in Mitrany, *A Working Peace System*, p. 159.
23 E. Haas, *Beyond the Nation-State*, ch. 1 & 2, See Sewell, *op. cit.*, part I.
24 See, for example, H. de St Simon, *De la Réorganisation de la Sociéte Européenne* (1815), Paris: les Presses Françaises, 1925, for proposals with a strikingly functionalist flavour.
25 A seminal work from this period is A. Salter, *Allied Shipping Control*, Oxford: Clarendon, 1921.
26 The most exhaustive tests have been undertaken by Haas in *Beyond the Nation-State*, which deals with the ILO, and Sewell, in *Functionalism and World Politics*, which is a study of economic development programmes in the UN.
27 This phrase was used by Robert Schuman in the Declaration of May 9, 1950, which led to the Coal and Steel Community.
28 The three Communities were merged in July 1967.
29 E. Haas, *The Uniting of Europe*, Stanford University Press, 1958, p. 16.
30 Haas, 'The Study of Regional Integration', *op. cit.*, pp. 630-36.
31 L. Lindberg, 'Political Integration as a Multidimensional Phenomenon Requiring Multivariate Measurement', *International Organisation* **24** (4), 1970, p. 652.
32 Haas, for example, describes integration as the product of 'an institutionalised pattern of interest politics, played out within existing international organisations': *Beyond the Nation-State*, p. 35.
33 P. Schmitter, 'Three Neofunctionalist Hypotheses about International Integration', *International Organisation* **23** (1), 1969, p. 164. See Lindberg and Scheingold, *Europe's Would-Be Polity*, pp. 134-9.
34 E. Haas, 'International Integration: The European and the Universal Process', the *International Political Communities*, New York: Doubleday, 1966, pp. 95-97.
35 For a critique of this empiricism, see O. Young 'Professor Russett: Industrious Tailor to a Naked Emperor', *World Politics*, **21** (3), 1969, pp. 486-511.
36 The lack of attention, in neofunctionalist theory, to external factors is discussed in J. Nye, 'Patterns and Catalysts in Regional Integration' *International Organisation*, **19** (4), 1965, pp. 870-84.
37 See, however, S. Scheingold, 'Domestic and International Consequences of Regional Integration', *International Organisation*, **24** (4), 1970, pp. 978-1002.
38 For the former's views, see W. Hallstein, *United Europe: Challenge and Opportunity*, Harvard University Press, 1962.
39 P. Schmitter, 'A Revised Theory of Regional Integration', *International Organisation*, **24** (4), 1970, p. 838.

40 For some preliminary tests of such hypotheses, see R. Cobb and C. Elder, *International Community*, New York: Holt, Rinehart and Winston, 1970, especially pp. 48-53, 120-8.

41 For example, Lindberg and Scheingold, *Europe's Would-Be Polity*, ch. 9.

42 J. Nye and R. Keohane, 'Transnational Relations and World Politics', *International Organisation*, **25** (3), 1971, p. 331.

43 See, for example, R. Cox, 'Labor and Transnational Relations', *International Organisation*, **25** (3), 1971, p. 579. Cf. also the chapter by Michael Hodges in this volume.

A Political Theory for the New Society
David Mitrany

C.E. Vaughan remarks somewhere in his massively learned history that in times of political upheaval political theory is impotent.[1] One can see the point: such are no times for debate. But now scholars, here and elsewhere, are heard to say that political theory is not merely dormant, but dead.[2] Stated so boldly, that must seem an extravagant paradox when all the world over countries are convulsed with political searching. Yet in a sense, in a deep sense, the assertion is greatly true: mostly it is politics without theory (as was the New Deal in America). None of the established theories can now contain the rushing waters of change that are surging over the world.

Modern political theory has never been sheer abstract speculation about some ideal of society; that was left quite consciously to the utopians. All the great contributions—of Hobbes and Montesquieu and Locke—were directed to contentious issues of the time, as was also the *Federalist*. And while emphasis may have been given to general form, to constitutions, the real concern was always with 'good' government; the virtue of the form was only relative as helping or hindering the good life of the community within. It is that relationship, the perennial balancing of state and society, that now seems shattered altogether, leaving little place or scope for a consistent political theory.

A few years ago the implications of this plight for the political scientist were put sharply, at about the same time, by two voices, one English and one French. The distinguished French jurist and judge who wrote under the pseudonym of Casamajor argued that our political practices had changed little but our circumstances had changed out of all recognition. 'It seems clear that we lack an elementary new insight; either we shall achieve this or we shall perish.'[3] The central issue was laid out more explicitly in an article on 'What Politics is About'. The 'historically unique achievements' of our science and technology 'present us with entirely new organisational problems. At no period in history has human capacity for political creation been subjected to such continuous unremitting strain', and this has rendered 'traditional ideas of "what politics is about" almost as obsolete as astrology or alchemy . . . In this unique historical context, if we are to win through, a supreme effort of political creativity is needed.'[4]

The strange aspect in the making of theory in our time and discipline is that while in relation to the state it is deemed to have lost any meaning, for the international sphere such a deluge of theory has gushed forth in endless variety from the academic springs, especially in North America, as almost to flood the field of political studies (and carry off the bulk of the golden loaves which the Foundations cast upon these academic waters). And the paradox does not end there. In a way it was natural after the shock of two world wars, and the appearance of doomlike new weapons, that western political scientists should

25

search anxiously for a prospect 'beyond the nation-state'. What earlier seekers had seen as a desirable advance now loomed up as a desperate necessity. We had to find the way to an international system with authority to purge world society, as we had to do in national society, of resort to force as the habitual way of settling differences and divisions. On the wider stage it was a more difficult but all the more pressing problem, but it was something which in modern times political scientists had learned to face and to solve within the national state.

The new international theorists did little of the kind. Some of them, a minority, skirted round the problem by simply prescribing a larger dimension—regional or continental or even global—of an established federal pattern.[5] (As a shipbuilder might simply multiply the dimensions of the same design for a powerboat and a river steamer and a transatlantic liner.) The great majority laboured hard indeed, but in ways strange to contemplate. They set out to uncover 'scientific' ways and laws for the making of an international system, using ingenious tools that, I suspect, would have stunned all the policy makers from Bismarck to Bevin. Three points might be made about the trend in general: (i) there had never been anything like it before in any field of political science, least of all in the international field; (ii) unlike the natural sciences, the trend showed almost as many approaches as performers—no unity of scope or method of comprehension, not even of language—and therefore the elaborate efforts could not precipitate a solid groundwork for an academic discipline;[6] (iii) there is no evidence that it has had any effect on actual practitioners and policy, nor any instances of political action based on one or the other of these 'scientific' models.

The matter of our study is thus replete with paradoxes. (1) Political stress in our time is unique in that it is universal. In previous periods political revolution overran one country or at most a region, but now the upheaval has spread, and at the same time, over the five continents. (2) A second and suggestive paradox is more a matter of our line of vision. In my student days political theory wrestled above all with the phenomenon of the state, its origins and nature and substance; a continuous questioning of the relation between state and society dominated the field, but even the historically-minded and liberal Sir Ernest Barker looked upon the national state as the ultimate in political creation. In a conservative mood one might worship it, in a radical mood one might hate it—as in the Marxist cosmology—but one way or another one could not get away from it.[7] That kind of introspection seems to have gone: not because the state has surrendered to Marxist doctrine and withered away, but rather because it has become so pervasive that it has absorbed all society into it. Now it hardly appears in argument or titles: the concern is with its working parts and ways as systems of political 'engineering', rather than its architecture, and their practical fitness in relation to changing practical ends. And the old passionate theoretical debates as to the seat of 'sovereignty' and power have vanished like the echo of distant cymbals.

No longer does the state enshrine the nature of society; it is the social current that determines, in perpetual adjustment, the make-up of the governmental system. In such conditions political science can no longer be other than pragmatical. Our society is experiencing a revolutionary stress without parallel in history. It affects every side of communal as of private life, and it touches and reverberates from every corner of the known world. With its threefold inter-related sides—social, political and technological—it is a revolution without a finite purpose or end, such as to reform a political system or displace a social power group or transform a system of property. Speaking sociologically, it is truly a 'permanent revolution', not that of Marx but in its very nature, without a clear horizon or spectrum or predictable end; a state of things in which the only constant is change itself.[8]

One can gain some insight into the central issue from another remark of Vaughan's, when he notes that Montesquieu was the first to introduce into the field of politics the view (adumbrated by Vico) that all knowledge is knowledge of relations.[9] Montesquieu regarded as central the relation between the form of government, with its prescribed rules and institutions, and the general social order; and he set out to 'prove that the whole social and civil life of every country depends, in the last resort, largely upon the particular form of government established in it'.[10] That was a natural logic when the issue was between arbitrary rule by monarchic 'divine right' and aristocratic privilege and the need to reform it towards constitutional government. But that is not the issue now. The relationship has been wholly reversed. No form of government, no constitutional or traditional claim is now immutably set: in the last resort the form of government and its laws and institutions are shaped and reshaped by the restless flux of the community's social pressures. 'Government' is no longer the guardian of a set social order, but the servant and instrument of social change.

These conditions pose two central questions for the student. Can there be any consistent theory at all as a guide to political organisation, or must it all be *ad hoc* improvisation? And as long as the international world is a medley of independent states, and the fundamental unit of the state is undergoing such uncharted transformation, what is the effect and meaning for international theory and the international system?

Today we are in the early stages of a wholly new political society; in the national range so all pervasive that one might call it the 'comprehensive state', for which, as a working system, we have no precedent in history.[11] The source of its uniqueness lies in the massive body of functions now vested in central government, summed up broadly in two categories of public responsibility: national security and social security; and both immersed in the new practice of 'national planning'. And all that functional concentration is taking shape under the pressures of an untamed scientific and technological revolution. The situation is new, but the ideological ingredients are those laid down by democratic Liberalism and Marxism, both products of the social transition of the nineteenth century; and when the arguments, on both sides, are put in nineteenth century doctrinal language, they not only sound archaic but are politically meaningless. Where are those 'self evident truths' that stood up so bravely in the American Declaration of Independence? Where the proletarian standards fluttering defiantly from the ruins of the State? It is all a battle of ideologies drained of ideas: no concepts fresh to our time, no political theory to have absorbed and make sense of the new problems and conditions.

National security had always been a responsibility of the central authority; indeed, as part of the consolidation of the national state it had been a preserve of the sovereign. But in the past (and relatively) its demands and its effects on the life of the country were limited. Now, if one includes research and other indirect aspects, national defence in leading countries probably absorbs close to half the value of the total national product, and it is especially relevant that unlike former times the organisation and demands of the new scientific defence go on undiminished even through years of peace. In 1952 President Truman rebuked as 'unrealistic' the 6-3 decision of the Supreme Court that taking over the steel plants by government could be justified only in case of war or invasion: 'In this day and age war is not only fighting, and defence . . . is a job for the entire resources of the nation'; and the President as Commander-in-Chief must be able to act at all times in the service of the nation's security.[12]

As for economic controls, even a sort of planning, they have been at work also in the past, under mercantilism. But, again, in those earlier periods social life was simple and mainly local, and the scope and impact of state intervention were correspondingly limited. As Professor Clinton Rossiter has put it in regard to the United States, the American President always was 'protector of the peace', now he is also 'manager of prosperity'.

The peculiarity of the trend is seen in the paradox that the greater the social change the less has politics, in the traditional sense, an active and controlling role. The more government *for* the people, the less government *by* the people. Most of the new states have quickly shut out the play of politics and taken up the bastard scheme of the 'one-party state'. In totalitarian states—apart from an ephemeral play with the 'corporative state'—the process has reached its logical conclusion by leaving no room for politics at all. It ends in a managerial state with a small ruling group deciding what is good for country and people; and having so decided proceeding simply by administrative action, changing at will governmental arrangements to fit the social plans; and with the Courts engaged in sustaining their decrees rather than a statutory body of law. 'It is a distinguishing mark of this kind of regime that there is nowhere any firm distinction between the state and the rest of society', but 'a forcible amalgamation of the two under the aegis of the Party' as the ultimate authority.[13] The full measure of the paradox comes out in the Marxist postulate of the 'withering away of the state' set against the Communist 'total' state, a sternly integrated governing machine which leaves no room for individual or group initiative, for material or mental adventure.

We can now see how some scholars came to think that there was no longer room for political theory. It would be difficult to fit into its traditional ambiance the pragmatical authority of a welfare state which refuses to be shackled to any constitutional pillars, which every day takes over by simple executive decision some fresh sector of society. And one can also see why so many of those who took up the international trails got lost in them. Though they looked at things less in terms of theory than of its actual embodiment they, too, felt the old self-confined state to be used up and that some new political construction was needed. But while dismissing the old limits they were unable to break away from the old conception, and seem to have taken for granted that, like the old, the new working ways must be woven within the stays of a fixed political-territorial frame. As a world dimension is not practical in our time, it had to be a lesser one, which inevitably meant a larger number of lesser ones. But as that is a solution that cannot meet the new global problems, the whole array of 'scientific' designs could only lead back to the very unscientific disunion of the old world.

As a witness of the cataclysmic transformation of the historical scene I confess myself greatly baffled by the rash of methodological efforts in pursuit of some 'scientific law' of international unity and disunity. There was nothing like it before the two world wars, when life in the world of states was more simple and predictable; there has been nothing like it since in the national field, though this is closer to our experience and steadier in its elements and problems. The quality of science is to give a more exact insight into how things work under certain conditions. In the flood of international methodologies, with every practitioner tending to use a contrived idiom of his own,[14] there is a risk that the more 'scientific', the less relevant it all becomes. Science is founded upon constants which impose their own unity upon all working in the particular field, but the international field is a turbulence of inconstants and of the unpredictable; and all the valiant efforts to fix and categorise them have in no way made them any less so. 'American labourers in the vineyard of international relations seem no closer to agreement on a paradigm for international relations research than were their predecessors twenty years ago.'[15]

The main weight of the new effort fell on the use of mathematical tools, to give precision to factors and conclusions and make prediction possible. The economists had done that lavishly in the inter-war period—and the matter they work with is quantitative in its very essence, which that of politics is not—and what did they achieve in the way of predictions or solutions?[16] Even under 'planning', with computers and new sophisticated formulations, all the forecasts and plans in developed as in undeveloped states have gone awry; and in economics executive policy can actually be shaped to follow executive 'plans'. They have miscarried even under Communist or other dictatorships, though these provide the only political framework in which economic and social policy could be decided and carried out upon a predetermined quantitative basis. Elsewhere social politics can never offer anything so 'scientific': economic issues of production may work under technical prescription, social issues of distribution now more than before must labour under political competition.

All these elements are bound to be more ravelled and magnified in the international sphere, and any 'scientific' model more divorced from the working reality. What help can 'decision-making' theory bring to the student when some ninety of the UN's 130 members are ruled dictatorially, policy changing mostly through violent changes of the whole regime? Given the anxiety for a stable international system it was natural enough that the 'integration' school should have had the widest appeal and following—though the relevant article in *The International Encyclopaedia of the Social Sciences*[17] notes that while they use the term widely, scholars are far from agreed on what they mean by it. In fact, with hardly an exception, to achieve any definition its practitioners have fallen back upon the regional dimension; but except for the EEC, which has grown out of its own special seed and momentum,[18] and as yet is far from an 'integrated union', every political-federal integration proposed or attempted since the war has failed, some of them tragically. And even so truncated and shuttered, what help has 'integration theory' brought to the working present, what insight into the prospective future?[19] Some followers of the 'integration' school have sought light from the history of past unions. Whether the union of England and Scotland or that which made the German Empire have anything relevant for our own international problem may be left open. But it is very relevant that in our time more political unions have broken up than have come into being; and the easy assumption that regional neighbourhood makes ready soil for political union should have been checked by the unhappy experience of Latin America and of the Balkans over the century-and-a-half since they have been free from outside domination. Neighbourhood does offer real ground, however, for a scheme of devolution that might encourage those countries to deal together, in the first instance, with their own regional problems and differences; this would relieve much of the pressure on the central organs of the UN, and in the process would show the benefits and spur the habit of local co-operation.[20] And, on the other hand, there is much to learn from the social history of international relations: how trade and finance, culture and communications, were 'integrated' at different levels and periods, not through political union but through changes and advances in particular fields of activity.[21]

If the present time is likely to prove a historical turning-point that will be, above all, because of such a dramatic change in the scientific-technological field. It is unique in its spread and variety, in its deep permeation of social life all the world over; but especially because every new invention, every new discovery is now apt to breed problems which, for the first time in history, are global in their very nature and in their scale. And that, inescapably, also projects the scale of the coming international system. Old habitual issues, trade and finance and so on, can still be pushed around by the ways and whims of individual states or their groupings. But satellites and other soaring marvels yet to come are free of any 'sovereign' land or air limits and so cannot be checked through diplomatic bargains and pacts, as little as these can control epidemics. Rather it is these new devices which impose their own measure upon the international system. Each in its own kind is governed by its own technical nature, and the controlling answers must be of the same kind. And as their mechanical skills and purpose are constantly being refined, the controlling answer cannot be tied to fixed terms and time limits, like diplomatic deals, but, like the technology itself, they must be adaptable to changing conditions and effects, under some continuing authority. Nuclear power, space travel, the exploration of the seabed—they all move upon a new plane of international relations and organisation, shaped not by any theory as to the political self-determination of the parties but by the technological self-determination of each of the matters involved.

In fact every such issue in recent times, from nuclear non-proliferation to pollution, has had to be dealt with through *ad hoc* specific agreements, each shaping its own controlling organisation and rules (so much so that in 1972 UNITAR felt impelled to arrange a seminar to look into the effects of that proliferation of direct contractual pacts outside the UN). All these rules and regulations in their varied but specific relevance are steadily building up a body of new international law, of positive administrative law, a true development in international government, while much of the old diplomatic international law, like much constitutional law, is ignored or falling into disrepute. The contrast between the two may be seen in that the most respected rule of traditional international law, the 'freedom of the seas', would if invoked actually stand in the way of any collective agreement on the exploitation of the deep seabed. The states themselves have had to work out the central principle of the new international condition. To be able to carry on their scientific-technological experiments and activities, they have set up in joint accord *non*-sovereign spheres in space and in the maritime deeps, a negative condominium in Antarctica, and so on. In other words, the new problems are leading them not to create sovereignty but to deny it, not to exclusive political integrations but to collective functional integrations. And so, as Ronn Kaiser has granted in the article quoted before, 'given the proper political environment, the old functionalist dream of world peace might be possible in a functional region that becomes world-wide'.[22]

If traditional political theory has little to offer for the understanding and guidance of the new welfare state, it can offer less for the new international condition. Yet while politically the two dimensions seem wider apart than ever, in their social philosophy and problems of government they are now close to the point of affinity; because the elements which set them upon their new course are the same for both. Traditional theory rested upon fixed constitutional positions and relations, the new social and technological problems are in constant flux and resist any attempt at such formal enclosing. Their needs are eroding the great tradition of democratic-representative government, and thus the sense and act of participation on which it depended. Hence the general lament about 'alienation'; and hence, paradoxically, the attempt to mend this with the old 'democratic' remedy of widening the electorate has only served to dilute still more the scope of popular initiative and control. All the aims of political democracy were to control government; all the claims of social democracy end in control by government. To quote Professor Rossiter again, 'the positive state is the administrative state'; and the administrative state all too easily can degenerate into a bureaucratic-autocratic state. The essential balance between executive and the representative factor could be restored only 'by bringing the citizen into the process of government on his own specialist level, as well as in his capacity as an elector'. Every individual is something of a specialist, and 'it is at the point at which his own life comes into contact with the state's regulations that his interest in politics can be most easily aroused'[23] — and, one might add, intelligently used.

The democratic dilution at work in the welfare state is bound to go deeper in the wider and more unstable international dimension. If constituencies now are too large and general elections too vague to make sense of popular participation in a single state, what meaning could they have in direct elections, say, for a European Parliament that might have to debate lines of social and economic policy to serve from Sicily to Scotland?[24] And even this would relate to only one 'region' and only to its own local problems; what would it be for the wider international sphere and its wider global problems? It is instructive for the similarity of the new character of government in whatever sphere that just as in old states a growing range of policy is settled outside Parliament, in the international sphere, as we have related, a growing range of problems are settled outside the formal workings of the UN. Yet because its agencies were opening a new world of communal action and did not have to fit into an established mould, many international experiments actually show an advance in democratic representation. While the nationalised sectors in Britain, for instance, or the TVA and other executive agencies in the United States and elsewhere are autonomous and outside any representative control, the specialised agencies of .the UN, like the ILO, were each provided from the outset with a small functional assembly to watch over its policy and performance. And as besides expert officials they include representatives of relevant professional bodies, the NGOs, they know what it is all about and can bring the views of their profession into the shaping of policy, while also taking back to their constituents the sense of that agency's policy and actions.[25] Their democratic value was well summed up by an earlier writer: bodies such as these may 'diminish the orthodox sovereignty of the states, but the power and sovereign rights of the people would increase because they would have a direct voice through their own delegates in all the agencies handling some of their affairs.'[26]

Here one may see not only the parallelism between the national and the international spheres in the new ways of government, but also the line that leads them together towards a working integration. Insofar as it points to a new phase in political outlook and evolution it is surely the very sign of our time—the sign not of power but of service (even dictatorships now justify themselves as service dictatorships). That is the inherent meaning of the planned welfare state, and I believe its political lines will soon work themselves out into a theoretical conception. And that conception will implicitly reach out beyond the nation-state, just as the philosophy of the welfare state has grown fortuitously into that of a welfare world (partly, again paradoxically, because the disruptive vagaries of national planning can only be met through international planning). Between the two, therefore, is not a political division based on 'sovereign' distinction, but a sociological continuity and affinity based on the new universal social aspiration, with inevitably similar ways of working towards the service purpose of our time.

The functional theory is a concept of social construction, and therefore implicitly of sociological relevance.[27] As a scheme of government it seems flexible enough to serve the varying needs of the time in whatever range. But it should be clear, given the difference in historical stages, that in the international range its task is the opposite of that in the national range. In existing national systems functional devolution can serve to check a cankerous executive centralisation (and at the same time make for more efficient administration). In the international sphere its scope must be rather to concentrate sectors of activity under some collective authority and so build up, gradually, the substance of an international society and of international government; until at a deeper level the two sides merge to the same ultimate purpose. Whenever it is used it can serve both ends at the same time because it is the only concept that breaks away from the long durance to the dogma of sovereign territorial division—which, after all, is only a modern invention and not a law of social nature. Hence, it is the only one which allows social organisation to find and follow its natural bent and range; the only one capable of adapting itself to our endless changes in needs and conditions without political upheaval. And all that and always patently for the benefit of all the peoples in the partnership.

Out of its straight and simple practical virtues the functional concept thus generates a unified political theory, one not bound to any ideology or dogma but to the living realities of the new service society; hence it is that so many of the new issues move quite naturally into the functional scheme of action without the need of theoretical advocacy. It can serve the international prospect above all, because it does not offend the natural attachments and attractions of nationality, nor links of religion and race or even ideology; because it answers truly and fully the old call for a 'league of peoples, not of governments', on foundations that all have in common and all can understand (even the illiterates), and which at all times can be tested in action for all to see as to its value in performance and its fairness in service. It works through that equally natural diversification of practical loyalties through which modern society has sought to be both collegiate and free. Political world government is not possible, but common government is both possible and necessary in those things which need to be governed in common. And that means that it cannot rest on contiguity of territory, but on the conjunction of social interests.

Notes and references

1   C. E. Vaughan, *Studies in the history of political philosophy before and after Rousseau,* ed. A.G. Little, Manchester: Manchester University Press, 2 vols 1925; new edition New York: Russell, 1960.

2 I myself in 1951 produced a paper with a 'Lament for Political Theory'; Mr Stuart Hampshire a little later seemed baffled that theory should have lost its voice just when two grand ideologies were clinched in mortal combat; and Mr Laslett announced with simple finality that for the time being political theory was dead.

3 'La Justice, l'Homme et la Liberté, review in *The Times Literary Supplement,* London, 25 November 1965.

4 *Ibid.* 18 November 1965.

5 William H. Riker, 'Six Books in Search of a Subject or Does Federalism Exist and does it Matter?'—review article in *Comparative Politics,* October 1969, pp. 135-146.

6 William T.R. Fox, *The American Study of International Relations,* Columbia Institute of International Studies, University of South Carolina Press, 1968, p. 116.

7 To give just a few of the titles between the wars: Hobhouse, *The Metaphysical Theory of the State*; Rathenau, *Der Neue Staat*; Follett, *The New State*; Wollsendorff, *Der Reine Staat*; Spann, *Der Wahre Staat*; Oakley, *The False State*; Grabowsky, *Der Motorische Staat*; Kjellen, *The Organic State*; Steiner, *Der Dreifache Staat*; Ziegler, *Autoritärer oder Totaler Staat*; Smend, *Der Staat als Integration*; Laski, *The State in Theory and Practice*; etc. etc.

8 In much the same words this was the argument I put by way of response to the general enquiry from the new Social Science Research Council, in July, 1966.

9 C.E. Vaughan, *op. cit.,* vol. 1, p. 260, 1925 edition—It is interesting that L.T. Hobhouse described the part of the political scientist as that of uncovering 'the relation of things'; and that Woodrow Wilson used the very same phrase (in the essay *The Mind of a Master*) when he said of Adam Smith that 'he was no specialist, except in the relation of things'.

10 *Ibid,* vol. 1, pp. 264-5, 1925 edition.

11 Past autocratic and such states had great concentration of power, but economic and social life was dispersed, locally and individually, with little national (let alone international) intercourse, and in the same degree less affected by the central 'autarchy'. In his famous 'horse-and-buggy' speech President Roosevelt pointed out that only some ten per cent of production entered into inter-state commerce at the time of the making of the Union.

12 *Mémoirs,* New York: Doubleday, vol. 2, p. 507.

13 G.L. Arnold (pseudonym of G. Lichtheim), *The Pattern of World Conflict,* London: Allen and Unwin, 1955, p. 116.

14 In *Hudibras,* Samuel Butler hit the point neatly:
　　'For all a rhetorician's rules
　　Teach nothing, but to name his tools'.

15 William T.R. Fox, *op. cit.,* p. 116.

16 The new tool is not even new at that. John Aubrey ('Brief Lives', London, Cresset Press, 1949 p. 275) recounts that when James Harrington (*Oceana*) set up the discussion group known as the *Rota* in 1659, (which met every night at 'The Turks Head', New Palace Yard), they were much troubled by Sir William Petty's 'arithmeticall proportions, reducing politie to numbers'. Almost three centuries later, Graham Wallas was 'really frightened . . . by the "experimental method" of Merriam and his disciples—which does not mean experiment at all, but the collection of observed facts with a definite attempt to prevent oneself

thinking about them. I am appalled at the amount of time and money and steady work and potential enthusiasm that is being wasted on "research".' (Letter to Walter Lippman, 12 Sept. 1927, kindly communicated by the late Miss May Wallas.)

17 New York: Macmillan, 1968, vol. 7, sec. III

18 The earlier regionalists simply assumed it to be a necessary intermediate stage between the nation-state and a world system; the new 'scientific' regional-integrationists have come to it rather from watching and analysing the growth of the European Union and then turning what they saw into a theoretical model for general application. It was not their theoretical work that guided the shape and process of this regional integration, but the practice of an actual integration which gave them ideas for their theoretical schemes.

19 It so happens that two encouragingly frank pieces of self-examination on this very subject appeared together in the *Journal of Common Market Studies*. In 'Toward the Copernican Phase of Regional Integration Theory', Ronn D. Kaiser wrote that neofunctionalism was in a state of crisis 'resulting from a collapse of basic assumptions. In short, it is becoming apparent that the methodological techniques of regional integration theory are meaningless without the substance of the process being patently clear'. And he quotes the self-criticism of Ernst B. Haas that 'a giant step . . . would be taken if we could clarify the matter of what we propose to explain and/or predict, (vol. 10, No. 3, March 1972, p. 207). On his part Professor Donald Puchala writes in 'Of Blind Men, Elephants, and International Integration', that 'more than fifteen years of defining, redefining, refining, modelling and theorising have failed to generate satisfactory conceptualisations of exactly what it is we are talking about when we refer to "international integration". . . . In the light of the reigning conceptual confusion in the realm of integration studies it is difficult to see why the field has acquired a reputation for theoretical sophistication. Rather, I should think that those of us in the field would be rather embarrassed at the fact that after fifteen years of effort we are still uncertain about what we are studying'. (*ibid.*, p. 268). And again, my theme is 'that our analytical models and our conventional frameworks have clouded more than they have illumined our understanding of contemporary international integration . . . We must, in other words, stop testing the present in terms of progress toward or regression from hypothetical futures since we really have no way of knowing where or how contemporary international integration is going to end up.' (p. 276-7).

20 A very early paper urged such a scheme of regional devolution on these very grounds, as most of the smaller states (with Switzerland an exception) existed in such clusters. But it also urged it because such regional groupings might serve as units for joint representation on any central organs so as to obviate the unreal and stultifying pretence at 'equality' between all member states, or their invidious division into 'classes' that would be involved in any scheme of weighted representation. David Mitrany, 'Minor States and a League of Nations: A Scheme of Devolution', *The Manchester Guardian*, 19 April 1919). Sir Winston Churchill mooted something similar in a world broadcast, 21 March, 1943: In a world institution 'side by side with the Great Powers there should be a number of groupings of states or confederations which would express themselves through their own chosen representatives, the whole making

a council of great states and groups of states'. (Reproduced in *'Onwards to Victory'*, *War Speeches*, ed. Charley Eade, London: Cassell, 1944, p. 37.)

21　See Maurice Mandelbaum, 'The Problem of Historical Knowledge', New York, Liveright Publishing Co., 1938, where he shows the habitual division into random time-epochs—Middle Ages, Rennaissance, etc.—does not make much sense. One has to follow up particular functional sectors, which tend to overlap in their differing history of progress or stagnation or decline.

22　It is not a little interesting to follow the play of the 'dimensions' in relation to the functional argument. The two authors mentioned before on the whole stay within the regional scale, and their own pictures seem familiar, but for some reason both strive to vary the baptism of the concept, surrounding it with a mixture of rhetorical overtones. Mr Kaiser chooses to describe 'a likely model for an integrated Europe of the future' as a 'regional conglomerate, analogous to Haas's "asymmetrical regional overlap".' 'The regional conglomerate would have the European Community evolving to the status of a central government, but in an incomplete fashion. The member states might become quasi-sovereign guardians of their cultural nations while the Community serves as the administrator of a relatively depoliticised economic commonwealth. The pattern of interdependence would vary between units, perhaps from issue to issue.—The regional conglomerate assumes that both the depoliticisation of economics and the transformation of identity will be incomplete and uneven.' (*op. cit.*, pp. 270-1). Puchala prefers to describe his version as a 'Concordance System characteristic of contemporary international integration'. 'Let it be noted that . . . a Concordance System need not be institutionally centralised. Transactions are channelled through institutions, to be sure, but the Concordance System may include any number of functionally specific organisations and any number of standardised procedures, while it includes nothing even vaguely resembling an overarching central government. In this way again, the Concordance System remains essentially an international system.' And he quotes in support Fagan's description of regional integration in Central America: 'In a sense, the integration effort was not one but several efforts, each issue being taken up by a different, largely autonomous institution.' (*op. cit.* p. 278). Still within the regional context there is a special interest in 'Europe's Futures, Europe's Choices', a study from the Institute of Strategic Studies, London, because it analysed systematically six possible 'models' for union in their political, economic and military implications; and then in a concluding chapter dismissing all the six saying that 'the functional solution bears the smack of reality as a general prescription for the world in the 1970's . . .' (p. 165) 'The mixed, functional Europe suggested here would be a more modest Europe than many people have hoped and worked for. *Functional Europe* may sound tame stuff to a younger generation fretting under the conventional wisdom of their elders. But it might, nevertheless, . . . offer a considerable intellectual and political challenge. For it may require a profound change in our concept of international co-operation.' (p. 167) (Alastair Buchan, ed., Chatto and Windus, London, 1969.) As to the 'world-wide' range mentioned by Mr Kaiser, such a picture was given by Mr Seyom Brown in the article 'Constructive Disorder in World Politics': 'On the traditional issues of trade, tariffs and international currency, the dominant coalitions of the past twenty-five years are falling apart. New issues are arising—economic exploitation of the oceans, the control of environmental pollution, increasing demands for nuclear energy . . . The goal should be the emergence globally of the kind of complicated webs of special interests and associations found in many of the advanced industrial nations . . . Civil wars are most rare where an interlocking of individual interests restrains those who would pulverize the society'. A new diplomacy would 'seek special opportunities for practical co-operative projects with those with whom one has general ideological disagreements . . . If we are to envision world community in these terms, the current disorder, with all its threatening aspects, might appear a time of constructive opportunity.' (*Brookings Institution Bulletin*, Washington D.C., vol. **8** (4), 1972.) It was all summed up by Professor Percy E. Corbett in the conclusion of his paper 'From International to World Law': 'My survey has, I hope, shown that a marked advance in integration has occurred in the last half-century and that despite setbacks it continues. The advance has been carried on by a partly fortuitous combination of private and public enterprise directed to particular tasks without overall definition of purpose or plan of concerted action. If there has been any underlying theory, it is of the functionalist type propounded in the last three decades by David Mitrany and his followers.' (Lehigh University Research Monographs, No. 1, October 1969). One curious and unexpected item might be added to this little selection on functional internationalism. Professor Gerda Zellentin relates that in a letter to Lenin, 14 March, 1922, the Soviet Foreign Commissar, Chicherin, urged 'functionalist strategies as a way to secure peace and counteract the League of Nations.' He suggested a world congress of all countries and colonies, with trade unions making up one third of the membership, and which under a unanimity rule 'would act as a moral authority'. For practical matters the Congress would set up technical commissions which would carry out 'our wide-ranging economic programme for reconstruction on a world scale' (such as the internationalisation of transport and of sources of energy, foreign aid 'from the strong to the weak', and so on). Bourgeois capital only knows how to exploit, 'but in the international commissions it will on the contrary be induced to invest for joint action for "the general good".' Against the lines on technical commissions Lenin wrote in the margin, *jawohl*, and underlined it. (*Intersystemare Beziehungen in Europa*, Leiden, Sijthoff, 1970, pp. 206-7.)

23 Dorothy M. Pickles, *Introduction to Politics*, London: Sylvan Press, 1951, p. 104.

24 See the other chapter in this book by David Mitrany. It is suggestive that about one-third of the huge bureaucratic establishment at Brussels consists of translators and interpreters.

25 David Mitrany, 'An Advance in Democratic Representation', *Associations*, Brussels, March, 1954; reprinted in *A Working Peace System*, Quadrangle Books, Chicago, 1966. See Lyman C. White *International Non-Governmental Organisations, New Brunswick, N.J. Rutgers University Press, 1951*. Also, Georges Langrod, 'Le Rôle du secteur privé de la cooperation internationale', *Associations*, Brussels, October, 1954.

26 Hans E. Fried 'The Frontiers of the Future', *Free World*, August, 1943, p. 11—See Robert C. Angell, *Peace on the March*, New York: Van Nostrand Reinhold, 1969.

27 Some of its critics have pressed the issue of 'separability', that one cannot

separate the functional from the political aspect and organisation. The fallacy of the argument would have been evident if I had used 'constitutional' as a base of distinction: 'political', admittedly, is very wide in its usage. But everywhere in the democratic West that is the very thing that has been pursued in numerous modern arrangements (nationalised boards in Britain, executive agencies in the USA); and that has been the invariable and inevitable pattern with international agencies, beginning with the Rhine and Danube Commissions, the International Postal Union, and so on. I suspect that the criticism rests on a confusion as to the steps of the process: a state's decision to participate inevitably is a *political* act, but once made it has to accept the *non*-political conduct and policy of the functional organ; just as national executive agencies become functionally autonomous once they have been brought into existence by the 'political' act of Parliament or Congress.

Neofunctional Theories of Regional Integration
Nina Heathcote

Can the international society of states acquire the procedural characteristics of a domestic political system? The neofunctionalist theory of integration asserts that it can, in particular that the integration process gradually erodes the national sovereignty of the European Economic Community member-states, transforming the Hobbesian anarchy into some form of irreversible political union. This is possible because, according to the neofunctionalists, in the post-industrial 'new' Europe the autonomy of the nation-state was already questionable.

Ernst Haas claimed the new-functionalist theory to be 'one of the most promising modes of analysis' available to students of international relations.[1] Nevertheless since 1958 he has found it necessary to revise the theory, first in 1967 as a result of the 1965 Community crisis, (see below pp.00) and again in 1970 (see below pp. 00). Unlike the orthodox functionalists, Haas believed integration would succeed most in a regional setting and took as his chief subject for investigation the European Community where he believed the nation-state to be in 'full retreat'.[2]

The theory attempts no less than a solution to the problem of international violence, first in Europe, and then, so it is hoped, by emulation in other parts of the world. It is concerned with integration whenever

> . . . the erosion of local autonomy (in this case state sovereignty) . . . may be based on deliberate and voluntary decisions by actors or . . . unintended consequences of such decisions, but . . . never . . . on force.[3]

Because of the change in the nature of international society, the nature of international conflict has also changed. As states lose 'attributes of sovereignty' they acquire 'new techniques' for resolving conflicts between themselves based on a consensus to settle differences by peaceful means.[4]

This is surely a challenging programme. Can sovereignty really be eroded as Haas envisaged? Has he not opened a Pandora's box in so boldly advocating 'new techniques' for conflict resolution? By dismissing the notion of sovereignty as an anachronism, Haas (like the earlier functionalists) asserted that both internal and external peace could be safeguarded without the ultimate sanction of force and thus had attempted to avoid the age-old dilemma: though sovereignty is a necessary condition of interstate violence, is it not also necessary for the maintenance of internal order? (To do away with the capacity for external coercion while retaining internally the power to coerce, though a familiar utopian objective, has not yet been managed in practice.) Or, as Bernard Crick poses, is not a government's ultimate power to enforce order internally and to maintain its state's integrity from external conquest necessary to its providing for the peaceful resolution of internal political conflicts?[5]

Functionalists understood that a future European superpower might indeed keep order between member-states, yet would recreate at the regional level the fundamental problem of power-politics. Replacing nation-states with structures like themselves only larger would not eliminate international violence. This led David Mitrany to criticise the founding of the EEC. Haas, on the other hand, though a leading neofunctionalist is now less confident of his earlier belief that by adopting a supranational government the EEC would avoid becoming a nation-state writ large.[6]

To assert that coercive power has become irrelevant to internal peace or to international order is to imply a fundamental change in the nature of politics. Not unexpectedly neofunctionalism (like functionalism) is anti-political, on the grounds that political activity (except when directed towards the promoting of welfare) is bound up with warfare, outdated and destined to decline. In the modern western state, politics has come to reflect 'a general consensus on the desirability to preserve and develop industrial society'[7]. Power for power's sake had ceased to be a motivating force of governments; defence, foreign policy and ideology mattered no longer.[8] As governments learnt that they could satisfy demands for welfare without recourse to violence, international conflict would become manageable. Haas at times represents high politics and welfare politics as distinct, e.g.

> . . . supranationality symbolises the victory of economics over politics. . .[9]
> . . . the supremacy of welfare-dominated policies is assured.

At others, he seems to suggest that in modern pluralistic, industrial states, welfare is the main interest of citizens and politics merely disguises this reality:

> . . . there is no longer a distinctly political function, separate from economics, welfare or education, a function which finds its reason for being in the sublime heights of foreign policy, defense and constitution making.[10]

The assertion in the last quote necessarily precludes all possibility of testing the hypotheses implicit in the first two.

Mistrust of politicians ensues from dislike of politics. Integration in the EEC would progress, in Haas's view, not by the efforts of individual politicians, but through governments, 'adaptive interest groups, bureaucracies, technocrats and other units with modest but pragmatic interests', and furthermore by incremental steps. 'Rational', welfare-oriented administrators (the EEC Commission) rather than ideologically motivated statesmen are to be responsible for leading the new technocratic Europe towards its supranational goal. Into their theoretical construction of supranationality, which administrators alone can understand and manage for the benefit of all, the neofunctionalists have smuggled the concept of an over-riding common interest, and betrayed the ideological bent of their theory.[11]

The neofunctionalists would object: bureaucratic rule is not intended to suppress political conflicts, but only to provide better means than parliamentary democracy can for resolving them peacefully:

> . . . political community exists when there is likelihood of peaceful change in a setting of contending groups with mutually antagonistic aims.[12]

The supranational method is alleged to offer appropriate outlets for a plurality of interests. Haas stressed the need for the setting up of central bureaucratic institutions whose task would be to channel conflicting demands into 'merging ideological patterns', i.e. to guide them into supranationality.[13] This important innovation exposed the neofunctionalists to the charge of crypto-federalism.

To show that integration would not result from political dedication to a federal state nor be dictated by central institutions (or any other agency), that is, that it would 'never (be based) . . . on force', Haas introduced the notions of system and process, which he claimed were neglected by Mitrany. Given the bureaucratic, pluralistic and industrial environment of modern Europe, interest groups each working for their own (perceived) self-interest would unintentionally converge to constitute a system[14] by means of the 'spill-over' process. It is the latter process and not 'force' that would automatically lead the EEC from economic to political unity.[15] The unintended consequences of performing tasks with which the political actors (interest groups, political parties, bureaucracies) entrust central institutions would in turn generate new problems which, if the new demands and expectations of the actors were to be met, could only be resolved by more integration and by granting new powers to the central authorities. Thus each further stage of integration is attained by a 'spill-over' from the preceding one. The impetus is supplied not by the efforts of a political movement sharing long-range aims (as in a federal undertaking) but in a short-term pattern of interaction.

In this way the supranational method can establish in the external order that procedural consensus otherwise typical of internal politics. When actors come to realise that their main interests require commitment to central institutions, they 'learn' to observe new rules of conduct without being coerced, without contrived agreement on the contents of proposals, or without sharing the purpose that integration should succeed. On the crucial question of movement towards supranationality, however, their choices are foreclosed by the logic of the integration process which determines the outcome.

Haas seems to regard the deterministic element of the 'spill-over' process as a kind of moderate determinism: 'moderate' because no one is coerced, the free will element is supplied by the willed purpose of the actors, 'determinism' because the 'automatic' (or—as he calls it—functional) element is furnished by the 'unintended' consequences of the actors' choices. Haas was more deterministic than he liked to admit, for integration was the sole outcome which he seriously considered to be possible.[16]

Haas's 'actors' differ from ants only by their occasionally combining for conscious promotion of integrative aims, and by their being aware of (merely short-term) self-interest. (Haas subsequently had to invent a new category 'dramatic political actors' to account for General de Gaulle's success in taking deliberate political steps against supranationality.)

> . . . neofunctionalists rely on the primacy of incremental decision-making over grand designs, arguing that most political actors are incapable of long-range purposive behaviour because they stumble from one set of decisions into the next as a result of not having been able to foresee many of the implications and consequences of the earlier decisions.[17]

This is often but not always true. What is remarkable is that what they as humans cannot do, the spill-over process will do for them. The down-grading of conscious political activity, upon the mere assumption that a regular patterning of events such as the 'spill-over' predetermines the course of international affairs, reflects the theory's sociological bias: man is the creature of circumstance.

The neofunctionalist theorists have thus contended that, as integration proceeded, the consensus characteristic of the domestic political system would be recreated at the Community level and so replace power-politics. The sovereign power of the state, no longer needed to supply the framework for peaceful resolution of internal conflicts and unfitted to discharge a like responsibility in the international setting, was in the process of being superseded by the authority of supranational institutions.

In 1967 Haas admitted that his hypothesis had been challenged by the events of the 1965 crisis: supranationality being disrupted in 'high politics' style by de Gaulle.[18] It is not clear why in a single footnote Haas attributed important aspects of this revision to two diametrically opposed interpretations in two separate studies of the Community crisis: Professor Lindberg's in which he argued the crisis confirmed the validity of the neofunctional 'spill-over' doctrine,[19] and mine which questioned that doctrine's validity. [20] Haas conceded that the 1965 clash between France and the EEC Commission was power-political. Nevertheless, he stopped short of renouncing his belief that a new supranational style was replacing power-politics and that national sovereignty was being eroded by means of the spill-over process. Instead he stated it with less conviction and in a logically weaker form: 'incremental processes . . . are always subject to reversal'.[21]

To salvage the theory Haas concentrated upon explaining the causes contributing to the disruption of his process: 'The functional logic . . . presupposes that national consciousness is weak and that the national situation is perceived as gloomy'. He now qualifies 'the functional logic' as follows: as the nation-state becomes stronger 'the very success of the incremental method becomes self-defeating as important elites recognise that welfare can be safeguarded without a strong Commission and overt political unity'. 'If integration has gone very far by then, no harm is done to the union but in Europe it had not gone far enough before the national situation improved once more'.[22] Thus unless the integration level reached a certain threshold the process might be interrupted by a strengthened expression of national consciousness.

We leave aside for the moment the fact that even in France, whose leader arrested the integration process, the evidence has pointed less to a nationalist revival than to a revival of state power—in general that the EEC is not an affair of nations or groups, but of governments. More to the purpose: that an apparently continuous progress towards integration was interrupted in 1965 puts in doubt the neofunctionalist thesis of a basic incremental process. But what calls for explanation is not why the process was disrupted, but why it is held that the thesis, in the amended form 'that integration and disintegration as two rival social processes are simultaneously at work'[23], should be retained. The amended theory is now so broad that it cannot be challenged by contrary evidence. On Haas's terms any interruption to the integration process can be interpreted as an expression of national consciousness and included in the amended 'explanation'. Is it not simpler, and at least as plausible, to approach each advance toward (or retreat from) integration as resulting from an act of political choice that entailed no spill-over and no subsequent 'learning'?

We can now question the theory's central contentions, that the international

41

system in post-war Western Europe was unstable, and that relations between member-states of the European Community were undergoing a qualitative change. But in practice supranationality has had little impact on the sovereignty of the EEC member-states; the Six's diplomacy seems no different from diplomacy practised by nations elsewhere. Progress in integration has proved deceptive, and its achievements have largely been limited to an industrial customs union and to common measures for protecting agriculture against competition from the outside world.

It is therefore surprising that in his ambitious move towards constructing a general theory of integration Haas, writing in 1970, glosses over these objections by flatly asserting that power-politics no longer plays a significant role in relations between member-states of the EEC.

The neofunctional and communications theories have neither been falsified nor have they demonstrated positive predictive prowess outside Western Europe.[24]

The theory would be

... concerned with tasks, transactions, perceptions and learning, not with sovereignty, military capability, and balances of power.[25]

Should violence-generating factors (e.g. considerations of balance of power and so forth) nevertheless appear decisive in promoting or in arresting integration, either phenomenon would by definition remove the study of inter-state politics in Europe from the neofunctionalist concern. The assumptions of the theory are taken as proven with respect to the EEC and the debate thus concluded. This of course implies that if empirical evidence accumulates in favour of power-political considerations, then the neofunctionalist theory is, on its own terms irrelevant, and has historical interest only.

However that may be, after 1965 the deterministic approach needed reformulation in probabilistic terms with the aim 'to explain the *tendency* toward the voluntary creation of larger political units'[26] This shift in terms at once raises the problem of measurement: unless Haas can establish and measure the variation of political integration with the incremental process, the basic assertion just quoted remains too vague to merit serious consideration. But recent neofunctionalist effort has not succeeded in producing numerical data or in constructing reliable measurement scales, without which statistical models are pointless. Measurement problems will be discussed again later in this chapter (pp.00); meanwhile one should keep in mind that statistical models break down except where there is a recurrent pattern implied by a process. At this point the most important objection to a statistical approach is that difficulties of measurement have indefinitely postponed putting the revised theory to the test.

Computer simulation, to which Haas next resorts, would in his opinion '... stretch ... our minds and give us a purchase on the future.'[27] Simulation cannot test a hypothesis (although it may be a guide) since a computer will yield no more information than is put into it, and what is left out, in this case power-politics, may be crucial. Again, a solution based on simulation assumes at least that a scale of measurement applicable to the reality is available and only minor or technical details (e.g. lack of time, complicated distribution of error) hinder an assault on the problem itself.

Contrary to what we should expect from the neofunctionalist analysis, disagreements between the member-states have been reconciled by diplomatic rather than by supranational means, and the propensity for conflict has if anything increased. The growing influence of the Council reinforces an impression that the EEC countries act on the basis of national interest, and in concert only when these interests coincide. All of this seems to imply that to exclude power-politics is to exclude most of what goes on in the Community, leaving the neofunctionalist theory with very little to explain and therefore with little explanatory power.

The main emphasis in the joint work[28] of Leon Lindberg and Stuart Scheingold is on identifying fluctuations in the course of integration as a basis for estimating its future prospects. They only hint at the effect of such changes on the nature of international politics, in particular on the question of international violence. Thus the reader is merely informed that authority would be shared between a collective decision-making centre (the Community) and the national systems on a basis of a 'symbiotic relationship'

> ... that will provide the most adequate, flexible, and responsive combination of resources for coping with the problems of the future. . .[29]

Their investigation is therefore more restricted than that of Haas and more concerned with methodology. Lindberg himself shares Haas's ambition to arrive at some form of universal law of integration by applying quantitative techniques, and his work both individually and jointly with Scheingold raises some important issues concerning the usefulness of abstract models and quantitative arguments.

To distinguish himself from the strictly neofunctionalist school, Lindberg has adopted a behavioural approach, applying David Easton's systems analysis to the study of European integration. The integration model he and Scheingold elaborate is less deterministic, and a more 'actor-oriented one', than Haas's, 'emerging out of neofunctionalist thought, but distinct from it in the extent of its voluntarism'. Actors, not economic forces, articulate demands and provide leadership for the promotion of integration.[30] In order to examine the theory it may be useful to sum up its basic propositions.

The basic model specifies that the decisions or output depend upon the variation of inputs and on their processing by the systems.[31] The inputs are

1 A continuous stream of demands which supposedly accelerate or reverse integration.
2 Leadership, the supply of which depends on the initiatives of national or supranational leaders.
3 Support, which though not strictly an activator of the integration process, provides a necessary favourable 'background' of mass and elite attitudes towards the collective system.

These inputs, if powerful enough, may activate four mechanisms (spill-over, side-payments and log-rolling, feed-back and actor-socialisation). As actors realise benefits from integration, their attitudes towards the system may change and generate new demands thus repeating the cycle, either accelerating the integration process, leaving it static, or else reversing it.

The term 'integration' is defined operationally[32] as an increasing function of

1 *Functional scope,* i.e. the range of decision-making functions delegated to central authority,
2 *Institutional capacity,* i.e. the extent to which the collective systems can process demands. It includes (a) the authority of supranational institutions to make decisions and to have them accepted; (b) intergovernmental agreements about decision-making rules and norms in bargaining.

The variables: scope, capacity, leadership, and support, are the resources at the Community's disposal for processing demands in order to alter the level of integration. Precisely how integration depends on these variables is not defined, but an equation is given[33] on the basis of which it is hoped to predict changes in the level of integration according to changes in these independent variables. This point will be discussed later.

Three patterns which identify the effects of decisions on the dynamics of integration are abstracted as:

1 fulfillment of tasks and obligations;
2 retraction or non-fulfillment;
3 extension of joint activities into completely new areas of decision-making.

Each of these three recurrent outcome patterns is said to be associated with a distinct 'process model' derived from the basic model of integration but at a lower level of abstraction. Separate models are needed allegedly because different variations and combinations of variables are said to be associated with each. As I understand the authors' argument, these may be summarised as follows:

Fulfillment is represented either by the *Forward Linkage* process model which implies growth in integration (i.e. an increase in scope and capacity) or the *Equilibrium* model, corresponding to a state in which activities are regularised or constitutionalised without changes in the levels of scope and capacity.

Retraction may be associated with either the Output-Failure or the Spill-back process models, which represent a withdrawal from a previously agreed area of activity and a decline in the levels of scope and capacity even to the point of complete disintegration.

Extension is represented by *Systems Transformation*—a model(s) of integration not yet devised; and refers to a situation in which obligations are expanded beyond the original treaty commitments.[34]

The purpose of these models is to help our understanding of the 'infinite complexity' of the real world,[35] and to predict the most likely integration outcome. So far Lindberg and Schiengold merely speculate on the relationship between variables for each outcome. The authors themselves concede that their evidence based on case studies is merely suggestive.[36] From their cursory examination of the factors which may account for successes or failures of integration in the different issue areas, they formulate a hypothesis concerning the future evolution of the Community as a whole. It is here that an effort is made to replace the neofunctionalist notion that deterministic 'spill-over' process ensures uninterrupted progress towards a political union with the proposition that the Community as a whole only tends towards equilibrium. This is to happen gradually, with other outcomes still to be expected in discrete issue areas. The sectoral approach is a methodological device, which (like Haas's two opposing incremental processes) helps the authors to account for the uneven course of integration since 1965.

In 1969, when *Europe's Would be Polity* was being written, the empirical evidence seemed more consistent with the hypothesis of equilibrium already attained, than with the over-optimistic spill-over hypothesis. For spill-over the authors substitute 'conservative dynamic' which is not automatic but depends on actors' perceptions of costs and benefits. Equilibrium sets in when actors reach a certain level of satisfaction and no longer wish to risk their gains in a crisis provoked by further integration, for by definition integration is said to imply stress and conflict.

> The European Community is . . . a crisis system that seems to advance most often as a result of very tense and explosive situations.[37]

Yet once established the equilibrium state can be disturbed only by a crisis. As actors perceive that, through inaction, the benefits of integration may be lost, they may prefer to accept the risks of a crisis in order to reactivate the dynamic of the system. The authors do not seem to consider other, equally logical possibilities, e.g. that costs would continue to outbalance benefits and might be generally recognised as doing so, at any level of integration.

Because their theory is posed in a statistical form, Lindberg and Scheingold are faced with similar measurement problems as is Haas: they must be able to measure relevant variables, otherwise statements about conditions associated with any of the proposed integration models and predictions about the Community's future are for the time being mere opinions.[38] Yet while it is asserted that quantification is possible, Lindberg's essay 'Political Integration as a Multidimensional Phenomenon. . .'[39] provides little more than a taxonomy of variables that require measuring, and no properly specified model is produced let alone tested. The conclusion of the article acknowledges the generally acceptable proposition that '. . . the political integration phenomenon is enormously complex. . .'[40] and states that the author's present contribution is in identifying the dimensions of variation on which integration depends.

The problem of measurement is discussed in some detail and interesting tables of descriptive statistics based on subjective measures are presented, but not much is claimed for these data.

> Of course, as they stand, these specific categories and codes are clearly inadequate for use as a serious research tool.[41]

Elsewhere Lindberg concedes that

> I will limit my discussion to fairly general suggestions as to what ought to be done, leaving it up to those with more sophisticated mathematical and statistical skills to work out the details of how to do it.[42]

Is he dodging the issue? If his dimensions of variation are to provide useful

45

independent variables in a mathematical or quasi-mathematical model, it is pointless to list items that require measurement without demonstrating that they can in fact be measured. Otherwise his propositions may remain interesting, but have been neither established nor refuted. His article thus confirms the view suggested earlier in this chapter (p. oo) that a statistical approach to the prediction or explanation of political phenomena such as integration may be mischievous. This brings together the following two criticisms or questions: (1) there are, as his own efforts indicate, good reasons to suppose that the difficulties of measurement are insurmountable, yet to refute his integration hypothesis critics must await his providing such measurement scales. (2) Moreover, the complex measuring enterprise is only justified if the model offers evident promise as a candidate for elucidating the current status of integration.

It is implicit in *Europe's Would-Be Polity*, and generally throughout neo-functionalist thought, that the evolution of international relations during quite short time-periods is characterised by recurrent patterns. The attraction of this approach to the study of integration is the possibility of projecting trends over longer time-horizons, and the prospect of a general explanation. The dangers are that much trivial information may be collected merely because it 'fits' regularities, and that vital information may be omitted because it defies classification.[43] But how has this approach clarified the realities of the European Community?

Consider for example Lindberg's attempt to defend the concept of process which he employs in his analysis of the 1965 crisis:

> It seems at least likely that de Gaulle has been *betting on* the permanency and irreversibility of integration, not challenging it. Far from denying the effects of spill-over and the political implications of economic integration, he has based his strategy on them while at the same time acting to limit their effects on himself. He has not intended to undo integration but to turn it to his own purposes. The other members of the Community are trapped by the logic of spill-over and by the web of relationships and commitments which have developed since 1950. . . . The theory of integration and of the spill-over process, seems to be strikingly verified by de Gaulle's actions (if turned on its head!)[44]

It is likely that de Gaulle 'based his strategy on the political implications of economic integration', but this does not automatically validate the 'theory of integration and of the spill-over process'. Indeed, de Gaulle was reacting not so much, to the political effects of economic integration as to a straight-forward power-political bid by the Commission. Obviously, the spill-over logic could not explain the subsequent slowing down of integration, and so the authors of *Europe's Would-Be Polity* account for that effect of the crisis by reference to another force, i.e. the conservative dynamic. The crisis:

> . . . had the paradoxical effect of constraining both those who would expand the scope of integration and those who would limit or roll back integration.[45]

Nevertheless it is important for the authors to make the case that at least one issue area, that of agriculture, was unaffected by de Gaulle's 1965 attack on supranationality:

... Thus while crises certainly affected the Community's overall institutional capacities, its impact on or relevance for the agricultural area is not clear.[46]

If *all* issue areas were significantly affected by a single act (e.g. de Gaulle's in 1965) then the sectoral approach and indeed the concept of process, though not actually invalidated, would lose much point. Lindberg and Scheingold spell out their view of the debate in the following terms:

... individual sectors or issue areas seem to tend toward equilibrium, and ... as integration proceeds, more and more sectors are likely to follow suit and the whole system may become ... more stable and more resistant to growth. Hence our projection of an overall equilibrium or plateau to be reached some time within the next several years:

and

It is an over-simplification to attribute the slow-down in integration that became apparent in the 1960s to the malevolence of one political leader, de Gaulle, or even to a 'lack of political will' among political actors more generally... Perhaps as important as these factors ... are the two trends we have stressed ... namely; the conservative dynamic set in motion by the integration process itself, and the possibility that the societal and international parameters that sustained and conditioned the growth of the Community from the 1950s to the mid-1970s are in the process of being transformed.[47]

To rebut those who attribute the slow-down in integration '... to de Gaulle...' one must show that after 1965 his policies did not affect the course of events. But the authors having no taste for detailed controversy about historical causation accommodate the counter-example as an 'over-simplification' in uneasy partnership with their notion of process.

The present writer dissents. In view of the fact that since 1965 integration has suffered reverses at all levels, there is not much explanatory power in the concepts of equilibrium and conservative dynamic.[48] After General de Gaulle prevented majority voting from coming into operation in the Council and attacked the authority of the Commission, the 'institutional capacity' of the Community has been weakened. The Commission has never recovered its prestige and the Council has never seriously attempted to revive supranational procedures. Divisions along national lines have been deepened by the recent trend towards conducting the Community's more important business in a sequence of semi-institutionalised summit meetings of Heads of Government. Such divisions are characteristic of relations between the EEC members as regards East-West relations, trade policies with the USA, attitudes towards world currency problems and as regards virtually all aspects of integration.

Thus more than just institutional procedures have been set aside. The prospects for economic integration are now in doubt. With the Agricultural Policy in serious difficulties, the Community may be slipping back into a mere customs union. This state of affairs suggests that on matters of importance the member-states have seldom allowed the 'Community method' to come into play. It is therefore premature to conclude along with *Europe's Would-Be Polity*, that

> The result of . . . merging of (national and Community) systems is that actors tend more and more to define their roles in terms of joint problem solving rather than as agents of one system or another.[49]

Recent events, such as the abortive attempt to establish monetary union, emphasise the irrelevance of such theorising. In 1971 the latter project broke down under the impact of divergent interests of the member-states (especially France & Germany) and of world currency problems for neither of which the theories here under discussion can account. Moreover, parity fluctuations have nearly destroyed the common market and single price system in agriculture. The Community can occasionally concert its policies in dealing with the outside world as it did during the Kennedy Round, and on some aspects of monetary and trade matters as in the 1971-72 negotiations with the United States, but this is a far cry from integration. Yet quite clearly there is plenty of scope for 'joint problem solving' in the Community on such matters as structural reform in agriculture, inflation etc.,—on which, (be it noted) the EEC has so far failed to act effectively.

If de Gaulle's single political act was crucial in arresting progress towards supranationality, if subsequent reverses in economic integration can be attributed to the interplay of competing national interests among states unwilling to surrender national sovereignty, and if most of the important decisions are made by the heads of member-governments, then disaggregating the process to examine sector-by-sector contributions is likely to prove both tedious and unrewarding. Under these circumstances the 'process' hypothesis itself (whether the process is supposed to be generating spill-over or a conservative dynamic) is superfluous.

The shortcomings of a methodology which relies heavily on abstracting data suitable for statistical models has implications for the behavioural approach wider than the theories of integration here examined. But integration theories provide an interesting case study. An analysis of Community affairs in terms of actors' responses to risks and benefits of integration is more attractive to the behavioural scientist than the 'traditional', i.e. historical approach, since it lends itself to the type of theoretical manipulation to which he is a priori committed. It is a misfortune for him when empirical evidence suggests the overriding importance of the single political act or of changes too irregular to be fitted into statistical models.

A requirement of such models is that many actors (viz. enough to establish system-dominance) participate. In the Lindberg-Scheingold model the emphasis is therefore on

> . . . the critical role of interest groups and of bureaucratic and technocratic elites in the (integration) process. . . Much of the dynamics of integration can be described in terms of the gradual mobilisation and commitment of an ever-widening circle of subgroup actors.[50]

Planned long-range policies, of the kind that are usually the prerogative of statesmen, are unlikely to emanate from the interaction of numerous actors with conflicting interests and aims. Statistical methods come into their own when dealing with broad and general questions arising from such interaction. But it is at least doubtful that integration in the EEC has been *mainly* the work of the 'ever-widening circle of subgroup actors' rather than of a few governments. Let us take the Common Agricultural Policy as an example in which interest groups did play an unusually important part. It is true that the demands of the German farmers to maintain the present high price levels for agricultural products contributed to the breakdown of the policy. But even though assimilating this information, the model appears to omit other vital, but possibly non-quantifiable information: on the currency crisis, the reasons for failure by national governments to solve problems of structural reform, German unwillingness to help subsidise French and Italian farming etc., all of which can be adequately explained in terms of competing national interests without reference to functional groups.

Models can be useful in suggesting a hypothesis or identifying a trend. But information must be interpreted with care. For instance, there is some force in the notion that national sovereignty is being eroded and the Community's strengthened as the range of activities subject to joint decisions increases. The transfer of sovereignty is said to take place as a

> ... movement *from* a situation in which individual national governments make all fundamental policy choices ... *to* a 'terminal' situation where all these choices are subject to joint decision in the European system.[51]

But to answer fundamental questions about the location of sovereignty one needs to know more: do states still retain the residual sovereignty which gives them the power to negate any given trend? If this power has not been exercised, then it cannot appear in the data; nor, of course, can it affect movements reflecting the Community's performance in completing tasks and fulfilling obligations. For these reasons it could be assumed for a time that national sovereignty was being eroded by the transfer of functions to the Community institutions. But de Gaulle's 1965 *démarche* reversed any such trend, and thus showed that the residual sovereignty of a member state could still upset the cumulative case in favour of progress towards integration.

It is potent criticism of the Haas and Lindberg-Scheingold approaches that until the measurement problem is overcome neither theory can be refuted, yet at the same time they do not provide much insight into every-day Community affairs. Significantly, the central problem of qualitative change in relations between the member-states receives less and less attention as theorists of integration occupy themselves with questions of methodology. With the passage of time their forecasts of European unification become less certain and less optimistic. Haas moves from the belief that integration will eliminate warfare to one that regional integration may in fact promote international violence.[52] Lindberg shifts emphasis from spill-over to an equilibrium of integration. 'Joint problem solving' cannot easily be reconciled with the rising of incidence of conflict between Community members; spill-over and equilibrium cannot characterise the mounting setbacks to integration. The complexity of the model-building involved has led integration theorists to exclude the Europeans states' relations with the rest of the world. Yet the monetary crises of 1971 cast doubt on those *regional* theories of integration that underplay or ignore the impact of events originating outside the local system. Similarly, Germany's central position on the continent strongly suggests that its relations with the superpowers may outweigh the advantages to it of cooperating with the members of the Community. The disruption of Franco-German relations in 1965 over the Multilateral Force (MLF) question, the possible consequences of Brandt's *Ostpolitik*, are developments which may overwhelmingly affect the prospects of integration. Rather than tackle such questions of substance, the theorists of integration have been seeking refuge in methodology.*

Notes and references

1 Ernst B. Haas, *Beyond the Nation-State*, Stanford University Press, 1964, pp. 3-4.

2 Ernst B. Haas, 'International Integration: The European and the Universal Process', in *International Stability*, ed. Dale J. Hekuis, Charles G. McClintock, Arthur L. Burns, John Wiley and Sons, 1964, p. 229.

3 Ernst B. Haas, 'International Integration', *International Encyclopedia of the Social Sciences*, ed. David L. Sills; Crowell, Collier and Macmillan, 1968, p. 522.

4 Ernst B. Haas, *The Study of Regional Integration: Reflections on the Joy and Anguish of Pretheorizing*, International Integration Series, Reprint No. 363, Institute of International Studies, University of California, n.d. p. 610 (Reprinted from *International Organisation*, vol. 24, (4), 1970).

5 Bernard Crick, *In Defence of Politics*, Pelican Books Ltd. 1964, pp. 178-9.

6 He thinks it possible but not likely that

... regional integration may lead to a future world made up of fewer and fewer units, each a unit with all the power and will to self-assertion that we associate with classical nationalism. The future, then, may be such as to force us to equate peace with nonintegration and associate the likelihood of major war with successful regional integration. (*The Study of Regional Integration, op. cit.*, p. 645.)

7, 9 and 10 Ernst B. Haas, *Technocracy, Pluralism and the New Europe*, Reprint No. 18, Institute of International Studies, University of California, n.d. pp. 70-71, 78. (from Stephen R. Graubard, ed., *A New Europe?*, Boston: Houghton Mifflin Co., 1964.)

8 Haas, *Beyond the Nation-State, op.cit.*, p. 47.

11 See Crick, *op. cit.*, chapter 5, 'A Defence of Politics against Technology', especially pp. 108-110.

12 Ernst B. Haas, 'International Integration', in *International Stability, op. cit.*, p. 230.

13 Ernst B. Haas, *The Uniting of Europe*, Stevens and Sons Ltd, 1958, p. 158.

14 Haas, *Beyond the Nation-State, op. cit.* p. 34

15 Haas, 'International Integration', *International Stability, op. cit.* p. 230.

16 Haas, *Beyond the Nation-State, op. cit.* p. 79.

17 Haas, *The Study of Regional Integration, op. cit.*, p. 627.

18 Haas, *The Uniting of Europe and the Uniting of Latin America*, Reprint No. 241, Institute of International Studies, University of California n.d., p. 325 (Reprinted from *Journal of Common Market Studies*, vol. 5 (4), June 1967).

19 Leon L. Lindberg, 'Integration as a Source of Stress on the European Community System'. *International Organization*, vol. 20, 1966. p. 234.

* I am indebted to Professor C.R. Heathcote of the Department of Statistics, Australian National University for general advice on the use of statistical models. However, the opinions expressed remain my responsibility.

20 Nina Heathcote, 'The Crisis of European Supranationality', *Journal of Common Market Studies*, Dec. 1966, pp. 166-9.
21 Haas, *The Uniting of Europe and the Uniting of Latin America*, op. cit., pp. 328-9.
22 *Ibid.*, p. 331.
23 Haas, *The Uniting of Europe and the Uniting of Latin America*, op. cit., p. 315.
24 Haas, *The Study of Regional Integration*, op. cit., p. 629.
25 *Ibid.*, p. 608.
26 *Ibid.*, (my italics).
27 *Ibid.*, p. 646.
28 Leon N. Lindberg and Stuart A. Scheingold, *Europe's Would-be Polity, Patterns of Change in the European Community*, Prentice-Hall 1970.
29 *Ibid.*, p. 309.
30 *Ibid.*, p. 282.
31 For the purposes of quantification, Lindberg later ('Political Integration as a Multidimensional Phenomenon Requiring Multivariate Measurement', *International Organisation*, Autumn 1970, pp. 649-731), expanded this already complicated model by the addition of more variables. A complete summary of his argument in that article is beyond the scope of this chapter.
32 *Ibid.*, p. 99.
33 *Ibid.*, p. 114.
34 *Ibid.*, ch. 4, pp. 101-140.
35 *Ibid.*, p. 138.
36 *Ibid.*, p. 135; 216.
37 *Ibid.*, p. 240.
38 e.g. Neither measurement nor adequate historical evidence support the following statement:
> ... growth opportunities *do not necessarily* vary directly with the scope and capacities of the system. Our model notation $dS=f(S+Su)(dD+dL)+e_n$ indicates that change (dS) is some function of the other major variables—including of course, the existing political system (S). *If*, however, an increase in the scope and capacities of the system is associated with growth only up to a point where the conservative forces take hold, then it is clear that the relationship between the system and support for the system is not linear but more probably curvilinear.

[*Europe's Would-Be Polity*, op. cit., p. 292. (italics added)].
Details of notation are unimportant for our purposes, since for the theory to have substance, estimation of the function must be possible whether it be linear, quadratic, or anything else; and for this, measurement of the variables is essential. The authors' 'not necessarily' and 'if', qualifying the above extract, indicate they are aware of the fact that as yet they have nothing of substance to communicate.
39 *International Organisation*, Autumn 1970.
40 *Ibid.*, p. 717.
41 *Ibid.*, p. 676.
42 *Ibid.*, p. 719.
43 For an illuminating discussion and criticism of the behavioural approach to social sciences see Hugh Stretton, *The Political Sciences*, Routledge and Kegan Paul, 1969, pp. 161-3.

44 Lindberg, 'Integration as a Source of Stress on the European Community System', *International Organisation*, 20, 1966, p. 240.
45 Lindberg, *Europe's Would-Be Polity, op. cit.*, p. 197.
46 *Ibid.*, p. 154.
47 *Ibid.*, pp. 305-6.
48 'spill-back' may be the more appropriate outcome pattern to apply, were one to describe the Community's evolution in Lindberg-Scheingold terms: 'spill-back' is an outcome pattern which is characterised by a decrease in sectoral scope or institutional capacities or both', *ibid.*, p. 199, see also p. 207: equilibrium at a lower level 'would amount to spill-back'.
49 *Ibid.*, p. 32.
50 *Ibid.*, p. 124.
51 *Ibid.*, p. 68.
52 Haas, *The Study of Regional Integration, op. cit.*, p. 645.

The Prospect of Integration: Federal or Functional?*
David Mitrany

On the day the European Consultative Assembly was to meet at Strasbourg for the first time, the *Manchester Guardian* welcomed it in a somewhat questioning editorial: It was altogether a 'strange experiment. Perhaps never before has an old aspiration seen the light so utterly unprepared for facing the world'. (6 August 1949). That might be said more generally of many plans, and even acts, which have gone into the effort for European union. The study of their implications has been trifling compared with the vast propaganda. The most assertive pleas have come from the federalists, and often they have claimed support from the success of the American union. That union was born in much simpler conditions than those facing twentieth-century Europe, and yet how searching and straight was the case that Madison and Hamilton and Jay argued in the eighty-six papers of the *Federalist*, in their appeal to the *minds* of the electors! If the effort to understand be tedious and irksome, Hamilton wrote in the fifteenth paper, 'you will recollect, that you are in quest of information on a subject the most momentous which can engage the attention of a free people; that the field through which you have to travel is in itself spacious; and that the difficulties of the journey have been unnecessarily increased by the mazes with which sophistry has beset the way'.

The perspective has been complicated by the use of the analogy with a single federal state by 'Europeans' within and outside the Six, and discussion often made elusive by the way many of them 'stick to the original concepts in spite of fundamental changes in European and international relations'.[1] The group set up some years ago by the Council of Europe to look into the problem of European unity conceded in its sober re-appraisal that 'no clear picture emerged from this intimate and searching discussion', only 'the need for genuine realism'; but 'M. Dennis de Rougemont, though he acted as chairman of the group, stuck to "federation" in an Introduction didactic and waspish in tone which read as if he neither heard what the group had said nor read the thoughtful summary which followed'.[2]

The study also admitted that the discussion left only a sense of the paucity of political inventiveness. One need therefore be neither for nor against the idea of European union to find genuine interest in any concrete instance of the anxious quest for some political idea that might work effectively beyond the nation-state and before the unlikely prospect of something like a world state. But for the reasons mentioned above the student still has to sort out some of the quite non-partisan issues that crop up continuously, such as what is 'political' and what is

*This paper is a revised version of an article first published in the Journal of Common Market Studies, December 1965. Reprinted with the permission of the author and publisher.

not, by working back to general findings of political science and even to traditional tenets of political theory. The scope of this paper is precisely such an attempt, inevitably a modest one, to clarify some of the political elements of European union. Only a relatively small part of the vast literature has concerned itself with the political side, and the bulk of this with 'diplomatic' aspects, such as the position of Great Britain and the cross-current of Atlantic Union[3]. Here we are concerned rather with the 'constitutional' side, and this not with actual structure and organisation, amply described and discussed elsewhere, but as a general system in itself and in relation to a wider international system.

A New Political System?

It would be natural to start from what exists, but on the political side one cannot do even that without some clarification as there are many divergences of mind among leading 'Europeans'. Most of them had from the outset called for a federal union. When initiating the first working institution, the European Coal and Steel Community (ECSC) though its charter said nothing of the sort, M. Robert Schuman insisted that it was but the first rung of a federal ladder; but later, in the group set up by the Council of Europe, both he and Mr van Kleffens spoke of nothing more precise than 'integration'. Nor did the Treaty of Rome include any political premise in its substantive part, but its preamble clearly if indefinitely stated the intention of the signatories to work for 'a closer political union'. The governments made some acknowledgment of this in the abortive Fouchet-Cattani proposals, and the 'European' view was given more precise and authoritative expression in the several reports prepared for the European Parliament by its political committee. But Dr Hallstein in the lecture he gave in London dismissed the whole 'distinction between economic and political unification as specious. . . What is called economic fusion is in fact a political process'.[4] To add to it defence and foreign policy 'would not represent a transition to another, the "political", sphere but would be merely the addition of further matters in a process which in fact already belongs to the political sphere.'[5] The division of views came out sharply in two speeches earlier in the same year. The German Chancellor, Dr Erhard, insisted in the Bundestag, 9 January 1964; that 'Europe cannot be achieved by automatic progress within the framework of the Rome Treaties, i.e. solely in the field of economic integration . . . It will take all our endeavours and all our political will to gather Europe into a unit that is not just technocratic but also political'. On his side, in his speech to the European Parliament on 18 June 1964, Dr Hallstein went so far as to list a 'specious political union' as one of the dangers facing the Community.[6]

Whatever may lie behind Dr Hallstein's line of argument, it entered deeply into the actual nature of the new European arrangement; and to find its place in the range of current political experiments it may help before discussing specific modes to ask in a general way what political union really implies. Dr Hallstein's argument no doubt is correct in this sense and degree: the Six being a group of independent states any decision to do something in common, from a solitary act to the EEC, can be taken only by the governments; and in all such cases the *agents* and the *decisions* are both political. But the *object* can be non-political (a commercial treaty or the ECSC), and the agency charged with the execution, even if autonomous, like the ECSC would essentially be an administrative organ. As Dr Erhard put it, in the

Common Market powers have been given 'not to what might be termed in any democratic sense a politically responsible body, but only to a joint administration'. Such an organ is competent to manage the activity put in its charge within the terms of the agreement, but not to act in any other sectors of the economic and social life of the members, let alone in any political matter.

Perhaps a point open to argument is how far such non-political activities can range without guidance and control from a political organ. Dr Hallstein again diverges from the predominant 'European' view when he insists that the EEC does not need such direction; he points out that the Treaty of Rome did not lay down a margin beyond which 'it can be implemented only on condition that "political union" has been achieved'.[7] In this he seems to be supported by Professor Kymmel who noted that Benelux was in effect a common market but without any political superstructure. 'In my view a common market or economic integration can be established and maintained without federation and without centralising all elements of economic policy in a supranational or federal body';[8] though Dr Hallstein, one must presume, would have liked to see all those elements centralised at Brussels—which happens to make all the difference.

To come back to the main argument, this particular difference of view affects only the range of non-political activities, but the position is very different where the object itself is political, for example, a diplomatic or a military alliance. Even if limited in scope and time (and though, like NATO, it may boast a Supreme Commander) it could never be wholly autonomous. The task itself can never be defined and limited in advance but must remain a continuous variable, reflecting changing situations; and situations changed by the conduct of the opposing parties as much as by the intent of the united parties, and so calling for equally continuous adaptations in policy. Every such decision, possibly charged with issues of peace or war, must inevitably stay with the responsible governments. But if they should reach the point where they want to unify and make permanent both the process of decision making and that of execution in foreign policy and defence, in what by its nature must remain a variable political sphere, that could only mean a common executive authority; that is—whatever its form and the process of gestation—a common government. Within possible constitutional variations, that is the essence of political union.

The six partners in the EEC, as Professor Kymmel pointed out, have never stated unambiguously how they saw the end-product of 'closer political integration'. All the student had to go by, as offering such formal evidence as there was, were the Fouchet-Cattani proposals and the *desiderata* of the Political Committee of the European Parliament; and all one could do was to see how these related to accepted patterns of political theory and experience. But even this is only half of the problem. There are two sides to any political picture—its form and its fitness. Form is the visible and classifiable element, but what makes it right or wrong is the second component of any political system, the social ambience in which it has to operate. If the governments, who must carry the consequences of their words, have shrunk from being more precise on what they had in mind, the 'Europeans' through years of insistent pressure have failed to probe into the utterly new social climate for which with unquestioning assurance they had offered an old transatlantic plant. As Thornton Read remarked some years ago, with a touch of impatient sharpness, 'In politics as in war certainty is a symptom of blindness'.[10]

The Regional Fallacy

The restlessness which now makes life uneasy all the world over springs from a combination of two revolutionary currents: (i) the end of the colonial era and the mass-production of new states; (ii) at the same time, a universal social revolution which through economic planning for social security and welfare is hardening every state, old and new, into something more truly 'organic' than anything known before. And all that has to be fitted into the high effort to build up a lasting international system of law and order; that is the world we are facing now. To pass the test of historic fitness any political experiment will have to take account of these two developments, which seem irreversible, and help to contain and guide them towards the creation of an international system of law and order, so that we may complete the democratic pyramid of responsible government. Perhaps in 1919 this ideal was premature. Nuclear power and the opening up of space have now made it the foremost priority, in which every other social aspiration—communal and individual, material and moral—is inescapably enmeshed. Reaction to the Second World War in fact brought out pleas from some for outright world government or world federation; others retreated into the idea of regional unions as an intermediate stage between the national state and the world.[11] As to this, it all depends whether regional unions are meant to become closed and exclusive, or simply units for administrative devolution within a universal system. 'Given the complexities of modern life and the restlessness of the mass of new states, the demands likely to be made upon any central international authority are bound to be very heavy, and perhaps excessive. It might be all to the good if that burden could be relieved by entrusting regional groups with the right and duty to deal in the first instance with any local issues through regional councils and regional courts, with the right of appeal to the central council and court should the local effort fail... Such a scheme of devolution would also have an educational value politically, in that it would encourage the local groups ... through the exercise of direct responsibility to learn the need for and the habit of give and take in their mutual relations... Proximity and even kinship have not always bred political tolerance between the states of a region. And regional devolution might also help, as a secondary advantage, to ease the awkward problem of formal equality through a system of indirect group representation in the central organs'.[12]

The possible use of such regional devolution has hardly been explored so far. But the regional idea would have vastly different consequences if used to set up closed political units. 'The new units would then not support but would cut across the jurisdiction and authority of any international system. The argument about the need for an intermediate step obviously is only valid if the regional unions are to be open unions; but if they are to be closed and exclusive, the more fully and effectively they are integrated the deeper must be the division they would cause in the emergent unity of the world'.[13] Most of its 'European' champions have seen their regional union as leading from the start, or by speedy stages, to a federal state; and experienced men like Robert Schuman, Spaak, Monnet and others have also seen it as an essential base for global unification. So had Mazzini and his friends been devoutly convinced that the nation-state was the essential gateway to a world at peace. But it is curious, and perhaps suggestive, that the idea of regional union should find favour now when it no longer makes sense politically or economically, and certainly not historically. It did not present itself at all to the mind of the two

Hague conferences at the turn of the century, and the Covenant of 1919 touched it but warily. A regional emendation was suggested in 1923, but quickly rejected; it was tried in the Locarno treaties of 1925, but achieved even locally no more than a momentary easing of strain.

Miss Sarah Wambaugh, the American jurist, pointed out some years ago that after the first World War Europe and Asia on the one side and the USA on the other had tried two opposite approaches to security, based on differing philosophies: the League system could not be tried out fully as long as America remained neutral; the American system had a free run. But insofar as they were regional systems neither worked. 'The League system did not fail because it was not regional, but rather because it was regional in effect.' 'Geographical association no longer corresponds to the actual interests of neighbours',[14] a view echoed more recently in a group appointed by the Council of Europe.

From an international standpoint this is merely stating the obvious. But even from a regional position it seems strange that it should spring into favour in Western Europe. The early European dreamers of world peace—Crucé and St Pierre, Kant and Rousseau and the rest—never thought of it: to them Europe was the universe. In later days of trade and colonial expansion Europe indeed wanted to embrace the universe; and the Concert of Europe was the controlling voice of the whole political world. Is there some meaning in the fact that this urge for European union should have come when Europe no longer dominates? Europe created 'nationality', but out of the same fount of liberating principles it also created internationalism. Yet now, when its ideas have spread to all the quarters of the globe and at last the prospect seems ripe for a general system, Europe is being urged to shrink back within the narrow comforts of her own walls. Western union—like Britain's connection with it—has been urged above all as essential for economic wellbeing, through the creation of a wide common market. A paper from the Council of Europe summarised the economic case in the simple proposition that national markets were too small, while world integration was impracticable.[15] The argument relied (i) on an outdated physical-political antithesis; and from that it proceeded to the 'specious' assumption that (ii) national markets were the normal economic working unit—ignoring the immense web of international trade and also the numerous trans-national links in all the main sectors of production.

It seems a doubtful issue, but I am neither competent to discuss it nor concerned with economic regionalism except in its political repercussions.[16] And as to these, whatever the material results, the mercantilist practices of economic planning will of necessity have to be applied still more forcefully in a regional union, which will have so many more strands to re-adjust and pull together, than in any one state.[17] There must be something in the fact that the Common Market of six sovereign states was from the outset placed under the management of an essentially 'bureaucratic' Commission. The same considerations apply with even greater force to the political factors. In their case the common interest cannot be visibly defined, while they often touch imponderable and fugitive sentiments. To build up a cohesive loyalty national movements have often had to disinter or invent all sorts of historical, 'racial' and emotional affinities; above all, to keep alive the fear of some common external danger. Regionalism, starting with more differences than affinities, would have to go even further in that conjuring performance. Western union has been argued all along as vital for putting Europe in a state of economic and political self-defence, 'to avoid coming under Russian domination without at the same time accepting permanent American overlordship';[18] though some supporters might wish to reverse the order of precedence of the two nightmares. Western man used to pride himself on his humanistic cosmopolitan outlook, but now even men of standing have come to talk of the need to develop a 'European personality'. It would not be fair to saddle them with all the aberrations of Count Coudenhove-Kalergi (the first recipient of the Charlemagne prize)[19] but what is that 'European personality'? Does it begin and end at the limits of the EEC? Even the formal Martino Report could say that 'there is no question of dissolving Europe in a wider *ensemble* in which her personality would be lost'![20] In the nature of things it must be something which while it binds also divides; and by implication also something which is not there, that has to be brought into being. Indeed, one general reason for demanding an elected parliament seems to be a belief that 'direct elections are the best, perhaps the only way of stimulating mass interest and participation in European unification.'[21]

The making of 'Europe' is not to be kept merely to economics and politics, it has to bring into relief also *'l'unité du patrimoine spirituel et culturel de l'Europe'*[22] A strange argument in such a serious source in view of the long sad history of Europe's political and religious divisions, more numerous and fiercer than the conflicts within Asia and the Americas; and now Europe is again split in half ideologically. If there is a 'unique characteristic of European civilisation, in contrast with Eastern and other civilisations, it is that it always has been an *open* civilisation . . . [and so] able to permeate the whole world with her political, social and cultural outlook and experience. . .'[23] 'When one thinks of the past humanistic glories of the ancient universities of Paris and Oxford, of Prague and Padova, how strange to be faced now, when science is opening up the farthest ways to outer space and the planets'[24] and when with our Ariel-like means of communication all knowledge is instantly 'universalised'—to be faced with a proposal for a European University where things are to be taught from a specifically 'European' angle, so as to reinforce Europe's cultural and scientific potential.'[25] Perhaps it is not odd but in character that this narrowing conception should have been put into the Euratom Treaty—although the new University is to teach also economics and politics, sociology and psychology!

Will the new 'third world', so eager for knowledge and development, and in which we have to compete with disruptive revolutionary influences, not suspect any cultural product labelled as distinctly 'European'? The very concept of a closed regional union is a contradiction of the historic European idea; and the farther it moves from the sheer material sector, the more does its synthetic nature stand exposed.[26] But even if these inbreeding efforts and devices—closed economic planning, exclusive political institutions, the cultivation of a regional patriotism—even if all this were to serve the goal of a (limited) European union, it can hardly bear the argument that it would also pave the highway to a wider international unity.

'Such seems the disposition of men', said Dr Johnson, 'that whatever makes a distinction produces rivalry.' The 'ecumenical' argument for European union has carried least conviction of all, and not only among outsiders. One may quote a few points of doubt from within the movement not because they are critical, but because they are evident and tend to restore the balance of view. As to 'inwardness', it seems likely that in its first period it would be 'so concentrated on the task of keeping a precarious union together and creating an identity of its own that

58

it would have little time and energy left for acquiring a global vision and tackling global tasks. It would not be the first time in history when a new nation would seek strength in isolation.[27] Dr Hallstein indeed saw that to be inevitable: 'There is no public association, no State and no association of States which does not begin by attending to the welfare and security of its own members. [This is] the *raison d'être* of every political community.'[28] As to outlook, 'the very penetration into these fields [foreign policy and defence]tends to divert attention among the Six from the aim of being a stepping stone for better international co-operation, to that of merely becoming a new 'big power'[29]—Dr Hallstein's 'sovereign voice'! 'There is no special reason to believe that a federal Europe would suddenly be guided exclusively by sweet reasonableness and self-restraint.'[30] As to the limits of the union, the search for a true European solution 'requires more than a solution of little Europe within the framework of the Six, the seven or the fifteen. The task which the European federalists set themselves in the resistance movement during the first post-war years to create in Europe the political and social conditions for an all-European peace still remains to be solved. This is a programme which does not accept as inevitable the *status quo* thrust upon us by Soviet policy'.[31]

The Federal Fallacy

Of the many ideas which have gone into the making of the 'European' creed the most persistent has been the idea of federation; and the federal idea in fact traverses most aspects and issues of European union, both in its internal organisation and in its relation to the wider international problem. It is an old idea, which has often appeared in plans for political union. The Republican call in the middle of the nineteenth century, with Victor Hugo in the lead, for a European union of 'free peoples' meant little beyond a Radical 'holy alliance' in the struggle against autocracy; and Cobden's shrill call in 1856 was pointedly aimed at Russia. The Pan-Europa vicariously urged after the First World War was both anti-Bolshevik and anti-Anglo-Saxon, though it never had any solid outline or more than a dubious and changeable support. The only British politician of rank to have favoured it openly, Leo Amery, was also the only one to have joined Beaverbrook's Imperial Crusade—a position as 'puristically consistent as that of the anti-Semites who applaud the Zionist ideal of a Jewish return to Palestine.'[32]

Of the inter-war schemes, alone that proposed by Briand in 1929 had a fairly solid core; it also is the only one to offer some comparison with the present ideas. Though M. Briand's scheme came before the nuclear explosion and the mass of new states, the overwhelming view then was that any European union must avoid all exclusiveness and remain an organic part of the League of Nations.[33] Nonetheless, at Geneva most governments feared that 'no matter what the intentions of its promoters, the continental union might drain the League of Nations of its substance and compromise its universality'—therefore they favoured economic but not political action.[34] As a concept European union could hardly have been a natural product as it never led to actual unity; the present call is something quite new—it goes further in scope, but as a consequence it also is narrower in outlook. As its protagonists hope to free Europe from the new American power by emulating America's successful federal formula, a brief look at that analogy should throw light on its fitness to produce a wider union under the conditions of our time.

When in 1935 the Supreme Court threw out the National Recovery Act, in spite of the desperate economic crisis, President Roosevelt pointed out that in the 'horse and buggy' days when the Federal Constitution was written some ninety per cent of the population lived in self-sufficient local communities. Even more to the point, democracy was then seen as meaning that government should do as little as possible, and the federal system was shaped to that outlook. It was an invention meant to deal with a revolutionary situation, and to unite thirteen undeveloped states, in an isolated continent, and with 'more common problems coming to them in the future than they had separate history binding them to the past'. The revolutionary situation of the nuclear age hardly answers to a pattern that gave every citizen an absolute right 'to carry arms'. To be at all valid, the analogy, in the first place, would have to answer not to what happened two hundred years ago under the conditions of the time, but whether the thirteen states, if each had grown by itself to full separate political and economic stature, could be induced to federate now.[35] Concrete evidence for an answer is found in the difficulties which all the federal governments have met since the war in the every-day performance of their new tasks—and in such non-political tasks as highways and banking and health services, and the like—in Canada and in Australia as in America; even in placid Switzerland, most of the referenda since the war have gone against the federal government. They have even been faced with threats of secession, in Quebec and Western Australia; and in the USA after two hundred years and a bloody civil war, the issue of State rights still remains a perennial irritant.

Sometimes these federal governments have had their right to act in international society challenged by subordinate units.[36] All this can still happen in federations which are well-established national societies. Yet the reaction is not unnatural. A federal system rests upon a settled balance of power; any addition to the central functions alters that balance, and with cumulative and permanent effect. Sometimes the attempt is made to restore an older balance. We have not taken enough note of the centrifugal internal regionalism which in recent years has arisen or hardened even in old unitary states—in Belgium as in Italy, in France and in Britain; and, significantly, in the new federation of India. India had been provided with a more modern constitution, and had inherited a unified administration and a strong sense of national unity forged in the struggle for independence. Yet she had been troubled by cross-regional strains which had not existed before independence and has had to accept new anachronistic subdivisions caused by such factors as language and ethnic factors. An experience so widely spread leads to the conclusion that one effect of centralised planning and policy is to repel local sections with a marked interest or characteristic of their own, and that the reaction inevitably turns to thoughts of dis-union. It should be obvious that the wider the geographical limits of a new union and the more disparate its parts, the more difficult it must prove to accommodate the sub-regions.[37]

The 'European' federalists have been so caught in a readily convenient formula that they have neither asked how it works where it exists, nor whether its origins bear any relation to the problem of uniting a group of old states in the present social ambience. It is this question of sociological fitness which is at issue here. But once again, first one has to interpolate a theoretical clarification because the tactical vagueness of the 'Europeans' has now been fed by a new thesis from Professor Carl Freidrich, who has a close knowledge of the European experiment and is an authority on federal matters. In two recent papers[38] Professor Friedrich has tried to replace the established meaning of federation, as a particular type of political union, with the idea of a 'process by which a number of separate political organisations, be they states or any other kind of associations, enter into arrangements for doing various things jointly; and any and all of such actions fall into a general 'federalising process'. Even in old federations he says, there is never a constant relation between unifying and diversifying forces, rather an oscillating process, with sometimes one and sometimes the other in the ascendant. That is no doubt true, but it is true of all government; and it is least true of federal government. A new union or association is not conceivable without some formal compact, whose main purpose is precisely to delimit the competence of the various organs. That is why it has to provide for an arbitral Court, which Professor Freidrich lists among the essentials of a federal framework; and why it generally puts stiff obstacles in the way of that 'process' of change—which Professor Freidrich thinks should be not as difficult as it is in the USA, but neither 'so easy that the federation will not hold together'. The very purpose of any such written compact or statute is to introduce an element of fixity in the index of power; and no political system is so fixed as a federal constitution. It is intended to withstand the constant pressures from the ordinary claims of government as from sectional interests, and so 'hold together' the whole. It has proved far easier to change the position and powers of the British Crown by what one may fairly call a functional adaptation, than it has been to change the position and powers of the federal authority in the USA or Canada or Australia by amendment of their written constitutions.[39]

'The function of a true political thinker', said the late Professor Hobhouse, 'is not to predict events, but to uncover causal connections.' When all political systems are shaken, as they are now, by a social revolution, it is all the more the part of the political scientist to try to pin down the true implications of the schemes and expedients of the practising politician; whereas the likely effect of such permissive teaching is illustrated by Dr Hallstein's lecture—to use an experienced and authoritative witness. He starts from a correct statement of established theory: 'The position is that federation is one state but that confederation is a league of states' (World Today, January 1965, p. 15). But after that his thought becomes elusive. The Community would leave to 'each member its ultimate sovereign power', but it had to be a 'firm union' (loc.cit p. 13) and it must speak with a 'sovereign' voice in world politics (loc.cit p. 14). To that end, after economic and social life, trade and foreign policy and 'the sinews of war must be made Community matters', leading to the 'integration of defence policy'. (loc.cit pp 16-17) 'Integration is thus a process and not a static thing, and this process is one that tends towards complete federation, that is to a federal state.' And the argument ends with the dismantling of his initial definition: 'The conclusion is that there is no hard distinction between federation and confederation, obliging us to choose' (loc.cit p. 17).

We have not been helped in recent times by similar inflationary uses of 'democracy'; yet that is an abstract generic term, which might be filled with any content, from laisser faire to Socialist planning. But terms of specific constitutional classification are meant to tell us within fairly clear lines what kind of political prospect we are called upon to underwrite with our votes. That is all the more important when facing a new and far-reaching political adventure and when the electorate in Europe has nowhere been canvassed by a special 'European' party or by an election on the clear issue of European union. Could candidates for a European parliament ask the electorate from Brindisi to Bremen simply to 'Vote for our federalising process'!

And here we come to those matters which are at the heart of the political issue, as of any political system—namely, the range of its functions and the conditions under which they are to be performed. Fortunately, there is one aspect on which all students of politics are likely to be agreed—the vast change in modern times in the nature of government and, as a consequence, in the respective positions of executive and parliament. The original intent of the democratic idea was 'that Government should be kept to a minimum, and that minimum was to be guided by an informed and sensible electorate and controlled by its independent representatives.' In all these respects we have gone far towards the opposite pole, even in democratic countries. 'Government now tends to be omnipresent and, where present, almost omnipotent, if we accept, as we must, Sir Ernest Barker's definition that government authority is "the sum of its functions".'[40] For any new federal experiment, if it is to be free to develop the modern attributes of a welfare society, the working prototype is likely to be not the US Constitution of 1787 but rather something nearer to the federal system of the USSR.

The two functions always conceded as belonging to a federal executive have been defence and foreign policy (and trade). Defence as recently as 1914 was still a matter of a limited force with a limited armoury; but which part of resources and of industrial potential could now be said to remain outside the range of Dr Hallstein's 'sinews of War'—and not only in time of war, but throughout the longer periods of peace? Which part of economic and financial policy is now outside the scope of foreign policy? Nor is it possible to set any limit to the spread of centralised public action: the continuous pressure from new inventions and discoveries, on which the economic sector is as dependent as defence, can generally be controlled and provided for only by some central authority. The political balance sheet of these considerations should be self-evident. If the all-inclusive union which the 'Europeans' want were to be based on a restrictive federal balance-of-power, it would not be capable of growing freely into the kind of planned welfare society which marks our time; whereas if it were to be set up without the traditional federal restraints, it must grow—as it will have more, and more mixed, elements to weld together—into a more unitary political system than any existing federation.[41]

The 'sum of these functions', not any preconceived formula, must in the end shape the character of an eventual European executive, and hence also of a European parliament. As executive and parliament will be the pivotal organs of any fully-fledged-union—we may ignore for this brief review the piquant question of who would be its head, an elected President with hereditary Kings and Queens under him, or perhaps the several national rulers by rotation—it is striking how perfunctorily they have been examined in the proflic literature on European Union; indeed, the nature of the executive has been given hardly a glance.[42] Most of the recent argument has revealed an anxiety about giving the European Parliament some real control over policy at the expense of the powers of the Council of Ministers—the 'popular' as against the 'governmental' factor. The argument has been put with cogency and urgency in the Martino Report and may be justified in itself—as long as the present arrangements last.[43] But it is dubious as a general argument, and peculiar in its immediate assumptions. It is peculiar that a body of delegated parliamentarians should think it possible to be transformed, and fairly speedily, into a representative parliament, with commensurate powers, without making it clear that this could not be until an equally representative common executive had taken charge of affairs—of affairs intended to spread quickly and widely into new fields. The making of a comprehensive union could hardly be left to an amorphous 'popular' assembly and a Commission of 'technocrats'.

And in a more general way, the expectation of commanding powers for such a parliament overlooks the actual contrary current, and one bound to prevail if the wish for full union is fulfilled. One could lay it down almost as a law of modern politics that the powers of executive and parliament are bound to move in inverse ratio to each other. There are three general reasons for this. First, the enormous increase in government activity reduces the possibility of parliamentary initiative and control; that is bound to be more acute in a multi-state union with its wider jurisdiction and therefore greater complexity in policy-making. Secondly, the same conditions have added weight to party organisation and constricted the independence of individual members (both admitted and justified by the late Lord Morrison in his book, *Government and Parliament*). One cannot forsee how party alignments and organisation would develop in an elected European parliament, but these difficulties would surely affect individual members.

The third reason is the most powerful. The wider the activity of the state, the wider its direct contacts and relations with organised groups of interest, a trend as conspicuous in Scandinavia as in USA. Many issues of economic and social policy are now settled, or modified in application, through private bargaining between government departments and professional and other organised groups, without benefit of Parliament.[44] A whole new system of policy-making has thus grown up, not through any arbitrary imposition but through the inescapable sweep and urgencies of planned government, a system of 'government by committee.'[45] This particular tendency, above all others, inevitably would be strongly at work in a new multi-state union. Its administration could hardly work unless it were preponderantly 'bureaucratic'.[46] The wider and more varied the jurisdiction to be encompassed, the firmer will its planning have to be, and in the same measure the less amenable to protracted debate and detailed control by a motley parliamentary chamber at the centre. Local variations in claims and interests, and the multiplicity of organised groups, could not be attended to in any other way so as to gain acceptance for uniform legislation and administrative rules. While, therefore, it is a fair claim that the present Communities (though it was not true of ECSC) fall short in democratic content as long as they lack a representative assembly, it is an illusion to think that in a 'more perfect union' an elected parliament would gather unto itself more power than is now left to national parliaments even in the best of democratic states. It is likely to be less: it will have neither the cohesion nor the acquired traditions of a national parliament; while the executive will be under greater pressure of public business but also less exposed to the watchfulness of parties and press and popular opinion. Warning that 'Europe is not a nation', the Secretary-General of the European Parliament, Dr H.R. Nord, went on to say that 'It follows that attempts should not be made to solve the problem of European parliamentary control merely by trying to make the European Parliament look more like a national one. We are faced with a new and original phenomenon and the future rôle of the Parliament should be assessed in the light of the distribution of power within the Community.'[47]

Because of the neglect of such an assessment some derivative aspects of the parliamentary problem have been passed by altogether. The European Parliament has for some years pressed for direct elections with universal suffrage so as 'to associate the peoples' in the work of political integration; though as members of their home parliaments they must be aware of the spreading apathy of mass electorates everywhere. Constituencies are too large for close contact and interchange, and public issues too many and too technical to allow for more than very broad party appeals at election time. What range of constituencies could serve for an oversize continental election—a million, two million names on the electoral roll? What kind of concrete 'European' issues could be put by candidates to so vast and mixed an electorate to make as good sense in Sicily as in Brabant, on the Ruhr and in Brittany, and so generate that common 'European consciousness'? And this brings up a final and a more serious issue than the awkwardness of electoral mechanics. A fair 'European consciousness' has been achieved at Strasbourg by the simple device of keeping anti-Europeans away. It was perhaps not unnatural to send to Strasbourg party-members who at least were in general sympathy with the institution.[48] But what is to be done about the new opposition, for instance, in full Communist representation in a direct general election? Only two alternatives seem possible: (i) submit to the fundamentals of universal suffrage and so let in from the start a powerful element opposed to the very idea of Western union, and ideologically allied to the hostile Communist world; (ii) or prevent full Communist representation and so pollute the democratic claim from the start. Moreover, such arbitrary ostracism might attract around them other dissident elements and so, paradoxically, on this issue, help to widen their national appeal and make their outcast status still more indefensible.

Perhaps there has been no more curious sidelight into the state of mind, or the tactics, of the 'Europeans' than the way they have all along assumed that direct elections with universal suffrage must bring them popular support. They have simply ignored the fact that such a direct electoral challenge would also provide the first occasion when the various groups and sections who for one reason or another dislike or doubt the idea of Western Union would be brought together into something like an organised opposition.

The Functional Alternative

Much of what precedes had to be given to a critical examination of the federal idea because what matters here is not its theoretical virtues but its fitness in practice for a particular multi-national association—even within the arbitrary limits of a region. That people should have turned to it is not unnatural: it seemed the only relevant formula because our political thinking has so long been rooted in the notion that every authority must be linked to a given territory.[49] For the rest, it is plain that European federalism has been a blend of myth and some very mixed sentiments.[50] That is proved in another way by the readiness of moderate 'Europeans' for something more flexible. 'The majority of us do not regard the unification of Europe with the emotions of people acquiring a new fatherland', wrote Professor Samkalden; there is a need for 'a diversity of new organisations for specific needs and interests', and a 'plurality' of them is already available in which the value of the communities, 'but also their necessary limitation, find clear expression'.[51]

New and original phenomena demand, as at other crossroads in history, suitable changes in the government of societies, and three such phenomena may be singled out as governing the present problem of international peace and development.

(i) The new scientific inventions and discoveries have raised political, social and moral issues which can be dealt with only on their own global scale. Not one of them is peculiar to Europe; in the nuclear field all that Western Europe could do is to add its own pile of nuclear bombs, but not to halt their fearful menace.

(ii) At the same time, the contrary prospect of twice the number of sovereign states entitled to follow their own will, and many tempted by a revolutionary mood to do so.

(iii) The third factor, cutting across the other two and confusing their relation, is the trend to neo-mercantilist planning. It has injected a political element into wellnigh all the manifold international activities and relations which formerly grew freely across most frontiers. That is the given equation. The key we have to find, as the UN Charter demands, is one which allows us 'to achieve international cooperation in solving problems of an economic, social, cultural or humanitarian character' in the attainment of common ends.[52] To have a lasting effect the answer must be global. In theory that could be done through a world state or federation; but even if it were desirable, such a monstrous construction is not likely to come about unless through conquest. Or it could be done by making use of the present social and scientific opportunities to link together particular activities and interests, one at a time, according to need and possibility, and giving each a joint authority limited to that activity alone. That is the functional way.

Let it be said at once that there is nothing new in that. Before the two world wars, it had been the natural mode of western international organisations, some public and many private, but since then we have actually fallen back from the ways of the liberal nineteenth century. 'Before 1914 world integration was proceeding steadily by means of firm treaties and relationships, open door arrangements and so on. In addition, a great number of pre-1914 agreements created what might be termed "abstract regions" through multi-lateral contracts under the authority of international law.'[53]

Now, as in former autocratic times, economic and social and even cultural relations have again fallen under the control of the state—'the State has almost become an organisation for the prevention of free international intercourse and the growth of a normal human society'. Fichte's eighteenth century mercantilist extravagence, *Der Geschlossene Handelstaat*, is looming before us as a twentieth century contingent reality. The trend is general, varying only in manner and degree, and informed with a ruthless pragmatism which permits any government in the name of its 'plan' to change policy and practice abruptly without regard to the effect on the interests and plans of other peoples and the hurt to international goodwill. As their problems are more acute and their ways less staid, the new undeveloped states are especially apt in resorting to such planned licence; and as at the same time they are now protected by the incipient collective system of the UN, they can indulge—as no Great Power would have dared in the days of so-called 'international anarchy'—in what is also a new phenomenon which can only be described as 'total sovereignty'.

That is the new world which somehow has to be brought back into reliable working relationships, to open up a prospect and provide the elements for international government. We do not know what kind of international system will work. But we do know that as government is only the framework that enables a social community to live its life well, international government can have little sense or body without a living international community. One new phenomenon at least opens up a positive and remarkable prospect in that direction. As was said before, the immediate impact of planning, with its spreading concern for social welfare and rights, is nationalistic. But in its 'external' aspect one central characteristic is that it is *universal*. I believe this to be a novel, a unique historical situation. In the traditional category of 'human rights' there have always been differences from place to place in attitude, conception and practice. But now, whatever their constitutional form or cultural tradition, *all* countries have adopted the philosophy and claims of social security; and hence, inevitably, also similar administrative machinery and practice.[54] If this reading be correct, two practical factors are already at work, and on a world scale, to which strands of functional cooperation could be made fast. One is the indispensable factor of a common outlook and purpose, which in this case puts into strong relief an evident identity of everyday social aims and policy. The other is the useful factor of close similarity in ways and means. Administrative law is implicitly 'functional' law, and so is administrative practice. Every functional link helps to build up a common legal order—as the ILO well exemplifies—specific but also concrete and cumulative, one which does not stay aloof in the atmosphere of diplomatic and juridical compacts, but which enters everywhere into the daily life of the peoples themselves.

Two general considerations may be cited in support of this thesis. A general wish for a collective security system was natural after the shock of two world wars and of the atom bomb; but new and remarkable were the first signs 'of a sense of world community, of international responsibility for local conditions everywhere. The idea of the welfare state, new as it is even in our own countries, is already broadening into a sentiment for a welfare world'.[55] The substantial and manifold efforts and contributions generally known as 'technical assistance', are tangible proof of that; not, as in the past, occasional charity in some emergency, but a continuous policy of aid now accepted almost as a responsibility by the richer countries. On the other side, the new states, politically tangled up in aggressively 'uncommitted' groups and leagues, have shown themselves eager to join the UN's special agencies and other such bodies 'because the balance of considerations is in favour of such participation', and they have come to look upon it 'as an international asset and a strengthening of their position in the world'. In spite of their political sensitivity the new states have shown little mistrust of such bodies, 'even where the activities of the international organisation within the State's territory is concerned'.[56]

Considerations such as these show why one can find both opportunity and promise in joint working arrangements as a way of building up an international community. But it also is a natural not a contrived idea pressed into an existing political mould. Generically speaking, it represents a general tendency which has grown out of the working complexities of twentieth-century society. Both devolution and integration tend to occur as much within states as between states. Socialist theory had contemplated some form of centralised control (state socialism or syndicalism or guild socialism) for economic sectors taken over from capitalist enterprise, but when it came to 'nationalisation' British Labour turned instead to the non-political device of autonomous boards and authorities. That has become the normal way for activities which are altogether new—aviation, atomic energy, and so on. The use made of it in existing federations is of special relevance here. In the United States in spite of an old and hard-set regionalism, departments of state (war, agriculture, the Federal Reserve Board, etc.) make use in their administration of functional regions ('single-purpose areas') which vary freely from service to service and seldom coincide with state lines. And so do the hundred or so executive agencies which have come into being especially since the New Deal—which was 'not fashioned theoretically out of economic or social creeds' but was the wholly practical response to the 'felt necessities' of a pressing situation. The clearest evidence can be found in the great experiment of the Tennessee Valley Authority TVA.

Because its own task could not be performed unless allowed to cut across the sovereign jurisdiction of seven of the United States, the TVA offers a good prototype for possible inter-state arrangements. But for this reason it is as well to deal first with a general point raised in this connection. To the argument that even in established federations reforming activities have often had to be diverted into functional by-paths, instead of the direct way of constitutional amendment, it has sometimes been retorted that functional experiments have been possible and effective in the United States precisely because they worked within a federal system.[57] But for the past century and a half a growing number of international unions and services have worked well without reference to political supervision or protection. In addition to the wartime combined boards with Canada the United States has been a party to substantial joint activities with neighbouring states—the Alcan Highway (a likely model for an eventual Channel tunnel), the St Lawrence Waterway, the Rio Grande project with Mexico—all of them without any offence to or intrusion by the federal constitutions of the three states.

On the other side, as mentioned before, there have been a great many cases when a federal constitution has stood in the way of internal functional developments. In the face of a pressing need for such river control as was eventually obtained through the TVA, repeated efforts by several Presidents since the beginning of the century had gone astray; it was only the calamity of the great depression which gave Franklin Roosevelt a chance to push through the bill which created the autonomous TVA. The TVA then had to fight off forty-one legal suits over a period of five years and on a variety of constitutional objections before it was allowed to settle down to its great work. 'The TVA really introduced a new dimension into the constitutional structure of the US, without any change in the Constitution; but it could do so only because it was a new administrative and not a new political dimension.'[58]

This is not the place to restate the political philosophy which informs the functional idea beyond saying that to prefer it to the constitutional approach is not to be timid, much less to be haphazard. 'It rests indeed squarely upon the most characteristic idea of modern democratic-liberal philosophy, that which leaves the individual free to enter into a variety of relationships—religious, political and professional, social and cultural—each of which may take him in different directions and dimensions and into different groupings, some of them of international range. Each of us is in fact a 'bundle' of functional loyalties; so that to build a world community upon that liberal conception is merely to extend and consolidate it also between national societies and groups.'[59] The argument has grown out of a definite view of the dilemma of our time: that we can neither ignore the deep roots of nationality in the search for material effectiveness, nor deny the pressure for social betterment for the sake of a hollow independence. In the face of this dilemma perhaps one may look briefly at the relative merits of the functional idea in regard to some of those issues which have been shown to raise difficulties for any comprehensive political union.

In the first place, the functional approach does in no way offend the sentiment of nationality. At the same time, if offers even to the weakest of countries, instead of an empty formal equality, the assurance of non-domination and equality in the working benefits from any functional activity in which it participates. And these assurances can be the more readily accepted because functional arrangements have the patent virtue of technical self-determination: the range of their task can be clearly defined, and that in turn determines the powers and resources needed for their performance. Internationally speaking, in this way abstract political 'self-determination' is translated into a reality of functional co-determination. Allowing for suitable variations, Miriam Camps concluded that even for the Common Market 'this pattern is likely to be followed in the future, and to be reinforced by the fusion of the Communities, the governments being willing effectively to shift authority to the Commission only when the limits within which the Commission can act have been fairly strictly defined.'[60]

These considerations bear closely on the central difficulty of democratic control. As was said before, even within democratic regimes control over executive administration has increasingly slipped away from Parliament. In Britain indeed we have enacted the paradox that industries and services 'nationalised' into public ownership have been removed from the public control of Parliament, beyond a general debate on their annual Reports. In this respect, at any rate, international development would seem to show an advance on national practice. For the discussion of general policy the UN has the Economic and Social Council; but the significant innovation is that, varying with its work, every specialised agency, including the ILO, has its own little functional assembly which meets periodically to review work done and lay down policy and fix a budget for the next period. Moreover, Article 71 of the UN Charter has given certain private international bodies, the non-governmental organisations (NGOs), a formal right to be consulted or an informal right to be heard in their particular sphere of interest; that establishes a sort of functional constituency which can influence the agency's policy, but which also brings to members an insight into the reasons for the agency's policy.[61] Through this arrangement 'pressure groups' are brought into the open and enfranchised, and the process of democratic representation is effectively restored. Delegates to these functional assemblies and their non-governmental associations know what it is all about and can judge whether a policy is valid and whether it has been carried out fairly; whereas policy-making at Brussels is virtually hidden from national parliaments and private associations.[62]

That 'people are bad judges of general considerations but good judges of detail' had already been said by Machiavelli. Such functional organs may 'diminish the orthodox sovereignty of the states, but the power and sovereign rights of the people would increase, because they would have a direct voice through their own delegates in all the agencies handling some of their affairs.'[63] Apart from such special bodies, the trend has grown in recent years as national departments negotiate directly and act together with opposite branches in other countries in many matters of a technical or practical nature; and often these contacts continue while there may be political friction between the respective governments. The extent to which the whole practice of foreign policy and relations has thus been revolutionised in step with the sweep of technical developments and the extension of public controls, may be seen from the mere fact that in 1853 there were three international conferences, about a hundred in 1900, but by 1953 their number had risen to some two thousand and is possibly twice as high now. 'And it is not merely a matter of numbers. We have travelled far from the glittering parade of princes at the Congress of Vienna to the working meetings of civil servants, scientists and technicians who in this way now link together sectors of their national life and sections of their national departments into a vast and growing network of peaceful and beneficial international relations.[64]

The clear definition of the scope and powers of a functional authority, and the watchfulness of people who know the work as well as the 'technocrats' themselves and have a direct interest in its good performance, cannot but serve to keep policy and practice fairly transparent. The ECSC was organised and worked well on such a basis; whether mixing the three communities will leave these advantages unimpaired remains to be seen. But having pressed out of sheer political zeal for the fusion of the three, many 'Europeans', as the Martino Report admitted, came to fear that in the process the clear supra-nationality of the ECSC might be diluted to the inter-governmental level of the others. It could not be otherwise: the wider and vaguer the range of its activity, the less is a technical organisation likely to be given the freedom of supra-national autonomy.[65]

The question of membership provides one final point of comparison. A federal system is bound to be closed and exclusive; a functional system is naturally open, and changes in membership can be absorbed without doing violence to policy and administration. A federal constitution is a balancing act in regard to a whole range of social and political factors: with any change in membership the whole structure may have to be re-organised and probably to be re-negotiated[66]—rather like the Austro-Hungarian *Ausgleich*, which Viennese wits dubbed 'Monarchie auf Kündigung' because of the inevitable crisis at each ten-yearly renewal. Miriam Camps, in fact, brought up this very point: at Brussels, too, 'there is too much reliance on crises as a technique for forcing decisions.'[67]

Professor Freidrich's recent thesis was particularly dubious on this point: he would like federal rules to be made so easy as to make it possible for some members to leave or for others to be added without breaking up the whole federation. From a wide international experience, on the other hand, Dr Beijen gave the clear warning that if one really wanted to extend the membership of the Common Market 'it is better not to speak of federation'.[68] Even with the EEC, far as it is from federation, the clause that leaves open the door for 'any European country' willing to join implies, according to Mr Nederhorst, full acceptance of 'existing economic institutions and political principles',[69] and it was not unnatural in the discussions on the Fouchet plan for the French to insist on unanimity for new admissions.

On a minor scale the contrast stands out clearly even within the existing communities. The ECSC and Euratom were straight functional bodies and could get on with their allotted task without offending the position of other countries, while remaining open to possible links with them. The scope of EEC is by comparison diffuse and subject to a continuous temptation to self-inflation (which the 'Europeans' deem a virtue); with a bureaucratic tendency because it is diffuse, and an expansionist tendency because it is bureaucratic. The more fields of activity are added unto it, for example, agriculture, the more acquisitive it tends to become;[70] and in the degree in which it is rounded up, it also hardens into a segregated entity. The point is that for service units like the ECSC and Euratom, as for all the specialised agencies of the UN and any future functional body, wider association means more points of co-operative contact; for a self-inflating organisation like the EEC, more fields of control must internationally mean more points of competitive contact.

Federation was an advance on empire as a way of joining under a common government a group of separate territorial units. But federation is not only inadequate but irrelevant when the general task is not to consolidate but to loosen the hold of the territorial-sovereign conception of political relations, and so find a way to world peace through the revolutionary pressures of the time. Even earlier, neither the parts of the British Empire nor of Latin America, with many social and historical affinities, have turned to the federal idea for political comfort. It has not served any of the post-war problems and situations. It has not proved acceptable to neighbouring groups in East Africa or the Middle East or the Caribbean inspite of pressing common needs and paucity of resources. It has not suggested itself as a remedy for healing the break between parts that had been formerly united. Some years ago, the late Mr Nehru and the Pakistani President agreed that their countries had many practical interests which could with advantage be managed in common; and more recently, the leaders of the two parts of Ireland also agreed to seek to ease an old enmity by doing just that. Would either case have had a better prospect—despite the present relapse—if one of the parties were to have said, 'We must federate first'? Quite a number of practical activities are carried out in common by or for the British Commonwealth, but would not the mere hint at some political underpinning cause many a flight from that functional association?

When it comes to the new scientific inventions and discoveries—aviation, wireless, atomic energy, space exploration—their own technicalities defy any arrangement below the global scale. So much so that, for example in broadcasting, states have to respect the mutual interest even where there is no formal agreement. There may still be claims for sovereign rights in the air above a state's territory; but with satellites and space travel we have in truth reached the 'no man's land of sovereignty'. Nor is there any workable dividing line between military and non-military usage of space: no means of self-protection is left, only all-round protection through some common authority. The programme for space exploration adopted by the UN General Assembly in 1962 was only a first step towards taking it out of politics; and the same intent clearly informed the Antarctica Treaty signed by twelve countries, including the Soviet Union, in 1959, which suspended all territorial claims and disputes for a period of thirty years, and instead provided for scientific cooperation and mutual inspection to forestall any military uses. If one may be allowed the expression, these are not 'federalising' but 'functionalising' actions; they could never lead to federation between the parties, but the Antarctica treaty—considered as a type—which now amounts to temporary neutralisation under a joint agreement, could well lead to permanent neutralisation under a joint international authority.

Before concluding, there are two points that need to be mentioned as they recur in almost every critical account of the functional approach. One is the central and difficult question of coordination. To a degree, insofar as it is raised as an abstract assumption, it reflects the difficulty which our political thinking finds to conceive of authority, in the tradition of sovereignty, without a territory. Even the Roman Pontiff had to be accorded the Vatican territory as a base for sovereign status, though it is less than a speck on the Pontiff's vast expanse of influence and authority throughout the world. Yet the criticism also has a core of evident truth in the fear that a variety of autonomous organs might work at cross-purposes with each other. It is a real problem, but is it not better to wait till the need arises and experience shows what the need is? To prescribe for the sake of traditional 'roundness' something more definite than the guidance and supervision of, for example, the Economic and Social Council, would be to distort the whole conception from the start. To try to fit the functional bodies into a common mould would take away some of their special merits in working efficiency and flexibility of membership; while to impose upon them a 'coordinating' authority with anything like controlling status would be to move again towards that accumulation of power at the centre which is in question here. We would be drifting back onto the political track and so miss the way to possible universality.

The second point is one of doubt, not infrequently heard: 'Where will the political will for such functional union come from?' It seems a curious question. If there should be no will for working together on such lines, limited to evident self-interest, how assume that there might be a better will for wider unlimited political integration? The question is not so much a criticism of the functional idea as a great doubt whether general international co-operation is possible at all. It may be an open question whether in 1945 we were too hopeful or too form-bound in our approach. In the view of Senator J.W. Fullbright, the UN has in a manner broken down because it was based on the assumption of a unity of outlook among the Great Powers; now we had to turn to a functional approach to build up an international community, to tackle concrete problems instead of spectacular attempts at world constitution-making.[71] The same question, whether they were too hopeful or too formtied applies to the 'Europeans' who gathered at The Hague, in 1948. Many of them now feel the need for 'a more cautious conception of integration'; 'if Europe is to pursue its fundamental goal, functional integration appears to be the only practical method of cooperation'.[72] And the 'fundamental goal' here means not local peace and strength, but world-peace and wellbeing. As to this ultimate goal, in the concluding volume to the series of inquiries initiated by the Carnegie Endowment for International Peace, 'The Nations and the United Nations',[73] Professor Robert MacIver concludes that the UN's main service to the cause of peace may lie not in its political activities, but in the development of the common or cooperative interests of the peoples in areas which lie outside or on the margin of the usual play of power politics.

Conclusion

This paper has been written from the standpoint of a student of political science—with an evident international bias. It has in no way been concerned with the question whether a European union would or would not bring prosperity to its populations, or whether it is a good thing for Britain to join it. As a student I have sought an answer to two questions: what kind of political construction was a European union likely to be and what would be its temper; for if, as I think, function determines structure, this also means that structure must affect practice. And, therefore, in the second place, what would be its relevancy to the prospects for a general international system?

Admittedly, thus to try to examine the 'European' idea is like trying to hold a line on a political rainbow with its many fleeting hues; and with one horizon among those who are clear that they were not seeking 'a new fatherland' and wanted Europe united that it may work the better for international union, and the opposite horizon falling in Dr Hallstein's camp. For Dr Hallstein was no less clear that they were after 'awakening a new European patriotism'; and that—while the old nations may be left to dream their national dreams (and after dismissing any idea of supplanting the national with the supra-national as 'another illusion')—that 'perhaps it is true that only States can act politically. Then let us create the European State—or is Europe finally to abdicate?'[74]

If the aim is political union, a 'United States of Europe', Dr Hallstein's picture, with all its tactical tergiversations, is clearly nearer the mark. Both lines of inquiry have led to the same point, that by its nature and tendency a political union must be nationalistic; and that as such it must impede, and may defeat, the great historic quest for a general system of peace and development. Under the pressures of a planned and radical social transformation it is bound to shape towards a centralised system—closed, exclusive, competitive; and whatever else it may do, such a system would hardly be suited to mediate between the new ideological divisions, or temper the raw nationalism of the new states to steer them towards the greener pastures of a mutual international community.

More likely it is that it would cause the tentative 'blocs' that so confuse policy at the UN, out of distrust of the old world, to harden into other 'unions' in emulation of it. Could a European union, in the long run, benefit its own peoples if it tends in the least to split the world afresh into competing regional sovereignties? Is not breaking through that dour barrier of sovereignty the ultimate test? In a world of a hundred and more states sovereignty can in simple fact never be dismantled through a formula but only through function—shedding national functions and pooling authority in them; unless we are to give up all purpose of wide all-round international sharing in the works of peace.

Notes and references

1 F. Alting von Geusau, 'Europe beyond the Six', in the special issue of *Internationale Spectator,* The Hague, 8 April 1965, p. 487.

2 From review of Max Beloff, *Europe and the Europeans* (London: Chatto and Windus, 1957) in the *Manchester Guardian,* 13 December 1957.

3 The contrast between the two sections is instructive. The bulk of the literature has dealt with the economic side of European union and covered about every problem and implication in what are informed and careful studies; this applies also to the small group of articles dealing with the legal aspect. The bulk of the political literature, apart from simply descriptive contributions, has been mostly propaganda filled with assertive generalities prescribing European union as a universal remedy for every political ill or social complaint.
Apart from the more historical study by Ernst B. Haas, 'The Uniting of Europe, 1950-57' (Stevens 1958; revised 1968, Stanford University Press), and the same writer's theoretical 'International Integration: the European and the Universal Process', *International Organisation,* Cambridge, Mass., Summer 1961, perhaps the most helpful was the special issue of *Internationale Spectator, op. cit.,* with twenty essays by well-known Dutch experts and scholars. A more international group contributed some useful papers to the Conference of the

Grotius Seminarium on *Limits and Problems of European Integration*, ed. B. Landheer, The Hague, 1963.

4 *World Today*, January 1965, p. 10.

5 *Ibid*, p. 18.

6 His repeated use of the term 'specious' suggests an indictment rather than a theoretical difference, but this is one of those internal issues that are outside my province.

7 *Op. cit.*, p. 19.

8 In *Internationale Spectator*, April 1965, p. 555—A relevant point arose at Geneva in discussions on the Briand proposal for a European union in 1929. 'It was generally agreed that the solution of economic problems involved the taking of political decisions. But in the same measure it was found repugnant for such decisions to superimpose a collective organism to free separate decision by the governments.' (Mirkine Guetzevitch and Georges Scelle, *'L'Union Européenne'*, Paris, 1931, p. 17.)

9 Dr Ralf Dahrendorf has recently argued that if the Council of Ministers had had to negotiate with the United Kingdom about the real political problems— sovereignty, a common foreign policy, and future institutions—the negotiations could never have succeeded.

10 *Military Policy in a Changing Political Context*, Center for International Studies, Princeton, N.J., December 1964, p. 11.

11 Already the League of Nations had been dismissed by Coudenhove-Kalergi in his 'Pan-Europa' as having an 'abstract character' beacause it lacked such intermediate regional unions.

12 David Mitrany, 'Delusions of Regional Unity', in B. Landheer (ed.) *Limits and Problems of European Integration*, The Hague, 1961, pp. 40-41.

13 David Mitrany, *ibid.*, p. 41.

14 *Regionalism and World Organisation*, American Council on Public Affairs with Institute on World Organisations, Report on Second Conference, 1943; published Washington D.C. 1944, pp. 49-50.

15 Research directorate of the Secretariat-General of the Council of Europe, *The Present State of Economic Integration in Western Europe*, Strasburg, July, 1955, p. 94.

16 As references to the economic success of the United States are especially persistent, one may refer to the paper by S. Dell, 'Economic Integration and the American Example', *The Economic Journal*, March 1959. It quotes the studies of the late L. Rostas to the effect that 'relative productivity is in no way related to the size of the market. This points to the fact that the optimum plant (or firm) and specialisation can be achieved within the limits of a smaller market.' (e.g. Swedish and Swiss metallurgical achievements). It quotes as 'particularly damaging' the findings of Erwin Rothbarth and others that United States industry was more efficient than British industry as long ago as 1870, if not earlier, when its internal market was smaller than the English market. It doubts whether regional *per capita* income differences are now any smaller in the United States, with its vast integrated economy, than in Western Europe with its patchwork of independent states. It thus refutes the assumption that economic integration by itself leads to greater productivity and to uniform development throughout a 'large' region.

17 See David Mitrany, 'The International Consequences of National Planning',

Yale Review, September, 1947—which argued, incidentally, that as radical reformers would be the foremost practitioners of planning, and as planning must be guided and controlled by the state, Socialists and Labour—even pure Marxists—will of necessity find themselves state-bound, will themselves be 'nationalised'.

18 Letter from a Liberal parliamentary candidate to *The Guardian*, 26 August 1961. Mr. Harold Wilson had much the same thought when he addressed the European Parliament 23 January 1967 (shortly before he was due to visit President de Gaulle in Paris): European union was essential if Europe was not to remain in a state of 'industrial helotry' in relation to the United States. And more recently M. Monnet told an American audience, 'I think that peace will be helped by the creation of larger units. . . You (the USA) are the strongest; you are the richest; you are the most powerful. But it's important that this feeling does not degenerate in time into domination'. (WNBC TV Transcript, 'Speaking Freely', 8 February 1970.)

19 In his search for a binding element he discovered a 'Western nationality', a European 'race', and even a 'European soul', emphatically different from the 'American soul'.

20 p.8 para. 47.

21 Hugh Beesly, 'Direct Elections to European Parliament', in *Limits and Problems of European Integration*, The Hague, 1963, p. 85.—He would also use some of the armoury of the P.R. man: 'The European flag, a European University, a European satellite, goods-trains marked "Europe"—all these will help in the gradual growth of a European patriotism.' *(Ibid*, p. 87)

22 Martino Report, p 6, para. 38—Even M. Monnet, when interviewed on the BBC (10 July 1969), refused to be restricted, he said, 'by economic and other technicalities—European union is a matter of civilization!'

23 Europe has had 'an unusually dynamic history'; 'the end of the European Age in history is not necessarily the end of Europe, or of a civilisation which, though inseparable from the European heritage, has ceased to be exclusively European'.—Oscar Halecki, *The Limits and Divisions of European History*, London, 1950, p. 21.

24 David Mitrany, 'Delusions of Regional Unity', *loc. cit.*, p. 44.

25 *Observer*, London, 28 May 1961.

26 Herman Jahrreis dealt closely and sharply with the 'European' idea, especially Coudenhove Kalergi's 'Pan Europa', from the stand-point of international legal development, in 'Europa als Rechtseinheit', *Abhandlungen des Institutes für politische Auslandskunde an der Universität Leipzig*, Heft 6, Leipzig, 1929,pp. 28 ff.

27 J.L. Heldring, *Internationale Spectator*, April 1965, p. 545.

28 In *World Today*, January 1965, p. 20.

29 Alting von Geusau, *Internationale Spectator*, April 1965, p. 488.

30 J.L. Heldring, *Internationale Spectator*, April 1965, p. 542.

31 *Ibid* p. 67—Even M. Jean Monnet, who among 'Europeans' stands on a level of his own, could claim through the recent declaration of his Action Committee that European union was the best way to achieve German re-unification. Does it not seem obvious instead, as Russia refuses to recognise the EEC and fears the consolidation of a Western political union in which she believes Germany would be dominant, that she would be less likely to give up her hold on the buffer formed by East Germany?

32 David Mitrany, 'Pan-Europa—A Hope or a Danger?', *Political Quarterly*, London, Sept.-Dec. 1933.
33 See for example Edouard Herriot, 'Europe', Rieder, Paris 1930.
34 Mirkin Guetzevitch and Georges Scelle, *L'Union Européène*, Paris 1931, pp. 16-17.
35 See David Mitrany, 'Functional Federalism', *Common Cause*, Chicago, November 1950.
36 The point is developed in David Mitrany, 'The Functional Approach to World Organisation', *International Affairs*, London, July 1948.—Indirect supporting evidence was offered a few years ago by the attempt of US Senator Bricker to make international acts subject to separate approval by the states.
37 It should also be obvious that the 'federalising process' (see below) will remain very brittle until fully accomplished. In the interim period nothing is agreed beyond an intention, as in the Rome Treaty, and any change of government in the participating states may bring changes of outlook and intention. 'Experience shows that political trends often change in certain countries with disconcerting swiftness' and sharply alter policy 'merely as a consequence of the normal working of democratic institutions and not because of any calculated Machiavellism.' (Jan Hostie, in *Regionalism and World Organization*, *loc. cit.*, pp. 57-8). Political attempts are bound to remain exposed to politics; the late Dr Hugh Dalton, for example, insisted that British Labour could join in European union only with other Socialist governments. Therefore, says Mr Hostie, 'international institutions must be built to withstand at least the likeliest of the political shifts'—which hardly seems possible through any fixed federal constitution.
38 Papers for an Oxford meeting on Federation, Sept. 1963; and for the Sixth World Congress of IPSA, Geneva, Sept., 1964.
39 Professor Friedrich's 'any kind of association' presumably could mean that OEEC and COMECON, EFTA and NATO and the Arab League are all engaged in a 'federalising process', whether they mean it or not. The confusing guidance which such terminological licence can produce even from an experienced scholar, was offered to the Oxford Conference by W.H. Morris-Jones, as quoted by Friedrich (Geneva paper, Note 10): 'The Commonwealth, although as a whole it is no kind of federalism, can usefully be regarded as a collection of partial, functional, intermittent federations, composed of different members at different times for different purposes.' Perhaps in fairness to M. Dennis de Rougemont one should note that years ago he had anticipated this free-wheeling 'federalising' conception in a pamphlet which said that European federation would grow by 'here an economic agreement, there a cultural affinity', two Churches sharing Communion, above all by private individuals creating 'a series of networks for the exchange of ideas'; indeed, there was apparently nothing political about such 'federalising', as a federation is formed 'not by working from the centre outwards or through the medium of governments'. *Totalitarianism and Federalism*—London: Federal Union, 1950.
40 David Mitrany 'Parliamentary Democracy and Poll Democracy', *Parliamentary Affairs*, London; Winter 1955-6, p. 17.
41 In the view of Dr J.W. Beijen, Dutch ex-Minister, financial expert and diplomat, 'Too often the Communities are still considered as merely a means to increase the economic strength of the area. In essence, their task in the social

field is fundamental.' The inclusion of agriculture enhances that aspect, for everywhere agricultural policy is 'foremost social policy and only secondarily economic policy.' *Internationale Spectator,* April 1965, pp. 466-7.

42 One of the Reports to the European Parliament mentioned a curious proposal, later abandoned, for an autonomous Secretary-General with powers like those of the United Nations Secretary-General, and with the sole task of pressing for integration.

43 *Op. cit.,* especially pp. 5-6.

44 A few years ago an American observer of the British administrative scene, Professor Samuel Beer, of Harvard, went so far as to describe what he had seen as 'quasi-corporatism'.

45 See P.E.P. study 'Advisory Committees in British Government', London 1960; and K.C. Wheare, *Government by Committee,* Oxford: Clarendon Press, 1965.

46 The European Commission itself has produced striking and open support for this point. In the *Statement* it sent to the European Parliament in July 1968, it declared that the existing Community Treaties should be replaced by a single treaty in which 'The single Commission must be given implementing powers, powers that enable it not only to take the initiative in Community progress but also genuinely to *manage* that Community, for the task of management grows each time a new Community policy comes into force.' (Italics are the author's). Dr Ralph Dahrendorf, himself a member of the E E C Commission, has recently described it as a 'bureaucratic leviathan with a mania for harmonisation.'

47 *Internationale Spectator,* April 1965, p. 689.

48 In France extreme groups have been kept away, and, for a time, Italy in effect excluded the Opposition (Murray Forsyth, *The Parliament of the European Communities,* P.E.P. London, 1964, p. 21.)—Even M. Monnet's Action Committee for a United States of Europe, supposed to include heads of parties and of trade unions from the six countries, had excluded Gaullists and Communists.

49 This came out partly in the criticism by M.J. Petot that the experience of the European communities shows the unreality of the 'functionalist' thesis that starting from small, autonomous specialised authorities one could build a complete state! A 'complete state' and its introverted nature happens to be the very idea which functionalism seeks to overcome internationally; see his 'Des Communautés Européennes à la Fédération', *Revue Générale de Droit International Public,* Paris, 1960, vol. 64(2).

50 'The fallacy starts when it is believed that the motives for political integration are as rational as those for economic integration.' The first are 'mainly mythical, which does not deprive them of a certain driving force. But this force is soon spent when it clashes with the deeper and older myths and loyalties of the national states.'—J.L. Heldring, *Internationale Spectator,* p. 544.

51 *Internationale Spectator,* April 1965, pp. 641-2.

52 U N Charter, Article 1.

53 Adolf Drucker, in 'Regionalism and world organisation', *loc. cit.,* p. 102—one should note the incisive work of Francois Perroux, who uses the conception of *'espaces économiques'* freed from 'the servitudes of localisation'. See his *Europe sans Rivages,* Paris: Presses Universitaires de France, 1954.

54 David Mitrany, Comment in the Human Rights Section, Sixth I P S A World Conference, Geneva, September 1964.

55 David Mitrany, 'International Cooperation in Action', *International Associations*, Brussels, September 1959.

56 Benjamin Akzin, *New States and International Organisations*, UNESCO Paris 1955, pp. 170-2.

57 See, for example, Andrea Chitti-Batelli, 'Functional Federalism', *Common Cause*, Chicago, April 1950; and David Mitrany's reply, November 1950.

58 David Mitrany, *American Interpretations*, London, 1946, pp. 18-20. As against this, one must note that President Roosevelt's only 'attempt at direct constitutional revision, to increase the membership of the Supreme Court from 9 to 15, was bitterly disputed and was defeated, though its effect would have meant much less of a constitutional inroad than the experiment of the TVA and the body of new federal executive agencies'. (*Ibid*, p. 22.)
See the view given recently by Daniel Bell (Columbia University, Chairman of the 'Committee for the Year 2000' of the Academy of Arts and Social Sciences): he said that for the new problems, the territorial division into 50 states and a mass of municipalities is 'no longer meaningful'. The need is for a 'comprehensive orverhauling of governmental structures to determine the appropriate size and scope of units that can handle the appropriate tasks'. It would be futile to try to reduce the number of states, but 'all sorts of state functions could be "detached" and taken over by multistate or regional "compacts". . . Even the favourite theme of regionalism would prove no real solution, for the definition of a region is not hard and fast but varies with different functions. . . One must first determine what is to be centralised and what is to be decentralised'. ('Toward a communal society', *Life Magazine*, 12 May 1967'.)

59 David Mitrany, *International Associations, loc. cit.* 1959, p. 647.

60 Miriam Camps, *What Kind of Europe?* London: Oxford University Press, 1965, p. 131.

61 Lyman B. White, *International Non-governmental Organisations*, New Brunswick, Rutgers University Press 1951. Each association 'constitutes a segment of world unity for the particular interest with which it deals, and an accumulation of such segments would serve to create a living world community.' (p. 12).

62 David Mitrany, 'An Advance in Democratic Representation', In *International Associations, loc. cit.*, March 1954.—The functional assemblies have sometimes been confused by critics with functional representation in general bodies like the economic parliaments popular for awhile after the First World War. But in economic parliaments the several groups were there to fight for sectional interests as in any ordinary parliament, whereas functional bodies represent one interest and one purpose common to them all, and the debate is about scope and ways and means.

63 Hans E. Fried, 'The Frontiers of the Future,' *Free World*, August, 1943, p. 11.

64 David Mitrany, Review in *International Affairs*, RIIA, September 1960, p. 228.

65 Under the several treaties the powers of the European Parliament are lower than those of the ECSC Assembly—e.g., in the matter of treaty revision. In fact, as pointed out in the PEP pamphlet, *Direct Elections and the European Parliament*, Oct. 1960, the ECSC Assembly, encouraged by the High Authority, had greatly widened the scope given to it in the Treaty, and instead of being only a *post facto* critic it actually helped to shape the policy of the Community.

66 That this may happen even in old federations was shown at the Canadian federal provincial conference in July, 1965. The Federal Government had decided to refer to the Supreme Court the question of title to seabed resources on the Pacific coast, but the Premiers of British Columbia and of Quebec 'led a furious attack on the Federal Government, claiming that the matter was one for political negotiations and not for judicial settlement'. The Premier of Quebec bluntly declared that he would not respect a Supreme Court decision, or allow exploration in the Gulf of the St Lawrence on the strength of a Federal permit. *The Guardian,* London, 24 July, 1965.

67 Camps, *What kind of Europe?* p. 93.

68 *Internationale Spectator*, April 1965, p. 470.

69 *Limits and Problems*, Landheer, The Hague, 1963.

70 The General, despite his dislike of integration, has done much to reinforce the commission's powers, by pressing for a common agricultural policy which it alone can administer. 'On its part, using the argument that it would be undemocratic to handle the large agricultural funds without democratic control, the Commission has put forward a scheme 'which would transfer much of the Council's powers to the Parliament, and, even more, to the Commission'.—*The Economist*, 8 May 1965, p. 638.

71 J.W. Fulbright, 'The concept of free nations', *Foreign Affairs,* New York, October 1961.

72 Professor Alting von Geusau, *Internationale Spectator, loc. cit.*, p. 488.

73 Robert M. McIver, 'The nations and the United Nations', in series *National Studies on International Organisation*, New York: Manhattan Publishing Co., 1959.

74 *Op. cit.,* p. 15.

Functionalism and Strategies for International Integration
Paul Taylor

One of the great difficulties in evaluating a theory as a source of strategies for integration is the nature of the end-situation, the preferred goal. Unfortunately a student of international integration must know that there are a large number of conceivable conditions in inter-state relations which could be described as integration. If, for instance, it is supposed that the emergence of a centralised decision-making structure is essential in the integration of states then an action which forms part of a strategy of nation-building might be judged as unhelpful. Yet nation-building and changing attitudes are essential elements in the building of that socio-psychological community which is particularly stressed in the writing of some scholars as an aspect of international integration.[1]

Insistence upon a particular element in the condition of integration must lead to the denial of the value of strategies which focus upon other elements. This is an unnecessarily restrictive approach: it means that no theory can possibly be judged as a fruitful source of strategies of integration except in terms of that one end-situation with which it deals. It also means that a crude demand for that end-situation must be judged a better strategy for integration than a highly sophisticated series of measures to obtain some other kind of integration. It is essential to the task of evaluating the fruitfulness of functionalism as a source of strategies for integration that the end situation should be defined in a very general way, in terms of general principles rather than specific conditions.

The strategies are understood to be those which are directed towards the achievement in two or more states of closer links between government and bureaucracies; non-governmental organisations, interest groups or business interests; nations, peoples or communities. These entities may be linked more closely together in any combination. It is conceived, however, that the essential consequence should be a net reduction in the pre-disposition of any of these entities to settle their differences by violent means, and there must be an increase in the value which is attached to cooperation. These principles of organisation must be generally accepted as legitimate. A strategy of integration is conceptualised as a series of actions which are held by an actor to be causally linked together in a sequence leading to this end situation of integration.

The sense in which a theory, such as functionalism, might be said to be more or less fruitful as a source of strategies for integration, can now be described. The potential rather than the actual achievement is here evaluated. The theory is fruitful if it suggests to the actor that existing trends which he detects in political, social and economic life, might or might not, culminate in international integration, and if it suggests to him specific adjustments which would steer reality closer to the desired end situation; the theory could also be judged as fruitful if the principles of behaviour and organisation which it presents are conducive towards effective action (i.e. the actor's understanding of the principles is confirmed by apparent success in the pursuit of the strategy). A theory's fruitfulness might be illustrated further by its ability to sustain optimism in the face of the postponement of the desired end situation; and it might also be judged in terms of its capacity to suggest to the actors a variety of alternative courses of action, and a large number of fall-back positions, when difficulties are encountered. This latter quality would sustain a certain subtlety of strategy, the ability to decide upon an alternative and indirect approach in the event of difficulties, rather than the insistence upon the full frontal approach which so often exposes weakness.

It need hardly be added that this chapter represents but a small beginning towards the study of strategies for obtaining change in the structure and nature of international society. Much of it is highly speculative and impressionistic. There is reason to suppose that the study of purposeful change, which may be linked with the wish to bring about normative improvements, is still in a peculiarly primitive state. So many plans for improving international society involve sophisticated descriptions of what the new world should look like, but fail to present anything but the most sketchy of accounts of how such a world might be realised. The strategies are so crudely conceived that they are frequently no more than a baying at the moon, or an assertion that the world should be what it is not.

What are the qualities of a theory such as functionalism which might make it more or less fruitful as a source of strategies for integration? It would be misleading to suppose that the answer to this question is simply to do with whether it is a good theory or a bad theory, that a good theory is more fruitful and a bad theory less so. This completely ignores the multi-purpose aspect of theories; they have a number of different purposes and qualities, and to be judged as good in one dimension is not necessarily to be so judged in others. An aspect of a theory, such as its fruitfulness in providing prescriptions, is not necessarily related to its strength as a descriptive theory. Functionalism has now survived since the 1930s in the sense that it attracted, and still attracts a following (indeed its adherents now are probably more numerous than ever before). This might entitle us to say that functionalism is a feature of international society which should be studied; it is a force to be reckoned with. But it indicates nothing about the dimensions of the theory in terms of the purposes and qualities which are normally attached to the theory in general. In this section the dimensions, in this sense, of functionalism are explored; as a first step it is necessary to discuss the various purposes which have been sought through theory.

The first purpose, though not necessarily the most important one, is that of description. The theory has the task of conjuring up in the mind of the observer and his audience an image of structures and processes which are supposed to reflect precisely those which exist. The question of whether there is, or can be, isomorphism between theory and reality is at this point left unconsidered. The important aspect is that the description contained in the theory should gain acceptance.

A second purpose is that of explaining a phenomenon and predicting changes in the relationships between its component parts. There is a dispute about whether explanation or prediction have logical priority over one another; but it can be agreed that the two activities are closely linked. To explain something involves predicting likely relationships between its constituent elements. Is the explanation which is presented in the theory necessarily a reflection of what happens in reality? A theory enables us to produce a view about dynamic inter-relationships and to postulate a cause and an effect; it is essential that what is postulated is convincing and that it should remain tenable in the face of the various tests, such as those involved in the scientific method, to which it may be subjected.

A theory may allow the predicting of what will happen in two different senses. First a prediction involves a conception of what will happen if a specific change is introduced in the phenomenon associated with the theory. The prediction in this case involves an experimental readjustment of part of the theory and relies heavily upon the power of imagination. For example, a student of international institutions imagines the consequences of depriving the Secretary General of the United Nations of his right to call the Security Council into session. Second a theory might be used for the prediction of tendencies in the real world, in the following respects: first the theory enables a decision to be made about those tendencies which are at present worth noticing and, secondly, it places them after projection in a context in which they can be judged. For instance, Malthusian theory disposes the observer to treat changes in the birth rate as a matter of some significance; projections of the birth rate, say to the year 2,000, are then granted a special significance in terms of, for instance, the availability of food. It is not just that the theory creates a view about the importance of existing tendencies: the theory is also fundamental to decisions about the implications of such tendencies in the future. This dual role of theory is worth stressing in view of the habit of treating current developments as if they had some in-built quality of importance: judgments involved in isolating and evaluating tendencies are inseparable from the context of existing theory.

The third general function of theory is its role in the formulation of prescriptions. This activity follows logically after that of description, explanation and prediction. Having described, explained, and, on this basis, predicted, the attempt is made to obtain a development or outcome which would otherwise not arise: this is to be achieved by introducing some new element into the existing situation. The prescription involves a recommendation which it is thought will improve the situation as judged by some standard which is external to the object of the prescription. Accordingly the recommendation has two dimensions: a view about the nature of the specific improvement (there should be a United Europe, or stable democratic government in Africa, or world government); and a view about the means which might be used to obtain that improvement (for instance, direct elections to an international assembly, or the setting up of a world army). These two views are the main elements of the prescription, with the second view involving a choice of appropriate strategy.

These are the three main purposes which are sought through the constructing of theory in the social sciences. But how does functionalism, a particular theory of international integration, fulfil these purposes and does its success in any of them affect its potential contribution to strategies of integration? Inis Claude has argued that functionalism is more of an approach than a theory: his argument is that functionalism served some of the purposes of theorising less efficiently than others, and that because of this the name theory was perhaps misleading.[2] The value of this judgment may now be assessed.

Functionalism's strength as a descriptive theory is that it clearly presents a view of the central principles of the process of international integration. It depicts present international society as divided by conflict over illusory goals suggested by nationalism and high politics. Governments are the main instruments of the pursuit of such goals and they are sustained by the misplaced loyalties of their citizens. The description of integration stresses an educational process; the description focusses upon attitude change. The experience of successful international integration—and the perception of the rewards in terms of welfare which that brings—is seen to shift loyalties away from national governments. People learn from experience; within a stable state they have learnt to cooperate. In the integration process they are weened away from nationalism as a consequence of realising the advantages of cooperation in the international realm.[3]

Other integration theories, such as that called neofunctionalism, which was developed in particular by Professor Ernst B. Haas, stress in their description of integration rather different elements.[4] In neofunctionalism integration is seen as 'the process whereby political actors in several distinct national settings are persuaded to shift their loyalties, expectations and political activities towards a new and larger setting'. The political actors are persuaded to do this by pressures from organised groups who have learned that integration is rewarding: they articulate demands for further integration to which the actors respond. Professor Haas argues, however, that 'integration is conceptualised as resulting from an institutionalised pattern of interest politics played out within existing international organisations.'[5] Unlike the functionalists the neofunctionalists do not stress the role of consensus in maintaining stability in society and in integration; rather society and the integration process are dominated by self-seeking interest groups who are restrained only by a common acceptance of the rules of the game. The pluralist model lies at the heart of the neofunctionalist description of society and it is also characteristic of their view of integration. To the functionalists however consensus is the essence: their working model is that of Gemeinshaft in the Tönnian sense.

Enough has been said to illustrate the point that the principles of organisation and integration with which these two theories are concerned are different. The question of which theory is closer to how things are in reality is a matter of judgment and convenience: it cannot be demonstrated that either neofunctionalism or functionalism is the right theory in that it has embodied the true principles. Someone who chose the functionalist principles could not be accused of error although he might be thought old-fashioned. The resolution of this puzzle remains as yet outside the scope of theorising and testing in the social sciences. The descriptive elements of functionalism remain unimpeachable.

Yet it is the case that judged by the standards of modern social science neofunctionalism contains a much more extensive and more sophisticated description of integration. The intention of the neofunctionalists was to adapt functionalism to the requirements of constructing propositions about society and integration which could be tested. Certain aspects of functionalism were rejected as unrealistic; other aspects were spelled out in greater detail; the attempt was made to produce a more rigorous theory in the sense that hypotheses were produced which it was thought could be tested according to the principles of scientific method. For instance, bargaining techniques at various levels of integration were analysed and their contribution to the furthering of integration was assessed; and the integration process was described in terms of formulae such as spill-over, task-expansion, politicisation and the interpenetration of bureaucracies. Whilst the functionalists were content in their description of integration to concentrate upon central principles, neofunctionalists attempted the construction of a comprehensive descriptive theory. This reflected a very considerable intellectual effort and it involved the considerable extension of the range of integration theory. That very little of neofunctionalist theory has been found in the light of empirical evidence to be more or less accurate than functionalism is in no way to detract from this achievement.[6] But neofunctionalism did not succeed in reducing the confidence of the older functionalists in the distinctive aspects of their descriptive theory.

It may be that the more ambitious quality of neofunctionalism as a descriptive theory has been a factor in depriving it of some of its attractiveness as a source of strategy and has contributed towards its occasional unpopularity in some areas of the world and among some groups. The pluralist model which is important among the assumptions of neofunctionalists has been thought to be impregnated with ideological considerations[7]: it is given the status of an objective analytical tool, whereas there is truth in the argument that it is a product of a particular social and political experience, in particular that of the late industrial-capitalist society in the United States of America. The functionalist principles, on the other hand, are linked with a more widespread and pervasive tradition: the liberal-rational notion that stability is linked with agreement, and that consensus has a higher moral quality than competitive self-seeking. Even in Communist countries these assumptions are a powerful force which occasionally erupt in a dramatic way. This may explain why functionalism is studied, and its principles analysed and discussed in Communist countries such as Poland[8]: in a paradoxical fashion the neo-functionalists' concern with science and objectivity has appeared in many eyes to give their theory a narrower ideological quality whilst functionalism clung to a broader and more secure base.

Functionalist and neofunctionalist descriptions of integration may be briefly contrasted here with a third approach. The description of international integration which is characteristic of federalism stresses the primary importance of the institutional and constitutional arrangements and relies heavily upon creative political decisions by key actors. Integration is to be obtained from the top down, concentrating upon arrangements among governments by which they might be contained within a unifying constitutional framework.

The essential feature is that the federal constitution should allow a measure of regional devolution: the parts are to have a degree of autonomy from the centre. And in the integration process the recognition of regional differences is the starting point of the deliberations about the unifying federal constitution. In one branch of federalist thinking it is supposed that no differences between regions are beyond reconciliation within a well conceived constitution; in a second branch it is argued that it may be necessary to limit differences in the interests of obtaining a minimum of agreement as a condition of the success of the federal constitution. In creating such conditions gradualist strategies, such as functionalism, may be employed.[9]

In fulfilling the second purpose of theory, that of explaining and predicting, functionalism has several special qualities which help those who would construct strategies for integration. It is not difficult to accept that one of the conditions of stability at the level of the local community is a certain minimum of agreement: order is sustained by a common acceptance of the general ends of social action. The functionalist explanation of integration involves the extension of this experience to the international level. There is no peculiar leap of logic; the same kind of situation is to be created internationally as has apparently been created locally, and the optimistic aspects of every-day life are to be seized upon and exploited in the general interest.

Federalist strategies of integration, in contrast, depend upon a kind of reasoning which is much less straightforward in that they involve an attempt to resolve opposing tendencies in argument. The value of consensus at the local level is recognised and this is accorded a high value in preserving stability; in the Federal system, however, the prospect of continuing disagreement is accepted and the role of constitutions in cushioning intra-regional tensions is stressed. The federalist strategy for obtaining integration involves politicians in apparently contradictory acts: they are to agree sufficiently to recognise the validity of their disagreements. Their rival claims, all of them, are to be recognised and yet there is to be sufficient agreement for them to be embodied in some kind of common constitutional structure. Functionalism is consistent in its view of what provides stability now, at local level, and what might come to sustain stability later, in the larger, integrated area.

The functionalist strategy has the advantage that the constitutional arrangements are a symptom of the level of agreement which has been obtained, rather than an essential instrument in protecting it. The federal constitution easily becomes the only thing which groups have in common, particularly when it has been introduced as a political solution to problems of diversity. (The alternative is for a federal constitution to be little more than an administrative convenience, describing what is from the point of view of political behaviour a centralised system).[10] This encourages the development of a situation in which the supporters of unity attach an almost totem-like significance to the federal constitution: the edifice must not be touched or tampered with in any way in case it crumbles completely and exposes the hollowness of the agreement which it protects. The Rome Treaty has at least one important quality in common with this kind of federal constitution. It has been treated almost as a sacred object, a manifestation of a spirit, which is touched at the risk of extinction.

In retaining the confidence of those who are thinking about strategies for international integration functionalism's manner of fulfilling the theoretical purpose of prediction is also helpful, though this is not to deny that a theory such as neofunctionalism might be nearer to meeting the requirements of good theory in modern social science. As Dr Harrison points out, it is most difficult to demonstrate that the functionalist predictions are inaccurate. They cannot be conclusively confirmed; but they cannot be positively refuted. The point may be illustrated by a summary of the predictive elements of functionalism. The predictions are arranged according to a judgment of the extent of the change which they involve.

Functionalism predicts that the people's views of what is important in the political realm will be affected by what they do, particularly in maintaining and improving material standards. Their experience of carrying out tasks in common will weaken value differences between two or more groups, and create a more favourable attitude towards each others' intentions. The greater the rewards of cooperation the stronger the effect upon value differences and the more likely are peoples' perceptions of what is important in the political realm to change. Rewards will be maximised by organising tasks if necessary in international institutions in those geographical areas and to that extent which allows the maximum efficiency. Loyalties towards national governments will be eroded as the international institutions increase available rewards and as the demand for further cooperation increases.

The earlier predictions have a powerful and immediate appeal as they seem to rest on what in most parts of the world is a matter of every-day experience. What people think about each other is related to what they do together. Later predictions follow in a number of increasingly ambitious, but linked steps. An important aspect of this is that the predictions of functionalism are each related to a different period of time and have a different status in the testing procedures of scientific method. The earlier ones claim less in the short term and in some regions can be confirmed by evidence of attitude change[12]; the later ones claim most in relation to the very long term, and the time available for their realisation is so extensive that they must evade the structure of scientific method. There are just too many attitudes changing through too much time with too many consequences. The chance is therefore increased that the predictive aspects of functionalism preserve optimism in the short term and hope in the long term in the minds of those who ponder strategies for integration.

It is a truism that more scientific theories such as neofunctionalism are by their nature more vulnerable; their authors are concerned to construct them in such a way that they can conceivably be refuted. One aspect of this is that the period of time in which their predictions are to be realised is much shorter than that available to functionalism. There is the prospect that in the short term events might be seen to contradict the prediction. In a theory such as neofunctionalism, which involves detailed predictive-explanatory elements, such as spill-over, incremental decision-making, and politicisation, it is expected that progress towards the postulated outcome will be positively achieved continuously in these various dimensions. A failure in any one of them is conducive towards a weakening of confidence in the theory's capacity to obtain any of its purposes: the various elements of the theory are seen to be highly interdependent, and therefore vulnerable to partial failure.

Neofunctionalist spill-over was apparently blocked in the EEC in the mid-60s, particularly after the 1965 crisis. This contributed to a period of profound neofunctionalist gloom, which was if anything deeper than that afflicting members of the Commission of the European Communities.[13] The theories had not been confirmed in the short term; the conclusion was that they were in some way wrong rather than that they needed a longer period in which to obtain isomorphism with reality. Neofunctionalism, in striving for a more scientific quality, contrived to be trapped by time: the various elements of its predictive theory were generally up for judgment in the same relatively short span.

There is however an irresistible logic to functionalism: a failure to undermine loyalties towards national governments, or to drastically encroach upon the area of political disagreement, can always be countered by requiring more time or more cooperation. If there is enough cooperation political attitudes must be affected; if the rewards of internationalism are high enough the nation-state is certain to be sacrificed; if the problem is serious enough a form appropriate to its solution is certain to appear sooner or later. The act of thinking about social and political problems implies an optimism which is sufficient to sustain these views.

It is in accordance with the neofunctionalist claim to be a more scientific theory that its prescriptive element is weak. It does indeed focus upon the explanation of the development of a political system among two or more states, and it could be argued that in attempting this it is particularly useful to those who would prescribe a regional super-state, such as a united states of Europe. But the theory itself strives for an impartiality in relation to such prescriptions. The prescription is implied rather than explicit. Functionalism, in contrast, has a very important prescriptive element: the prescription is not spelt out in detail in terms of the structures of the end situation, but the principles are clear: there is to be a working peace system, a fruitful, functional cooperation, as opposed to a system of threats and violence. Again it is interesting that in functionalism it is the principles that are evoked in the prescription, whilst the details of the organisations which are to be established or the ways in which they are to work with each other, are left unconsidered. Functionalists were concerned to avoid the accusation of constructing Utopian systems;[14] they have argued that they could not know the future so to prescribe for it in detail was a futile exercise. There has to be change, undeniably, but the prospects for change were contained in a future which could be but dimly perceived. What was stressed was the need to seize upon opportunities for practical improvements in the existing situation, and, by this method, to make it more likely that favourable tendencies would lead to a better world.

Professor Gellner has distinguished between an *episodic* and an *evolutionary* approach towards progress: the *episodic* approach involved the view that progress could be obtained in a single step, that there could be a stage of dramatic improvement leading to a new plane of existence where things would be better than they had been; the *evolutionary* view in contrast involved the belief that there must be a steady improvement, that no plateau of improved existence could be reached, and that new systems would evolve from the present in ways which could not be foreseen.[15] Progress would continue steadily up a slope of evolution; it would not be halted at the next highest step. Functionalism's approach towards progress is evolutionary rather than episodic, whilst federalism, in that it implies the prospect of obtaining grace at a stroke of a constitution writer's pen, is episodic.

It was intended that in the proceeding paragraphs a profile of functionalism should emerge in terms of the purposes usually attributed to theorising. In order to attain credibility in the minds of those who are concerned with constructing strategies for international integration a measure of success in fulfilling each of these purposes is necessary. Such a profile is necessarily highly impressionistic but it is hoped that enough has been said to justify a comparison. Functionalism is less ambitious and less sophisticated than neofunctionalism as a descriptive theory. It is as sophisticated as federalism in its description of the major principles involved in the organisation of existing society. And—to sharpen the point—it is certainly much more sophisticated in its description of the world than the peace schemes of John Lennon and Yoko Ono.[16] Functionalism is more ambitious and sophisticated in its explanatory and predictive aspects; and it is most ambitious in its prescriptions. The Lennon-Ono approach is also sophisticated and ambitious in its prescriptive elements, but it is very weak indeed in the descriptive and explanatory ones. It lacks the ability to generate confidence over time in its prescriptive value.

Professor Claude's view that functionalism is an approach rather than a theory involves a judgment about the theory's profile: it is indicative of functionalism's greater concern with presenting a clear view of the central principles involved in explaining, predicting, and prescribing international integration, rather than with the formulation of a comprehensive descriptive theory, constructed according to current views about scientific method.

The attempt has been made to discuss the theory of functionalism in wider terms than those suggested by current views on good scientific method. The qualities of a set of ideas about social action in their appeal to individual actors are too easily strangled by science: their ability to generate and sustain a quality of optimism, to illuminate thinking about possibilities for change, to survive as a feature of international society, is not increased under scientific tutellage. Indeed precisely the opposite may be the case: the success of a theory in fulfilling several of those purposes which are normally attributed to it may be adversely affected by the attempt to meet the requirements of good social science as they are at present conceived. In considering functionalism's value for those who are concerned with formulating strategies for international integration it was necessary to consider much more than its scientific status; it was necessary to conduct an enquiry into the conditions of its social success in the community of scholars and international civil servants.

In the development of international organisation there are several points at which a functionalist influence may be detected. Early functionalists strongly supported the introduction of economic and social institutions into the structure of the League of Nations: there were a number of individuals who then realised the possibilites in approaching the problem of war from two directions, from above, through specific devices designed to act with governments when war broke out; and from below, through economic and social cooperation which could reduce the chance of war by changing attitudes and removing some of the problems of educational or material deficiency. This latter approach is reflected in the proposals for improving the machinery for economic and social cooperation in the League in the Bruce Report of 1939.[17] This report contained ideas which shaped the arrangements for economic and social cooperation of the United Nations, in particular, the Economic and Social Council. Many of the specialised agencies of the United Nations reflect functionalist thinking and they can be seen as part of a functionalist strategy for obtaining world peace. Some of the founding agreements, such as that of UNESCO, refer to this role in the assertion that 'war begins in the minds of men'.

In the range of international institutions which at present exist there is considerable evidence of the impact of functionalist ideas.[18] The work of organisations such as the specialised agencies of the United Nations acquire a purpose in the light of functionalism which they would not otherwise have. And the servants of these agencies frequently, consciously or unconsciously, reflect functionalism in their views: the theory grants a purpose and value to their careers.[18] The explanation of war contained in functionalism places them in a process of establishing a working peace-system. (Functionalism as a general explanation of war is brilliantly placed in its intellectual context by Kenneth Waltz in his book *Man, the State and War*.)

The great wealth of functionalist literature cannot be explored in detail here. A concern with the possible, a movement from the here and now by small steps into the future, is a characteristic of this writing. The functionalist mind is disposed to discover a unique balance between what is necessary and what can be done. William Reisman's article is a good example of this approach: it embodies many functionalist qualities.[19] The problem of the enforcement of international judgments and awards is located; what has to be done is the discovery of ways of effecting enforcement; what elements in the existing situation might be developed, and how does our knowledge of existing stable communities assist us to locate these elements? Is it possible that international organisations could make more use of a sanction which in existing communities is frequently used—the fine? What existing agencies in international society could conceivably effect this kind of economic sanction? International economic agencies clearly have potential in this direction and should be explored and it is with this potential that Reisman's article is mainly concerned. Other writings which also have this practical quality include Paul Hoffman's *Peace Can be Won*, the work of C.W. Jenks, and articles which are too numerous to mention here. There are also a large number of writers who have been indirectly influenced by functionalism, through for instance neofunctionalism in drawing up strategies for obtaining goals such as regional integration.[20]

In the face of this literature the cynic might yet discount the practical achievement of functionalism. The defendant must point out that theories which involve an acceptance of the inevitability of conflict, even violent conflict (the so-called realists) tend to make capital out of man's less praise-worthy characteristics, and in crying for a realistic acceptance of the world perpetuate its faults in a self-fulfilling-prophecy. The starting assumptions of functionalism are at least optimistic in accepting that man might be good enough to achieve something better. A judgment between the two in terms of their morality is at least not difficult to make.

In the constellation of theories of integration functionalism is a focus of thinking, a core subject around which other theories revolve, a matrix of philosophical and scientific problems.[21] The student of international integration is faced with only two possible alternatives in thinking: either he arranges his thoughts so that he is drawn into a vortex of which functionalism is the centre; or he is drawn towards the reassertion of the powers and supremacy of governments and accepts the approach of power politics. In either case he will find no easy way out because from the point of view of strategies for integration each is a nexus of problems, a starting point in a debate about strategies, rather than a view of the correct path.

The interests of students of international relations form part of a strategy of integration. Changes in such interests may indeed change what the world is like; the existing pattern of scholarly interests is a good reflection of the prevailing view of the world. It is one of the peculiarities of social science theory that the world might become the kind of place which it is thought to be. A strategy of integration might therefore include an appeal that scholars should choose more carefully among the two poles of concern which have always been accepted as the range of the subject: discord and collaboration, conflict and cooperation, war and peace. Of course, to ignore discord is to take the risk that the existing mechanisms for attempting, for instance, the peaceful resolution of disputes, or the maintaining of the balance of power, might falter. But there should surely be at this time a greater concern with the other pole: problems of collaboration, cooperation, and peace-building. This is not primarily because they might help in the solution of practical problems, like how to avoid unnecessary discord about the deep sea bed, or pollution, or space, but because the changing focus may involve a changing view of what the world is like, which may indeed eventually change the world itself. The changing interests of scholars towards the functionalist sphere of influence themselves form part of a strategy of integration.

A central problem in a choice between the functional and political poles revolves around the question of whether all significant functional cooperation must be initiated by governments, and whether their interests and interactions must be decisive. If the answer to this question is 'yes' then the student is persuaded towards the pole of conflict and a concern with high politics in his studies; if the answer is 'no' then functionalism is immediately attractive. The most important single step in undermining the position of the realists is to establish that this is not a matter of self-evident truth, or simple fact, that there is, in other words, room for doubt about the primacy of governments in initiating integrative ventures. There are, of course, numerous occasions on which the role of governments appears to be decisive in that their acts are those which immediately lead to the setting up of the functional organisation. Yet this appearance may conceal a number of possibilities: it may be, for instance, that the government is responding to interests which have been defined elsewhere. To state the case at its strongest: the appearance of the primacy of governments may sometimes conceal the fact that they are the instruments through which an emerging international interest is expressed.

Sources of such an international interest are too numerous to mention in detail; there are so many contexts in which it may be articulated in its various dimensions. They encompass the whole web of international interactions, the emerging matrix of international systems. More specifically they include non-governmental organisations, transnational business and interest groups, and the conditions and substance of attitude-change in the process of building an international socio-psychological community. It is not argued that such interests always or even usually prevail: it is sufficient to establish that the fact that governments have acted is an insufficient indication of the primacy of their interests. The sense of talking about the separate interests of governments changes as functional cooperation proceeds.

It may be that governments could interrupt functional ventures if they subsequently discovered a view of their discrete interests and that, as Inis Claude has pointed out, functional organisations are dependent upon a political umbrella.[22] It is difficult to escape the conclusion that this is less likely as the period and rewards of functional cooperation increase: the umbrella becomes incongruous as the sun begins to shine. To expect governments to rediscover themselves is to dispute the essential character of the terrain, like a plan to parry an attack by lions in central London. It could happen, but . . . Governments may also be dissuaded from seeking exclusive political interest through functional institutions by the complexity and technical nature of the joint undertaking. In many areas like air traffic control, or reducing pollution of the narrow sea lanes, action needs to be taken quickly by an authority which has been allowed an area of independent initiative. Government intervention could stop the action: the cost of this would be expected to be conducive to restraint on their part.

Linked with this problem of the relationships of governments with functional projects is that of the importance of the values which they are thought to protect. In the language of those who prefer to think in terms of hard-headed calculations the problem is whether the citizens can be bought off: can other values be set against those which are thought to derive from the state in such a way that the former are irresistibly more attractive? This is indeed the realistic centre of functionalism: the answer must be that everyone has his price. The assumption is that the drama and adventure of high politics is a luxury which man can ill-afford. The functionalist strategy depends upon a belief that there are indeed a number of carrots which are juicier than the nation state, and that they will flourish in a working peace system.

Functionalism, and the theories which have been contrasted with it as possible starting points for thinking about integrative strategies, may now be related to each other in a comprehensive strategy. Functionalism, neofunctionalism and federalism are unequal in their capacity to sustain the conditions of good strategy-building if the context of theorising is ignored; this point was established in the previous sections. They can, however, be related in an ideal complement in which the one is used to create the context within which are established the conditions of success of the other. If they are viewed as alternatives the weaknesses of some of the theories are apparent; if they are viewed as the elements of a comprehensive strategy then the special values of each may be exploited.

Functionalism is fundamental in that it is concerned with the building of socio-psychological community. In this it creates the essential basis of agreement on which can be superimposed the pluralist community of competing interest groups of the neofunctionalists; strategies at both these levels create the conditions in which it becomes increasingly easy to add the dimensions of constitutional unity in the federalist strategy. Each theory can be conceptualized as including a set of tools which are suitable for operating in turn at each of the three levels of socio-political organisation in the contemporary state: the people, the organised non-governmental groups, and the centralised decision-making structures. In a comprehensive scheme of integration at each of these levels the conditions of success are established in the integration of the next lowest level. In this way the *Gesellschaft* features of neofunctionalism are grafted on to the *Gemeinschaft* features of the functionalists, and the creation of common constitutional structures reflects the pervasive results of gradualism rather than a miracle of political creativity. This process may be conceptualised as proceeding at the regional or universal level; but, clearly, a concern with global integration such as is reflected in functionalism, would require some balanced relationship between the two. A triumph of regionalism creates new problems of integration.

Present approaches toward the European Assembly and its powers and functions are a good example of the mistakes in integrative strategy which may result from the failure to distinguish sufficiently clearly between these phases of integration. Lack of theoretical clarity has led practitioners and some scholars to confuse two purposes: that of obtaining further integration and that of introducing into the present institutions in Brussels some device for obtaining greater representativeness and responsibility in the Commission and Council. It is a characteristic of federalism that its supporters usually insist upon discovering in the present conditions the outlines of what they desire; the Assembly is to be the Parliament of a future Europe.

Functionalism's concern with values and the definition of a more general interest underlines the need for obtaining first the conditions in which a directly elected, more powerful Assembly could possibly succeed. To set up such an Assembly in the absence of such conditions could lead to a retreat from integration; it could expose the weakness of the pattern of support, the absence of that minimum of agreement without which no Assembly can work. First things, after all, must come first, even if they come slowly. Indeed many of the appeals in the federalist literature for a directly elected Assembly, or for voting in the Council by majority, seem to amount to a confession of failure, an acknowledgement of the weakness of the strategy: they amount to a recognition of opposition, an expression of the fear that someone in a system of unanimity might oppose their schemes effectively. The very manner in which their schemes are formulated sometimes implies the confession that they cannot succeed.

Federalism continuingly reminds politicians of what it is they are being asked to yield: political arrangements are necessary in order to get beyond existing political arrangements. The implication is that the question is so important that it cannot be left to existing politicians. In the early 1970s the approach of the Commission of the EEC frequently illustrated this failure of federalist tactics. The Commission repeatedly argued that questions such as medium term economic policy involved political questions and that the Brussels institutions should therefore be given greater political powers. Governments were continuously reminded in this tactic that this was indeed a political question and they became more determined to keep it within their control. Functionalism, on the other hand, disposes actors towards more subtle methods: it involves changing the criteria in terms of which decisions about political importance are made. Why remind governments that something of value is being taken from them? The political significance of such questions as economic integration should be played down rather than amplified, and governments are to be approached in such a way that they are not continuously reminded of their own importance.

The defence rests there. Functionalism as a source of strategies for obtaining integration is a unique mixture of elements. It generates a feeling for the wealth of things which can be done: it has the capacity to sustain optimism in the face of temporary set-backs. It maintains credibility in its descriptive aspects; it is conducive towards the development of more sophisticated strategies for obtaining the improvement of international society. At the heart of this mixture is one element which is perhaps the extraordinary achievement of the theory: it creates a powerful sense of the links between the very short term and the long term, between what can be done now, and the goals which eventually might be obtained. It combines hope for the future with a realistic view of the present.

Notes and references

1 By Karl Deutsch and David Mitrany. Politicians in the Third World also stress this factor in 'nation-building' to obtain stability in their states.
2 See *Functionalism: Report on the Conference at Bellagio*, Carnegie Endowment, 1970, pp. 6-7.
3 See Paul Taylor 'The Functionalist Approach to the Problem of International Order', *Political Studies*, October 1968, pp. 393-410.
4 See the excellent analysis and critique of neofunctionalism by Ronn D. Kaiser, 'Toward the Copernican Phase of Regional Integration theory', in *Journal of Common Market Studies*, March 1972, pp. 207-232.
5 Ernst B. Haas, *Beyond the Nation State*, Stanford, 1964, p. 55.
6 See Professor Haas's own evaluation in 'The study of regional integration: reflections on the joy and anguish of pre-theorising', in *International Organisation*, **24** (4), 1970.
7 See A.H. Somjee 'Pluralist-Behaviouralist paradigm in political science', in *Political Studies*, December 1971. See also newsletter of the American Organisation of Political Scientists called *Caucus for a New Political Science*.
8 See A.J.R. Groom, 'Functionalist theories and East-West cooperation in Europe'; paper delivered to the International Studies Association Conference, New York, March 1973.

9   See Friedrich von Krosigk, 'A reconsideration of federalism', *Journal of Common Market Studies*, March 1971.

10 See J. Rosenstiel, 'Some reflections on the notion of Supra-nationality', *Journal of Common Market Studies*, Oxford, 1963.

11 See below, pp. 00.

12 See, for instance, R. Inglehart, 'An end to European Integration?', *American Political Science Review*, March 1967; and D. Puchala, 'Patterns in West European Integration', *Journal of Common Market Studies*, December 1970.

13 Karl Heinz Neunreither refers to this in a discussion of spill-over in 'Transformation of a Political Role: reconsidering the case of the Commission of the European Communities', *Journal of Common Market Studies*, March, 1972, p. 243.

14 See Paul Taylor, 'The Functionalist Approach to the Problem of International Order: a Defence', *Political Studies*, **16**, 1968; p. 405.

15 Ernest Gellner, *Thought and Change*, Weidenfeld and Nicolson, 1969 (2nd Ed.) pp. 4-12.

16 The ex-Beatle and his wife embarked in 1969 upon a scheme for world peace through a kind of popular, religious, 'quietist' conversion.

17 See Victor-Yves Ghébali, *La Réforme Bruce, 1939-40*, Genève, June 1970. See also Ghébali's paper, pp. 00 ff.

18 See below, pp. 00-00.

19 William M. Reisman, 'The Role of the Economic Agencies in the Enforcement of International Judgments and Awards', *International Organisation*, **19** (3), Boston, Autumn 1965.

20 An impression of the impact of functionalist thinking on the student of regional and universal international institutions may be readily obtained by glancing through the footnotes in the last ten years in the two leading journals in the subject: the *Journal of Common Market Studies*, Oxford, quarterly, and *International Organisation*, Boston, quarterly.

21 It is interesting that federalists who turn to the study of strategies for integration frequently compromise with functionalism; one hybrid is Functional Federalism; see Carl J. Friedrich, *Europe: an Emergent Nation*, New York, 1969.

22 *Functionalism: Final Report of the Conference at Bellagio, loc. cit.*, p. 17.

Functionalism and World Society
A J R Groom

Functionalism is both a description and a prescription. As a description and explanation of phenomena in world society it has been used by practitioners and academics alike. As a prescription they have similarly used functionalist ideas as a basis for developing one of the major approaches to international organisation and to the study of world society in general. While functionalism is largely inexplicit and untestable,[1] it is never the less an extraordinarily seductive mode of thought which has not been effaced by the passage of time.[2] This mode of thought which, in its prescriptive form, is no more than a fuzzy set of hypotheses expressing a loosely integrated set of values, cannot claim to be a scientific theory which links together probablistic statements with deductive properties. This chapter seeks to examine functionalism both as a description of world society and as a prescription for a 'working peace system'. The starting point describes the history of the concept of functionalism.

Functionalism in its Conceptual and Historical Setting

The major approaches to international organisation, although containing descriptive elements, are essentially prescriptive. They can be grouped under several headings. No institution, no writer, falls entirely into any one category yet the distinctions serve the purpose of delineating different conceptual frameworks. These frameworks or approaches, which all seek to further peace and security if not always justice and participation, may be described as 'centralist', 'realist', 'gradualist', 'statist' and 'functionalist'.[3] 'Centralist' writers take the nation state as their model and they contrast the peaceful nature of relations within the state, which are increasingly concerned with welfare, with world war and international social anarchy at the world society level. The analogy of a government at the world level comes easily: it is world government, whether federal or not, with a centrally enforced world law. The hope is that world government will bring, on a world scale, what has been achieved on the national level. But such a new 'Leviathan' could only come into existence if it was imposed since the concept ignores such factors as the plurality of values and the demands for participation and independence in contemporary world society. Such an enforced world law would not resolve conflicts, at best it would merely repress or redefine them.

The 'realists' accept that world government is not presently feasible and that it could only come about as some variant of imperialism. Thus instead of seeking some new 'Leviathan' to produce order they attempt to strengthen the threat system with which we are familiar at the world level—collective security or the balance of power. Their model, like that of the centralists, is a power model of world society in which the main bulwark of orderly social relations is seen as a monolithic (centralist) or differentiated (realist) threat system to back up the *status quo* which is under constant threat from revisionists.

A different, 'gradualist', approach, which has its antecedents in the old idealist school, formed by a *mélange* of nineteenth century liberalism, pragmatism and radicalism, rejects the 'realist' image of man as being subject to a drive to dominate unless held in check by a threat system—be it overt or covert. In this approach man is amenable to reason and, if allowed to consider matters in a proper manner, he will act in a reasonable way. A threat system is not necessary to induce socially acceptable behaviour provided that the appropriate framework is available. The assumption is that what is reasonable is self-evident and therefore the principal requirement is the construction of a framework which will allow self-evident rationality to be recognised. Thus a rational framework is constructed on the basis of a set of ideals in the belief that normative behaviour would be induced from these ideals within the framework of a constitutional mechanism designed to facilitate this. Standards would be set and states would be gradually drawn towards accepting them because of their very reasonableness. This would be particularly so if the states were the product of self-determination and organised along liberal democratic lines. Thus gradually a new framework for world society would come into being. However, if any recalcitrant state or group should indulge in deviant behaviour and reject the self-evident rationality and reasonableness of the standard set it would, after due pause for reflection, be coerced into socially acceptable behaviour.

The 'statist' views the nation-state system, and particularly the European nation-state system, as being a natural super-organism. Thus, while international cooperation and coordination may be convenient and desirable for certain limited purposes, to submit to any higher body would be unnatural and, ultimately, self-defeating. The prime locus of loyalty and satisfaction of needs is the state and it is to the state the individuals and groups will turn for protection and wellbeing in times of crisis. Any form of international organisation which does not recognise this verity will not, and cannot, succeed.

'Functionalism', as a conscious approach to world organisation, dates back to the early years of the century and its origins lie in the development of functional organisations in the last century.[4] The functionalist argument starts from the basic notion that form should follow function. In other words, a particular functional system of endeavour delineates itself through transaction patterns and a suitable organisational frame for that system is determined by the needs of the function being performed. Functionalists argue that there is no need for a fixed constitution written in advance because the framework is developed and (ideally) modified as the function being fulfilled changes. The implication of the functionalist mode is to see a multiplicity of forms and levels of organisation each reflecting a system of transactions which may or may not produce institutions at the world level. In any case the relationship between institutions at the world level would itself be determined functionally and it would not necessarily imply a world government. Thus the primacy in organisation is given to transactions and not to constitutions, and boundaries are functionally determined and not state determined. The institutional framework is primarily a function of behaviour and only secondly a constraint upon it. Thus, functionalists argue, a 'working peace system' will evolve that will tend to diminish conflict by allowing cross-cutting loyalties, by developing super-ordinate goals, by removing barriers to intercourse and by creating a sense of security through fulfilling a necessary function rather than through a threat system. The development of a 'working peace system' is thus contingent upon a learning process in which successful cooperation in one dimension spills over into other spheres. The strategy therefore suggests itself that functional organisation should start from those spheres in which welfare is maximised through trans-national cooperation so that the domain of legitimised politics gradually expands while that of power politics gradually contracts.

Functionalism in this sense is usually associated with the name of David Mitrany. Mitrany's ideas have been formulated in a more rigorous manner, quite drastically modified and then tested by a number of neofunctionalist writers whose work will be referred to below and in other chapters.[5] Functionalism has also been used as a strategy by practitioners, such as Jean Monnet, in order to arrive at a goal, a functionally organised federal state such as a united Western Europe, of which functionalists would not approve.[6] This chapter will concentrate on Mitrany-type functionalism.

These broad approaches to international organisation have found some reflection in and have been based on the development of international institutions since the Congress of Vienna. Several broad trends in international organisation can be identified: namely, security organisations based on threat systems, adjustment organisations based on a gradualist approach, and functional organisations reflecting on-going systems of transactions. However, many organisations contain elements from a variety of approaches combined in ways that are not always complementary.

Security organisations have always been salient since they are dealing with high politics. They have been based on the notion of shoring up the existing order by the threat of coercion, whether through a balance system or a collective security system. The concert system of the nineteenth century emerged as an attempt to preserve the *status quo* after the upheavals of the French Revolution. It also developed as a mechanism whereby the great Powers sought to devise rules of behaviour (often at the expense of others) which would enable them to protect themselves against the consequences of their own new found military strength and ambitions which derived from the ideological motivation of nationalism and the logistic base provided by the industrial revolution. The system was doomed to failure since it could not allow for systemic change, indeed, its very premise was homoeostatis, although it did permit great tactical flexibility. This system continued, with new actors and variants in organisation, after the great holocaust of 1914-18 in the shape of the League of Nations' security provisions at the formal level and, informally, the Conference of Ambassadors and the Monroe Doctrine. After the second collapse of 1939-45 it was again resurrected, with modifications, in the shape of the United Nations Security Council and the bi-polar alliance systems. Underlying all of these security systems—be they formal organisations, the balance of power or collective security—was the attempt to create a threat which would compel deviant actors to conform with the desired behavioural norms as formulated by the *status quo* Powers.

Coexisting with these threat systems were various adjustment procedures of a gradualist character which sought to mitigate the harsher elements of power politics. Throughout this century arms control and disarmament have been sought after as a means of making power politics safer, and occasionally, as a means to alter the rules of the game so that power politics no longer predominates in security matters. At the same time adjustment procedures such as arbitration, conciliation and mediation have proliferated. Efforts to secure acceptance of new standards of behaviour in many fields have been made. The general tenor of these moves has been to provide more responsive procedures for dealing with the conflict endemic in any situation (but not inherent in man or groups) than mere threat systems.[7] In many spheres these adjustment procedures have been so internalised that there is no realisation of endemic conflict. Conflict, in common parlance, means that these internalised adjustment procedures have failed and that the conflict has become real in the sense that no legitimised means of resolving it exists. This relatively infrequent occurrence—both quantitatively and qualitatively if all transactions are considered—attests to the success of adjustment procedures. It may also be due to the growth of functional organisations.

Prior to the nineteenth century few transnational functional organisations existed. World society was relatively atomistic and the billiard ball model was in many ways an apt description. However, with the growing demand for cross-national transactions due to the industrial revolution, but with the opposite trend of the growing impediment to such transactions created by frontiers due in part to the nationalist upsurge following the French Revolution and the decline of *laissez-faire* philosophies, functional organisations began to be created as a response to a felt need. Functional international organisations enabled frontiers to be traversed for low politics but left undisturbed for high politics. 'One world' problems emerged, such as posts and telegraph, and have continued to emerge, such as pollution, and have demanded 'one world' answers. Some of the functional organisations which grew out of these felt needs were inter-governmental, a few were hybrid, but the vast majority were non-governmental inter- cross- or trans-national organisations. Such organisations often reflect transaction patterns and incite intergovernmental bodies to respond to new demands.[8] Without the all-pervading web of non-governmental organisation the world would be a very different, and less pleasant, place. Here is the heartland of functionalism.

The Relevance of Functionalism

What is the relevance of the 'theory' of functionalism as a description and as a prescription? This raises several questions, notably its ability to describe contempory world society, its claim to be a working peace system, its attitude to the state, its appropriateness as an approach to pressing world problems, and its standing as a prescription in terms of its own values of participation, flexibility and responsiveness. These questions do not exhaust functionalism's claim to relevance and, in any case, these claims are not conducive to rigorous testing so that any assessment remains personal and ridden with uncontrolled and largely uncontrollable values. While this is very regrettable such an assessment is worthwhile since it is a contribution to that inter-subjectivity that is at the basis of all science, whether rigorous or not.

Functionalism as a Description of Contemporary World Society

The literature on international relations reveals two competing general models of world society—the billiard ball model and the cobweb model. The dichotomy between the two models is crude but it serves the present purpose. The billiard ball model takes the state as the basic unit of analysis. States are seen as atomistic units, discrete, essentially complete in themselves and clearly defined in their competence and authority. However, while legally they are sovereign and equal, they are not so in fact. They are organised hierarchically on the basis of an amalgam of pressures conveniently placed under the rubric of power. They are thus like billiard balls of varying sizes knocking together on a billiard table. States are conceived of as the principal actors in world society and the nature of the transactions of all actors is held to be ultimately based on power.

Such a model may well have corresponded to the Europe of the seventeenth or eighteenth century with its largely atomistic but slowly emerging state system based on competing dynasties with relatively few non-politico-security transactions. At that point the boundaries of economic, communication, ethno-cultural, administrative and security systems may have been co-terminus or insignificant, but this is surely no longer so. Major systems boundaries are diversifying in different functional dimensions: some are getting bigger and some are getting smaller. They are no longer co-terminus nor are they without significance.

The cobweb model recognises this. It sees the world as a myriad of systems of transactions acting within and across a variety of functional dimensions. The formal state system is but one of these, albeit a highly important one. The relationship between the actors in these systems is not always characterised by power politics. Indeed, although there is a great role differentiation this differentiation is usually based not on power but on a legitimised acceptance of a functional differentiation. While power politics can and does exist the functionalist can point to the working peace system of the everyday world that is the chief characteristic of the cobweb model. The world is in fact organised largely on functional lines.[9] The functionalist takes this description as his starting point for prescription. His aim is to devise an organisational framework which reflects this world and one which will, hopefully, enhance its properties as a working peace system. If the differing size of systems in various functional dimensions is a potential source of conflict (and this is especially likely to be so if some of the systems boundaries such as those of the state are impermeable) then functional organisation may be one way of giving it an appropriate framework. This is not to say, as some functionalists assume, that the functional mode of organisation is *necessarily* the key to a 'working peace system' which brings groups actively together as opposed to one which enforces 'peace' through a threat system which imposes differentiation and coerces behaviour.

In another respect the functionalist can claim that his model is an appropriate description of world society. The tenacity of the functionalist mode of thought against many criticisms may reflect a certain stubbornnesss and rigidity of mind but it may also reflect a certain relevance. The exponential proliferation of functional organisations, both inter-governmental and non-governmental, is incontestable: there are now hundreds of international inter-governmental organisations and thousands of international non-governmental organisations. The latter in particular are, *prime facie*, at least some evidence of relevance. Many practitioners also think in functional terms, whether they be the progenitors or servants of functional organisation. This is not always immediately evident, due to the disinclination of practitioners to formulate their rules of thumb in a theoretical manner and to their lack of the intellectual tools (but certainly not the intellect) to do so. It is, nevertheless, a real indication of the relevance of functionalism. For example, the current proposals of East European Governments and quasi-official representatives on all-European cooperation (and security) are an eloquent instance of this.[10]

Finally, the continued academic interest in the approach attests to its relevance as a description of at least part of contemporary world society as well as to its attraction as a prescription.

A Working Peace System?

The prime prescriptive concern of functionalists is to eliminate war. The problem of 'securing the peace' was the immediate cause of the flowering of functionalist ideas that can be conveniently gathered under the rubric of 'superordinate goals'. If individuals, groups or states need to co-operate in order to secure an end which can only be achieved through co-operation and which they each separately, and for their own reasons, desire, then if this goal is sufficiently important they will be forced to work together and suppress or resolve their conflicts. The result of failing to suppress or resolve their conflicts would be to forego the desired 'superordinate' goal. The realisation and perception of common needs and interests, or super-ordinate goals, puts a damper on antagonisms between parties in dispute, for the dispute prejudices their common but separately perceived welfare. The general proposition has considerable experimental backing in diverse fields.[11] The difficulty of course lies in instilling a realisation and acceptance of common needs and interests in a conflict situation where stereotyping, tunnel vision and the like abound. Nevertheless, the approach appears fruitful. By starting with the technical or non-controversial aspects of international relations an ever increasing web of ties between actors can be built up on the basis of meeting needs by fulfilling commonly-desired functions. The functionalist hopes that a reduction in the likelihood of conflict will thereby occur and that the habit of cooperation will spread from one functional area to another. Compromise, the argument runs, is also likely to be facilitated in the remaining areas of dispute. In other words, the delineation and fulfilment of superordinate goals will engender a learning process so that the extent of non-controversial relations between units will expand and that of conflicting relations contract. Peace would not be dependent upon the nuclear deterrent, the balance of power or collective security but upon a web of common needs and interests. Individuals, groups and states would be induced to cooperate by the utilitarian and rational maximisation of welfare that they all seek. Dysfunctional conflict would be eliminated. Loyalties would not be polarised on one of the conflicting units but would be differentiated between several actors, and this cross-cutting in different spheres—economic, ethno-cultural, political—would diminish the likelihood of conflict. But to what extent will a multi-polarity of loyalties develop? Will there be a learning process between different areas of functional endeavour?

In his study of the International Labour Organisation (ILO), Haas remains sceptical of functionalist claims, although he is far from rejecting them.[12] He points out that the cooperation of groups results from the convergence of separate perceptions of interest and not from spontaneous surrender to a common good. This does not necessarily eliminate a learning process but Haas sees this in the form of task expansion, whereby the powers and competences of the ILO grow over the years in its own sphere, rather than as a spill-over effect into other areas. As a functionally specific international programme develops, and its organisation with it, and as behavioural norms and procedures are built up, so are mechanisms for dealing with conflict over these norms. However, the experience of the ILO seems to suggest that they will not spread into a *general* international code. It seems that while task expansion comes more easily than spill-over into other areas, there is no automaticity in either. If they are to come about at all they must be striven for.

Lindberg's analysis of the same phenomena in the European Economic Community (EEC) is more sanguine from the functionalist point of view.[13] This may be the result of a more conscious seeking after task expansion and spill-over on the part of the EEC Commission than that of the ILO's Governing Body. The different experience of the two organisations underlies the need for scepticism concerning any functionalist claims to automatic task expansion or spill-over. It rarely seems to happen on its own. However, if it is sought, and especially if the institutional and political environments are permissive, then task expansion and even spill-over can and do take place. But the difficulties are considerable. For example, if each organisational framework is functionally specific then membership will vary from organisation to organisation which will inhibit the learning process, although the cross-cutting may still act as a conflict dampener. In addition, functional organisation is based on instrumental ties which may not engender attitudinal ties to a similar degree. For a firmly based 'working peace system' both instrumental and attitudinal ties are necessary.

Both Haas and Sewell[14] reproach the functionalists for their supposed distinction between power (political) relations and welfare relations. They consider this distinction to be untenable in practice. The functionalists insistence that 'welfare' is the most propitious area for the development of peaceful cooperation from which such cooperation will expand by a learning process to more contentious areas is thus undermined. The critique of Haas and Sewell on this point is indeed telling to the extent that functionalists do in fact assume that power relations are a synonym for politics and that the welfare, or the economic and social area, is non-political. As the economic and social area can certainly be characterised by power relations at times, the distinction between power and welfare relations, while analytically attractive, is not founded in practice. But nor is the facile assumption that politics consists of power relations. In fact relations in all spheres—social, economic or other—may be dominated by power or they may not. Few, even adepts of the power politics school, would argue that all social relations are characterised by a ubiquitous struggle for power. It is notoriously difficult to give an operational meaning to the concept of 'power' and this may in part account for the furious argument between the power politics school and their opponents. Let it suffice to say that in some relationships the behaviour of an actor is changed by some form of unacceptable pressure from what it otherwise would be, while in other relationships the behaviour of an actor is decided on criteria that are acceptable to it. The former may be termed a power relationship and the latter a legitimised relationship. Most social relations can be located on a scale stretching between these two poles, as they contain elements of both. This is equally true of transactions in all dimensions. If politics is concerned with the allocation of values, structures, roles, means and goals, then the way in which this is done may be on a power basis or on a legitimised (or mutually acceptable) basis. Thus the crucial distinction is not between politics and welfare, as the functionalists would have it, but between power and legitimised relations in any particular sphere. If the functionalists could accept this distinction then they could escape from the damaging critique of Haas and Sewell. Functionalism would then concern itself with ways of augmenting the degree of legitimisation in social relations, but it would still be faced with the problem of how to start and sustain the spread of legitimised politics.

Functionalism, federalism, systems analysis, integration theory and regionalism share a concern over the effects of the contemporary state system. On the one hand the state is the repository of intense loyalty by citizens and groups and the organising medium for many of the essential elements in modern life. As such it cannot, and to a certain extent should not, be 'abolished'. On the other hand, the state promotes and perpetuates differences between peoples and its frontiers hinder the free working of cross-national functional systems. Not only does the state fail to fulfill all welfare needs but it also fails to provide security in an age when deterrence is unsure and defence is unacceptable. The functionalist does not attack the state system frontally but he seeks to solve the problems of nationalism and sovereignty by circumventing them. Frontiers are to be made meaningless by the transfer of the appropriate parcel of 'sovereign rights' from the state to a functional organisation. Systemic forces and a learning process are then relied upon by the functionalist to lead to the transcending, rather than the defeat, of the old order. The argument is that as more and more systems are organised on functional lines then not only will the diffusion and cross-cutting of loyalties make conflict less likely (because it is more dysfunctional) but the state, insofar as it no longer fulfills a function, will 'wither away'. Thus the individual or the group will be able to satisfy its needs in whatever area or system it wishes without any impediment on the part of the state.

Clearly this is an attractive notion, but is it a practical one? Obviously loyalties to the state and frontiers are not going to disappear overnight nor are cross-national functional organisations based on systemic needs going to materialise quickly. The functionalist does not suppose that they will and so, for the time being, he is stuck with states. Indeed, neofunctionalists are content to see functional organisations solely with states as members whereas the essence of functionalism is that membership of a functional organisation should be based on ability to contribute to the system. Manifestly in most cases this would involve a large non-governmental membership. To a surprising degree the neofunctionalist adopts the image of the billiard-ball model while the functionalist has that of the cobweb model. Moreover, both often associate the state with the political system and the political system with power politics. Are these assumptions justified?

Historically, it has been argued, an important factor in the evolution of states has been the coincidence of the boundaries of important systems, such as the communications, economic, administrative systems and so forth, so that they could be consolidated and treated as one—the state—with one consolidated decision making process for all the principal systems—its government. Hence the state could be likened to a billiard-ball—a cohesive unit with a hard exterior, its frontier. Nevertheless, this remained a coincidence and consolidation of separate systems, although they did reinforce each other. The demands of modern technology and of participation require a separation of these different systems so that each can be organised according to its needs for its proper working, as they often no longer coincide with state boundaries or with each other. For example, the dominant security and economic systems in which Britain acts extend far beyond the boundaries of the United Kingdom, while the principal administrative and ethno-cultural systems are devolving within the boundaries of Britain, and some are becoming autonomous within the state as, for example, in the case of the nationalised industries or public services. These have considerable independence from the state and do not necessarily respect its boundaries. They tend to be an independent actor rather than a sub-system of the state.

Each system, economic, ethnic or whatever, has within it a political function, that is, a means whereby goals, means and roles are allocated. When the frontiers of many systems coincided with state boundaries then these separate political functions for each system could conveniently be merged into a general politico-legal-administrative system or government whose fiat ran within the boundaries of a state. If, however, these systems are separated, then the political, or rôle and goal allocatory function, belonging to each system will also have to be separated. The state will then have a diminished political rôle and 'wither away' toward being a legal system. The essential point is therefore to conceive of the state primarily as a legal system with additional general administrative functions. Within and across the state's territorial boundaries a web of systems operates, each with its political process, some with and some without a predominantly power basis. The essence, for the functionalist, is to allow these systems to operate freely and without hindrance and to render to each its political or decision-making process. Thus those who are concerned will participate, be they states or other groups, and if participation is commensurate with interest then the possibilities of satisfaction, efficiency and peace will be augmented.[15]

This is not to argue, nor indeed would the functionalist necessarily argue, that if all systems were free to follow their needs, unimpeded by states or institutional forms that were unrelated to the function, then there would be no conflict between systems. There is no 'invisible hand' which ensures that if only systemic needs are fulfilled then all will be well. The interests of different systems may well conflict. For example, the needs of the economic system for oil may conflict with the needs of the ethno-cultural system in the area where the oil is to be found. This conflict will continue if systemic goals are considered to be fixed, whether or not it is temporarily settled by the exertion of superior power by one system. For the conflict to be resolved, that is, for the new situation to be self-supporting without the use of power and acceptable to or legitimised by all the actors, then systemic goals must be subject to variation. For systemic goals to change a system must have a feedback mechanism that can relay the effects of past policy and a political process whereby an assessment of alternatives can be made in terms of the cost of continuing the conflict and the cost of choosing an alternative. An alternative is always available, in theory, even though it may not be perceived by the parties, since there is always more than one value that is held by a party even if it is only articulated as simple opportunity cost. For this reason conflict is essentially subjective, although it may not be seen as such by the parties.[16] If the cause of a conflict can be located, and if the continuation of the conflict is considered to be more costly than altering the present policy of the system, then the conflict is perceived to be dysfunctional or self-defeating. Thus there will be peace to the extent that all systems respond to feedback and have a political process which can recognise when feedback is indicating that the policy being followed is dys-functional to the extent that in maximising one value a party is failing to achieve the totality of its values, that is, the pursuance of one goal is detrimental to other goals.[17] Such a recognition must also include the ability to act.

But what if one or all of the parties to a conflict refuse to respond to feedback, refuse to recognise a conflict's dysfunctionality and continue to thrust the burden of change on the environment? What if one value is perceived to be so salient that it must be pursued at all costs? In these cases, where the policies of different parties remain incompatible and there is no attempt to alter them, conflict will continue and the relations between the two parties will be characterised by the assertion of power. That these parties, or, as in the previous example, these systems, are organised on functional lines will make not one iota of difference to the basis of the conflict, although it will make a difference to the form of the conflict. The organisational forms of ethno-cultural and economic systems do not usually have armies at their disposal whereas states do. The essential elements in the avoidance of conflict are therefore information on the cause and cost of a conflict and a willingness to respond to feedback by changing policy or goals. (It should be noted that there are two forms of steering in response to negative feedback. The first merely involves tactical adjustment in the means of seeking a fixed goal. The second involves an adjustment of goals.) The organisation of the world on a functional basis might alter the form of conflict, it might mitigate conflict, but it would not, *ipso facto*, eliminate conflict, nor do all functionalists claim that it would. Power politics at the appropriate systems level can still occur. The central points of interest to the conflict analyst are still the flow of information and the way that it is processed, rather than the form of organisation of the actors.

The concern of this brief survey is to relate the doctrine of functionalism to some of its principal aspirations—the elimination of conflict and the creation of a working peace system—in the light of recent research on international organisation. By diminishing the dependence (and loyalties) of individuals and groups on the state and by increasing their dependence on a multiplicity of organisations for the satisfaction of their needs, the functional organisations may thereby decrease the use of armed force. If loyalties and interests are spread over many units, actors and systems, then there is a greater probability that war will become a matter of cutting off the nose to spite the face. War with oneself is more easily recognisable as dysfunctional than war with others. Moreover, as more and more actors no longer have armed force at their disposal, and as they are cross-national they will find it difficult to request states to supply it, then the form of conflict is likely to be non-violent. However, it is difficult to assess the impact of more functional organisation on the incidence of conflict. This will presumably depend upon the degree to which it is able to increase the satisfaction of felt needs, and the efficacy of the learning process on which so much depends yet about which so little is known.

Participation, Welfare and Development

Among the goals that a functionalist mode of organisation aspires to are those of responsiveness and welfare. One aspect of responsiveness that is evident in contemporary world society is the ubiquitous demand for participation. In addition, practically all forms of social organisation now feel the need to stress their concern with welfare. The UN, for example, responded to this by declaring the 1960s as the 'Development Decade'. It is thus apposite to consider functionalism in the light of these three phenomena—participation, welfare and development.

Participation. Demands for participation are evident at all levels of social organisation and in all functional dimensions. Sometimes they are dramatic, as in the case of workers and students in Paris in 1968; sometimes they are mediated by demands for independence, as in the case of colonies; sometimes they are personal, as in the case of children alienated from their parents; sometimes they are forced into time-honoured channels, as in the case of workers striking over seemingly trivial issues. Certainly the phenomenon is one of the major issues of our time.

What in fact does a demand for participation mean? Is there a common drive or demand that makes it worthwhile to consider seemingly diverse phenomena together? It is not easy to avoid the impression that 'participation' is, in that eloquently vulgar American phrase, a 'gut feeling'. Those demanding participation do not feel that, at the relevant level in the relevant system, they have a sufficient say in the decision-making process on matters which they deem to be important. When such a feeling spreads to different sectors of an individual's life and throughout areas of a group's field of social action and endeavour, then a feeling of disorientation or alienation beings to grow. There is, presumably, some point at which mounting dissatisfaction at the way in which values, goals and means are allocated in different areas merges into a general demand for change or participation such as was manifest in France in May and June 1968. Normally inertia is induced by satisfactory participation in most areas of an individual's or group's activities so that unsatisfactory participation can be accepted in other areas.

There seems to be no one form or degree of participation. A sense of participation is a subjective factor. Because an actor participates if he *feels* that he is participating, there can be no objective criterion of participation, at any level or in any system. Participation has to be given an operational definition in terms of a given actor in relation to his aspirations in a particular system at a particular level at a particular time. The degree and form of satisfactory participation is an ex-post concept, that is, there is enough when no serious dissatisfaction is expressed. This serious dissatisfaction must also be given an operational definition in terms of a specific situation and in particular the possibility of structural violence being legitimised by a 'happy slave' must be borne in mind. The difficulties in giving some day-to-day meaning to demands for participation when these demands are generalised are herculean, yet the consequences of ignoring them—further alienation leading to revolution or war—are such that they cannot be avoided.

Many attempts have been made to suggest ways in which a response can be given to these seemingly diverse, incoherent, yet real and basically similar demands. It is sometimes thought these demands can be met by changing the hierarchy of decision-makers in a particular system. But this has not always proved satisfactory since participation is not necessarily correlated with a prominent place in the hierarchy in decision-making, but with a perceived satisfactory role. The latter may be great or small: to participate is not necessarily to be the most important decision-maker but to play a subjectively relevant role which in some cases may entail no more than being part of a parameter-forming tacit consensus. Thus constitutional reform is no panacea. For example, Robert Triffin has suggested an ingenious reform of the French political system,[18] but this will be of little avail if the electors do not feel that they participate, and there is no guarantee that the reforms will elicit this response. Indeed, as Michael Crozier has pointed out, 'On one hand, people would like very much to participate in order to control their own environment. On the other hand, they feel that if and when they participate, their own behaviour will be controlled by their coparticipants'.[19] Thus formal participation may only be a palliative. In any case full liberal democracy is difficult to establish in a penetrated state system since the penetrating elements may have an important influence, yet they are represented, at best, by proxy, and at worst, not at all.

Perhaps most work on participation has been done in industrial relations. It has been suggested that participative decisions are more likely to take into account the needs and interests of all parties. Participation reduces alienation and increases identification and thus, paradoxically, by relinquishing hierarchial authority control is increased. But this assumes a substantial commonality of interest which may not be perceived by the parties, especially in the short run.[20] Nevertheless, this experience is encouraging.

One view would state that the demands for participation should not be met, for to satisfy them at one level would only lead to further demands. This view sets little store by a policy of 'appeasement' since it argues that the demands can never be satisfied, they can only be held back. Moreover, appeasement will never satisfy demands as they will increase in scope with success. Such a view equates demands for participation with the demand for 'power', which it sees as almost inherent, so that social relations are characterised by an everlasting struggle between the 'haves' and the 'have nots'. At the international level this gives rise to the balance of power and threat systems or collective security. The standpoint of this chapter, while acknowledging that such phenomena are not unknown, is that in the real world, in day-to-day relations—and these are the ones that are relevant—a satisfactory level of participation for actors, be they small or large groups, can exist. Is the functional approach a possible way to achieve this at the world level? Will organisation along functional lines enhance responsiveness and perhaps thereby increase an actor's perception that it is participating in what it feels is a relevant manner in what it considers to be a relevant system of transactions?

The functionalists' prime concern is to separate different systems one from the other in order to let each be organised as suits it best without restricting it to the confines of the state. Similarly the size and extent of sub-systems will be decided by the function they are seeking to perform. The polarisation of systems around the constitutional forms of the state will be reduced. Whatever the level, form will follow function, be it in the factory or in the economic system. The separation of systems into their respective functional area and their freeing from the confines of a constitution and a state's territoriality may increase the possibility of access to the political process of the allocation of goals and rôles by the actors concerned. The possibility to participate will be increased because an organisation will be concerned with a function and with those who fulfill it and not, on the cross-national level, just with states. The form is to fulfill a need and if one of the needs is participation then the form must strive to reflect this. The notion is that a greater flexibility in organisation will enhance the possibility of participation. It will not, however, guarantee it any more than will reform of formal structures such as that suggested by Triffin. It is a question of probabilities. There is no inherent reason why a functional system should not be highly unresponsive, power-ridden and non-participatory. Moreover, it is not known when, why and how often such regrettable characteristics will manifest themselves in a functional organisation. The functionalist can only suppose that functional organisation will promote access to the decision-making process in ways in which actors will deem to be subjectively participatory. This hypothesis has not been tested but it is attractive as a way forward when compared to the more tried, and often failed, alternatives on which the changes are rung as man battles with the problems of the twentieth century using the weapons of the nineteenth century. If the functionalist's peace system 'works' then it is more likely to be participatory than that of the centralist, the realist, the gradualist and the statist. If it does not, the stale formulae of the other approaches will remain in a world which is unlikely to be the worse for the functionalist experiment.

To summarise the argument, the present international governmental organisation (IGO) system reflects the billiard ball model of international relations and, even though partially organised on functional lines, it tends to down-grade cross-national transactions. Yet state boundaries are often inappropriate in a world where economic and security systems are sometimes continental in size, or a-territorial, and in which other systems are devolving from the state to smaller territorial units or even escaping from the state. If the IGO system reflected this, rather than hindered it, participation would not necessarily be thereby increased, but it might be facilitated. Thus, at present, many cross-national systems are disenfranchised in the IGO framework, although they are represented in the international non-governmental organisation (INGO) framework. There is therefore a need, with which the functionalist would concur, for a greater integration between the IGO and INGO systems in order to reduce this disenfranchisement which creates a climate of non-participation.

This prescription will be examined below but it can immediately be seen that the balance between the requirements for participation on a territorial basis and those for participation on a corporate basis will be problematic. Even if they are taken as given there remains the question of what is to be decided at what level. Moreover, this formalisation may have an alienating effect, along the lines suggested by Crozier, and create new divisions at a different level of society. In any case, it has already been argued that representation cannot be automatically equated with participation any more than the latter can be equated with legitimisation, consultation and on-going control.[21]

Welfare, like participation, is one of the promises of functionalism: the functional mode of organisation, it is claimed, will enhance welfare and satisfy more efficiently felt needs. Indeed, the two issues intersect. Taylor has argued that modern man has substituted the welfare system of the state for that of the extended family.[22] This has led to a crisis of participation, since while welfare is dispensed it is not necessarily dispensed on terms and in forms acceptable to the participant.[23] Moreover, welfare programmes are often not related to the range of systems of interaction in which the actor participates but are restricted to one system—that of the state.

It is a truism to say that, in theory, functional organisation will increase 'welfare'. By definition a functional organisation will only be set up if there is a need for it. (In practice, however, functional organisations are created for a variety of other reasons, some of which bear little relation to felt needs or to a function being performed or one considered to be desirable). If the function is now satisfactorily organised then there is no need to change it. However, if there is a barrier to the proper satisfaction of needs, particularly a state or constitutional barrier to the proper satisfaction of needs, then, in theory at least, functionalism will increase welfare. But what of practice? The studies of Haas, Sewell and Lindberg of semi-functional organisations dominated by states reveal that even in these merely relatively propitious circumstances, from the functionalist point of view, the record is largely one of the increasing satisfaction of felt needs. At the INGO level there is *prime facie* no evidence to suggest that functional organisation is detrimental to the perceived welfare of actors. Indeed, such organisations may be unlikely to persist in the face of such perception since INGOs may be less likely to be able to enforce continued membership than IGOs. But the evidence is inconclusive and the welfare hypothesis of functionalists has not been tested.

Inis Claude has argued against the functionalists' notion that increased welfare and the more efficient satisfaction of felt needs will lead to a working peace system.[24] He points out that there is no correlation between low economic development and 'aggressivity' and cites the fact that the Second World War was instigated by a highly developed country, Germany, and not by a developing country. But this view is simplistic in that it has the notion of an 'aggressor' rather seeing the war as the almost inevitable concomitant of a system of non-legitimised role differentiation. The Second World War may well have been 'unnecessary', but not for the reasons that Churchill gave. Rather it resulted from a structure the responsibility for which rested with many actors. Today conflict abounds in the developing world for reasons similar to that which motivated a highly developed Germany in the thirties. Claude's argument is thus too facile. If conflict results from imposed structures, unfulfilled expectations and non-legitimised role differentiation, can the functionalist offer a remedy? In seeking to enhance welfare and satisfy needs rather than 'deter aggressors', in seeking to promote participation the functionalist has a plausible hypothesis, but he has not shown that functional organisation will necessarily promote these goals.

Development and welfare are closely related terms, although there is tendency to use the former in a *tiers-monde* context and the latter with reference to the developed world. Functionalism is a developed world concept which has excited little or no interest on the part of *tiers-monde* scholars and practitioners. This raises the question of the extent to which functionalism is culture-bound and only appropriate to the developed world.

Some scholars in the *tiers-monde* are fearful of functional organisation for they see this as facilitating the penetration, control and exploitation of the South by the North in the form of non-governmental organisations such as multi-national corporations. Although functional organisation may, in this context, bring technological innovation to a developing country, it can also operate as a new mechanism of monopoly, dependence and deformation leading to capital outflows, loss of resources, a brain drain and monetary problems. Functionalism would also be instrumental in leading to an island economy.[25] On the other hand representatives of multi-nationals sometimes claim that they are virtually philanthropic institutions and little mention is made of profit. This is not the place to argue the merits or demerits of multi-nationals since the purpose is merely to point to the fears of scholars and practitioners in the *tiers-monde* that functional organisation could lead to greater exploitation. In the light of such fears practitioners and scholars cling to national sovereignty and the state apparatus as a barrier against exploitation. The functionalist needs to demonstrate to them that other countervailing powers will protect the weak in a particular functional dimension.

This question leads to another: how can a functional system be made responsible and responsive to the needs of all its participants, and, furthermore, responsive to the needs of the totality of functional dimensions? How can the functionalist give an assurance that he is not merely exchanging a system of powerful states for a network of systems dominated by powerful interests allied, perhaps, to the rump of powerful states? The simple answer is that he cannot: there is no guarantee that a functional system will not be dominated by power politics. The functionalist can only pin his hopes on cross-cutting, responsiveness, increased satisfaction of felt needs and enhanced welfare as well as an improved sense of participation. Failing this he will need to resort to building countervailing powers and thus open the way back to the very balance of power policies from which he is seeking to escape.

A Prescription

Functionalism, as a prescription, is a promise not a panacea: it is a promise that if we follow some simple axioms a working peace system may result. But because of its nature, it is hard to see whether the promise is being kept. In brief, it remains a hypothesis. Yet it is a promise which has relevance since it is based on systems of transactions. Its normative prescriptions may prove to be erroneous yet they do suggest a practical proposal. This proposal is for a greater integration of the systems of IGOs, INGOs, autonomous national boards and sub-national organisations.

If the cobweb model of world society has some significant correspondence with reality then the functionalist approach to organisation is one way to give that reality on organisational form which emanates from and responds to behavioural patterns. The present form of organisation is too wedded to the state system and is straining to match a transactional system. Such a matching already exists to a certain extent through the INGO network and it is being strengthened through its proliferation. But there is a great need for the integration of elements of the state-organised IGO framework with appropriate parts of the INGO network. Indeed, Article 71 of the UN Charter foresees such developments and many of the Specialised Agencies have analogous articles which allow for consultation with and the limited participation of non-state actors. But they are too little used. For example, UNCTAD developed in response to a felt need during the UN Development Decade. But governments are not the only actors in the development process: multi-national corporations, co-operatives, unions, universities, aid-giving bodies and many others have a role to play. UNCTAD's debates are unreal to the extent that these bodies do not play an appropriate role. One organisation, the ILO, has a mixed structure, with representatives of governments, labour and management, which reflected the capitalist world of fifty years ago. It is debatable whether it still represents even this small part of world society, but the success of the ILO in face of the vicissitudes of the last half century is encouraging in suggesting that such mixed governmental and non-governmental structures can be made to work to the benefit of all.

At the moment, as Judge and Skjelsbaek point out,[26] there is antipathy between the IGO and INGO systems. This is both unnecessary and dysfunctional. Much could be achieved if IGO secretariats and IGO members sought actively to integrate their INGO equivalents where and to the extent that a felt need exists. This is not a call for 'anarchy' nor for an organisational revolution: it is a call for many organisations and for more relevant ones; it is a call for greater control and for greater flexibility in its exercise. This proposal seeks after a means 'to weld together the common interests of all without interfering unduly with the particular ways of each' as Mitrany put it some thirty years ago.

A Problem

Let us assume that the world is organised along functional lines. John Burton has argued very cogently that this is already the case at the national level.[27] If this is also the situation at other levels of world society we shall be faced, indeed we are being faced, with a new world. This world consists of a myriad of autonomous bodies—IGOs, INGOs, nationalised industries, public services and so forth—criss-crossing the face of the earth. We are moving rapidly towards a *Gesellschaft* the like of which is unfamiliar. At the individual level each person, at least in developed societies, is becoming a bundle of rôles which are increasingly difficult to integrate into a whole. The growing number, the great variety and, above all, the rapid change in rôles is causing a degree of personal distress that cannot be other than disquieting. Alienation, anomie, withdrawal, mental sickness are widespread in developed societies and their treatment is a cost which needs to be related to the 'benefits' that supposedly come from a drive towards *Gesellschaft*. We thus need to preserve elements of *Gemeinschaft* as our societies become more and more rational, achievement-oriented and organised as task forces.[28] Functionalism cuts both ways in this process. By being task-oriented it promotes a *Gesellschaft* but by cross-cutting and the learning process it promotes shared values and a sense of *Gemeinschaft*. Once again we return to the key to functionalism as a prescription, namely, the spillover from one dimension to another of shared values generated by cooperation for functional goals. Without such spillover functionalism as a prescription is fatally flawed. Unfortunately the evidence concerning spillover is conflicting and incomplete.

A further aspect of the same problem emerges as we move towards a cobweb model of functionally organised world society, namely, that of control. In cybernetic terms, who steers? Mitrany envisaged some international planning agencies whose function would be to coordinate, to look to the future. Their rôle in a functionally organised world would be very important since functional organisations are based on present systems of transactions and the role of the planning agency would be goal-setting or at least goal-suggesting. To this extent the notion that 'form follows function' is attenuated. Although the planning agency might be tied to a particular functional dimension Mitrany clearly foresees an overall political coordinating authority which would be some form of 'world government' made up of functional bodies rather than state units.

Mitrany's planning agencies are one answer to the question 'who steers?'. However, he does not appear to have developed his thoughts on this matter in any detail (nor, for that matter, have anarchist writers who are faced with a similar problem, although the anarchists deny that it exists). The question 'who steers?' assumes that someone does. Historians and politicians often talk of steering the ship of state and journalists frequently refer to a particular figure being a strong hand at the helm. Most academic models of decision-making assume that there is some degree of control at both the macro and micro levels. But these models are being increasingly challenged. Lindblom and Braybrooke[29] have offered a model of disjointed incrementalism which has a good deal of intuitive explanatory power. Units may act in a goal-seeking manner at the micro-level as, for example, when a civil servant 'pushes paper' from his in-tray to his waste-paper basket or out-tray, or in the management of an airport. But is this also true at the macro-level? The contributors to *The Management of Britain's External Relations* did not think so.[30] The Lindblom-Braybrooke model suggests that there is no general overall control of policy. The dominant characteristic of decision-making at the macro-level is not a dichotomy between power and steering but rather a situation of drift.

If this model is as good a reflection of reality as *prime facie* it appears to be, what are its implications in a functionally organised world? If the billiard-ball model of world society is accepted then presumably the concentration of loyalty, expectations, and satisfactions on the state counteracts, to a certain extent, the tendency to drift, since the state is so salient and the object of and generator of such shared loyalties as to ensure that the drift is in the same direction. But what of a functionally organised world in which loyalties, expectations and satisfactions emanate from a variety of organisational frameworks? If disjointed incrementalism characterises decision making at the macro-level in each functional dimension what is there to ensure that the 'drift' in various dimensions is in the same direction so that world society does not disintegrate? With IGOs, INGOs, Ministries, Public Services, Nationalised Boards, NGOs and other groups organised functionally, but making policy in a disjointed incremental way, the functionalist is hard pressed to explain why world society will not be a disintegrating society and one in which, at the macro-level, there will not be the same elements of alienation, anomie and the like that now exist at the micro-level. His main line of defence is probably that no actor is a member of only one functional dimension, whatever the level of analysis. Since actors straddle more than one dimension their activities in different dimensions create mutually shared values or articulate previously inarticulated universal values. Such universal values as independance, participation and welfare have been commented upon above. These values are, however, mediated by culture to a degree that they may not be universal in their behavioural effects, even if they are in their origin. Thus once again, as a prescription, functionalism is no more than a promise of a working peace system since the hypotheses on which it is based remain untested.

Summary

Functionalism is not a theory but one of several approaches to international organisation. It is a relevant response to the organisational demands of a world society that increasingly resembles the cobweb model. Its claim to be a working peace system is based upon a false dichotomy between politics and welfare. The real difference is between power politics and legitimised politics and these can be found in systems of interactions in all functional dimensions. Functionalism is overly sanguine in its reliance on an automatic learning process to spread the domain of legitimised politics. Thus, by itself, the functionalist mode of organisation will not necessarily lead to the diminution of conflict. Equally, while functionalism seems likely to increase participation and welfare, it is no guarantee of it. This is particularly true of the *tiers-monde* where it may become the vehicle of exploitation. Nevertheless, there are grounds for recommending an increased resort to functional organisations in contemporary world society and, in particular, for an increased integration of the present IGO and INGO frameworks.

109

Notes and references

1 See next chapter by R.J. Harrison.
2 The bibliography gives abundant evidence of this.
3 For examples of each respectively see: G. Clark and L.B. Sohn, *World Peace Through World Law*, Cambridge: Harvard University Press, 1958; Hans J. Morgenthau, *Politics Among Nations*, New York: Knopf, 1948; efforts at standard-setting in the work of the ILO; Charles de Gaulle, Press Conference, 15 September 1960; David Mitrany, *A Working Peace System*, Chicago: Quadrangle, 1966.
4 I am grateful to Michael Hennessy for pointing out to me that 'functionalist' ideas were quite common among anarchist writers of the nineteenth century. They thus pre-date functionalists in the international organisation held. Moreover, modern anarchism with its emphasis on responsiveness, participation, consensus and the transactional basis for organisation has much in common with the functionalist mode.
5 See chapters by Charles Pentland and Nina Heathcote.
6 For example see Mitrany's comments in his chapter.
7 Endemic conflict occurs randomly between an actor and its environment. It is exceedingly rare that an actor's output meets with the required response from the environment. For example, to satisfy thirst there are many options—water from a stream or a tap, beer in a public house, coffee in a coffee bar, etc. It is very unlikely that thirst will be quenched without a subsequent decision, that is, when we become thirsty we are in conflict with our environment. Such conflict is endemic in life. We resolve such conflicts in a routine acceptable way, in this case, by going to a stream, tap, public house or coffee bar, so that we do not *appear* to be in conflict. We would be in conflict in the common parlance meaning of that term if the routine acceptable way of quenching thirst did not appear to be open to us.
8 See chapter by Anthony Judge and Kjell Skjelsbaek.
9 See chapter by John Burton.
10 See also the conclusions of Alastair Buchan (ed.), *Europe's Futures, Europe's Choices*, London: Chatto and Windus, 1969, reputedly written by the Foreign Office member of the team. The chapter by Thomas Weiss and Jean Siotis (pp. 173 ff.) examines the views of the heads of various inter-governmental agencies.
11 See Muzafer Sherif, *Group Cooperation and Conflict*, London: Routledge and Kegan Paul, 1966.
12 Ernst B. Haas, *Beyond the Nation State*, Stanford: Stanford University Press, 1964.
13 Leon Lindberg, *Political Dynamics of European Economic Integration*, London: Oxford University Press, 1963. In Lindberg's *Europe's Would-Be Polity*, London: Prentice Hall, 1970 (with Stuart Scheingold) and in their edited volume on *Regional Integration*, Cambridge: Harvard University Press, 1971, the views expressed are closer to those of Haas. A major difficulty arises in the time scale that is allowed for the learning process to work and for spill-over to occur. Should it be five years, ten or a lifetime or more? This exemplifies the difficulties in 'testing' functionalism.

14 J.P. Sewell, *Functionalism and World Politics,* Princeton: Princeton University Press, 1966.

15 I am grateful to a colleague, C.R. Mitchell, for access to the theoretical and empirical work he has done on this problem. For example, the enforcing of the state boundary between Somalia and its neighbours, with the consequent disruption of a cross-national ethno-economic system, was a major cause of inter-state conflict in the Horn of Africa. When the state boundary was made porous to the parties in the ethno-economic system, conflict subsided.

16 For a thorough discussion of these problems, see J.W. Burton, *Systems, States, Diplomacy and Rules,* London: Cambridge University Press, 1968, and J. W. Burton, A.J.R. Groom, C.R. Mitchell and A.V.S. de Renck, *The Study of World Society: a London Perspective,* Pittsburgh: International Studies Association Occasional Paper no. 1, 1974.

17 For a discussion of this question see A.J.R. Groom, *Peacekeeping,* Bethlehem: Lehigh University, International Relations Monograph No. 4, 1973.

18 Robert Triffin, 'Une democratie de participation', *Le Monde,* 9 July 1968.

19 Michel Crozier, quoted in Eric Norlinger, 'Democratic Stability and Instability: The French Case', *World Politics,* October 1965, p. 131.

20 For a discussion of these problems see A.S. Tannenbaum, *Social Psychology of the Work Organisation,* London: Tavistock Publications, 1971, chapter 7.

21 For a discussion of the problems see A.J.R. Groom and Paul Taylor (rapporteurs), *Functionalism: Final Report of the Bellagio Conference,* New York: Carnegie Endowment for International Peace, April 1971.

22 Paul Taylor, *International Cooperation Today,* London: Elek, 1971, p. 136.

23 A similar problem is raised by Richard Symonds in a paper (mimeo) to the Political Studies Association Conference in 1967 entitled 'Some Administrative Problems in International Organisations and in their programmes of Technical Cooperation', when he discusses (p.9) tighter UN General Assembly control of the Specialised Agencies' Technical Cooperation Programmes.

24 Inis Claude, *Swords into Plowshares,* New York: Random House, 1964 (third revised edition), p. 353.

25 For a cogent discussion of these problems see the paper of Marcos Kaplan in the Bellagio Report, *op.cit.* See also chapters here by Michael Hodges and R. Harrison.

26 Chapter by Judge and Skjelsbaek.

27 See chapter by John Burton.

28 For a full discussion of these problems: See Amitai Etzioni, *The Active Society,* New York: Free Press, 1968.

29 See Charles E. Lindblom and David Braybrooke, *Strategy of Decision: Policy Evaluation as a Social Process,* New York: Free Press, 1963.

30 Robert Boardman and A.J.R. Groom (eds.), *The Management of Britain's External Relations,* London: Macmillan, 1973.

Testing Functionalism
R J Harrison

'Thus the unfacts, did we possess them, are
too imprecisely few to warrant our certitude.'
(James Joyce, *Finnegan's Wake*, Viking Press, 1967, p. 51.)

Mitrany's influential essay, 'A working peace system',[1] now widely regarded as the
authoritative statement of the functional argument, was highly speculative. Its
author has said that, as a sociologist, he tried to introduce a more sociological
approach into the study of international relations.[2] The fruit of his effort bears the
stamp of his training and personal experience. He has acknowledged that, in
particular, the experience of the Tenessee Valley Authority had been, for him, a
formative element and he was 'impressed with the way that the requirements of
solving a problem could transcend political difficulties and constitutional formulae.'
Functionalism was an approach conditioned by such experiences rather than a
systematically worked out theory. It is, in a way, invidious to subject something as
impressionistic, speculative and idealistic as this to rigorous criticism, reformulating
it as a coherent theory of international change for the purpose of 'testing' it. Yet it
is an approach which has exercised a profound influence, many scholars having
confessed its importance in their own intellectual development. Mitrany himself,
because of the succinct strength of his exposition, has become generally accepted as
the authoritative exponent of, if not a theory, a mode of thinking about
international politics which had many adherents in the inter-war years and the
Second World War and provides the most popular rationale for the work of the
many international organisations now performing functional tasks, mostly under
the aegis of the United Nations Organisation (UNO).

Thus, though the evidence which can be adduced to test the expressed or
underlying premises is, in the nature of the thesis, severely limited, its examination
is worthwhile. A review of it does not pretend to put functionalism on a scientific
footing, but in attempting it, we are committing functionalism, somewhat
inappropriately, to the methodological imperatives of science, albeit social science.
The attempt, therefore, raises the usual methodological problems of the social
sciences acutely.

Methodological Problems

Since a body of explanatory theory relating to the social environment has been in
existence for some time, built up by philosophers, historians, economists, through
perceptive and intuitive observation of the social order, it is not surprising that
there has been some controversy between those who prefer this 'classical' approach
and the new force of self-styled 'social scientists'. Hedley Bull, for example, has

criticised the 'scientific approach' in its application to international politics. He presents, as an alternative, the classical view that there is very little of significance that can be said about international relations; that general propositions about this subject must derive 'from a scientifically imperfect process of perception or intuition, and that these general propositions cannot be accorded anything more than the tentative and inconclusive status appropriate to their origin'.[3] We must 'appreciate our reliance upon the capacity for judgment in the theory of international relations'; Mitrany's work is clearly in such a 'classical' tradition. It raises some empirical questions, but they are generally 'of so elusive a nature that any answer we provide to them will leave some things unsaid'. Bull's further comments, though unacceptable in their general application, are apparently quite well directed to the idea of 'testing' functionalism: 'It is not merely that in *framing* hypotheses in answer to these empirical questions we are dependent upon intuition or judgment (as has often been pointed out, this is as true in the natural as in the social sciences); it is that in the *testing* of them we are utterly dependent upon judgment also, upon a rough and ready observation, of a sort for which there is not room in logic or strict science, that things are this way and not that'.[4] To conclude the debate in such terms, however, would be very short-sighted if scientific method can add something to the logical status of explanation relating to the social environment.

The question on which this is dependent is one Hedley Bull raises. Is social enquiry liable to logical rules applied in the scientific spirit of ethical neutrality? Of a negative answer one can only say that it must rest on some intuitive philosophical position, itself not absolutely susceptible, therefore, to logical refutation. A positive answer provokes the very practical question whether the nature of the material, though it may not preclude ethical neutrality, nevertheless raises insuperable barriers to the application of scientific procedures. A first answer to this question would be that it is impossible to equate the whole range of social phenomena in this respect; that, for example, a higher degree of comparability and accuracy in quantification is possible in the study of electoral behaviour than in the study of the behaviour of states in military alliances. The data peculiarities of each subject of social enquiry are different. Thus, though it is possible to generalise very broadly about the methodological difficulties of social science, there are special problems which arise in the context of a theory of functional integration of the global society.

General Problems of Method

To oversimplify, all social scientists have to contend, more or less, with two problems. The first is one of terminology. Human behaviour, whether or not it may be studied with ethical neutrality, is not itself ethically neutral. Explanation must take account of such factors as prestige, loyalty, religion, legitimacy, which change their connotation in time and place, or, with little or no difference in connotation, produce quite different behaviour patterns in time and place. For example, an intense national loyalty may involve habitual compliance with the commands of a ruler or it may mean that the ruler is the focus of all the conflict and discontent within the national community. Evidently, such traditional and popular explanatory categories, with their changing emotional and ethical connotation, are defective. There is a serious terminological problem for the social scientist. It is

113

being met in part by the development of a new language of sociology. The process is slow because it is evolutionary rather than controlled.

The second general problem is the absence of the experimental situation, and the consequent problem of bias. Essentially, experiment requires the isolation of variables to determine their causal significance. The answer of the social scientist is the comparative method, which has the same underlying logic as the experiment. Sets of variables are compared, to establish, by agreement and difference, the necessary connections between them. The difficulty for the social scientist is that control is virtually impossible and he must, therefore, select those variables for comparison which he considers significant. In selecting some and dismissing others, a value judgment is exercised in the initial comparison.[5] So numerous are the concurrent factors which might be relevant in social phenomena, that subsequent repeated attempts to falsify the hypothesis can only hope to reduce the possibility that a wrong selection or a false hypothesis was made. However, as hypotheses formulated by other social scientists are tested and compared and a general theory begins to emerge, the problem of selecting which variables are relevant for comparison becomes less subject to the initial bias, more closely governed by the theoretical orientation.

Special Problems

Functionalist theory does not escape these difficulties of terminology and bias. The term 'community', for example, is used to refer to an ideal global system within which economic and welfare integration advanced by a web of functional organisation have created a consensus based on common welfare interests. It is a community defined by Mitrany, following Hobhouse, as the sum of the functions carried out by its members.[6] Each of us in this conception is a collection of functional loyalties so that building a world community involves merely an extension of such loyalties.[7] In more mystic vein, 'the community itself will acquire a living body not through a written act of faith but through active organic development.'[8] Both Sewell and Haas in studies of functional organisations of international cooperation, have understandably found it difficult to evaluate and use this conception of community. It is very general. It appears to be, in Mitrany's hands, interchangeable with 'society'. It is a term which, in popular usage connotes a sense of identity, of close social bonds with high normative content, and limited territory. It is a term, the elements of which sociologists have been at pains to refine in order to dispel some of its hazy penumbra. Sewell, therefore, notes resignedly that for the functionalist the word "community" often follows "international" or "world"; the term's usage further implies that a "community" has attained superior attributes of a largely unspecified nature'.[9] Haas, for his part, found it necessary to refine the term for analytical use. 'Like the functionalist, then, we may think of modern nation-states as communities whose basic consensus is restricted to agreement on the *procedure* for maintaining order and settling disputes among groups, for carrying out well-understood functions. Unlike that of the functionalist, this conception pre-supposes agreement merely on the *means* for achieving welfare, but not on the content of laws and politics, not on the substance of the functions'.[10]

Another instance of the terminological problem is the way in which, in identifying functionalist elements in the 'incrementalist' strategy of European integration, a host of neologisms like 'identitive power', 'spill-over', and 'feedback' have been coined by its students. Defined by stipulation to avoid the confusions of popular and professional usage, discipline in their use by other writers has proved hard to attain.

The second general problem, the existence of bias is also apparent. The functionalist argument as we have noted bears the stamp of Mitrany's training and experience. He exhibits, in common with many other sociologists, social psychologists, and psychologists who have offered a contribution to explanation in international politics, a tendency to neglect, ignore or discount the importance of the political framework of action. It is an aid to the understanding and evaluation of the thesis also, to recognise that it took shape in the interwar years and during the second world war in the writings of Reinsch, Potter, Cole and others.[11] Mitrany's own original contribution was in 1933.[12] It, therefore, shows a contemporary concern with nationalism as a threat to peace and produces a strategy designed to secure its erosion. Subsequent interest by a number of American and European writers in more limited regional integration reflects the respective concerns with bloc cohesion and superpower dominance in the bi-polar international environment.

We cannot overcome these problems in testing functionalism. We can only attempt to minimise them by using the terms Mitrany uses where possible, without attempting to give them greater precision than they have in his writing, and by trying to evade the problem of bias by setting out what we consider to be the essential problems to be tested and by drawing on as wide a disciplinary range as possible for evidence which can be related to well-tested theory.

Propositions

Essentially, the thesis is a set of propositions about the nature of community and, arising from those propositions, about how to create, by self-conscious effort, a world-wide community, free from war. The propositions can be reduced to five about the nature of community, and two dependent strategies:

1 Economic and welfare interest provide a basis for community.[13]
2 The nation-state system is without any permanent basis. It is divisive, violent, and blinds ment to their real needs and interests.[14]
3 The satisfaction of economic and welfare needs, creates common interests, though specific interests may differ in kind and degree.[15]
4 The elements of world community are already in existence in trade and other aspects of interdependence.[16]
5 Political discussion, particularly constitution building, by directly touching upon sentiments of national dignity, is divisive and prejudicial to community building.[17]

The strategic propositions which follow:

1 Specific functional tasks of economic and welfare cooperation, outside the area of political conflict, will create a community of interest and feeling which will ultimately make national frontiers meaningless.[18]
2 The organisation and scope of this activity can be functionally determined, varying according to the task. Any necessary coordination between tasks can be allowed to arise in the same way, without the deliberate elaboration of a constitutional framework (though this is not altogether precluded.)[19]

115

The evidence which appears to be most relevant to these propositions comes from the community studies of sociologists and social psychologists, the contribution of these two disciplines to the study of international politics, the sub-discipline of international relations, empirical experience with international organisations, a specialised literature which attempts to provide quantifiable indicators of the state of international society using available statistics, survey data etc., and the manufactured evidence of simulation and gaming.

Community Studies

The sociological and social psychological evidence from community studies is ambiguous. If, as Haas interprets functionalism, it posits the development from international Gesellschaft into Gemeinschaft[20] (or if the 'community' envisaged is merely the international application of Gesellschaft) the assumed evolutionary consequences would be disputed among sociologists. Many sociologists regard the normative bonds associated with the concept of Gemeinschaft as essential to stable 'system' operation and a necessary preliminary to the contractual or Gesellschaft conception. As Etzioni says, 'normative bonds are part of the definition of a collectivity because units which lack those are unstable and cannot serve as the building stones of a theory. As Durkheim pointed out, any contractual relationship requires a precontractual underpinning; i.e., societal bonds that are only utilitarian (not to mention only coercive) are inherently unstable. Units that command only strong utilitarian bonds ... may break up when, following a change in the environment, culture, or make-up of the actors, the relation no longer "pays". If some units that are linked by a high level of transactions maintain a stable bond despite such changes, this is not because the transactions bind them firmly, but because the units are also tied by normative bonds.'[21] To a considerable extent, studies of the economic modernisation problems of newly independent states fabricated by colonial powers support this view. Part of the problem is identified as the inadequacy of economic incentives in the absence of a pre-existing community cohesion and will.[22]

Some sociologists would accept the possibility of the evolution of Gesellschaft into Gemeinschaft. If 'system maintenance' be accepted as equivalent to, or analogous to community building in its functional requirements then Talcott Parsons' theory of functional imperatives in the organisation of society recognises this alternative.[23] The four imperatives, goal attainment, adaptation (or mobilisation of means), integration (exacting compliance), and latency (value creation and maintenance), may be regarded, according to Parsons, as the four phases of any social action-cycle. The most functional cycles, with respect to system maintenance, are from latent to integrative to goal attainment to adaptive (Gemeinschaft to Gesellschaft) or, in reverse from adaptive to latent. Like Mitrany, Parsons assumes the rationality of social processes, a conformity of choice of means with ends. The adaptive to latent cycle, evidently, depends heavily on this assumption.[24] The Parsonian analysis, however, though at this general theoretical level providing support for the functionalist thesis, incorporates the idea of the polity and its sanctions as the instruments of goal attainment and compliance. The polity is a sub-system which has the generalised capacity, or power, to mobilise the resources of the society for the attainment of its collective goals. Empirical studies, whether coincidentally relevant or directly based on it are *a priori* more relevant to neofunctionalism or federalist-functionalism which does assume the existence of central institutions which have or acquire the capacity to fulfil this instrumental role.

Yet another hypothesis is that even with the existence of the polity the development of Gesellschaft is inherently detrimental to, and takes place at the expense of, Gemeinschaft. Such a development is regarded as characterising the advanced industrial societies. Haas notes that 'a modern political community tends to lack the warmth and devotion we associate with ascriptive ties and communities based on primary contacts or loyalties . . . we may think of modern nation-states as communities whose basic consensus is restricted to agreement on the *procedure* for maintaining order and settling disputes among groups . . . the modern nation state, then, is a Gemeinschaft that looks and acts very much like the Gesellschaft we associate with our international system. Instead of being intimate and cosy it functions like a large scale bureaucratic organisation. Its tasks may involve the maximisation of the welfare of its citizens, but not necessarily in the sense of aggregating all their demands and hopes into a general consensus'.[25]

Not all sociologists would agree with Haas that this much 'cooler' community is 'no less a community'. It has a number of disturbing characteristics. The social outcome sanctioned by generally agreed norms in less developed societies are sanctioned in the advanced industrial societies by law and the state. In issue areas where sectional commitment to goals is high the use of the power of the state in conflict resolution strains the commitment to procedures to which the consensus is restricted. The Parsonian latency phase cannot fulfil its role of normative adjustment and creation. The sociology of advanced urban industrial society, therefore, is very much indebted to negative concepts like alienation, anomie, apathy, drop-out, protest, and like manifestations of stress and dissatisfaction with a society which, as Marcuse has so eloquently pointed out, continues to deliver the economic and welfare 'goods'.[26] Such an interpretation of this evidence is apparently in conflict with the functionalist conception of consensus built upon common economic and welfare interests.

However, Marcuse, Bell and others[27] place a very different interpretation on the same evidence. These negative concepts are essential to the directly contradictory thesis (which clearly supports the functionalist position) that current radical expressions of alienation may be related to the consensus society, a society whose economic and welfare efficiency makes dissent appear to be an irrational oddity, confined to a minority. In this view, the development of Gesellschaft in the advanced industrial society produces a condition of ultra-stability, a decline in ideological diversity and its replacement by a single unifying ideology of materialism. Dissent finds no representation in orthodox politics and hence exhibits the peculiarities of protest politics.

There is no way, at present of coming to a conclusion on these disputed interpretations of the same evidence. The weight of empirical studies however tends to support the view that Gesellschaft developments tend to undermine existing Gemeinschaft (a premiss of the functionalist argument) and that alienation rises with the relative importance attached to utilitarian sanctions. Mayne, Tonnies, Weber, Durkheim, Redfield, Mayo, Schmalenbach and others regard this transition within a society as disintegrative rather than an integrative factor. Whether it be temporary or permanent, a rise in alienation and the disruptive effects associated with it would appear to be a likely concomitant of functionalist success in making national frontiers 'meaningless'.[28]

It may be that the irrationalities of nationalism or some other form of exclusionist localised loyalty play a necessary role in the psychological well-being of individuals. There is considerable evidential support for the view that seemingly irrational modes of human behaviour, with immediately negative economic effects in some cases, appear to contribute to the achievement of non-economic goals. At the level of small community studies there is evidence, for example, of the severe social problems resulting from slum clearance and town planning, with the dissolution of patterns of mutual aid, companionship, commercial services, neighbourhood supervision of children and other bonds. The importance of irrational modes in the behaviour of workers in industry, the impact of industrialisation on traditional cultures in 'developing' countries, are among other relevant studies, raising doubts about the primacy accorded to utilitarian motives and bonds in the functionalist conception of international society.[29]

Other studies suggest that a necessary part of the concept of community as a basis of social cohesion is the existence of an outgroup which can be perceived as the enemy. Gunnar Myrdal's *Beyond the Welfare State* points out the utility of the anti-imperialist nationalist stance of the newly independent states of Africa and Asia as a cohesive force, often the only force available for mobilising the energies necessary for development.[30] Three case studies showing the apparently vital role of the enemy in politics have been presented by D.J. Finlay *et al*. The enemy in this view satisfies the system need for an antithesis as an instrument of unity. If not available it must be created or the social and political edifice of control weakens or disintegrates or changes into a new and unpredictable form.[31] Considerable ingenuity has gone into the manufacture of evidence to assess the factors which determine the cohesion of groups. In experiments supervised by Henri Tajfel at Bristol a number of local schoolboys were divided into two groups by trivial and then by random selection criteria and in the performance of various assigned activities began immediately to discriminate against each other in favour of the groups to which they had been assigned.[32] This and other group experiments tend to support the neo-Hobbesian enemy-outgoing thesis of group cohesion, casting doubts on the concept of international community.[33] Such experiments can at best, of course, be regarded only as suggestive of explanations of international behaviour.

Subject to that caveat one of the most carefully managed, pre-researched experiments in intra- and inter-group behaviour, that conducted by M. Sherif *et al*, confirms the findings of inter-group discrimination and hostility, shows a positive relationship between increased inter-group conflict and enhanced ingroup solidarity, and shows that the most effective way of bringing groups together is against a common enemy. However, the Sherif experiments were designed to answer a very wide range of questions and they demonstrated also that though contacts between groups in deliberately non-competitive situations, in persuasive situations (including appropriate religious environments) in which the virtues of amity were extolled and in situations affording pleasurable activity to the individuals of both groups, did not break down group hostility and conflict, group relations were improved when they were assigned tasks or given goals which could be achieved by cooperation. 'Cooperation between groups arising from a series of super-ordinate goals will have a cumulative effect toward reducing the social distance between them, changing hostile attitudes and stereotypes and hence reducing the possibility of future conflicts between them.'[34]

What the further results of decreasing hostility and conflict between groups may be, the Sherif experiments do not indicate. There is, however, apparently relevant evidence of a non-experimental kind on the effects of reducing or eliminating inter-community conflict. Studies of inter-tribal relations in Africa, South America and the Pacific have provided corroborating evidence of the importance of the displacement of aggression on to outgroups as a factor of group cohesion. They indicate intra-community fission may be a result of the suppression of tribal warfare.[35] It would be impossible to test directly, the proposition that, in an attenuated form, the same factors were at work within and between modern states, but the presumption is not unreasonable.

Functionalism is, in a sense, based on a socio-psychological abstraction from the facts of international life. In international trade, improved world-wide communications, and in other aspects of international interdependence, Mitrany sees a burgeoning community, the development of which is arbitrarily restricted by the activities of the sovereign states.[36] Before considering the attempts by social psychologists to detect a correlative internationalism we should notice briefly, that a great deal of evidence is available on trends in international transactions of all kinds which makes possible the more precise definition of this element of the functionalist argument. A detailed review and evaluation of the apparent indicators of international interdependence would be a task of such magnitude that it is obviously out of place in this essay. We can, however, offer a few general observations and impressions about this data as it relates to functionalism and the premiss of growing interdependence. First, we may observe that the development and use of modern means of communication is very uneven, reflecting the differences between the developed and the under-developed countries, and the centrally planned and market economies. There is a more marked pattern of intra-regional than international interdependence and the pattern grows clearer with the increasing pace of technological advance.

To take one obvious example, television satellites capable of beaming the same programme throughout the world have little significance over Africa and Asia where there are relatively few receivers. The following table shows world estimates of television and radio receivers for 1968.

| | No. of telev. rec's. | | No. of radio receivers | |
	Total mills.	per 1000 inhabitants	Total mills.	per 1000 inhabitants
World total	236	68	674	194
Africa	0·87	2.6	15·1	45
N. America	92	298	336·7	1090
S. America	8	47	28·3	157
Asia	23·5	12	76·5	39
Europe	81	178	128	281
Oceania	3·2	173	4	216
USSR	27	113	85·5	359

Adapted from UNESCO *Statistical Yearbook 1969* (Paris, 1970) pp. 619 and 636.
Figures for Asia include Japan, and country-by-country comparison points up the differences more sharply: see *op. cit.* 1969, pp. 618-645.

The pattern of mail traffic, telegraph service and use of telephones shows the same gross disparity. More significantly, increases in international trade and travel are also concentrated among a few countries, namely the advanced industrial societies. The following table gives an estimate of 1969 exports from developed and developing market economies, and from centrally planned economies to the same categorised destinations.

From	Exports to world	Developed	Developing	Cent. planned
World	272,710	191,240	52,260	27,790
Developed	193,190	147,900	37,460	7,140
Developing	49,780	36,400	10,270	2,600
Cent. planned	29,750	6,940	3,960	18,060

Adapted from U.N. *Statistical Yearbook 1970* (New York, 1971) p. 410; (f.o.b. value in millions U.S. dollars).

Even tourism, which might be expected to benefit underdeveloped, 'unspoilt' countries, is concentrated in the exchanges between the developed countries. Ten developed countries in the 1960s spent and received from seventy to eighty per cent of the total value of international tourism.[37]

The impact of advanced technology as an element in the economic and defence independent capabilities of the existing nation-states is also uneven in its effects on inter-dependence. The *defi americain* which recommends European technological cooperation is not a significant policy consideration for the poorer countries, attempting to modernise. In the defence field, the development of intercontinental ballistic missiles and atomic warheads has reduced the importance of territory and distance as security factors primarily for those few countries which can afford to possess them. Other states continue to provide conventional defence against the equally conventional forces of their presumed enemies. The super-powers have consequently found their long-range deadly weaponry inadequate for a wide range of strategic and political purposes. They have, themselves therefore, maintained conventional national forces.

The trends in international communication and trade, and other transactions would have to be subjected to content analysis to explain the linkage which may exist between interaction-interdependence and the development of international community, capable of resolving problems of change peacefully after the functionalist model. The existing evidence however does not demonstrate a necessary link between interaction *per se* and this conception of integration. There is evidence that international communication, including exposure to mass media with its content of foreign news, international travel, international business contacts and educational contacts, does affect attitudes, often positively. However, increased friendliness is related to such factors as the degree of similarity in values and cultures of the countries of interchange. Exposure to a very different culture through transnational participation may result in simple national stereotypes being replaced by very much more highly differentiated images of foreign countries in the minds of participants but it does not necessarily result in a greater sympathy and friendliness towards the country concerned.[38]

Pool[39] has found that many other factors may be considered determinant variables affecting such changes. They include travellers' own images of themselves and their cultures, hosts' images of themselves, travellers' image of the outside world and the country visited, the hosts' image of the country from which the traveller comes. The type and circumstances of travel also helps to determine the result of such contacts: whether the trip had a clear purpose, whether it was official, whether a traveller was alone or part of a group, whether his companions were fellow nationals or not, whether the contacts with host nationals were personal or official, involved cooperation in joint tasks or competition and bargaining, whether the traveller knew the host's language. Living arrangements, duration of stay and all the facts affecting the ease or hardship of the travel experience were also important. One of the more striking examples cited by Pool[40] of the operation of such factors is the case of American negroes who have gone to Africa to what they felt to be their homeland, only to find that if Africa was home they had become alienated, unable to accept most of the cultural, economic, political and even dietary implications of life in an African community.

In general, these investigations support the view that it is purposive, cooperative contacts which are most favourable to the development of friendly attitudes but they also indicate the importance of possible opposing and cross-current variables, not taken into account in the functionalist thesis. It should be noted, also, that the studies referred to in Pool's survey are not concerned specifically or even primarily with interactions and transactions which arise as a result of international functional cooperation or which occur within the relevant organisations. In this connection the work of students of regional European organisations, attempting to find operational indicators of community integration, is worthy of attention.[41]

The least controversial indicators presented in this study context, however, are those which provide evidence of political community. Integration towards political community is defined, with variations, by reference to the transfer of loyalties and expectations to a new centre which has institutions with decision-making power in key areas. Thus the functional scope and relative importance of authoritative central decision-making is one general test-category. It may be elaborated by distinguishing the various functional sectors or issue areas in which the authoritative resolution of conflict is likely to be required. An attempt is made to weight sectors by reference to such factors as their presumed integrative 'spill-over' potential, judgment as to their importance in relation to the powers of government in other sectors, or by the type of conflict resolution they stimulate. These factors must be related to decision-making outcomes, and to the resources or assets available to central institutions to secure compliance. The multi-dimensional assessment of central authority can then be expressed relatively to other loci of decision-making within the community—particularly the member states.

Another accepted indicator of political community is the existence of demands, their scope, and the organisational scope and resources of the actors articulating demands. For example, the relative importance of regional and national parties and pressure group activity in generating demands and exercising effective influence is regarded as a useful indicator of community progress, though difficult to make operational.

Lindberg has elaborated such indicators in a suggestive discussion of 'Political Integration as a Multidimensional Phenomenon Requiring Multivariate Measurement',[42] which should be consulted. He lists twenty-two 'issue areas', suggests weighting criteria, and outcome and resource evaluation criteria. He also considers demand flow conditions to be fulfilled in advancing integration. These categories could be adopted to some degree as tests of the international development of functional cooperation and its effects. Lindberg's issue area weighting would provide a rough guide to progress in the international assumption of functional tasks relative to national responsibilities. And, within a functional area, the source and strength of demands on the international organisation and their effectiveness at this level would also indicate progress along functionalist lines. Such questions have indeed been asked, in a few cases, in studies of international organisations.[43]

However, one other indicator used by students of European Community development, though not very appropriate for *direct* application at the present rudimentary stage of international functional development, does present findings with analogous force for functionalism. Political systems are sustained by the consensus which exists on procedures, and on the general responsibility to obey the laws which derive from such procedures: in effect, a conception of legitimacy. Such a conception is likely to be the most dependable basis of support for authority. On this assumption, research has been carried out into European integration which tests attitudes to common institutions. Inglehart, Lindberg, Scheingold and Dennis, working in collaboration with the European Community Information Service have conducted attitude surveys for seven Western European countries, Preliminary findings have been reported by Inglehart.[44]

He suggests that an original permissive consensus which enabled a small elite to work in almost conspiratorial fashion to launch the Schuman Plan, and the EEC and Euratom, has been clearly sustained over some twenty years of experience with these organisations. Odd fluctuations in the size of this consensual support are linked to the more dramatic events in the life of the community or the nation concerned. The only marked long-term reversal of opinion in favour of European integration was in Britain, and was a result of the 1967 veto. Testing the intensity of Europeanism by asking questions about specific proposals representing different degrees of supra-nationalism, in such sample categories as educational peer groups, age groups, parent-child groups, has shown, Inglehart argues, that the younger and more highly educated respondents are more favourable to integration, and that, therefore, as these cohorts succeed their parents in positions of influence the prospects for European supra-nationalism developing are enhanced. He argues, on the other hand that with the reversal of opinion in Britain 'If British entry does not take place in the immediate future (it) ... may become an increasingly remote possibility at any future time.'[45]

If the methods and the tentative conclusions of this group of students of European integration, including the presumed feedback linkage between central institutions with functional tasks, elite attitudes, and public opinion, be accepted, then there is an analogous possibility of attitude development at the international level, based on a functionalist strategy. However, the value of this kind of analysis is still a subject of debate. Thus, Deutsch, Edinger, Macridis and Merrit, in an attitudinal survey at the elite level arrived at quite different conclusions:

> The next decade of European politics is likely to be dominated by the politics of nations states, and not by any supranational European institutions. In this regard and for this period, the views of President de Gaulle, that only nation-states will be obeyed and supported by the population, and the view of Raymond Aron,

that there will be no European federation—even for the next twenty years—seem to be borne out by the great preponderance of the data that we have examined.

Within France, and within Germany, the various elite groups generally are closer in their attitudes to each other, and to the mass opinion of their own country, than they are to the opinion of their counterparts in the other country.[46]

Inglehart argues that the contradictions between his own study and that of Deutsch are not as profound in detail as they appear in the general conclusions. Nevertheless, this kind of study has to be seen in the light of studies of 'public opinion' over a longer period[47] which have demonstrated the instability of issues, the contrasting durability of opinion, or attitudes, on grand or simple matters like party and ethnic loyalties and images of other countries, and the relative ignorance of, and weakness of preferences in international affairs. We do not really know how to classify Europeanism or internationalism in this framework of reference so we can have little confidence in the durability within a particular age 'cohort', of such motivations. Only testing, preferably of the identical sample, over many years, could dispel this particular, critical, uncertainty.

Some American political scientists seem prepared to take to the very dangerous and marshy ground which leads from the observation that communications, transactions, and interactions do, in a complex way, have an effect on attitudes. They assume the link between interdependence and integration, and use communications and transactions as indicators of integration. Karl Deutsch was the pioneer of this technique in his *Political Community and the North Atlantic Area*[48] but the difficulties and dangers of the method are illustrated by Bruce Russett in his *Community and Contention*, a study of the relationship between Britain and America in the twentieth century.[49] Russett takes five so called normal years, 1890, 1913, 1928, 1938 and 1954, and for each of these years ascertains the number of treaties and executive agreements signed between Britain and the USA relative to the rest of the world, the size of diplomatic delegations in the two countries in comparison with other countries, various measurable aspects of newspaper comment (confined to the London *Times* and the *New York Times*), trade in goods and services, investment, shipping, tourism, other kinds of travel, mail, telegraph, telephone. He does offer, as a check, an historical account of Anglo-American diplomacy since 1890 and a separate historical account of the military link.

The history he finds is one of nearly simultaneous conflictual and cooperative behaviour, difficult, therefore as Russett admits to relate to the concept of integration.[50] He even offers his own warning about the caution which must be used in interpreting the 'hard' data of communication, attention, and transaction. This does not prevent him, once in his stride in the quantitative marathon from voicing confident absurdities like the following.[51]

In summary, we have found in this chapter clear evidence of expanded Anglo-American capabilities in two areas: British films in America, and American magazines in Britain. In two other cases—American movies in Britain, and British magazines in the United States—the trend was either ambiguous or changing. But in five other cases—mail in both countries, telephone and telegraph messages combined in both, and migration to America—the evidence

123

clearly points to diminished capabilities. This evidence is not quite as one-sided as in the preceding chapter on elite links, where the totals of the capabilities for responsiveness showed that four indicators were up, three neutral, and thirteen down; but the bulk of the data points the same way in both cases. When we take the combined totals—six up, five neutrals and eighteen down, plus the four declining indices produced in Chapter 3—we have grounds for serious concern about the state of the Anglo-American alliance.

Anyone who examines the figures presented by Russett for his various indicators will recognise a multitude of other factors having little relevance to Atlantic community cohesion which contributes to the changes shown. Changes in the power status of Britain during the period surveyed, changes in the mode of communication, additions to the kinds of transport available, are clearly all potential determinants of the indicators he uses. Yet Russett is something more than a mere industrious tailor to a naked emperor. He has examined directly by survey rather than through indicative statistical aggregates the relationship between attitudes and cross-cultural contacts. He has shown the linkage which does exist between direct personal economic interests in another country and favourable attitudes toward that country. But that major part of his argument which rests on his transactions, communications analysis, illustrates the main objections to this approach. There is no way of proving that an intensive pattern of communication between states will result in a closer community with greater elite responsiveness; or conversely that a developing sense of community will give rise to a greater volume of transactions. Mere quantification without content analysis of communications can tell us little about the motives and processes which lead to the security community to which they allegedly contribute or which they indicate. If a correlation can be established between transactions/communications and the development of community in a number of cases, (for example, by checking against historical accounts like the one by which Russett fails to prove his point) we achieve only an indication of community rather than an explanation. This would be a very minor step forward, achieved by some very costly research, though it would be a step forward, providing us with an additional criterion for selection of periods and areas the study of which might yield the materials of an explanatory theory. At present however, the approach must be regarded as failing to offer a reliable test of functionalism.[52]

A certain amount of work has been done which focusses more narrowly on the processes and effects involved in personal contacts occurring in intergovernmental organisations, drawing especially on the activities of the United Nations. At this level particularly, we would expect the community of interest to become operative and national frontiers relatively meaningless. Chadwick F. Alger presents a survey of this literature, which concerns itself for the most part with the diplomatic activities of the Assembly and Security Council, in his 'Personal contact in intergovernmental organisations.'[53] It is clear that membership of international organisations does produce changes in inter-governmental communications, providing continual access to countries which do not have a wide diplomatic representation abroad. Diplomats find that contact through international organisations are less formal, less bound by considerations of rank, more frequent and facile.

Beyond the study of diplomatic contacts, the focus of interest has been on the

Secretariat serving the diplomatic site, and more narrowly on the dramatic role of higher officials like the Secretary-General or his accredited representative as head of a delicate peacekeeping mission—none of which is of much interest as a test of functionalism. Of the less numerous studies which examine the role of experts and permanent members of Secretariats, the findings generally confirm functionalist expectations, showing that officials tend to develop and pass on norms for the organisation.[54]

A great deal of work, of varying degrees of general relevance to the functionalist thesis, has been done, sometimes without any clear theoretical orientation, on international organisations.[55] No dramatic contradictions about the role of international functional organisations emerge from such research. The findings in some respects confirm functionalist expectations, in other respects, disappoint them.

International bodies do become an important source of common information for governments, thus removing one element of possible disagreement in approaches to problems. More significantly, officials act as 'non-national monitors of relations among national representatives and of the health of the organisation'.[56] Tenure, expertise and detachment from national dependence are factors which tend to increase their influence on policy. Paradoxically, the national representiveness of an official is also important. It helps in the achievement of organisational viewpoints which member governments are likely to accept and in the provision of persuasive, trusted, intermediaries between governments and international organisations, securing that degree of consensus on specific issues without which technically competent and loyal Secretariats can achieve little.[57] For this reason, dual or overlapping roles, between national and international duties, for some officials, may be regarded as an asset in relation to functionalist goals.

Of vital importance to the functionalist argument, however, is the role of international functional organisations as consensus or loyalty-producing mechanisms in a context wider than the temporary specific issue. Such a consensus-producing role depends to some degree, on the organisation having a capacity to respond to functional requirements, a response which will be evident in structural development, procedures, and ethos. Some light on this question has been shed by a small number of studies, specifically directed toward testing functionalism, examining the operation of functionally specific international bodies.

Sewell's examination of United Nations programmes financing economic development was intended as a direct empirical test of the functionalist thesis. Sewell examines the work of the International Bank for Reconstruction and Development (IBRD), which arose to meet a common need, and evolved in function and structure in a way which mirrored the development of the need itself.[58] Problems arising in its operation, particularly the requirement of a government guarantee for all its loans, gave birth to the International Finance Corporation—an international body with the Bank's Vice-president as its head—which could make loans to private enterprise without the government guarantee exacted by the International Bank. Thus the functionalist strategic proposition that tasks will determine organisation and structure is apparently confirmed.

Sewell, however, has reservations about the adequacy of an interpretation confined to this technical functional self-determination process. 'It is all well and good to say that programme A's functional autonomy is due to the desirability of

125

such an arrangement, but how—if at all—are we to know in *advance* that it will prove to be desired as well as desirable.'[59] The creation of the International Finance Corporation (IFC) is an example to which we can again turn to explain why this doubt arises in Sewell's general conclusions. The IFC was not the only suggestion designed to avoid the loan guarantee problem and it is far from clear that it was, functionally, the most desirable. A report, which may or may not have originated with IBRD staff, was presented to the President of the United States in March 1951, recommending the setting up of the International Finance Corporation which could make loans to private enterprise.[60] By 1954, backing by the United States Treasury had been achieved, and the statute for the new agency rapidly followed—and was approved by the General Assembly in 1955. Thus the International Finance Corporation came into being and was preferred to other proposals, like Rao's UNEDA (a public international grant agency in which less-developed member states were more interested) because it was more in line with United States policy, not because it was necessarily the optimum organisational response to a functional need.

The same example illustrates yet another of the general findings of the whole study, that the non-controversiality which, at least initially, determines which tasks are selected for functional cooperation, is rarely, if ever, operable. As Sewell points out, Mitrany, in *A Working Peace System*, illustrated his thesis with a hypothetical International Investment Board and an International Development Commission, and the agencies which Sewell himself treats were chosen for the similarity of their functions to those that Mitrany evidently had in mind. They did not prove non-controversial.

As a test of attitude change on the part of participating states, the study in no wise vindicates the functionalist thesis. 'We sought to fit out our perception with the provisional expectation of seeing functional activity as the training ground for cooperation. Yet in viewing these slices of functional life, we perceived not so much habituation in agreement as the trappings of continuing conflict'.[61] The theme, therefore, of Sewell's final interpretation is that:

> 'The functionalists completely neglect the context of the activities they propose to explain, except as they take that context to be the ultimate beneficiary of functional endeavor. In the narrowness of its focus, the functional interpretation cuts off an understanding of the very dynamics which give rise to these activities and affect every aspect of their existence. To say "function" or "technical self-determination" is of itself to imply the overriding importance of a spontaneous motive and directive force which must be rejected, at least on the basis of this investigation'.[62]

Functionalism, in other words, is virtually a mono-causal explanation of social activity, summed up in the dictum that 'a community may be regarded as the sum of the functions performed by its members'. Like all mono-causal explanations, it is inadequate.

Another specific examination of the functionalist hypothesis by reference to international organisations of functional cooperation is the examination of the International Labour Organisation by Ernest B. Haas in *Beyond the Nation State*. Haas offers a reformulation of functionalist theory to take account of deficiencies in the original formulation which had been revealed by the studies of people like Sewell, Engle and Goodman.[63]

First, because of what he calls 'the fuzzy manner in which progress towards world community is related to the leadership of the expert',[64] he attempts to provide greater clarity by introducing a theory of 'interest politics' as the dynamic element. From this there follows the second modification, that any so-called 'common good' realised must be an unforeseen consequence of group conflict emerging as policy decision. 'There is no common good other than that perceived through the interest-tinted lenses worn by the international actors, but international interest politics causes the tinting to fall into converging patterns, and functionalism sensitises us to spotting the tasks responsible for the pattern'.[65] Haas goes on, in his refinement, to correct the functionalistic neglect of the role of law by offering a conception of the generation of norms through interest group activity, in an integrative process.[66] Other propositions which he rejects or modifies are that power is separate from welfare (upon which depends the proposition that power politics can be by-passed), that through the process of learning, initially power-oriented governmental pursuits evolve into welfare-oriented action, that experts *per se*, as distinct from 'expert managers of functionally specific bureaucracies at the national level'[67] can advance welfare integration, and that personal political loyalties are the result of satisfaction with the performance of functions by an agency of government—a proposition which, though true in part, is one from which all nations with ascriptive status patterns must be excluded.

Functionalism thus refined on the basis of 'the empirical evidence that has accumulated about the actual behaviour of international organisations'[68] becomes the paradigm for Haas' investigation of the ILO. The investigation vindicates the refinement exercise, and in the process provides further evidence relevant to the original thesis. The study shows the effects of political developments and international environment upon the working of the organisation. For example, the emphasis in the field of formal agreements has been on the drafting of texts of basic human rights. This emphasis was a result of Western pressure reflecting the climate of the Cold War, and the standards laid down were adopted, for the most part, only by the European and Commonwealth governments. Then 'the bifurcation of industrial interests between the West and the newly emerging countries manifested itself strongly in the attempt to regulate international conditions of industrial competition, by means of global collective bargaining in the Industrial Committee'. There was, as a by-product of the divergence of views on these issues, some 'new institutional machinery claiming some degree of supervisory power', and voluntary groups did avail themselves of such new scope for action as this afforded them, but, in general, the ILO 'was the victim of the inability of the major actors to fashion a coherent global economic and social machinery. The Organisation was too technical to lose all relevance; but it was not technical enough to be immune from the effects of the political winds that swept the world'.[69] This specific finding, like other findings in this study, tends to confirm Sewell's rather pessimistic conclusions. In Haas's own summation 'The hypothesis advanced in our paradigm were verified with respect to the internal growth of the Organisation, with respect to the impact of the environment on the Organisation. They were proved false, by and large, by the experience of forty-five years of attempted international standard-setting in the labour-welfare field; the environment was not markedly influenced by the programme'.[70]

It should be stressed that the analysis of the internal growth of the ILO reveals a pattern very like that which Sewell describes in his parallel study. The unqualified proposition that organisation will be functionally determined cannot be sustained. The Organisation responded mainly to external demands of a political nature. The appointment of directors, who can exercise a considerable influence on pro-grammatic re-evaluation by virtue of their position, was one of the more obvious ways in which external forces modified the influence of the permanent bureaucracy and its experts. The institutionalisation of worker and employer participation, a feature which distinguishes the ILO from most other international organs has been another factor, international political divisions having made themselves felt at this level. The study, in sum, shows that norms and procedures developed which were not specifically related to the original functional role laid down for the organisation, nor to any developed general consensus about how that role should be modified. They developed rather out of interpersonal and intergroup adjustments. New programmes like the technical assistance programme depend on the goals of one set of 'clients' and their adoption by segments of the Office, not the whole staff.[71] The pattern of influence of internal actors, including experts, is certainly not determined solely or even principally by functional requirements, nor by the precise nature of the expertise in question but by many other factors, especially the external political environment.

These findings must modify the functionalist view that the activities of functional organisations taken in conjunction with universal welfare needs will be productive of a value consensus transcending national frontiers. They are not inconsistent with Gunnar Myrdal's judgment, based on his experiences as Executive Secretary to the United Nations Economic Commission for Europe: 'In the typical case international organisations are nothing else but instruments for the policies of individual governments, means for the diplomacy of a number of disparate and sovereign nation states ... an intergovernmental organisation ... becomes im-portant for the pursuance of national policies precisely to the extent that such a multi-lateral coordination is the real and continuous aim of national govern-ments'.[72] Where international organisations have attempted to escape from this fundamental limitation on their activities, through leaders who have attempted to create an organisational ideology—like Julian Huxley, first Director General of UNESCO, or Boyd Orr of the Food and Agricultural Organisation, who proposed new organisational structures to meet perceived functionalist needs—they have failed; in both these instances the Director General resigned.

The problems of selecting, ordering and weighting the evidence which leads to these general conclusions may be illustrated by random example. Haas' effort to provide objective evidence of the degree of fulfilment of the functional tasks of the ILO serves to point out the complexity and near intractability of the data relevant to the testing of functionalism. Thus, the work of the Committee of Experts on the application of Conventions and Recommendations is evaluated by counting cases where the State concerned takes one of four kinds of action: full remedial, partial remedial, failure to remove infraction, denunciation of Convention.[73] On this category-count Haas judges the Committee successful—that is, in its specific task. This technique, however, bristles with evaluational difficulties. All cases are weighted equally. Yet there are presumable differences in the numbers of member states affected, significant differences in the reasons for failure or success, such as ideology, tradition, impact in different economies, wealth of affected states and differences in the potential spill-over effect of policy decisions. The problem of weighting the importance of the example as a whole also arises. What is the meaning of the task in functionalist terms—does it indicate commitment to procedure or to substance, and how important is the committee in relation to the work of the parent organisation? Are the norms on which compliance is sought externally task-oriented, or internally survival-oriented?

The possibility of reducing the complexity of analysis by using experimental techniques raises the question of the use of simulation and gaming in international relations and its potential value as a test of the functionalist thesis. Richard Snyder's warning about the present development of these techniques is, however, an indication of its limitations. 'At this stage in the development of the social sciences and especially at this stage of the development of simulation techniques for analysing international relations, most experiments belong in the discovery stage of science building, not in the verification phase'.[74]

The technique does, however, as Snyder points out, offer us an otherwise much less accessible opportunity to study the perceptions, evaluations and choices of participants in structured situations. The problem of selection of relevant variables, of reducing large numbers of variables to clusters for the purpose of simulation and gaming, the problem of assessing how far the level of abstraction from reality of the game affects its potential application to the real world, are major problems to be overcome. Because of them, gaming and simulation cannot replace other techniques of analysis; they can only supplement them. To some extent, however, these problems can be overcome by the repetition of experiments which alter the selected variables in a controlled way as a check on the original selection. Another problem of the simulated situation is that though every effort may be made to correct it, the game is system-oriented rather than state-oriented: the national actors are represented, they may in fact be the dominant element in a game, but there is the absence for the players of a sense of high stakes, an absence, too, of a sense of responsibility on the part of the participants acting as governments, deriving from the fact that they will not have to bear the results of their decisions. Reality resumes when game-time ends. Real states can be introduced to help the players overcome this absence of a sense of drama and there may be considerable scope for the improvement of techniques by such methods but, gaming and simulation in international politics are largely useful for training and teaching, they can in no sense be considered a replacement for existing research techniques.

A particular problem in relation to functionalism is the problem of time reality in gaming. Gaming is least vulnerable to this problem in simulation of crisis situations, but functionalism is a theory of evolution of attitudes and thus direct testing of its strategies is hardly feasible. The nearest related phenomenon which has been tested by gaming and simulation is 'learning'. A number of experiments have demonstrated the learning capacity of the participants in a series of games or simulation and its effect on modifying behaviour. Thus the simulation study of deterrence theory by Raser and Crow, designed specifically to study the effect of the capacity to delay nuclear retaliation on international politics, employing multiple runs, showed some evidence of learning capacity.[75] A number of international behaviour studies under the rubric of project Michelson,[76] the basic purpose of which is to explore the premises underlying the concept of strategic deterrence were concerned with learning theory in international relations.

The detailed conclusions of these studies do not suggest that learning in international relations is ever likely to be a continuous process nor is learning in the sense demonstrated by these experiments necessarily a rational process. It operates differently in different situations, according to the mode of communications between actors, and a whole range of variables which are frequent though not necessarily regular elements in international politics. Thus the relevance of this kind of research to the functionalist thesis is that international relations offers a great variety of learning contexts. The learning process in carrying out functional tasks could therefore be altered, countered or promoted by such unpredictable different learning contexts. Crises for example[77] arising outside the scope of the functional task will tend to influence the perceptions and the behaviour of actors, reducing the likelihood that their responses to one another's actions will be considered and rational.

Another kind of indirectly relevant manufactured research is the research into simulated alliance and coalition formation and the development of cohesion. Denis Forcese, for example, has examined the relationship between relative power of states and alliance cohesion in thirteen simulation experiments, and artificially separates as determinant factors of cohesion, defence, economic and ideological elements. At first sight, therefore, the experiments offer an analogous test of the importance of economic factors in international cohesion. The findings[78] reveal that defence is the most frequent motive for alliance formation. They show that economically based alliances or coalitions are the longest sustained. The application of such findings to the functionalist supposition that economic and welfare interest will provide the basis for community is, however, subject to the difficulties that the findings stand in need of considerable interpretation. The frequency and the periodic nature of alliance formation for defence purposes could be regarded as indicative of the high priority of the defence factor in international relations. Just as the economic/welfare organisation like the ILO can persist through crises and world war, so the economic patterns in the gaming situation persist, as the reflection of the lower priority of economic concerns. There is also a sense in which the finding is an artifact of the game, in that the game takes place in a context of threat where clearly the defence factor has the highest priority.

Beyond intergovernmental cooperation for functional purposes (actual or simulated) lies the area of non-governmental international organisation. The scope of activity in this area is wide: vocational, academic, ideological, humanitarian, linguistic, artistic. It includes the direct promotion of the internationalism which is the functionalist goal by means of bilateral and multilateral 'friendship' clubs and associations, and by support of the work of official international bodies. The political impact of most of these activities is marginal and their cumulative integrative effect is not apparent. However, one kind of organisation in this category, the multi-national business corporation, though not a new phenomenon, has become increasingly important in the international environment. In 1971 197 enterprises had a total sales volume in excess of one billion US dollars.[79] Slightly less than half the sovereign states had a lower gross national product. A global scale of investment and marketing operations sustains these giants.

Because it is ostensibly an international functional organisation, though private, the multi-national corporation deserves consideration as a test of the theory in spite of its not coming within the scope of Mitrany's original thesis. As an international employer of labour and management the great corporation is interesting to the functionalist in its internal operations. How far does the service of the corporation develop the international view, transcending nationalism, anticipated in inter-governmental bodies? What of the 'corporation spirit' deliberately engendered in this environment? Whether it may be equated with internationalism in the functionalist mode is extremely doubtful. The utilitarian and status sanctions of the corporation produce an overt identification which transcends national boundaries, but the nature of the loyalty of 'organisation man' and its breaking strain have yet to be established. The career interest of the host national employee is in maximising the local investment and operation rather than the optimal international dispersal. The problem is that no multi-national companies are, as yet, truly multi-national in their employment policies and interest orientation. Dr Ernest Woodrofe, Chairman of Unilever, in his speech to the Unilever Annual General Meeting in 1972 attempted to draw a distinction between great American firms with overseas subsidiaries like Ford Motors, which does the bulk of its business in the United States, and firms like Unilever for which the country or countries of origin account for a minority of sales. The distinction, however, cannot be maintained very far beyond this point, and is, therefore, almost meaningless. Unilever, like other multi-national companies, is controlled by a board made up from its countries of origin—in this case Holland and Britain. Chief executives of the multi-nationals, almost invariably, are nationals of the country of origin. In host countries the mixture of nationalities is between that of the parent and the host, bilateral rather than multilateral. As a matter of policy Unilever recruits 90 per cent of the senior management in each host country locally, but this is hardly a contribution to internationalism.

In the last analysis, it is the interests of the parent company that determine investment holding, internal costing and the pattern of diversification of interests. The corporations are not concerned and are particularly well-placed to avoid the concern of governments and intergovernmental organisations with problems like structural and regional unemployment, environmental improvement, provision of health services and pensions schemes and other aspects of welfare (other than that of their own employees) which might provide the basis of international community in the functionalist mode.

There is no evidence, furthermore, that the contribution of the great corporation to the general welfare through managerial expertise, research and development, economies of scale and other factors affecting productivity is any better than, or even as good as, purely national firms in the advanced industrial societies from which they spring and in which their operations are concentrated. Multi-national capital is not risk capital. There is an inhibition on any innovations which disturb an existing pattern of expansion of international operations. There is the slowness of decision-making in comparison with national firms, as Dr Woodrofe complained, 'whose relative smallness makes speed of decision easier', and there are the much weightier managerial and organisation problems of the vast conglomerate. The effects of these disadvantages can be seen in profit margins which, though very difficult to assess, because of their international distribution, do not appear to be any higher than the average of national firms.

Because neither states nor intergovernmental institutions can at present accommodate the task of regulating the multi-national corporation, it may be hypothesised that existing international structures may be strengthened to deal with them. This is the beguiling principle that need will dictate. The problem, however, is, once again, that the multi-nationals are not truly international but national in their control and interest orientation, though their operations are global. They are manifestations of the national power and even, on occasion, instruments

131

of the national policy of the leading industrial nations—the United States first, followed at some distance by Japan and Western Europe.[80] According to one estimate, by 1975 some 300 corporations, 200 of them American, will own 75 per cent of all industrial assets in the non-communist world. The distribution and control of the mammoth companies, therefore, as Modelski points out, 'confirms and is intimately related to the existing unequal pattern of the distribution of the world's wealth: it does little to ameliorate the strains and stresses produced by this distribution'.[81] Controls, or some kind of transformation of the multi-national company which would make it contribute to the functionalist welfare world, however badly needed, are both in a remote, highly speculative future. They are certainly not dominant trends in the present development of intergovernmental cooperation, domestic policy and company operations.

We have explored in this paper a number of propositions which have their place in the functionalist approach to the problem of building an international society. They have their most authoritative expression in the writings of David Mitrany, but Mitrany was much more explicit about what ought to be done than about what would follow from his prescription. The attributes of international society are left for the most part unstated. There is a hint that the improvement of communications and other technological changes have created interdependence and that this is an aspect of the peaceful international society. There is a hint that attitudinal change, prompted by the recognition of common needs and common solutions will be another consequence of functional integration making national frontiers meaningless. Nations, though perhaps retaining many aspects of their present character, would no longer conflict with each other because they are involved in a web of functional cooperation, eschewing politics. In this international society, experts and the representatives of world-wide sectional interests would 'get on' with the job in hand. Organisation would develop according to the requirements of the task.

These are the suppositions, or hints of suppositions, for which we have sought 'evidence' over a wide field of published work. We have been conscious throughout, however, that we are examining propositions about social, economic and, to a degree, cultural, integration which, even more than propositions which may be made about political integration, are difficult to reduce to a form in which they can be tested.

Notes and references

1 D. Mitrany, *A Working Peace System:* An Argument for the Functional Development of International Organisation, (London: RIIA, 1943).
2 A.J.R. Groom and P. Taylor (eds) *Functionalism:* Final report of the conference, Bellagio, 1969 (New York, Carnegie, 1970), p. 14; see also 'The functional approach to World organisation' in *A Working Peace System* (Chicago: Quadrangle Books, 1966), p. 157.
3 'International Theory: the case for a classical approach', *World Politics* (April, 1966), p. 361.
4 *Ibid.*, p. 367.
5 See Gunnar Myrdal, *Objectivity in Social Research* (New York: Pantheon books, Duckworth, 1969).
6 *International Congress on Mental Health, Proceedings on the international*

conference on mental hygiene IV (London: Lewis and Co., 1948), p. 84 quoted by Sewell J.P., *Functionalism and World Politics* (Princeton: Princeton University Press, 1966), p. 17.

7 Mitrany, 'International cooperation in action', *International Associations* XI September 1959, p. 647.

8 *A Working Peace System* (1943), p. 10.

9 J.P. Sewell, *Functionalism and World Politics* (Princeton: Princeton University Press, 1966), p. 29 ff.

10 E.B. Haas, *Beyond the Nation-State* (Stanford: Stanford University Press, 1964), p. 39; see also his remarks on terminological confusion, *ibid.*, pp. 26-7 and p. 27 ff.

11 Paul S. Reinsch, *Public International Unions* (Boston: Ginn and Co., 1911); P.B. Potter, *This World of Nations* (New York: Macmillan, 1929); G.D.H. Cole, *The Intelligent Man's Guide through World Chaos* (London: Gollancz, 1932), esp. pp. 642-59; see also L. Woolf, *The Way of Peace* (London: Benn, 1928). Woolf's essay on the international extension of the cooperative idea has the germ of much of the functionalist argument; see also Sewell, *op.cit.*, p. 7 ff. for other references.

12 *The Progress of International Government* (Newhaven: Yale University Press, 1933).

13 Mitrany, *A Working Peace System* (1966), p. 17.

14 *A Working Peace System* (1943), p. 6; see also N. Angell, *The Great Illusion—Now* (Harmondsworth: Penguin Books, 1939), p. 269.

15 *A Working Peace System* (1943), p. 32.

16 *Ibid.*, p. 13.

17 *Ibid.*, pp. 21, 22-3.

18 *Ibid.*, pp. 26-7.

19 *Ibid.*, pp. 35-39.

20 *Op.cit.*, p. 26. We do not define these terms. The task has not been accomplished by any sociologist including Tönnies. However, the words indicate, very generally, the difference between task-oriented relations, based on contract and on the promotion of special interests, particularly economic interests; and relations of greater emotional depth based on status and agreed norms, without specific task orientation. 'Gesellschaft' connotes more readily relations between elites, 'Gemeinschaft' a totality of relationships in a territorial setting, but this connotative distinction is sometimes conveniently divorced in use from the contractual-normative distinction (as in this case by Haas). In the present paper we have assumed that the international community or society which is the functionalist goal is multi-dimensional, involving both elite and mass attitudes, contractual and normative bonds. Whether Mitrany's own conception is more limited is a moot point.

21 A. Etzioni, *The Active Society* (New York: Free Press, 1968), p. 98.

22 See e.g. L. Binder, 'National integration and political development', *American Political Science Review* 58 (1964), pp. 622-31 and S.N. Eisenstadt, *Modernisation: Growth and Diversity* (Bloomington, Dept. of Govt., Indiana University, 1963), p. 7; and W. Folz, 'Building the newest nations' in K. Deutsch and W. Foltz, *Nation-Building* (New York, Atherton Press, 1966), pp. 117-31.

23 A. Etzioni's three-part concept of integrating power derives from the Parsonian imperatives; see his *Political Unification* (New York: Holt, Rinehart, 1965,

pp. 38-9) and his 'The Epigenesis of Political Communities at the International Level' *American Journal of Sociology* (Jan., 1963), pp. 407-21.

24 *The Structure of Social Action* (New York: McGraw Hill, 1937), pp. 698-9. See *Economy and Society* (Glencoe: Free Press, 1957), pp. 48-9, 77.

25 *Op.cit.*, p. 39.

26 H. Marcuse, *One Dimensional Man* (London: Sphere Books, 1968), pp. 19, 24-5; see also Georges Vedel (ed) *La Dépolitisation* (Paris: Armand Colin, 1962); Morton A. Kaplan (ed) *The Revolution in World Politics* (New York: Wiley, 1962); Edward Shils, *The Torment of Secrecy* (Glencoe: Free Press, 1955); and E. Mizruchi, *Success and Opportunity: A study of Anomie* (New York: Free Press, 1964); S.K. Weinberg, *Social Problems in Modern Urban Society*, 2nd ed. (Englewood Cliffs: Prentice-Hall, 1970).

27 Daniel Bell, *The End of Ideology* (New York: Collier, 1962); Robert Lane, 'The Politics of Consensus in an Age of Affluence' *American Political Science Review* (Dec. 1965), p. 884; Ulf Himmelstrand, 'A theoretical and empirical approach to depoliticization and political involvement', *Acta Sociologica*, VI, 1962, p. 83; S.M. Lipset, *Political Man* (London: Mercury Books, 1963), especially pp. 404-17.

28 For a discussion see R. Konig, *The Community* (trans. E. Fitzgerald) (London: Routledge and Kegan Paul, 1968); and for a first-class analytical history of this sociological tradition in the 19th century see R.A. Nisbet, *The Sociological Tradition* (London: Heinemann, 1967), pp. 47-106.

29 R. Redfield, *The Primitive World and its transformation* (Harmondsworth: Penguin, 1968); W. Low, *The Social System of the Modern Factory* (New Haven: Yale University Press, 1947); H. Bracey, *Neighbors* (London: Routledge and Kegan Paul, 1964). J. Jacobs, *The Death and Life of Great American Cities* (Harmondsworth: Penguin, 1965) and *The Economy of Cities* (Random House, 1969); T. McGee, *The Urbanisation Process in the Third World* (Bell, 1971); I.L. Horowitz, *Three Worlds of Development* (London: O.U.P., 1966); E. Mayo, *The Social Problems of an Industrial Civilisation* (New York: Macmillan, 1933); S. Nosow and W. Form, *Man, Work and Society* (New York: Basic Books, 1962).

30 *Op.cit.* (London: Duckworth, 1958), p. 155; see also R.W. Cox (ed), *International Organisation: World Politics* (London: Macmillan, 1969). Cox notes that, *à propos* of developing countries, 'a major function of international organisation has become the promotion of national rather than international integration' (p. 39).

31 D.J. Finlay, O.R. Holsti and R.R. Fagan, *Enemies in Politics* (Chicago: Rand McNally, 1967), p. 22.

32 See *The Times*, 18 December 1971, p. 2; also H. Tajfel 'Experiments in intergroup discrimination' *Scientific American* 223 (Nov. 1970), pp. 96-103.

33 For a powerful statement of the argument that conflict is essential to the maintenance of society, see L.A. Coser, *The Functions of Social Conflict* (London: Routledge and Kegan Paul, 1956). F.M. Thrasher, *The Gang* (Chicago: University of Chicago Press, 1927); K. Lewin, R. Lippitt and R.K. White, 'An experimental study of leadership and group life' in H. Proshansky and B. Seidenberg (eds) *Basic Studies in Social Psychology* (New York: Holt, Rinehart and Winston, 1965), pp. 523-37; M. Sherif and C.W. Sherif, *Social Psychology* (New York: Harper and Row, 1969), pp. 129-45; and

J.P. Scott, *Aggression* (Chicago: University of Chicago Press, 1958).

34 Sherif and Sherif, *op.cit.*, p. 255.

35 Robert A. Levine, 'Socialisation, Social Structure and Intersocietal Images' in H.C. Kelman (ed) *International Behaviour* (New York: Holt, Rinehart and Winston, 1965), pp. 45-69; R.F. Maher, *New Men of Papua* (Madison: University of Wisconsin Press, 1961); and R.F. Murphy, 'Intergroup hostility and social cohesion', *American Anthropologist*, 61, 1959, pp. 17-29.

36 *A Working Peace System* (1943), p. 13.

37 See H.P. Gray, *International Travel—International Trade*, (Lexington, Heath Lexington Books, 1970), pp. 34-44, see also K. Deutsch, 'Toward an inventory of basic trends and patterns in international politics' in J.N. Rosenau (ed), *International Politics and Foreign Policy* (New York: Free Press, 1969), p. 503.

38 For statistics of international interchange of persons, see R.C. Angell, 'The growth of transnational participation', *Journal of Social Issues* 23 (1967), pp. 108-29; and for a guide to relevant studies see L. Smith and C.M. Smith, *International Communication and Public Opinion* (Princeton: Princeton University Press, 1952).

39 Ithiel de Sola Pool, 'Effects of Cross-National Contact on National and International Images' in Kelman, *op.cit.*, pp. 104-29.

40 *Op.cit.*, p. 124.

41 See J.S. Nye, 'Patterns and Catalysts in Regional Integration', *International Organisations*, 19 (4) (1965), pp. 870-84, and his 'Comparative Regional Integration: Concept and Measurement' *International Organisation*, 22 (4) (1968), pp. 855-880 and *Peace in Parts* (Boston: Little Brown and Co., 1971); and E.B. Haas and P.C. Schmitter, 'Economics and Differential Patterns of Political Integration: Projections about Unity in Latin America' *International Organisation*, 18 (4) (1964), pp. 705-37; and E.B. Haas and M. Barrera, 'The Operationalisation of some variables related to Regional Integration: a research note' *International Organisation*, 23 (1) (1969), pp. 150-60; P.C. Schmitter, 'Further notes on operationalising some variables related to Regional Integration', *International Organisation*, 23 (1) (1969), pp. 327-36; and K. Deutsch, *Political Community at the International Level: Problems of Definition and Measurement* (New York: Doubleday, 1954); R. Inglehart, 'An end to European Integration?' *American Political Science Review*, 61 (1) (1967), pp. 91-105; W.E. Fisher 'An analysis of the Deutsch Socio-Causal Paradigm of Political Integration' *International Organisation*, 23 (2) (1969), pp. 259-90; B. Russett, *International Regions and the International System* (Chicago: Rand McNally, 1969); B. Russett, *Community and Contention* (Cambridge: M.I.T. Press, 1963); O.R. Young, 'Professor Russett: Industrious Tailor to a Naked Emperor' *World Politics*, 21 (3), (1969). The concept of the pluralistic security community which involves no central political institutions or authority is elaborated by K. Deutsch in his *Political Community and the North Atlantic Area* (Princeton: Princeton University Press, 1957). It has characteristics which conform with functionalist expectations. In such a community relations are predictably peaceful, conflicts being resolved by compromise or avoidance. The concept is not, however, particularly useful as a test of functionalist theory of change since it is stated by reference to given conditions to which the compatibility of major values, the capacity to respond to mutual needs quickly and without resort to violence, and mutual

predictability of behaviour are the most important. The evolution of these conditions is treated in very general terms. The concept is more useful in the context of regional or alliance cohesion between like actors.

42 Leon Lindberg, in *International Organisation*, **24** (4), (1970), pp. 649-731.

43 See below, Inglehart, pp. 25-30, and see Cox, *op.cit.*, pp. 17-25 *et passim*.

44 R. Inglehart, 'Public Opinion and Regional Integration', *International Organisation*, **24** (4), (1970), pp. 764-95.

45 *Ibid.*, p. 795.

46 K.W. Deutsch *et al.*, *France, Germany and the Western Alliance: a study of elite attitudes on European Integration and world politics* (New York: Scribner's, 1967), pp. 298-9; see also R. Ingelhart, 'An End to European Integrations?' *American Political Science Review* **61** (1967), pp. 91-105.

47 See e.g. G. Almond, *The American People and Foreign Policy* (New York: Harcourt, Brace and World, 1950); G. Almond and S. Verba, *The Civic Culture* (Princeton: Princeton University Press, 1963); James N. Rosenau (ed) *Domestic Sources of Foreign Policy* (New York: Free Press, 1967); K.J. Holsti, *International Politics* (Englewood Cliffs: Prentice Hall, 1967), pp. 155-91; H.C. Kelman, *op.cit.* The complexity of factors involved in attitude change is well brought out in M.J. Rosenberg, 'Attitude change and foreign policy in the cold war era' in J.N. Rosenau, *Domestic Sources . . .*, pp. 111-59. See also S.N. Eisenstadt, *From Generation to Generation* (New York: Free Press, 1956); W. Albig, *Modern Public Opinion* (New York: McGraw Hill, 1956), especially pp. 332-367.

48 *Op.cit.*

49 *Op.cit.*

50 *Ibid.*, p. 26.

51 *Ibid.*, p. 125.

52 See, however, *International Organisation*, **25** (3), (1971), pp. 329-758. This entire issue is devoted to 'Transnational relations and world politics', and is generally optimistic about the potential of this methodology. A comprehensive bibliography is included.

53 Kelman, *op.cit.*, pp. 523-61; for suggestions on research techniques for measuring the internationalisation effect see H.R. Alker, 'Supranationalism in the United Nations' in J.N. Rosenau (ed), *International Politics and Foreign Policy* (New York: Free Press, 1969), pp. 697-709.

54 Kelman, *op.cit.*, pp. 537-8.

55 See the list in E.B. Haas, *Beyond the Nation State*, pp. 524-5; and see R.J. Yalem 'The study of international organisation, 1920-1965: a survey of the literature', *Background*, May 1966, **10** (1), pp. 1-56. C.F. Alger 'Methodological Innovation in Research on International Organisation' in J.A. Robinson (ed), *Political Science Annual*, 1969-70, **2** (Indianapolis: Bobbs-Merrill, 1969), pp. 209-40; also his 'Research on Research: A decade of quantitative and field research on international organizations', *International Organization*, **24** (3), 1970, pp. 414-50.

56 Alger in Kelman, *op.cit.*, p. 537.

57 Alger, *op.cit.*, p. 539.

58 *Op.cit.*, p. 246.

59 *Op.cit.*, p. 251.

60 *Op.cit.*, pp. 108-111.

61 *Op.cit.,* p. 287.
62 *Op.cit.,* pp. 287-8.
63 Sewell had completed the dissertation on which his book is based in 1962; see also H.E. Engle, *A Critical Study of the Functionalist Approach to International Organisation,* unpublished Ph.D. thesis (Columbia University 1957) and N.E. Goodman, *International Health Organisations and their Work* (New York: Blackeston, 1952).
64 *Op.cit.,* p.30.
65 *Op.cit.,* p. 35.
66 *Op.cit.,* p. 46.
67 *Op.cit.,* p. 49.
68 *Op.cit.,* p. 47.
69 *Op.cit.,* pp.437-8.
70 *Op.cit.,* p. 444.
71 See e.g. *op.cit.,* pp. 179-81.
72 *Realities and Illusions in Regard to Intergovernmental Organisations* (London: Oxford University Press, 1955), pp. 4-5, quoted by Haas, *op.cit.,* p. 98.
73 Haas, *op.cit.,* p. 258.
74 R.C. Snyder, 'Some perspectives on the Use of Experimental Techniques in the study of International Relations' in H. Guetzkow, *Simulation in International Relations* (Englewood Cliffs: Prentice-Hall, 1963), p. 7; for a survey of the literature see P. Smoker, *International Relations* (Oakville: Canadian Peace Research Institute, Peace Research Reviews, 3, 6, 1971).
75 J.R. Raser and W.J. Crow 'A simulation study of deterrence theories' in D.G. Pruitt and R.C. Snyder, *Theory and Research on the causes of war* (Englewood Cliffs: Prentice-Hall, 1969), pp. 136-149; see also J.R. Raser 'Learning and Affect in International Politics' in J.N. Rosenau, *International Politics and Foreign Policy* (New York: Free Press, 1969), pp. 432-441.
76 See T.W. Milburn, 'Intellectual History of a Research Program' in Pruitt and Snyder, *op.cit.,* p. 266.
77 *Ibid.,* p. 278.
78 D. Forcese, *Power and Military Alliance Cohesion: thirteen simulation experiments* (Ph.D. dissertation, Department of Sociology, Washington University, St. Louis, 1968).
79 'The Fortune Directory', *Fortune* (August 1971), p. 150.
80 120 US companies (manufacturing and mining) had sales over $1 billion, and 77 outside the US. The pattern of international banking, ranked by assets, is similar. 'Fortune Directory' *op.cit.,* pp. 150-157.
81 G. Modelski, 'The Corporation in World Society' in *The Yearbook of World Affairs 1968* (London: Stevens and Sons, 1968), p. 76.

Part Two
Problems and Dimensions

The League of Nations and Functionalism
Victor-Yves Ghébali

The League of Nations is currently viewed as having been a collective security institution which undertook some endeavours in the functional sectors of international relations. Its contribution to functionalism is thus regarded as having been limited to the Bruce Report of 1939, a document which inspired the drafters of the UN Charter. In other words, it is asserted that the League rested overwhelmingly—if not exclusively—on the negative principle of 'keeping Nations peacefully apart'. Indeed, Professor Mitrany's early conceptions of functionalism were developed along with a critique of the League of Nations whose weakness 'lay in the fact that it was limited to the task of organising stability'; the League failed, he assumed, because it could not further in international affairs the process of peaceful change, that is to say 'automatic and continuous social action, continually adapted to changing needs and conditions'; at any rate, the Covenant was 'concerned primarily with defining the formal relationship of states, in a negative sense, and only vaguely with initiating positive common activities'[1].

Our purpose is to reconsider the League's place in the history of the functional approach to international organisation and to show that if collective security was the fundamental aim of the League of Nations, in fact it was also based, to a significant extent, on the positive principle of 'bringing nations actively together'. In analysing the practical and theoretical contribution of the League, we will use the expressions 'functionalism' and 'functional cooperation', although the League officially referred to 'technical cooperation', 'non-political cooperation', and also later on, with the Bruce Report, to 'economic and social cooperation'.

The Idea of Functional Cooperation and the Drafting of the Covenant

Although the ideological stream of thought underlying the League of Nations movement of 1914-19 was overwhelmingly inspired by hatred towards a world strife which 'need not have happened', and although its proponents were advocating above all the setting up of an international device to prevent recurrence of such dreadful events, functional cooperation occupied a place in the mind of the framers of the Covenant.

In 1919, the devasted economies, the disrupted transit and communications systems, as well as the threat of widespread epidemics and drug consumption, created among European statesmen a sense of urgency regarding intergovernmental collaboration to resolve problems which were beyond the capabilities of any one nation-state to resolve. Besides, the Peace Treaties involved many political decisions with functional aspects: German reparations, internationalisation of waterways, and so forth. Moreover, a body of experience in international functional cooperation already existed as a consequence of the International Administrative Unions of the

141

prewar period and of the organs established to facilitate inter-allied cooperation in the fields of shipping, food and raw materials[2]. If functionalism as such was not yet organised into an elaborate body of principles, there was, nevertheless, some theoretical thinking on the concepts of 'international administration' and 'international government'[3]. During the war, this trend found its expression particularly in the writings of Leonard Woolf, spokesman of the Fabian Society. In 1916, Woolf published a book entitled *International Government*[4] in which he praised the achievements of such long-established bodies as the Universal Postal Union (UPU) and the International Telecommunications Union (ITU), and drew attention to the necessity of expanding their work and coordinating their action.

The importance of Woolf's ideas in the history of functional development of international organisation cannot be exaggerated: the functional provisions of the Covenant were derived from the writings of a number of British officials—more particularly Lord Robert Cecil and General Smuts—who borrowed heavily from him. One of the earliest major documents concerning the future League which was based upon Woolf's line of thought was mooted in the Foreign Office in the first half of November 1918 by Sir Alfred Zimmern. It envisaged the League not only as a revised version of the European Concert and The Hague Conferences System, but also of International Unions and Inter-Allied functional bodies. More particularly, it proposed entrusting the League with the task of acting as a link between Public International Unions in order to control and supervise their activities; the creation of new bodies of that sort, as well as of standing international commissions of study and inquiry, was also considered. In the mind of the drafter, this seemed to be 'the best way of dealing with the *prevention of war*, as a long-distance problem, as contrasted with the short-distance problem of *restraining resort to violence*[5]. Lord Cecil selected this Foreign Office memorandum as a basis of work; he included these ideas in the several British draft schemes for a League of Nations which were informally submitted to the United States with the intention of reaching a common position[6].

As to General Smuts, his main contribution was to provide functional cooperation with a strong justification in a pamphlet entitled *The League of Nations. A Practical Suggestion*[7] which he published in December 1918. 'Peace and war are resultants of many complex forces,and those forces will have to be gripped at an earlier stage of their growth if peace is to be effectively maintained', stated the author in a penetrating foreword. He added that the League should not be 'confined to the prevention of wars or the punishment of an unauthorised belligerent, but would be extended to the domain of ordinary peaceful intercourse between the members of the League. Thus the League must be 'a great organ of the ordinary peaceful life of civilisation', because 'it is not sufficient for the League merely to be a sort of *deus ex machina*, called in in very grave emergencies when the spectre of war appears; if it is to last, it must be much more. It must become part and parcel of the common international life of states, it must be an ever visible, living working organ of the policy of civilisation. It must function so strongly in the ordinary peaceful intercourse of states that it becomes irresistible in their disputes; its peace activity must be the foundation and guarantee of its war power'[8].

All the founding fathers of the League were not equally convinced of the necessity of providing in the Covenant some room for functional cooperation. President Wilson considered the League as an instrument of high politics. The French shared his view and, moreover, wanted the League to be used to protect the harvest of the Allied victory. In the course of the Paris negotiations, however, the British succeeded in overcoming their mild indifference or opposition. The British functional proposals became—with minor amendments—articles 23 and 24 of the Covenant. Article 24 seemed especially significant, for it provided that all existing or future public International Unions should be placed under the League's direction[9]; its aim was obviously to make the League the apex of all kinds of intergovernmental cooperation. As to article 23, it authorised the League to deal with the specific problems of traffic in women and children and traffic in opium, as well as with questions related to commerce and health[10]; its weakness was that it allowed the League to work in such fields only subject to present or future intergovernmental agreements[11]. If, given the limited scope of this study, we disregard the ILO's operation and article 25 dealing with national Red Cross organisations (which proved to be unimportant), then the League Covenant emerged as a mainly political document with a few functional exceptions. The preamble to the Covenant, which also was of British origin, emphasises the subordination of functional cooperation to collective security. It stated the pledge of member states 'to *achieve* international peace and security' and only 'to *promote* international cooperation'. However, in theory, article 24 opened wide prospects for the League in the realm of functional cooperation.

The League's System of Functional Cooperation

The early development of functional cooperation within the League followed a quite different course from that anticipated. Article 24, to quote Stanley Bailey, became 'the Cinderella of the Covenant'[12]. That article was never fully operative for at least three reasons[13]. Firstly, after the United States Senate rejected the Versailles Treaty, the US government opposed, as a non-member, the placement of International Unions, in which it was participating, under the control of the League. Secondly, the League encountered strong resistance within the International Bureaux: their secretariats alleged that control by the League would do more harm than good in so far as it would subordinate them to a body less universal in membership and enmesh them in 'politics'; as a matter of fact these excuses masked long-established bureaucratic conservatism and national vested interests, since some Bureaux were mere extensions of host countries' administration (e.g. Switzerland and the Berne Bureaux; Italy and the International Institute of Agriculture) and vested interests were too strong to be overcome. In the third place, League members were reluctant to implement article 24 fully lest this should overburden the League's budget. They also feared that in broadening the League's activities they would so increase its prestige as to provide grounds for a gradual encroachment upon national sovereignty. It was as if the drafters of the Covenant realised that they had gone too far in the text of article 24.

Accordingly, article 24 was narrowly construed. It was considered not to be automatic even for existing Bureaux. The 'direction of League' amounted to no more than tokenism. In the last resort, as pointed out by Bailey, 'the League has built a large and well-equipped hotel, but the guests are slow in arriving'[14]. Indeed, only six International Bureaux—none of a major importance—were placed under the League's direction between 1921 and 1931[15]. The strongest and most powerful organisations, such as the UPU, the ITU, and the International Institute of Agriculture, remained outside the League's jurisdiction. Relations were maintained

TABLE I - STRUCTURE OF LEAGUE'S FUNCTIONAL BODIES (1938)

	Council type body	Assembly type body	Secretariat type body*	Additional permanent bodies
Organisation for Communications and Transit (1921)	Committee for Communications and Transit and auxiliary bodies (permanent and *ad hoc*)	- General conference* - *Ad hoc* conferences	Communications and Transit Section of the League's Secretariat	None
Economic and Financial Organisation (permanent as from 1923)	4 standing committees and auxiliary bodies (permanent and *ad hoc*): - Economic Committee - Financial Committee - Fiscal Committee - Committee of Statistical Experts (coordinated by the Co-ordination Committee as from 1938)	*Ad hoc* conferences only	Economic and Financial Section of the League's Secretariat	None
Health Organisation (permanent as from 1923)	Health Committee and auxiliary bodies (permanent and *ad hoc*)	- General Advisory Health Council (Permanent Committee of the *Office international d'hygiène publique*) - *Ad hoc* conferences	- Health Section of the League's Secretariat - Eastern Bureau (Singapore)	- International Centre for Research on Leprosy (Rio de Janeiro, 1934)
Intellectual Cooperation Organisation (established formally in 1931)	International Committee on Intellectual Co-operation and auxiliary bodies (permanent and *ad hoc*)	*Ad hoc* conferences only	Intellectual Coöperation Section of the League's Secretariat	- International Institute of intellectual Cooperation (Paris, 1926) - International Educational Cinematographic Institute (Rome, 1926)* - National Committees on Intellectual Cooperation - International Studies Conference (1928-1933)**

TABLE I (Continued)

	Council type body	Assembly type body	Secretariat type body*	Additional permanent bodies
Social Questions bodies (1922)*	Advisory Committee on Social Questions and *ad hoc* auxiliary bodies	*Ad hoc* conferences only	Social Questions Section of the League's Secretariat	None
Opium bodies (1921, 1928, 1933)	3 standing committees and auxiliary bodies (permanent and *ad hoc*): - Advisory Committee on Traffice in Opium (1921) - Permanent Central Opium Board (1928) - Supervisory Body (1933)	*Ad hoc* conferences only	Opium Section of the League's Secretariat	None

*latest re-organisation in 1936.

*Abolished in 1938

*Prior to the merging of Sections into Departments

*closed in 1937
**Autonomous body as from 1934.

145

with them only 'on the basis of negotiation between equal and independent parties'. The original idea of the Covenant drafters was replaced by a 'system of mild and friendly cooperation'.[16]

But the demand for functional cooperation was of so strong a nature that a loop-hole, provided for by Article 23, was early devised. Indeed, since functional cooperation could not be developed on a satisfactory basis outside the League, an irresistible and spontaneous trend led to the creation of *special League bodies* for that purpose. Article 23 became the keystone of the whole League system of functional cooperation, although nothing in its letter or spirit had destined it to play such a role. The solution worked out did not even follow League constitutional rules: while article 23 was supposed to operate fully 'subject to and in accordance with the provisions of international conventions existing or hereafter to be agreed upon', most of the functional bodies were created *prior* to any international legislation.

Article 23 gave birth to two categories of standing functional institutions: *Technical Organisations* (Organisation for Communications and Transit, Economic and Financial Organisation, Health Organisation, Intellectual Cooperation Organisation) and *Technical Commissions* (Social Questions Commission, Opium Commissions). Initially, there was a legal difference between organisations and commissions. Article 23 (c) entrusted the League itself with 'the general supervision over the execution of agreements with regard to the traffic in women and children, and the traffic in opium and other dangerous drugs'; permanent commissions assisted by a relevant section of the League Secretariat were thus created for these purposes. Such a device was considered insufficient to meet the requirements of Article 23(e) and (f) under which *member states* were called upon to 'make provision' and to 'endeavour to take steps' in order to maintain and secure freedom of communications and transit and equitable treatment of commerce, and to promote public health. Although those 'provisions' and 'steps' remained vague, it was thought necessary to build a more elaborate machiney. The original inclination centred around the creation of agencies more or less similar to the ILO, but this was dropped and the result was the emergence of hybrid and unautonomous bodies called 'Technical Organisations'. A look at Table I demonstrates however to what extent Technical Organisations followed the institutional patterns of the ILO, *viz.* International Unions. Each organisation usually consisted of: (a) an advisory committee of experts assisted by several ad hoc or standing sub-committees charged with specific tasks; (b) periodic and/or ad hoc conferences; (c) a technical section of the League's Secretariat; and (d) additional bodies such as International Institutes whose peculiar situation *vis-à-vis* the League can be explained by the fact that they were created according to needs and means.

With the passage of time, the substantial difference between the two categories of bodies largely disappeared. Apart from formal status[17], only the degree of institutional complexity differentiated Organisations and Commissions. An Organisation was nothing more than a Commission around which more numerous and complex bodies were orbiting (see again Table I). Neither Organisations nor Commissions did enjoy autonomy like the ILO: they were part of the general institutional framework of the League and their expenses were included in the League's general budget. However, while the ILO possessed an independent policy-making organ, they were subordinated to the Council and Assembly, being only advisory to them. Moreover, the ILO had an independent secretariat, while each functional agency was serviced by a relevant section of the League's Secretariat. In other words, constitutional status provided a common denominator between Technical Organisations and Commissions. According to a Council resolution of 19 May 1920, which was approved in a slightly amended form by the Assembly on 8 December 1920[18], these agencies were created as subsidiary bodies to facilitate the work of the political organs of the League—which appointed their members—and to assist governments to fulfill their international duties by establishing direct contact between their technical representatives. They were independent in so far as their internal working was concerned. They remained under the control of the League's political organs which were committed to verify whether their proposals respected the principles and spirit of the Covenant. The Council acted on the basis of recommendations by its 'rapporteurs' for technical questions, and the Assembly supervised the functional work by means of its second and fifth committees and later on also its seventh committee (notwithstanding the supervision of its fourth—budgetary—committee). Such a political framework of functional cooperation was subject to constant evolution in the 1920s.

Functional Cooperation in the 1920's: Growth and Outgrowth

Despite limited resources of money and staff and, in many instances, the relative newness or unprecedented scale of problems to be solved, the League's functional bodies produced in the 1920s an impressive range of achievements. This result was due to the impulse given to functional activities by first-rate directors or officials such as Sir James Arthur Salter (of the Economic and Financial Organisation), Ludwik Rajchman (of the Health Organisation), Bernardo Attolico and Robert Haas (of the Organisation for Communications and Transit), Dame Rachel Crowdy (of the Social Questions Section), and Jean Monnet (Under-Secretary-General, entrusted with the supervision of Technical Organisations). Under the leadership of these people, most of whom had wartime experience in inter-allied functional cooperation, able functional units were established in the League's Secretariat and began to operate from the early 1920s.

The League's fields of interest could be divided into four arbitrary categories: (a) economic and financial problems (including population questions) and related matters of communications and transit; (b) educational problems ('Intellectual cooperation'); (c) social problems, a category which in the League's terminology covered child welfare, the suppression of traffic in women and children, the suppression of obscene publications, (d) drug control and health problems—which were also to a large extent of a social nature. Humanitarian problems are not listed above because of their narrow scope and the political approach in which they were tackled. The protection of minorities had a political character, only a limited number of States was involved with this. The Mandates regime did not apply to all non-autonomous territories, but only to those detached from the defeated powers of the First World War; slavery questions so far as mandates were concerned were treated as part of the general responsibility in the Secretariat's Mandates Section; the Refugees problem was essentially considered from a political point of view. However the High Commissioner for Refugees enjoyed a great degree of administrative autonomy. There was a standing commission for the question of slavery. However it was not a functional technical commission in so far as it was not serviced by an independent Secretariat section, but rather by the Mandates Section of the League Secretariat.

Assistance to refugees in the League framework was carried out under numerous and complex mechanisms:

— from 1921 to 1931, there was a High Commissioner (Fridtjof Nansen) whose jurisdiction covered Russian and Armenian refugees as well as certain categories of refugees from the Near East and Asia Minor. The High Commissioner was assisted, as of 1922, by an Advisory Committee of Private Organisations for Refugees and, beginning in 1928, by an Intergovernmental Advisory Commission for Refugees. In addition, as from 1924 to 1928, the manpower, immigration and repatriation problems raised by refugees were handled by the ILO;

— after the death of Nansen in 1930, the legal and political protection of refugees was taken over by the League Secretariat. As for the humanitarian protection, a special International Bureau—the Nansen International Office for Refugees—was established for a limited duration (1931-1938) and placed under League direction according to Article 24 of the Covenant;

— from 1933 to 1938 (during the period of existence of the Nansen Office), there was also a High Commissioner's Office for Refugees coming from Germany which functioned in two distinct stages:

from 1933 to 1936, the High Commissioner, James G. McDonald, although appointed by the League, submitted his reports to an autonomous governing body and his office—located in Lausanne and shortly after in London—had no link whatsoever with the League. This odd procedure was initiated by the League itself which did not want to displease Nazi Germany whose notice of withdrawal had not yet expired.

a more directly 'League period' goes from 1936 to 1938. Following the effective withdrawal of Germany and the development of Nazi foreign policy, the High Commissioner's office was integrated into the League structure. The League appointed a new High Commissioner (Sir Neill Malcolm in replacement of McDonald who had resigned) and established his mandate in such a way that it would expire at the same time as that of the Nansen Office.

— from 1939 to 1946 the mandate of the Nansen Office and that of the High Commissioner's Office for Refugees coming from Germany were taken over by a single High Commissioner's Office which had its headquarters in London under the direction of Sir Herbert Emerson.

Technical organisations and commisions performed the following main functions:

1. **International legislation**. This was the basic function of the League's technical organisations and commissions in the 1920s. It was generally thought that coordination of national units would succeed only if an increasing number of binding universal rules were established by intergovernmental conferences convened under the League's aegis. Whereas few or no general international conventions in functional fields existed before the First World War, the League was able to develop within a decade more than thirty such conventions covering a wide range of issues, from the international regulation of railways to the control of manufactured drugs, from the suppression of counterfeited currency to the standardisation of sera, from the simplification of customs formalities to the protection of industrial property[19]

2. **Technical assistance**. Technical Organisations responded to requests for assistance from governments by providing expert advice or by carrying out specific

tasks on the spot. The Health Organisation cooperated with many public health authorities in reforming their health services. The Communications and Transit Organisation played a role in the reorganisation of the Austrian and Bulgarian railways. The most outstanding work in this field was, however, done by the Economic and Financial Organisation when it devised an ambitious reconstruction scheme for Austria, which was then on the verge of financial bankruptcy and political chaos; it provided for a twenty years loan granted by the European Powers and guaranteed by a supervision over Austria's public finances exercised on behalf of the League by an appointed commissioner-general (1922-26). The success of this plan made it a ready model easily acceptable by other governments applying for financial help. The same organisation contributed to the introduction of a new currency in the Free City of Danzig and realised banking reform and stabilisation of currency in several weak countries[20].

3. **Advice to League political bodies**. The League Council and Assembly often enlisted Technical Organisations in studying the non-political aspects of security problems. During the framing of the 1924 Memel statute, the Organisation for Communications and Transit determined the rules governing the use of Memel's port. In the same way, it appointed experts to solve many difficulties related to Danzig harbour and railways or to report on the machine-guns incident at Szent-Gothard on the Austro-Hungarian frontier. It also proceeded in 1927 to a full study on the best ways to ensure the working of the League—as far as communications were concerned—in time of emergency. As a result of the Organisation's recommendation, the League decided to set up *Radio-Nations*, a wireless station. As to the Economic and Financial Organisation, it assisted for instance in the drafting of the 1922 German-Polish Convention on Upper Silesia, and the Convention on Financial Assistance to States Victim of Aggression (1930).[21]

4. **Supervision of international conventions**. As a general rule, international agreements concluded within the League's framework provided for their supervision by the relevant international functional bodies. For instance, in the field of narcotics, international functional control was agreed to by the States and was one of the most indisputable of the League's successes; governments were required to send reports on the actual application of international conventions, and also on consumption, manufacture, imports and exports, illicit transactions and seizures, estimates of narcotic requirements, and so forth. In the light of this information, as well as of their own enquiries, the League's bodies recommended action and if necessary called for explanations by certain countries or asked the Council to apply sanctions[22].

5. **Data collection and publication**. The Epidemiological Intelligence Service of the Health Organisation centralised information concerning the outbreak and spread of infectious diseases. The same Organisation had in Singapore a bureau covering the Eastern and Far-Eastern regions; its bulletins were broadcast to health administrations and to ships sailing on the Eastern seas. The Economic Intelligence Service of the Economic and Financial Organisation regularly issued many valuable statements dealing with production, trade, balance of payments, commercial banks, and so forth.[23]

6. **Conciliation**. The Communications and Transit Organisation was authorised to act as a conciliator in disputes arising out of the conventions on communications and transit adopted within the framework of the League. It also had a similar

function in relation to disputes on the interpretation of clauses of the Peace Treaties dealing with communications. Out of seventeen disputes before the League in connection with the Peace Treaties, fourteen were settled by means of the good offices of the organisation[24].

The development of these functions, together with others which cannot be mentioned in this brief study, did not always proceed smoothly because of the mistrust of certain governments. Speaking in the name of the Dominions, Canada, for instance, as early as 1920, raised the problem of the representation of non-European countries, arguing that it was difficult for such countries to send experts to the increasing number of meetings in Geneva. At the same time, the opponents of functionalism charged that one ILO was 'quite enough'. Underlying this criticism was their dissatisfaction with the increasing cost and the growing autonomy of that organisation. Their main argument however was that the League should not divert its money and energy from pursuing the fundamental task of world peace. Straying too far into non-political fields could only damage the League's prestige. Behind these reasons, one can find the same major concern that led to article 24's failure: the fear that the League might encroach upon the domestic jurisdiction of Member States.

A confrontation between the opponents and proponents of functional cooperation occured twice in the League's history. The first instance took place in the Assembly of 1920 when the draft schemes for Technical Organisations (Organisation for Communications and Transit, Economic and Financial Organisation, Health Organisation) were discussed. While the overwhelming majority of the Assembly was ready to adopt these schemes, the British Dominions opposed vigorously what they regarded as the creation of new ILOs. Eventually, under a compromise suggested by Lord Robert Cecil, it was decided that these bodies should be created: (a) with a consultative status to prevent them from making any decision binding for Governments; and (b) on a temporary basis but with the understanding that they could be granted permanent status should they prove to be particularly effective at moderate cost[25]. This requirement was fulfilled and by 1923 the Health Organisation as well as the Economic and Financial Organisation became officially permanent. (The Organisation for Communications and Transit was permanent from 1921 because its statute was adopted as an official instrument by the Barcelona Conference on 1921.)[26]

A few years later, the United Kingdom totally reversed its initial position. Its representatives were now finding that League functional bodies were going too far and too fast. Consequently in 1926, the British government submitted to the Seventh Assembly a memorandum asking for a definition of the League's 'sphere of action' out of a legal interpretation of the Preamble and of Articles 3 and 4 of the Covenant[27]. A sharp exchange occured between the British Empire delegates and the French representative who refused to proceed to any legal definition because 'to define is to limit, and to limit is to restrain'. While admitting that the maintenance of peace was indisputably the primary object of the League, the French delegate denied that peace could be ensured only by formal political Council meetings or be manufactured by the machinery of international law. He also developed arguments with strong functional connotations:

'There are certain evils so serious and deep-rooted that the countries suffering from them constitute a definite element of unrest in the world . . . that peace cannot be regarded as secure until they have been eradicated (. . .) If the tribune god-head of the League,—arbitration, security and disarmament—is to come down on earth and live among us, preparing the way for peace, we must create the proper atmosphere for its reception. We must teach the nations that the interests which they have in common are more numerous than those which divide them and are also more real, more profound and more permanent. Collaboration and co-operation between the peoples create an atmosphere favourable to the maintenance of peace.'[28]

Given the negative reaction of France and other nations, and the real difficulty of arriving at any sound definition of what should come within the League's purview, the discussion was postponed until the next Assembly. But in 1927, Britain surprisingly withdrew its memorandum from the agenda, stating that the 1926 debate had satisfied her major claims.

The non-acceptance of the British view allowed the League's functional bodies to develop in many ways. The scope of Technical Organisations and Commissions expanded as numerous problems came within the international sphere. Coping with these new responsibilities necessitated a development of institutional structures. New committees were added to existing ones (such as in the field of narcotics control—see Table I) and subsidiary bodies proliferated within almost all Organisations and Commissions. One remarkable feature of that process was the emergence of 'International Institutes' set up and financed by host governments placed at the disposal of the League as auxiliary bodies to the Intellectual Cooperation Organisation[29]. To a certain extent, International Institutes were an indirect application of the original provisions of Article 24 and the British government raised doubts about the legality of their affiliation to the League[30]. At any event, because of their proliferation, the bodies dealing with intellectual cooperation—a concern not even provided for in the Covenant—and which were centred around a Technical Organisation, received the status of Technical Organisation in 1931[31]. This over-all evolution was accompanied by constant and substantial increases in budgets and personnel[32]. In addition, the control of the functional bodies by the Council and Assembly became progressively a formality. These political organs had neither the time nor the expertise to exercise real supervision over bodies which were becoming more and more specialised. The Council often approved the proposals of the functional committees automatically without any discussion—unless the rapporteurs acting for the committees asked for an official decision on a particular point. The real 'master' of the functional agencies was indeed the Secretary-General. He assisted the Council and Assembly rapporteurs in the preparation of papers which were frequently drafted by him or his collaborators. Moreover, the amount of the Secretariat's assistance to Technical Organisations and Commissions depended upon the Secretary-General's good will as head of the League's internal administration. In this connection, Sir Eric Drummond, the first Secretary-General, who was 'cautiously following rather than anticipating developments . . . supplied these (functional) services with the needed personnel and administrative support, often overcoming considerable difficulties. . .[33] Because of Drummond's attitude, the League's functional organs mushroomed until the eve of the world crisis.

A favourable balance-sheet of League functional achievements within this period is easy to establish especially if one chooses to test it against political achievements. In the area of security, the League could claim only one major success (the resolution of the Greek-Bulgarian incident). In the functional field, the instances were more numerous and sometimes more significant: the financial rescue of Austria and other weak countries, the campaign against various infectious diseases in Europe and outside Europe, world wide drug control, and so forth. However, all this meant very little, if anything, to national public opinion. These activities were less moving and dramatic in nature than political problems which faced the League. Nevertheless with the good will of governments, the benevolence of the Secretary-General, and the ingenuity of first-rate officials, the League in the 1920s enjoyed a golden age of functional cooperation. This image was to be altered to some extent in the 1930s.

Functional Cooperation in the 1930s: Re-adaptation and Setback

In the second decade of the League's history, functional cooperation received two successive and severe blows. The first was the Great Depression which shrank the League's income and resulted in a drastic curtailment of the League's activities. The changes introduced by the crisis were nevertheless more qualitative than quantitative in nature. The crisis undermined and destroyed the spirit of international cooperation built up laboriously during the previous decade. As a consequence, a part of the League's achievements in the 1920s came to naught and many projects quickly became obsolete. League functional bodies played no significant role during the Depression. Being only of an advisory character, they could do nothing once the majority of governments decided to seek national instead of international solutions to problems.

This did not mean, however, that functional cooperation was brought to an end or was even at a standstill. Quickly, and pragmatically, the relevant bodies redefined their objectives and adjusted their methods to the new systemic conditions. Since the time was obviously no longer propitious to a further development of international legislation, this standard method was largely discarded. Instead, the League choose to follow new processes which were more informal and more flexible. The League organised numerous meetings 'limited to certain groups of States which had the same kind of problem to face, either because of geographical propinquity, or because of some other common feature'. These meetings were called 'not to draft precise texts, but to exchange information, to receive the advice of disinterested experts, to lay down general principles'[34]. When formal conventions were prepared, they were 'to be accepted by governments as models in negotiating and drafting such bilateral agreements as they might make with other countries'[35]. Moreover, League functional agencies focused their attention less on governmental action than on 'the cares and interests of the individual and his family'[36]. They became deeply involved in problems which were as much domestic as international such as housing, nutrition, standards of living, conditions of rural life, and so forth. The Economic and Financial Organisation succeeded in effecting a most remarkable adaptation[37]. Its effectiveness can be seen particularly in the area of double taxation where, following model treaties drafted by the League's Fiscal Committee, some 300 conventions were concluded by a number of governments within a few years.

Old procedures continued also to be followed. For instance, League functional bodies still assisted the Council and the Assembly in handling political and security questions—among them the Saar Plebiscite and the preparation of economic sanctions against Italy. Technical assistance far from being interrupted was even expanded. After 1931, all of the League's technical Organisations and Commissions had been joining in an effort to provide China with assistance on an unprecedented scale[38]. The Health Organisation developed the Chinese Central Health Station and undertook sanitation and veterinary work in certain Chinese provinces. During the Sino-Japanese dispute it also sent medical units with medical stores to China. The Economic and Financial Organisation designated agricultural experts to cope with urgent problems. The Communications and Transit Organisation helped the Chinese National Economic Council in road construction and water conservation. The Intellectual Cooperation Organisation helped Chinese students abroad to adapt their training to the new requirements of China. To a large extent League functional agencies helped modernise China and, in a sense, this appeared to be a substitute for the protection the League was not able to give to China against Japan. Thus, in the final analysis, the functional agencies effectively survived the economic crisis while, on the other hand, many of the League's political acheivements collapsed. In the 1930s, as Ranshofen Wertheimer said: 'the technical work of the League stood out as the chief evidence of the League's continued utility and vitality'[39].

The positive effects of functional re-adaptation were however partially offset by the administrative changes introduced within the League's Secretariat when the French financial expert Joseph Avenol succeeded Drummond as Secretary-General in 1933. Avenol wanted to substitute French administrative practice for Drummond's administrative practice which he regarded as laxity. He was particularly upset by the relative autonomy of the functional agencies. In spite of his background, Avenol cared little for functional work (with perhaps an exception for financial questions). He was convinced that 'the ultimate fate of the international technical work depended exclusively on the political work and that success in the political field would solve all technical problems. Translated into concrete action, this meant that the League's political work, its *raison d'être*, should under no circumstances be overshadowed by secondary activities. In case the League's political activities decreased, technical and non-political services had to be maintained in their pre-established normal proportion to the political work'[40] Soon after assuming office, he gradually curtailed the basic customary prerogatives of the functional bodies. This was realised at a first stage, in 1933, with the setting up of a new coordinating Central Section within the Secretariat. His antifunctional policy culminated in 1936 when the Council adopted the 'General Regulations on Committees'—a restrictive document, in the drafting of which he took a prominent part[41]. Every Technical Organisation and Commission was compelled to bring its terms of reference into line with the new rules whose supervision and implementation fell within the purview of the Central Section. The situation was even worsened by the departure of some of the remaining pioneers of the 1920s: Sir Arthur Salter had already left the Secretariat in 1931; Robert Haas, who was serving in the most autonomous Technical Organisation, died in 1935, and Rajchman, the man who was behind the whole enterprise of assistance to China, was dismissed in 1939 for his anti-appeasement feelings. Moreover, as a consequence of the introduction of the French administrative system, the devolution of responsibilities, and initiative, were constantly discouraged and 'the Directors lost much of their executive responsibility. They came more and more under the supervision of the Secretary-General, who often remained anonymous, but acted through an increasingly powerful Central Section which assumed in many respects the role of the *cabinet* in the French meaning of this term'. The members of sections—formerly the backbone and the living spirit of the Secretariat—became 'mere mechanical executors of their tasks, discouraged from taking responsibilities and considered exchangeable in their duties'[42]. At the beginning of 1939, the League's political organs decided—as a consequence of their general policy of budgetary economies undertaken in the previous year—to initiate a series of administrative contractions and mergers in the Secretariat. This led to the emergence of three 'departments', each of which regrouped a certain number of the old sections (*viz.* technical organisations 'and commissions' secretariats)[43]. The constitutional setback was complete.

The League's Official Adoption of Functionalism: The Bruce Report (1939)

Several factors induced the Secretary-General to change his views on the respective roles of collective security and functional cooperation in the late 1930s. The Munich Agreement which culminated in a surrender by the League's major Powers to the Nazis marked the start of the evolution of his views. The very fact that League principles and ideals had been trampled upon by their legitimate custodians gave full evidence that they intended to prevent the League from playing any political role whatsoever in world affairs for the years to come. Such a prospect confronted the Secretary-General with a difficult choice: acceptance of this fact meant the end of the League as a political forum while resistance would have provoked a major break with Member States. The only way he could secure a vital role for the League as an active institution was to embrace the very programmes he had previously rejected. Very soon he proceeded to give fresh impetus to functional cooperation and to promote it as an end in itself.

Certain facts warranted such a solution. The success of the ILO offered food for thought. Moreover the League's functional agencies were proving effective in spite of all setbacks (in 1939 they were taking 60 per cent of the League's budget). In adapting to the new conditions of the 1930s, they had 'opened up new springs of popular interest and support'[44]. But various weaknesses of the institutional system had also been revealed, such as overlapping activities, absence of a real supervisory body, and lack of wide publicity. These were due to twenty years growth without any coherent design. A demand for constitutional change began gradually to take shape. Among the leading advocates for change was Stanley Bruce, Australia's high commissioner in London and also its representative at the League meetings[45]. Reinforcing this trend were two reports submitted by Lord Cranborne, British delegate at the Committe of 28—a body which had been charged with an overall examination of League's reform following the sanctions' failure[46]. The Cranborne Reports showed that while the League of Nations as a political institution was dying from a lack of universality, its functional activities had actually been quasi-universal for many years. Indeed, the functional agencies had long served as an important link between the League and the many States which withdrew from it, and also the United States[47]. At that time, the American participation extended to almost all functional bodies on an *ad hoc* basis, Lord Cranborne's implicit conclusion was that an extension of functional activities would be the best substitute for political universality.

The 1938 Assembly, which was in session during the Munich events, endorsed the Cranborne Reports and solicited the opinion of Non-Member States on a possible expansion of their cooperation with the League[48]. Only the United States responded to the Assembly. While making no concrete proposal, the American reply constituted the warmest tribute ever paid by a government to the League. More particularly, it was the first favourable over-all declaration issued by the United States on the League since the sad days of 1920[49]. Significantly it was followed by informal reports that the United States government would possibly accept a closer and even a more formal association with the League's functional bodies, should they be endowed with more autonomy[50]. This was a decisive factor in leading the Secretary-General to embrace functionalism.

As the Nazi threat to Danzig materialised, the Secretary-General convinced the Council, on May 27, 1939, to set up a small committee, presided over by Bruce, to study appropriate measures to ensure the expansion of League's machinery for dealing with technical problems, and to promote the direct participation of all nations in the efforts made to solve those problems. This was the starting point of the so-called 'Bruce Reform'. Bruce's role was actually a limited one. He lent his prestige to the programme of the Secretary-General who, in turn, was influenced by Alexander Loveday, director of the Economic and Financial Organisation[51].

The Bruce Committee composed of seven non-governmental experts was actually dominated by Joseph Avenol, who conducted the discussions on the basis of a working paper bearing his signature. The Committee produced a remarkable document entitled 'The Development of International Cooperation in Economic and Social Affairs', more commonly known as the 'Bruce Report'[52]. The Report recommended the establishment of a new body—the Central Committee for Economic and Social Questions—which would replace the Council and Assembly in the direction and supervision of League functional work. States not belonging to the League could become members of the Committee on the same footing as League members, given that they contributed to the Committee's expenses. Thus a new category of League membership devoid of any political responsibility was provided for. The Central Committee was to consist of twenty-four governments elected by the Assembly and not more than eight experts co-opted by the Committee for their special qualifications. The inclusion of non-governmental experts in a decision-making League body brought the League close to the ILO procedure. All matters were to be decided by a majority vote: the Central Committee was a more 'democratic' organ than the Council in which unanimity was a general rule. Furthermore, the reform envisaged special annual reports by the Secretary-General dealing with the Central Committee's work, notwithstanding the annual Report of the general League activities; this meant that the League's functional work would henceforth 'be organised at the Assembly, without being overshadowed by the debate on foreign policies'[53]

The most significant innovation was, however, to be found in the conception of international organisation implicitly embodied in the Report. The departure from the original emphasis of the Covenant can be seen in the assertion of the Bruce Report that: 'The League is not and *has never been* an institution concerned solely with the prevention of war', and that it is its non-political work 'which is now an essential element in the promotion of peaceful civilisation'[54]. More striking functional arguments are to be found in the memorandum submitted by the Secretary-General to the Bruce Committee and which the Committee retained as a basis for its recommendations. In this document, Avenol considered that functional

155

work should be promoted 'as an end in itself requiring no justification by reference to its indirect results'. In his opinion,

'all States who desire to collaborate in this work, whether Members of the League or not, should feel that they can do so without having to take into consideration any possible repercussions of a political character. They should feel that they have at their disposal a machinery which it is a part of their normal administrative action to use at every point where the national administration finds the need of consultation on the international aspect of any question which it may be considering; just as one Department within a national administration consults another when any problem presents aspects which fall outside its own special sphere of knowledge'[55].

Reading between the lines of the Bruce Report, one must come to the conclusion that the major approach to world peace carried for twenty years—collective security—was not the soundest approach, and that to perform their supreme function, international organisations should focus not upon the political issues dividing nation states, but rather upon those functional activities likely to bring them participating actively together.

The League issued the Bruce Report only a few days before the outbreak of the Second World War. The document was favourably received in many quarters, but it came too late. 'If it had been established in 1936, the (Central) committee could perhaps have come to the rescue more effectively in regard to the League's technical work, but at the end of 1939 there was no longer any hope of reviving the technical activity of the League'[56]. The reform was formally adopted by the Assembly in December 1939 and first steps towards its implementation were taken in the Spring of 1940. Military developments, however, brought to an end all possibilities of a full implementation.

The League survived until 1946 and performed some valuable functional work during the Second World War. League commissions continued to supervise effectively international conventions dealing with drug traffic control and addiction. The health services still provided valuable information and advice to governments. The economic and financial services, which were transferred to Princeton University, produced many outstanding studies dealing with such concerns as population, currency, commercial policy, customs unions, economic depressions, and many post-war problems. Finally, the League assisted and cooperated with functional wartime agencies including UNRRA, the Inter-Allied Committee on Post-War Requirements, and the Interim Commission of FAO[57]. The basic principles of the Bruce Report were vindicated in 1945 with the drafting of the United Nations Charter, which included two chapters (of eighteen articles) devoted to functional cooperation; more particularly, it vested the whole responsibility for functional cooperation in an Economic and Social Council acting under the authority of the General Assembly; the Economic and Social Council was to a great extent a direct off-spring of the League's Central Committee for Economic and Social Questions[58].

Thus, in two decades a complete reversal of the principles embodied in the Preamble of the Covenant had taken place: the League had not succeeded even in *promoting* collective security while it had actually *achieved* a considerable degree of functional cooperation.

Conclusion

The League of Nations experiment in functional cooperation justified to a very large extent some of the major arguments advanced by David Mitrany in his *A Working Peace System* (1943).

The League tested fully the fact that form follows the function. The emergence of Technical Organisations and International Institutes within the framework of the League was an indication that the functions of world society were evolving much faster than the legal order and political institutions established by the 1919 peacemakers. Each of these functions was, in addition, tackled by bodies which differed in structure and in methods of work according to the dimension and nature of the problem at hand, as well as the need and means of the moment.

The process of functional cooperation proved not only irresistible, but also cumulative. Many functions generated others and this led, particularly in the 1920s, to a constant extension of League activities, which brought some governments to protest against the organisation's 'indefinite aim'. Nevertheless, in the same period, the League's agencies helped to develop the idea that world society was itself a simple basic unit rather than composed of self-sufficient national units.

The creation of a genuine tradition of international cooperation was to a certain extent due to the introduction of new élites—technical experts—in international affairs. The taking of functional activities from the hands of professional diplomats and their devolution to experts free from national bias who developed an *esprit de corps* as a result of working together on a permanent basis, was perhaps one of the most valuable innovations of the League.

Finally, since the functional agencies were opened to non-League representatives, whether governmental or not, and since they proceeded through the 'way of natural selection', binding together the interests which are common, where they are common, and to the extent to which they are common[59], the net effect was to achieve a considerable degree of universality, a condition for which the League's political organs had been striving for many years, but had failed to achieve.

The League of Nations' contribution to international organisation is twofold. From a theoretical point of view, the League promoted the idea that functional cooperation could be treated on its own merits, *viz*. that functional cooperation had a direct rather than an indirect contribution to bring to world peace, and that an international organisation was more likely to succeed if it approached issues on the basis of common interests rather than divisive conflicts. On a more practical level, the League was the first institution which set up the first effective barriers to 'ignorance, disease and poverty'.

Notes and references

1 *A Working Peace System* (London: Royal Institute of International Affairs), 1943. (pp. 35, 37 and 28 of the 1966 reprint by the Chicago's Quadrangle Books).
2 For a fair account on this subject, see James A. Salter, *Allied Shipping Control. An Experiment in International Administration* (Oxford: Clarendon Press, 1921), XVI-372 p.
3 See Louis Renault, 'Les Unions internationales. Leurs avantages et leurs

inconvénients', *Revue générale de droit international public*, Tome III (1896), pp. 14-26; Pierre Kasansky, 'Théorie de l'administration internationale', *id.*, Tome IX (1902), pp. 353-367; Raymond L. Bridgeman, *World Organisation* (Boston: Ginn and Co.), 1905, VI-172 p., Léon Poinsard, *Comment se prépare l'unité sociale du monde. Le droit international au XXe siècle, ses progrès et ses tendances* (Paris: Bureaux de la Science sociale), 1907, 115 p.; Victor H. Duras, *Universal Peace by International Government* (New York: Broadway Publishing Co.), 1908, 186 p.; Paul S. Reinsch, *Public International Unions. Their Work and Organisations. A Study in International Administrative Law* (Boston: Ginn and Co.), 1911, VIII-189 p.; John A. Hobson, *Towards International Government* (London: Allen and Unwin), 1915, 216 p.; Leonard S. Woolf, *International Government. Two Reports Prepared for the Fabian Research Department together with a Project by a Fabian Committee for a Supernational Authority that will Prevent War* (Westminster: Fabian Society), 1916, 259 p.; Francis B. Sayre, *Experiments in International Administration* (New York: Harper and Bros), 1919, 200 p.

4   *Op.cit.*

5   Alfred Zimmern, *The League of Nations and the Rule of Law, 1918-1935* (London: Macmillan), 1936, p. 194 (original italics).

6   See David H. Miller, *The Drafting of the Covenant* (London: Putnam), 1928, 2 vols.; *passim*.

7   Jan. C. Smuts, *The League of Nations. A Practical Suggestion.* (London: Hodder and Stoughton), 1918, 71 p. (quoted in Miller, *op.cit* 2, p. 23).

8   Miller, *op.cit.*, pp. 23, 24-25.

9   Article 24: 1. There shall be placed under the direction of the League the international bureaux already established by general treaties if the parties to such treaties consent. All such international bureaux and all commissions for the regulation of matters of international interest hereafter constituted shall be placed under the direction of the League.
2. In all matters of international interest which are regulated by general conventions but which are not placed under the control of international bureaux or commissions, the Secretariat of the League shall, subject to the consent of the Council and if desired by the parties, collect and distribute all relevant information and shall render any other assistance which may be necessary or desirable.
3. The Council may include as part of the expenses of the Secretariat the expenses of any bureau or commission which is placed under the direction of the League.

10 Article 23: Subject to and in accordance with the provisions of international conventions existing or hereafter to be agreed upon, the Members of the League:
(a) . . .
(b) . . .
(c) will entrust the League with the general supervision over the execution of agreements with regard to the traffic in women and children, and the traffic in opium and other dangerous drugs;
(d) . . .
(e) will make provision to secure and maintain freedom of communications and of transit and equitable treatment for the commerce of all Members of the

League. In this connection, the special necessities of the regions devastated during the war of 1914-18 shall be borne in mind;

(f) will endeavour to take steps in matters of international concern for the prevention and control of disease.

Paragraphs (a), (b), and (d) are respectively relevant to conditions of labour (a provision fully implemented by the ILO's creation), just treatment of native inhabitants of non-autonomous territories (a point covered by Article 22 related to Mandates), and supervision of trade in arms and ammunition (a question more related to disarmament).

11 For a legal interpretation of Article 23, see Jean Ray, *Commentaire du Pacte de la Société des Nations, selon la politique et la jurisprudence des organes de la Société* (Paris:Sirey), 1930, pp. 648-666.

12 Stanley H. Bailey, 'Some Problems of Article XXIV of the Covenant', *American Political Science Review*, Vol. XXV, No. 2 (May, 1931, pp. 420-421.

13 Listed in Bailey, *op.cit.*, and in George A. Codding, 'The Relationship of the League and the UN with the Independent Agencies: A Comparison', *Annals of International Studies*, No. 1 (1970), pp. 65-87.

14 Bailey, *op.cit.*, p. 418.

15 International Bureau for Information and Enquiries Regarding Relief to Foreigners (1921); International Hydrographic Bureau (1921); Central International Office for the Control of the Liquor Traffic in Africa (1922); International Commission for Air Navigation (1922); International Exhibitions Bureau (1931); Nansen International Office for Refugees (1931).

16 Zimmern, *op.cit.*, p. 306. On the legal relations between the League and International Bureaux, see LON docs. C.48. 1921, C.196. 1921, A.94. 1927, A.107. 1927, A.71. 1928. XII, C.233. 1928. XII, A.296. 1928. XII.

17 It should be noticed that the OCT was the only Organisation endowed with formal and written statute. As for the other Organisations, their statute was embodied into one or several Council and/or Assembly resolutions.

18 LON, Minutes of the 5th session of the Council, p. 186 (Council Resolution); LON *Official Journal, Special Supplement*, January 1921, p. 12 (Assembly Resolution).

19 For more details, see *Annuaire de la Société des Nations, 1938* (Genève: Editions de l'Annuaire de la Société des Nations), 1938, pp. 321-329. See also 'List of Conventions with Indication of the Relevant Articles Conferring Powers on the Organs of the League of Nations', LON doc. C.100. M.100. 1945. V.

20 For specific details, see *Ten Years of World Cooperation* (Geneva: League of Nations Secretariat), 1930, pp. 183-195; 'The League of Nations Reconstruction Schemes in the Inter-War Period', LON doc. C.59. M.59. 1945. II.A. See also LON doc. 1930. II. 16

21 Martin Hill, *The Economic and Financial Organisation of the League of Nations. A Survey of Twenty Year's Experience* (Washington: Carnegie Endowment for International Peace), 1946, pp. 226-228; *Ten Years of World Cooperation, op.cit.*, pp. 226-228.

22 See Bertil A. Renborg, *International Drug Control* (Washington: Carnegie Endowment for International Peace), 1947, XI-276 p.

23 See *Ten Years of World Cooperation op.cit.*, pp. 205-206 and 235-237

24 See LON doc. C.D.C.I. 1, Annex IV.

25 LON, *The Records of the First Assembly. Plenary Meetings (Meetings Held from the 15th of November to the 18th of December 1920)*, pp. 323-392, 411.

26 Council Resolution of 10 September, 1923 (LON *Official Journal*, 1923, p. 1303) (Economic and Financial Organisation); Council Resolution of 7 July, 1923 (LON *Official Journal, 1923, p. 936 and 1045-1046), and Assembly* Resolution of September 15th, 1923 (LON *Official Journal, Special Supplement* No. 11, p. 11) (Health Organisation). For the statute of the Organisation for Communications and Transit, see LON docs. C.662. M.265. 1923. VIII, pp. 90-95; C.C.T. 79 (2) and Addendum; C.95. M.48. 1938. III.

27 See LON doc. A.102. 1926. V., Annex.

28 Records of the Seventh Ordinary Session of the Assembly. Text of the Debates, LON *Official Journal, Special Supplement* No. 44, Geneva, 1926, p. 124.

29 The International Institute of Intellectual Cooperation was created by the French government in 1926; the International Educational Cinematographic Institute was created in 1928 by the Italian government (which also set up in 1928 the International Institute for the Unification of Private Law). In the 1930s, the Brazilian government offered the International Center for Research on Leprosy.

30 LON *Official Journal, Special Supplement* No. 54, p. 179. The establishment of the International Relief Union in 1927 is another instance of the indirect implementation of Article 24. The IRU was an International Bureau whose statute, although referring only to Article 23 (f) and 24, included actually all elements placing the Union under the authority of the League.

31 See LON doc. A.23 1931. XII.

32 Egon F. Ranshofen-Wertheimer, *The International Secretariat. A Great Experiment in International Administration* (Washington: Carnegie Endowment for International Peace), 1945, pp. 158-161

33 *Ibid.* p. 161.

34 F.P. Walters, *A History of the League of Nations* (London: Oxford University Press), 1960, p. 750.

35 Martin Hill, *The Economic and Financial Organisation of the League of Nations. A Survey of Twenty Years' Experience; op.cit.* p. 73.

36 Walters, *op.cit.*, p. 750.

37 See Alexander Loveday, 'The Economic and Financial Activities of the League', *International Affairs*, Vol. 17, No. 4 (November-December 1938), pp. 788-808.

38 See Norbert Meienberger, *Entwicklungshilfe under dem Völkerbund* (Winterthur: Verlag P.G. Keller), 1965, XVI-150 p. Y.C. Hoe, *The Programme of Technical Cooperation between China and the League of Nations* (Honolulu: Institute of Pacific Relations), 1933, 30 p., mimeographed.

39 Ranshofen-Wertheimer, *op.cit.*, p. 163.

40 *Ibid.*

41 The background and contents of these Regulations are brilliantly analysed in Vladimir D. Pastuhov, *Memorandum on the Composition, Procedure and Functions of Committees of the League of Nations* (Washington: Carnegie Endowment for International Peace, roneogr.), 1943, pp. 28-50. For the text of the Regulations, see LON *Official Journal*, 1936, pp. 131-133.

42 Ranshofen-Wertheimer, *op.cit.*, pp. 155-156.

43 *Ibid.*, p. 87
44 Walters, *op.cit.*, p. 757.
45 *Ibid.*, p. 759.
46 See LON docs. C.367. M.249. 1937. VII and C.368. M.250. 1937. VII. On the Committee's work, see S. Engel, 'League Reform. An Analysis of Official Proposals and Discussions, 1936-1939', *Geneva Studies*, Vol. XI, Nos. 3-4 (August 1940), 282 p.
47 See Martin Hill, 'Memorandum on the Existing Cooperation between the Technical Organisations of the League and non-members States and States under notice of withdrawal', LON Archives, 1933-1946, 50/38620/38332.
48 Assembly Resolution of September 30, 1938 (LON doc. C.L.193. 1938, VII)
49 'The United States and the League, the Labour Organisation and the World Court in 1939. An Annual Account by a Group of Americans in Geneva', *Geneva Studies*, Vol. XI, No. 1 (February 1940), p. 22. For Cordell Hull official letter to the League, see LON doc. C.77. M.87. 1939. VII.
50 Letter from Arthur Sweetser to Joseph Avenol, February 22, 1939 (LON Archives, 1933-46, 50/37281/8871).
51 On Loveday's views, see his memorandum to Sean Lester dated July 7, 1939 (LON Archives, 1933-46, 50/38743/38332).
52 LON doc. A.23. 1939.
53 *Ibid.*, pp. 19-20.
54 *Ibid.*, p. 7 (author's italics).
55 LON doc. C.D.C.I. 1, p. 8.
56 Pastuhov, *op.cit.*, p. 78.
57 For more details, see LON doc. A.6. 1946, pp. 22-44.
58 A brief comparison between the general aspect of these bodies is to be found in Victor-Yves Ghébali, *La Société des Nations et la Réforme Bruce, 1939-1940* (Genève: Centre européen de la Dotation Carnegie pour la paix internationale), 1970, pp. 78-82.
59 Mitrany, *op.cit.*, p. 69.

Functionalism and the Specialised Agencies
Allan McKnight

Whatever one's concept of functionalism, inter-governmental organisations (IGOs) form a vital base against which to formulate and test functionalist theories. IGOs are not a recent phenomenom. The oldest which is still active is the Central Commission for the Navigation of the Rhine (CCR). Its creation having been agreed at the Congress of Vienna, negotiations for its constitutive treaty took fifteen years and it came into being in 1831. Another still active is the International Bureau of Weights and Measures (BIPM), founded in 1875. Two others, Universal Postal Union (UPU) (established 1874) and International Telecommunications Union (ITU) (established 1865) are members of the UN family. Others founded in the nineteenth century but now defunct included IGOs dealing with: the navigation of the Congo (1885), the Cape Spartel Light in Tangier (1865), the regulation of North Sea Fisheries (1882), Penology (1872), the protection of trade in time of war (1856), Pan American railways (1890), Quarantine control in Egypt (1881) and the uniform nomenclature for causes of death (1900). These are the germs of functionalism. The formation of IGOs to deal with specific subjects, globally or regionally, has continued unabated, apart from the period of the two World Wars.

This chapter, however, concentrates on the UN 'specialised agencies' in the sense in which that term is commonly used in the discharge of United Nation business, as, for example, in the reports of the Advisory Committee on Administrative and Budgetary Questions (ACABQ) to the General Assembly and in the oversight by ECOSOC of programmatic activities relevant to economic and social affairs. This yields nine agencies from the UN family and the International Atomic Energy Agency (IAEA). The latter is an autonomous body in the formal legal sense but is linked to the United Nations and a number of its specialised agencies by relationship agreements and is considered as a member of the UN family.[1]

The resulting list of specialised agencies upon which this chapter is based is:

ILO	:	International Labour Organisation
FAO	:	Food and Agricultural Organisation
UNESCO	:	United Nations Educational Scientific and Cultural Organisation
WHO	:	World Health Organisation
ICAO	:	International Civil Aviation Organisation
UPU	:	Universal Postal Union
ITU	:	International Telecommunications Union
WMO	:	World Meteorological Organisation
IMCO	:	Inter-Governmental Maritime Consultative Organisation
IAEA	:	International Atomic Energy Agency

162

The common feature of these agencies is that each has an independent constitutive treaty. evolved within the aegis of, or taken over by, the United Nations, providing for independent governing bodies and independent budgets, and answerable to ECOSOC.

The exlusions must be pointed out. First, there are the four 'financial' agencies which are only loosely tied to the General Assembly and ECOSOC.[2] These are:

International Monetary Fund (IMF)
International Bank for Reconstruction and Development (IBRD)
International Finance Corporation (IFC)
International Development Association (IDA)

Second are those agencies listed by the Yearbook of International Organisations (YBIO)[3] as members of the UN family but which are not specialised agencies. They are:[4]

General Agreement on Tariffs and Trade
UN Children's Fund
UN High Commissioner for Refugees
International Narcotics Control Board
UN Conference on Trade & Development
UN Development Programme
UN Industrial Development Organisation
UN Institute for Training and Research
UN Research Institute for Social Development
World Food Programme.

The importance of other IGOs, of which there were, in 1972, 250 or so, must not be ignored. In membership they range from three to ninety-three states; memberships seems to be a matter of free national choice although in a few exceptional cases there is evidence of political bloc abstentions; many are regional, many are global. Several have more members than the smallest of the UN group. The IGOs outside the UN system deal with such fields of endeavour as social conditions for bargees, industrial property, banking, tourism, law, nutrition, pest control, research and development, communications, customs, fisheries, transport, insurance, pollution, commodities, oceanology and planet and animal production and diseases. For most IGOs, the functional interest is highly specific. An exhaustive study of IGOs as an aspect of functionalism would need to take account of all these organisations. This would be a mammoth task and this chapter is confined to the ten IGOs identified above, as the specialised agencies of the UN family.[5]

It is interesting to consider the ten agencies from the point of view of their dates of creation, numbers of staff members, annual expenditures and numbers of member states.[6]

The two oldest specialised agencies are ITU and UPU. ITU has the aims of improving the national use of telecommunications by promoting technical facilities and their operation, improving their efficiency and making them generally available. An important modern activity is the regulation of broadcasting frequencies. UPU aims to organise and improve postal services and to promote international collaboration in the postal field. *Inter alia* it serves as a central point for mediating

163

	Date of creation	Estab. posts 1970	Expend. 1970 (US $M)	No. of members
ILO	1919	1404	34.25	121
FAO	1945	2493	39.90	119
UNESCO	1945	1920	44.27	125
WHO	1946	3040	75.77	128
ICAO	1944	545	8.17	119
UPU	1874	95	2.01	141
ITU	1865	478	7.89	137
WMO	1947	204	3.50	122
IMCO	1948	107	1.26	68
IAEA	1956	860	14.84	102
		11 146	231.86	

in financial questions related to international postal services. It now administers and directly executes postal projects as part of UN programmes of technical cooperation, as does ITU in the field of telecommunications.

Although ICAO was founded in 1944, it may be taken as in direct line of succession to the International Commission of Aerial Navigation (ICAN) established in 1919 when the first passenger carrying flights between European countries were being planned. ICAO's aims are to develop the principles and techniques of international air navigation and to standardise facilities throughout the world to ensure safe and orderly growth, and particularly to encourage the development of airways, airports and air navigation facilities. It is enjoined by its statute to ensure that the rights of its member states are fully respected and that each member has a fair opportunity to operate international airlines. It assists the less developed member states to establish facilities which meet international standards, and it provides considerable technical assistance to train national personnel.

One other specialised agency, ILO, survived from the 1919 Peace Conference. At that conference it was recognised that social injustice could result in such unrest as might constitute a cause of war. The aim of ILO is to raise working and living standards throughout the world by laying down minimum standards. It concerns itself also with the sub-aims of furthering full employment, the training and transfer of workers, effective rights to collective bargaining, cooperation of labour and management, social security, industrial safety, family welfare, and educational and vocational opportunity. That social justice and population welfare is a matter of international concern received greater recognition in the agencies constituted within the UN family after 1945.

Leaving ILO aside, it is significant that ITU, UPU, ICAN and ICAO were established with a clear recognition that certain communication services transcend nation states and cannot be provided unless an international mechanism is created whereby national officials can foregather and ensure the provision of the service across state frontiers. Among the specialised agencies created after 1945, WMO and IMCO to a large extent fall in the same category, as does WHO in its epidemiological recording and control activities.

IMCO, although established in 1948, did not legally come into existence until 1958 due to tardy ratification by states operating large gross tonnages. Its aim is to provide machinery for cooperation on technical aspects of merchant shipping, particularly safety of life and of navigation and to encourage the removal of hindrances to international shipping. IMCO's potential role, which has been neglected for years, is growing rapidly under the impact of world concern with pollution of the oceans and the need for both preserving them and making their resources, particularly of fisheries, available to man; and this at a time when giant tankers (whether carrying oil or chemicals) increase alarmingly the dangers of environmental damage from illegal discharge of wastes, or from stranding or collision.

WMO aims to foster world cooperation in achieving a network of stations whose meteorological observations are rapidly fed into an international system for wide dissemination to aid weather forecasts. A major function is standardisation of observations and reporting. It is particularly concerned with the application of meteorology to air and sea transport, and agriculture (for example, in protecting crops against insect pests and diseases.) Its most spectacular achievement is the World Weather Watch which began in 1968 and which involves high speed exchange of satellite and conventional data.

IAEA has the grand aim of accelerating and enlarging the contribution of atomic energy to peace, health and prosperity throughout the world. By its statute, IAEA is particularly concerned with safety standards in view of the insidious health risks of radio-activity. Its standards are essentially international because there is much international movement of radio-active materials and because, in all but a few locations, radio-activity released in a nuclear incident will cross state borders.

The three other specialised agencies, UNESCO, FAO and WHO, were greatly influenced in their inception by a concern with social justice such as had led to the creation of ILO. In each case there was a realisation in 1945 that in the aftermath of war, the problems of illiteracy, hunger and health demanded world wide action

The objective of WHO is to attain for all people the highest possible level of health, health being accepted as a state of complete physical, mental and social well-being and is not merely identified by the absence of disease or infirmity. In pursuance of these objectives, the WHO has acted as a general coordinator on international health, assisted governments with public health services, stimulated work to eradicate epidemic, endemic and other diseases; promoted improvement of nutrition, sanitation and other aspects of environmental hygiene, promoted maternal and child health and fostered activities in the field of mental health. Examples in practical terms of its activities are the campaign for the eradication of malaria and the central information service concerning spreads of epidemics. It is concerned with quarantine, health statistics, standardisation of pharmaceutical substances, public health and medical research. Some of its activities serve the needs of the world as a whole, while others are primarily directed to the under-privileged in developing countries.[7]

FAO aims to raise the levels of nutrition and the standards of living of all people and to secure improvements in the efficiency of production of all foods and agricultural products and their subsequent distribution. Above all its aim is to ensure mankind's freedom from hunger. This wide aim leads FAO to be concerned with fisheries, forestries, cereals, live-stock and soils and the obverse problems, such as pests, diseases and misuse of land and other natural resources, which affect agricultural production, marketing and prices. Under the FAO entry in the Year Book of International Organisations, well over fifty subsidiary bodies, inspired by FAO, are listed, which deal with individual products or forestry or fisheries or a pest in a particular region.

UNESCO has the overall aim of promoting collaboration among nations through education, science and culture in order to further universal respect for justice, for the rule of law and for human rights, and for the fundamental freedoms for all people without distinction of race, sex, language or religion. Particular aims are: to give fresh impulse to popular education and the spread of culture; to diffuse knowledge; to encourage cooperation among nations in all bi anches of intellectual activity; and to initiate international methods aimed at giving all people access to printed and published materials produced by any of them. It directs its activities to natural sciences, social sciences, human sciences and culture, communications and education generally. It has a wide web of cooperative arrangements with intergovernmental and non-governmental organisations. Apart from a continuing effort in the educational field, there have been spectacular activities such as its stimulation of research on arid lands, hydrology and oceanology; its Nubia campaign and its efforts to preserve Venice and Florence are well-known.

This brief sketch of the ten agencies indicates, not only the wide range of the functions contemplated in the statutory aims prescribed at the time of their formation, but the further diversification which has occurred as they have developed their programmes of activities. The pursuit by the ten agencies of these activities, many of which are highly specialised, has created a significantly large area of functionalist effort.

Each specialised agency brings together in any one year a large number of people and puts others in touch with member states with whom they would not normally be connected. This process operates within the secretariat of each agency by reason of its multinational staff, through engaging consultants as expert advisers to member states, through advisory services performed by the Secretariat and, last but not least, through its governing organs.

All specialised agencies have a similar broad statutory provision about staff, namely, that the staff is neither to seek nor to receive instructions from any government, and, consistent with competence, is to be recruited on as wide a geographical basis as possible.[8] Each agency has a multi-national staff (commonly over fifty nationalities are represented). The process of people of varying nationalities combining together to serve a common functional institution is established at the birth of the agency. Due to staff turnover, the numbers involved over a decade much exceed the number of staff employed.[9] A prime activity of the agency is to provide advisory and consultancy services to the less developed member states. This takes the regular staff to many countries where they must work in association with national officials in making investigations of needs and feasibility, providing advice, and sometimes services. Five of the agencies maintain regional or branch offices—FAO (6), ICAO (5), ILO (26), UNESCO (5), WHO (6)—which furthers the process. Moreover, the advice or assistance sought by a state often requires the attachment of an expert. The agencies frequently recruit a consultant for the period of the mission, financed either by the agency itself or by UNDP under its technical assistance programme. Most agencies also have a fellowship programme for the training in advanced countries of nationals of the developing countries in the skills relevant to the agency's specialised field. For example, WHO has awarded 32 000 fellowships.

No attempt is made here to quantify accurately the number of people enveloped in an international function as secretariat staff, consultants, or fellows under training. The staff of the ten agencies totalled 11 146 in 1970. The number of fellows and expert consultants would be of the order of another 5000. The governing organs of the agencies consist of an executive board, variously titled and comprising usually about 30 states, and a general conference of all member states. The frequency of meeting of each organ varies as between agencies. The members of delegations to a general conference would total in each agency about 500 officials and for executive boards between 50 and 100 at the least. The average number of officials attending such meetings annually is estimated at approximately 3000.

In addition, every year each agency holds a number of conferences at which a specialised subject is discussed. Attendance varies but on the average a scientific conference will attract an attendance of 100-200. Most agencies also hold meetings of small groups of top experts for the purpose of obtaining definitive advice on detailed questions. Some of these panels are standing committees; some are delegates of the governing organs; and some are advisory to the Secretariat. A detailed questionnaire to the ten agencies would be necessary to quantify the number of people involved, but, as an example, a relatively small agency like IAEA holds some ten scientific conferences and twenty to thirty panel meetings each year. This results in an annual total of some 2000-2500 specialists from member states joining in international discussions under the auspices of IAEA. A conservative estimate for the ten agencies would seem to be 15 000 persons per year under this head.

Taken together this means that approximately 30-40 000 persons are, in any one year, directly participating in international intercourse under the aegis of the ten specialised agencies, either as career staff members, staff members on fixed term appointments, experts and consultants, fellows under training, delegates to meetings of the governing organs, or attendees at specialised conferences, committees and panels. An individual may be involved only in a single meeting or he may participate for a few months or years, or he may spend a virtual life-time as a career international civil servant. Over a decade, allowing for various terms of association with the specialised agencies, the number of people participating directly would be between 150 000 and 200 000.

Apart from this direct participation, there is also indirect involvement at the national level in the affairs of the specialised agencies. This involvement is often continuous for a long period of years and affects a large number of persons from junior officials to Ministers.

Practice varies in different countries as to the allocation of ministerial responsibility for the various agencies. In some the foreign ministry maintains a strict and direct control using the specialist departments and agencies as advisers only in formulating national policies towards each particular agency. In most, foreign ministries perform a coordinating role which in many cases is loose, and the task of examining the business of the agency and formulating a national policy is performed by the specialist ministry or agency within the national administration. The result in that in all national administrations there is a core of officials outside the foreign ministry who have a deep interest in the business of the specialised agencies, particularly where it allows a specialised, national, departmental minister to perform on the world stage. Many office-holders, who before 1945 never lifted their eyes above national horizons, are now frequently aware of the international dimensions of their work.

What is the effect of this large-scale direct and indirect involvement in the affairs

167

of the specialised agencies? It certainly does not constitute a wholesale shift of loyalty and faith from national institutions to government through international institutions. Much depends on the type of participation by the individual concerned. At one end of the spectrum of participation is the scientist or technician who attends a single meeting on a highly technical subject such as the non-destructive testing of materials or the purity standard in the manufacturing process for a particular pharmaceutical. Meetings on such subjects may be repeated every few years to review new knowledge and techniques and an individual may attend two or three times in a decade. This type of participation resembles the habitual international intercourse among the scientific community to discuss common problems; the specialised agencies merely increase the opportunities for such intercourse.

Next in the spectrum are meetings to discuss a scientific or technical subject where the meetings usually constitute a series and the identity of the attendees is constant because there is a need to reach international agreement on technical standards for the conduct of particular activities. Examples are legion and a few chosen at random are the discussion of the safe transport of nuclear materials, traffic lanes for aircraft and for shipping in congested waters, the content of oil discharged on the high seas and standardisation of meteorological data. The technical nature of the subject and the often compelling need for world rules usually leads to accords but the process may be time-consuming since national interests are often initially divergent, largely due to considerations of economics and trade, particularly where the international standards require modification of equipment in national use. Participants in the two types of specialist discussions mentioned probably obtain the greatest degree of satisfaction from participation in the specialised agencies.

The greatest frustrations to functional action occur when there is a political difference which needs to be resolved as a prerequisite to technical discussions. Political differences occur most of all in governing organs and within the secretariats, and persist commonly in relation to the programmes to be pursued and the consequent budgetary appropriations to be made.

The composition of national delegations to the governing organs and their attitudes also varies. No agency is completely non-political and none is completely political. The extent to which political considerations or functional and technical considerations dominate proceedings is a reflection of the prevailing political climate. A general observation can be ventured. In the early years of an agency's existence politics dominate the discussion until a consensus emerges as to the programmatic activities of the agencies and the level at which they should be conducted. Thereafter the content of debates becomes more functional and technical and the representatives are less likely to be diplomatic. This was certainly the writer's experience in IAEA, which can be illustrated by two examples. For the first few years of IAEA's existence, the annual discussions of the Board of Governors on the programme and budget occupied on average about ten working days, notwithstanding previous consideration by a committee of the Board. Now it occupies a few hours and the prior committee consideration is also much shortened. The second example concerns the system of safeguards controls designed to ensure that nuclear material is not diverted to military uses. This was a subject of bitter political debate for the first five years (1958-63) and the technical rules for such a system were disputed as vehemently as the political basis. Once the United States and the Soviet Union formed a common political will to take action to halt the spread of nuclear weapons (culminating in the Non-Proliferation Treaty of 1968) the political differences withered away; the discussions became increasingly technical; political ambassadors ceased to sit as representatives and their chairs were filled by scientists.

A side effect of the specialised agencies is that foreign ministry officials, usually trained in the arts of Edwardian diplomacy—that is private bilateral dealings, dominated by political considerations—now spend some years of their careers, both in the early and late stages, associated with specialised agencies where the issue is functional or technical and the quest is for a public, multilateral consensus. The effect is impossible to measure; it is accompanied by many other factors, such as the emergence of new states and the democratisation of the foreign service in most, if not all, states, new and old.

Although the specialised agencies have operated over a quarter of a century and involved a large number of people in their functional activities, it would be unrealistic not to recognise that there is considerable disenchantment with some of the specialised agencies and the UN family in general. This springs partly from disappointment with progress on the two main (and interrelated) problems facing the world, namely disarmament and development. The failure to meet the development goals spreads into the specialised agencies who are intimately concerned with the process, except for funding. But there are more mundane causes. Conditions of service in the UN family are superior to those in all but a few favoured national administrations and this leads to a certain amount of jealousy on the part of national officials.[10] Standards of overall executive direction and management, particularly in programme and budgeting and establishment control, are often not in the first class. Incisiveness in action leaves much to be desired; deliberative and administrative procedures are cumbersome and time consuming, particularly when inter-agency consultation is necessary. Budgets tend to grow at a rate which, after allowing for inflation, may exceed the growth in GNP of the main contributors.[11] As with most bureaucracies, there is a strong tendency to empire building, with a strong will to preserve jurisdictional functions set out in the separate constitutive treaties of the agencies. For example in the field of atomic energy, techniques using radioactive sources are important in agriculture and medicine, and IAEA has under its statute been properly concerned with these techniques. IAEA is similarly concerned with the health and safety of workers in the nuclear field, commencing with underground uranium mining. But these are also fields within the statutory purview of FAO, WHO and ILO.

This type of situation calls for a rational division of activity and function which may be achieved in two ways. The first is for the division of labour to be resolved in national policies towards the specialised agencies and the question resolved among member states in the governing organs. But it is rare for the representatives of an individual country in the various agencies to be consistent as to the desirable division. A coordinated division could also be achieved by the executive heads of the agencies.[12] Here there are some hopeful signs. In the last five years there have been numerous combinations through committee structures. The FAO entry in YBIO lists 25 committees on specialist subjects on which FAO sits with another specialised agency or another IGO. FAO and IAEA even possess a joint operating division of secretariat members.

The system of specialised agencies already provides a significant sector of functionalist activity in international affairs. Without their efforts in producing agreed regulatory regimes, many activities, presently accepted as commonplace, could scarcely be conducted. Within their present statutory aims, there is more need for international regimes to govern existing activities and the future will throw up more problems which need regulation on an international basis, since divergent national standards would be chaotic. For example, any serious attempt to tackle the problems of the environment will require, after the initial political consensus to act, concerted international action to fix technical standards, to give them the force of law and to provide mechanisms for ensuring compliance..

On the horizon is a more alluring functionalist prospect, namely, the granting of an exclusive competence for a particular operational function to a specialised agency. At this point it should be noted that, at the Chicago conference which evolved the ICAO statute, the Australian delegation proposed that international air transport should be conducted by a single world international airline. If the Baruch Plan had been accepted in the late 1940s, atomic energy would have been monopolistically operated by an international agency under the control of the United Nations. These proposals are often dismissed as unrealistic. I prefer to think that they were merely two or three decades ahead of their time, as monopolistic nationalised coal mining and rail transport would have been viewed in 1910 or 1920. A single world airline would have avoided the current over-capacity, the inane competition for passengers, pollution problems, and over capitalisation, with a net result of cheaper air transport for all. An atomic monopoly under the aegis of the UN would probably have spared the world the peril and waste of resources of the nuclear arms race.

There is now evidence to support the view that certain activities should, within the next decade, be conducted operationally and managerially by a specialised agency or IGO with various degrees of delegation to national authorities. Overall control would be exercised by the international organisation concerned. An interesting example of the trend is the reconstitution at a Conference in Washington in 1970 of the International Telecommunications Satellite Consortium (INTELSAT). It is not at present a member of the UN family. It possesses 69 members who are national agencies representing the member states; unfortunately it has no members from Eastern Europe. After the Washington Conference it has been described as 'an international public utility'. Its member states, while free to operate their separate systems, will be obliged to consult the organisation. With the mounting pressure within the UN Second Development Decade for the use of satellites for natural resource surveys, INTELSAT should, within ten years, be a specialised agency responsible to the UN for the operation of a satellite system to provide communications and telecast educational programmes, to conduct resource surveys and to verify disarmament. Likewise with WMO. If science and technology leads us in the 1980s to weather modification by man and climate engineering, world operation and management would be desirable.

In short, the specialised agencies are already responsible for regulating a large number of technological activities[13] at least to the extent of prescribing standards. Observance of those standards is often left (as also in many cases is their adoption) to the individual will of the member states. The adoption of agreed standards is a constant practice of functionalism. Currently there are other fields where world standards should be developed. New technologies will throw up more needs for international regulatory regimes which will probably include prohibition of particular activities. The process of expanding international regulation will be slow, due partly to the inertial tradition of the nation state as the supreme source of law making and law enforcement. Modification of this attitude in favour of world law making is not aided by the current disenchantment with intergovernmental organisations. Improved efficiency in operation and management of IGOs is hampered by the traditional emphasis on the sovereignty of the nation state. In time, both will yield to the realities of the needs for international regulation of functional activities. One problem, scarcely touched as yet, is the association with functionalist law making of the representatives of the people, parliamentarians or their equivalent. The process is too exclusively in the hands of executive governments and shrouded in confidentiality in the formative stages. But increasing thought is being given to the means of associating popular representatives with the process of international decision-making on functional subjects, particularly in science and technology.[14]

Notes and references

1 The degree of interest in, or oversight of, specialised agencies by ECOSOC varies. It is naturally strongest in those which have a functional responsibility closely related to the development process. IAEA has a responsibility also to the Security Council in respect of its safeguards controls which are designed to ensure that nuclear materials are not diverted to the manufacture of nuclear weapons. This responsibility to the Security Council is at present unique. If other specialised agencies are asked to assume tasks in relation to the verification of disarmament accords (for example World Health Organisation (WHO) in relation to biological warfare agents) they may also become subject to a responsibility to the Security Council as well as ECOSOC.

2 Except for IMF these agencies have relationship agreements with UN and their policies are frequently debated in ECOSOC and UNGA in the context of the development process.

3 This source has been invaluable to the writer. References are to both the 12th Edition (1968-9) and the 13th Edition (1970-71).

4 This fails to give a complete picture. Some of these 'sub-agencies' have their own governing body of inter governmental representatives. Others without the benefit of such a group submit reports which are individually debated in the General Assembly. But the list ignores those departments of the UN Secretariat which have specific operational functions. Among these one must single out the Division of Transport and Natural Resources. This division, which appears to possess little intellectuality or imagination, on the whole operates as a dead hand on many of the activities and proposals of the specialised agencies.

In addition, it fails to show the place in the total structure of the many inter-governmental commissions and committees under ECOSOC which deal with such subjects as statistics, population, social development, human rights, status of women, natural resources and the application of science and technology to development. It also fails to show the extent to which the specialised agencies have stimulated the creation of new IGOs, as UNESCO has done with the International Oceanographic Commission and the extent to which they have breathed new life into IGOs which were semi-comatose, as FAO has done with the International Poplar Commission.

5 In any examination of functionalism, the population of non-governmental organisations is very important. They number over 2000 and cover many diverse fields. See chapter OO;

6 Compiled from Y BIO and ACABQ reports.

7 All specialised agencies have an express or implied function to further the development process. With WHO it is most explicit but the other specialised agencies perform the function as executing agencies for UN DP.

8 Regrettably this is a counsel of perfection. Recruiting is a slapdash affair, based on a formula of number of posts being in direct proportion to the percentage of assessed contribution to the budget. This yields staff of varying competence and integrity, with consequent effects on staff morale and the confidence of governments in the agencies. In fairness it must be recognised that the competence of staff and the standard of executive administration in national administrations are also infinitely varied. In the writer's limited experience, the two states which consistently produce governmental papers which are most impressive are Singapore and Trinidad and Tobago.

9 Staffing policies vary somewhat among the specialised agencies on a basis of simplistic political considerations, which have little concern with efficiency. Original concepts of an international civil service (with its concomitant dedication and devotion) have yielded to a current concept of staffing by which about 30 per cent are career men and 70 per cent on fixed term contracts. The 30 per cent tend to be confined to infrastructure staff, such as interpreters, translators, and administrators, while the scientists and experts change periodically. The period varies between different agencies ranging from two years to seven years; it lacks a consistent pattern because of varying policies among executive heads as to extensions of contracts. This subject deserves real study; what is needed is a managerial base to replace the amateur diplomatic base on which it is currently and accidentally determined.

10 The important thing is that this jealousy exists although it is less than rational in ignoring the family problems of living in a foreign country.

11 These causes of disenchantment are stated here from the point of view of the national official involved. But there are equally serious effects within the secretariats. Lack of dynamic executive leadership in the agencies and constant (often carping) criticism in the governing organs tends to create a circuitous lack of agency dynamism and government confidence.

12 Although the UN family has possessed the Administrative Coordination Committee (ACC), consisting of the executive heads of the agencies and sub-agencies, since 1947, it does not seem to most observers to have been very effective. Perhaps it again reflects a lack of emphasis on modern management and too much reliance on diplomatic amateurism.

13 Although international functional activity is concentrated, particularly in the specialised agencies, in subjects with a high technical content, it does exist in other fields but usually on a regional basis outside the UN family, for example, co-operation in the field of custom taxation. In 1939 the League of Nations, for example, was working on treaties to provide for co-operation in the prevention of income tax evasion.

14 As an example relating to science and technology, see the proceedings of the Council of Europe's 3rd Parliamentary and Scientific Conference 10-14 April 1972.

Functionalism and International Secretariats: Ideology and Rhetoric in the UN Family
Thomas Weiss and Jean Siotis

If we consider functionalism as a guide to international action, it seems appropriate to ask a number of questions about its impact on the perception and behaviour of a given set of international actors. In an attempt to evaluate its impact on the United Nations' family, we have chosen to look at one limited but important aspect of international secretariats' behaviour: the rhetoric of heads of secretariats when they are called upon to provide 'ideological' explanation for their actions. The expressed views of heads of secretariats or of important units of the United Nations Secretariat, are to be considered as one of many indicators which would have to be studied before we can reach any valid conclusions concerning the impact of functionalism as a set of action guidelines on those who are responsible for the work of international secretariats. However, short of this more ambitious study, a brief examination of such pronouncements will help us formulate hypotheses which could form the basis of a larger study.

Functionalism purports to describe—and prescribe—the process whereby the non-controversial, welfare activities of international organisations lead in the long-run to the performance by them of those duties presently performed by individual nation-states. The process of integration is seen as a movement away from zero-sum competition of sovereign states toward the omega point of world community. Since international organisations are the vehicle to be used in this transition, it is not unimportant to see to what extent their secretariats—at least in the tenor of their rhetoric—are conscious of their functionalist role.

In evaluating the degree to which the rhetoric of international secretariats are consciously functionalist, we are proposing four general criteria: (a) The most important is the link with a working peace system: a leader must be conscious of the eventual contribution of a welfare project to peace. (b) The rhetoric must look upon tasks and their spill-over into other areas (task expansion) as a sought-after goal. What is important is programmed organisational flexibility (the spirit of reform as an alternative to revolution or anti-revolution) and not simply pragmatic organisational expansion. (c) Rhetoric must concentrate on welfare. It is important to underline cooperation in non-controversial projects which benefit individuals and not only their societies. (d) In the case of specialised agencies, the organisational role as an institution in the larger UN system is crucial. Calculations of a common interest in the good of the whole system as well as a preoccupation with bringing nations together (and not just keeping them warily apart) are necessary. Before looking at the secretariats themselves, it would be useful to keep in mind three historical roots of ECOSOC activities: the Bruce Reform, Soviet opposition and the impact of Federalism.

While the League is not usually analysed in terms of functionally specific projects, purely welfare ones gradually assumed a large degree of importance. One

173

observer notes that 25 per cent of 1921 budget and at least 50 per cent of the post 1930 budgets provided for technical cooperation projects.[1] In addition, after the budget reached its highest level in 1932, only non-controversial League activities escaped budgetary cuts, although Secretary-General Avenol actively prevented their further expansion. The Bruce Commission, whose report was completed in 1939, attempted to analyse functionalist possibilities before the word itself had become 'fashionable'.[2] The League was of course trying to make a virtue out of a necessity. While that virtue, namely technical cooperation, is not unimportant, it is necessary to remember that such welfare projects were often begrudgingly acknowledged and not actively sought.

All of the governments at Dumbarton Oaks supported the principle of Article 55 of the UN Charter 'but the Soviet Union expected the new institution to deal with international problems in the broadest sense and they stressed promotion of the general welfare as the long-term foundation of peaceful relations . . . The Soviet Union wanted the entire organisation confined to security enforcement in a narrow sense.'[3] To a certain extent, the Soviet Union had adopted a position analogous to that of the United States at Paris in 1919 in which Wilson's obsession with collective security forced the delegates to push Smuts' functional suggestions off the agenda although they were eventually included in articles 23-25 of the Covenant.[4] In looking at the failure of the League, the Soviet leaders concluded that its activities had been too disparate. The United States and Britain agreed essentially with this analysis. However, their solution was not to ignore the problem but to attempt to find a better distribution of UN activities. Therefore, postwar security arrangements would also have to promote general social welfare which would diminish the tensions underlying war. While this was the positive part of great power motivations, there was also a rather negative one. The USSR finally agreed to welfare projects as part of the super organisation because of the United States' insistence that it was necessary to compensate the smaller states for their diminished security role.[5]

Finally, it is necessary to recall the federalist influence. Mitrany's pamphlet was published in 1943 without much fanfare, while federalist efforts in trying to update the League were a rather widespread phenomenon. The organisational principle of 'consent on the international level'[6] —and not technical determination—was central, but an active role for welfare projects was also necessary: 'Peace under modern conditions cannot be a static condition of life achieved by the renunciation of war . . . Peace must be a dynamic and continuous process . . . Peace involves whatever international organisation is necessary under the conditions of the times to protect the interests and promote the progress of mankind.'[7] In this total effort, Mitrany's welfare projects were important, but their authority was not to derive from technical needs, but rather from an 'international machinery with authority'.[8]

The pressures for the inclusion of welfare projects in the UN were thus diverse, but hardly functionalist. Eventually, paragraphs 1-3 of the Dumbarton Oaks proposals agreed to both 'maintain international peace and security as well as international cooperation in the solution of economic, social and other humanitarian problems'. A familiarity with these historical pressures is helpful in examining the rhetoric of 'UN family' officials, because this foreshadows the working hypothesis of our paper. The UN Secretaries General have imprecise views about the role of functionalist efforts and thus are rather 'half-hearted' in emphasising them. They admit little connection between an initial emphasis on welfare and world order because their attention is focused upon the role of the UN as a vehicle for solving political crises. On the other hand, the Directors General of specialised agencies (and possibly heads of technical units within the UN) assume different ideological postures. The ideological links between their individual tasks and a peace system are closer because therein lies the very justification for such agencies, in spite of the fact that they tend to become ends in themselves.

This chapter is an attempt to verify these themes by looking at some major statements (especially reports and speeches) of organisational heads. In the first part, we shall examine some pronouncements by the three Secretaries General of the UN. In the second part, we shall refer to five agencies: two rather functionalist secretariats, the ILO and UNCTAD; two agencies which demonstrate the non-functionalist property of deifying their own tasks, the WHO and World Bank; and finally to the special case of the Economic Commission for Europe secretariat during the 'tough years' of the Cold War.

Functionalism and the UN Secretariat

Trygve Lie Article 55 of the UN Charter justifies a concern with welfare projects 'with a view to the creation of conditions of stability and well-being which are necessary for peaceful and friendly relations among nations'. In his 1951 *Annual Report,* Trygve Lie recalls the dual role: 'its functions are not only "peace keeping" but "peace creating"'.[9] This would suggest that Lie was quite concerned with functionalist logic. However, on further reading, one finds that the few elements of functionalist rhetoric are mixed with more constitutional (or Wilsonian or federalist) elements which are his primary concern.

In regard to the links between ECOSOC tasks and peace, Lie stated 'it is by unspectacular means such as these that the United Nations, its commissions and specialised agencies are doing some of their most constructive long-range work, the object of which is to remove the underlying causes of war'.[10] However, by reading all of his report, the overwhelming impression is that he is concerned with the Cold War which plagued the world and his organisation. Technical assistance does not lead to peace but goes hand in hand with peaceful efforts. His definition of the world organisation in 1946 was that it was 'for the maintenance of peace and security and the promotion of the welfare of humanity'.[11] In such a conception, the functional tasks were a portion of day to day concerns, but in the final analysis they would not by themselves lead to world government because the 'United Nations is no stronger than the collective will of the nations that support it'.[12]

The fact that welfare and technical assistance had been an expanding part of the UN and that these had helped millions of people may seem ample evidence of task-expansion and an accentuation of welfare concerns. However, Lie's calls for disarmament or arms reduction to finance welfare projects[13] reflect a reversal of Mitrany's logic. For Lie does not see welfare activities expanding to stop war, but hopes rather that negotiations to stop war can expand welfare projects. Furthermore, his organising principle is not technical self-determination but rather a more voluntarist one: 'I am more than ever convinced that the United Nations can, and should, be a place where the combined *common sense* and *determination* of the peoples will find its voice and take a real part in the framing of the future of mankind'.[14]

Lie does, of course, perceive links between welfare and cooperation and other activities. Economic coordination, for instance, can 'reduce the basic causes of unrest and violent upheaval in many parts of the world; at the same time it could, by increasing the utilization of unused resources, so expand the world economy and world trade that all countries would benefit'.[15] However, while all of his reports refer to interdependence as one of the foundations of a more peaceful world, the second organisational goal—the prevention of conflict—clearly predominates: 'to prevent a new world war from breaking out is the main reason for existence of the United Nations'.[16] The functionalist dictum of bringing nations peacefully together has yielded to the requirement of keeping them less violently apart.

Although elements of functionalism are present in Lie's rhetoric, he is more concerned with the UN as a sought-after supranational organ with primary responsibility in security matters. In his final report in 1952, however, a new functionalist possibility arises.[17] The conflict between East-West was necessarily an ideological one that could be solved by negotiations. However, the North-South problem was to be seen more as an economic and technical problem in which the potential for 'a working peace system' existed.

Dag Hammarskjöld The first two reports by Dag Hammarskjöld in 1953[18] pursue this theme and it assumes more importance at the end of the Korean conflict. The changing stress in the organisational rhetoric on functionalism is striking. The relevance of welfare activities to the peace system is seen as direct and important, because even the ultimate UN authority in preventing conflict 'will depend also on the solution of the underlying economic and social problems that are behind the pressures leading to international conflicts'.[19] The potential for task expansion is great: 'It is unavoidable that this (focus on ECOSOC) should be so when one considers the virtually limitless possibilities of useful and legitimate action opened up by article 55 of the Charter'.[20] He finds the subordination of welfare concerns to security understandable, although it presents short run difficulties.[21] His mandate is to bring nations together because rising populations and poor living conditions are 'more dangerous in the long run than the conflicts that so monopolise our attention today'.[22]

In the 1955-1956 reports[23] we find evidence of a greater uncertainty on Hammarskjöld's part. While functionalist ideology is mentioned there seems to have been a change in the Secretary's General view after three years in office. There is no longer the enthusiasm or optimism which had marked his earlier functional pronouncements, as a more traditional concern with the diplomatic role emerges. In his introduction to the 1957 report[24] the weight of the Suez and Hungarian crises was so heavy that in a special section entitled 'The Role of the United Nations', he does not mention welfare projects at all. He only speaks of the UN as 'an instrument for negotiating among, and to some extent for, governments'. In the rest of the report and that of 1958[25] 'economic development' becomes the main subject of ECOSCO activities and concern, but it is never linked with larger goals and there is even a proposal to link activities to those of national governments, hardly a hoped-for functionalist evolution.

The 1959 introduction once again evaluated the organisation's role, and was considered an important enough policy statement to be reproduced and distributed in the UN pamphlet series as 'A Review of the Organisation in World Affairs'. Is it not significant then, that only six per cent of the text (less than that devoted to the ICJ or the personal role of the Secretary General) was devoted to ECOSOC and all of the specialised agencies? In addition, the content of this insignificant section was an administrative reform which would give to the UN the 'same significance in the economic field as the one which is entrusted to it in the political sphere'.[26] Hammarskjöld thus admitted that technical assistance had been much less important than the political field: he was proposing very little alteration of organisational focus.

Hammarskjöld's move away from functionalist rhetoric toward a more Wilsonian version of the UN continues in his last two years in office. 'The main field of useful activity of the United Nations ... must aim at keeping newly arising conflicts outside the sphere of bloc interests'.[27] While he does regret the 'conventional thinking which sees the Organisation only, or mainly, as a machinery for negotiation',[28] he is himself nevertheless preoccupied with preventive diplomacy rather than with active functionalism. In fact, in his final report, he categorises the organisation as falling between that of a conflict negotiator and an executive.[29] The expression of the choice in these terms seems to indicate an acceptance of the primary importance of the UN's role as a political agency, rather than as a generator of functionalist schemes.

U Thant The concern of the third Secretary General with functionalist ideology is shallow. His first report underlines poverty as being more dangerous than ideology,[30] and treats it as a technical problem which can be solved by the Development Decade. He feels that men must dedicate themselves to the task 'of making the Charter of the United Nations a living hope for all humanity; to eradicate poverty as a prime cause of conflict; and to strive energetically and purposefully toward the general welfare of mankind, as a basis for a just and enduring peace'.[31] However, the emphasis on development does not seem to have arisen from a conscious ideological concern with functionalism, but rather as a pragmatic organisational reaction to the needs of member states. With more than two thirds of its members considering themselves in the category of 'developing' nations, there was bound to be a concern with welfare. However, the insertion of all major ECOSOC projects into the Development Decade was in no way evidence of a perceived link with a peace system, nor did it reflect ideological task expansion, nor did it mirror a comprehensive view of the UN role. It reflected the organisational inability to override the concerns of a vast majority of voting members.

For Thant, as for his predecessors, a negotiated solution to political crises was the primary goal of the UN. Therefore, the objective political climate became a most crucial consideration. From 1966-1969, the Secretary General's opening paragraph in each annual report dealt with the impact of Vietnam. '[The] international political situation has not improved. . . These are conditions which, even if they strongly underline the need for the United Nations, are at the same time not conducive to the most effective action of which the Organisation is capable'.[32] In other words, political conditions inhibit effective technical co-operation. Thant is thus denying the most basic of functionalist beliefs by saying that politics is not separable from welfare. He is placing himself clearly on the side of the realists who would also agree that: 'The ultimate strength of the Organisation ... lie[s] in the degree to which its aims and activities are understood and supported by the people of the world'.[33] While human rights and emphasis on development were certainly increasing welfare concerns of the UN, Thant does not see their potential to erode conflict levels. Conflict can be stopped only by a positive commitment: 'There is but one true answer to violence, duress and intimidation among states; the answer must be found in a *resolute rejection of violence* and a determined resistance to it by the vast majority of men'.[34]

Thus, at a maximum, one could say that welfare concerns are 'an essential part'[35] of UN activities. In the rhetoric of the UN Secretaries General it is clear that functionalism has frequently been subordinated to the requirement of solving pressing political problems. The original goals of the organisation were to maintain peace and to promote the conditions necessary for a durable working peace system. In reaching this goal there were two classic methods: primary emphasis on codifying consent (Wilsonian) or on non-controversial projects to erode hostility gradually so that consent is possible (functionalism). The latter 'peace by pieces' has not been reflected in the UN Secretariat's organisational ideology, since the functionalist path is always interrupted by the need to recognise the primary political interest of governments.

Functionalism and Specialised Bodies

At this point, we shall examine briefly the rhetoric of executive heads of four specialised agencies and of the Economic Commission for Europe. By definition, specialised agencies exist to satisfy specified welfare goals, and thereby contribute to the maintenance of peace. Thus, we would expect to find more elements of functionalist ideology in the statements of their Directors General. In their origins all ECOSOC activities are dependent upon the search for security, yet this is accompanied and limited by the well-known organisational tendency to over-emphasise personal contributions. This leads us to expect a loose relationship between functional tasks and a working peace system in the sense that the programme in a specific issue area, not larger goals of a working peace system, is more immediately important.

Old Functionalist Roots: ILO The agency with the oldest functionalist heritage is the International Labour Organisation and it actually provided one of the best examples of welfare cooperation for the Bruce Commission and Mitrany. The opening sentence of its 1919 and 1972 Constitution is based upon the functionalist premise that 'universal and lasting peace can be established only if it is based upon social justice'. The means chosen during the early years were based on the social reform philosophy of Albert Thomas. The actual work of the ILO even in the immediate post Second World War years did not change to problem solving, but rather continued with drafting labour standards. The preoccupations with a functionalist strategy, as well as logic, had to wait until the appointment of David A. Morse in 1948 for their realisation. As Ernst Haas has written of Morse: 'His name has been linked with an approach to international labour problems that stresses technical assistance, education, and promotion activities in preference to legislative action . . . Morse's approach is as firmly anchored in a conception of 'situation' and 'need' as the earlier Functionalism. The source of the need is the impact of technology on society'.[36]

Morse's reports and speeches are filled with functionalist propositions. In his view, the move from standard-setting to active and promotional campaigns was justified in the long-run as a contribution to peace because disease, poverty, ignorance, and poor living conditions were unacceptable in the international system. 'It is discernible even to the most unenlightened that these are the ugly facts of life and that rapid improvement of these conditions is essential to the elimination of international strain, to the easing of international tension, and to the promotion of world peace'.[37] While the ILO ideology of Morse is the more realistic because it purports to find solutions to specific problems which are *among* the real threats to peace',[38] there is nonetheless an essential link with a total working peace system.

The expansion of ILO activities—especially with United Nations Development Programme funds—represented in part a pragmatic organisational willingness to expand its role. At the same time, however, the move away from legislation toward promotional programmes and direct action pre-dated the influx of UNDP funds. This was a direct and conscious result of Morse's desire to fulfil his highest organisational principle, 'universalism'. After the return to Geneva of the Socialist Countries—which Morse had actively pursued—the organisation had to please the USSR at the same time that it attempted not to alienate the liberal values of western trade unions. The solution was the instigation of non-controversial projects instead of value-loaded resolutions.

Welfare is the sole focus: 'Action to promote respect for human rights is a corollary to the ILO's activities directed toward the improvement of the material circumstances of life and is of fundamental importance to the achievement of the organisation's objectives as laid down by the Constitution...'.[39] In a key re-evaluation in 1960, the Office felt that 'the main objective will remain social progress, pursued in a climate of freedom, founded on increased productivity, and directed toward higher standards of living'.[40] Thus, while the economic benefits to be derived from economic development can themselves be considered as functionalist objectives, the International Labour Organisation goes further in this direction. It is self-conscious about its concern with the social welfare component of economic growth by ensuring that all growth remains compatible with individual welfare.

It is only in our last category of criteria that Morse's ideology falls short of success. Because of its fifty-three year history, the ILO has evolved a more distinctive and autonomous view of the UN than other secretariats. It does not consider its role as necessarily integrally linked to larger UN goals. Furthermore, the organisation has always been a spokesman for labour interests and looked upon itself as a pressure group for them, making confrontation instead of common calculations necessary. However, the final ideological commitment of the office under Morse, the World Employment Programme,[41] emphasises the maximum use of labour forces—instead of capital intensive methods—as the best road to development as well as providing the maximum welfare for the population. The 'sales approach' for this is truly functionalist in that it stresses that employers or governments are no longer 'enemies', but are linked in a complementarity of interests. This recognition is necessary to maximise the benefits of economic growth for workers.

The Third World's Functionalist Representative: UNCTAD The United Nations Conference on Trade and Development (UNCTAD) has, since 1964 rapidly become recognised as the official institutional framework for Third World demands for economic growth through trade. The Preamble to the 'Final Act' of the 1964 Conference conforms to our functionalist scheme, 'Recognising that universal peace and prosperity are closely linked and that economic growth of the developing countries will also contribute to the economic growth of the developed countries . . . the State signatories of the Final Act are resolved, in a sense of human solidarity, to employ international machinery for the promotion of the economic and social advancement of people'.[42]

Despite the wording of Article 55 of the UN Charter the great Power conception of economic and social affairs reflects a concern with preventing the recurrence of the economic experience of the 1930s.[44] Even if one disagrees with this unkind interpretation of motivations, GATT, IMF, and IBRD are hardly spokesmen for the interests of the economically less-developed world. In the fashion envisioned by Mitrany for the development of a new international organisation, UNCTAD arose to meet the needs of the Third World for an institutional structure. The importance of this need was noted by Raul Prebisch: 'The report is founded on the conviction that practice and action in the field of trade and development is second to no other responsibility which the United Nations, established to maintain peace, must face in the 1960s'.[44] Despite this auspicious foundation, the ideology of Prebisch is rather ambiguous in it functionalist roots, mainly because UNCTAD is so acutely political in taking the side of the 'have nots'.

There is, however, a perceived link between the institution's immediate goal and world peace: 'A notable feature of the debate was a general consensus that the search for a universal peace and the continued prosperity of the developed countries were linked to the economic growth of the developing countries'.[45] The motivation for this peace is based upon the threat of further violence: 'The marginal and redundant labour forces are building up a really explosive mixture in the peripheral communities. Everything depends on whether there is something to set it off. The detonator is very near at hand; it is to be found in the resentment and understandable dissatisfaction of all these dynamic elements when they fail to find sufficient opportunities for satisfying their vital ambitions'.[46] In this struggle, however, UNCTAD speaks for the 'group of 77' and does not remain neutral: Prebisch feels that 'the United Nations is of great significance in providing support for the weaker part of the world's political and economic system'.[47]

In the second category, task expansion, UNCTAD is typically functionalist. Prebisch resisted every pressure by the developed countries to restrict its tasks, and exerted a continual and conscious pressure to develop the organisation's role as the central focus of development efforts. 'In order to adapt them continuously to the requirements of the situation'[48] Prebisch emphasised that the organisational structure must remain flexible in problem solving: 'And if the ways of dealing with them proposed here are not acceptable, others will have to be sought which are'.[49] The development of UNCTAD itself reflects movement from requests to positive action. Reacting against politically-tied aid and the infringement of independence which resulted from it, UNCTAD members singled out trade as a specific project and vehicle for development. Thus, 'there was a widespread readiness to move from the area of generalities to that of specific tasks'.[50] Prebisch tells us in 1964 that, 'What is required is positive action',[51] and his exhaustive listing of quantitative targets, preferences, and the like are certainly a guide to action.

Not wishing to be 'unrealistic',[52] he felt that the organisation should concentrate on particular questions of international trade and finance that appeared to have reached a stage where agreement was possible, or those which were so crucial that immediate discussion could facilitate a solution when the international situation had changed. There are reasons why the UNCTAD programme in practice could be considered non-functionalist: the goals are not chosen as part of a strategy for building a working peace system, but are rather uncoordinated responses to immediate, pressing problems. And the solutions Prebisch recommended can hardly be considered as non-controversial, for present UNCTAD projects and proposals clearly reflect the political difference of opinion between the haves and have-nots, with UNCTAD clearly on the side of the latter. Similarly, the rhetoric from the top echelons of the United Nations as well as that of Prebisch referring to common interest calculations is ambiguous in its view of functionalism. 'In adopting this target [five per cent growth] the United Nations explicitly recognised that its achievement is a matter of international as well as national concern'.[53] Prebisch also denies that his aims 'would be incompatible with the clear economic interest of the industrial countries . . . Actually, the periphery could offer a vast new frontier for the expansion of trade.'[54] However, this rhetoric is rather implausible because the tangible benefits to the advanced countries are produced only in the long-run. In the short-run, they are required to make sacrifices which could prove unacceptable.

In summary, Prebisch's speeches and writings about UNCTAD clearly show functionalist elements, although there are some implied departures from the theory. We cannot improve on Gosovic's summary: 'It differs from the political organs of the United Nations in the sense that it is less political, more functionally specific, and technically oriented . . . On the other hand, it differs from the general type of specialised agencies because it is less independent, more intensely political, more functionally diffuse, and less technical at this stage of its growth'.[55]

Sclerosis of Functionalism: WHO   The third organisation to be discussed is the World Health Organisation. Its constitution states that 'the health of all peoples is fundamental to the attainment of peace', and the assigned task is certainly fertile ground for common calculations in a non-controversial area. Despite these facts, the rhetoric of the organisation is rather unenthusiastically - if at all—functionalist as health for health's sake has gradually become the organisation's main goal. One of the most obvious functionalist activities for the UN—largely because of the League precedent—was in the area of health. The Brazilian delegation in the WHO commission in 1947 quoted the 'functionalist' Cardinal Spellman that 'medicine [is] one of the pillars of peace',[56] at the same time that an independent study group saw the functionalist constitution of the WHO as 'the most far-reaching and, in a sense, revolutionary of multilateral agreements'.[57]

The first Director General, Brock Chisholm, reflected immediate post-war enthusiasm for functionalist solutions in his rhetoric. He felt that WHO projects 'will not only contribute immensely to the spread, efficiency and social acceptability of economic development, but will ultimately demonstrate the truth of one of the cardinal principles of the organisation—namely—that raising of physical, mental and social health standards will help to establish a happier and more peaceful world'.[58] He consciously sought to enlarge the role of the WHO from an emergency reference service on communicable diseases like malaria and tuberculosis to 'a system which can be said to embrace any form of assistance needed by countries for the general protection and care of health'.[59] The emphasis of all projects was on individual welfare, and Chisholm talked frequently of common perspectives and interdependence: 'The growing realisation of governments that

181

many health problems require for their effective solution the united action of all the nations'.[60] In his last report he stated that 'nothing short of complete world-mindedness is acceptable'.[61]

Marcolino G. Candau became Director General in 1953 and at first seemed to continue Chisholm's functionalist focus on eventual world order: 'WHO's role in promoting world health as comprising only one part ... of a general framework of all national and international efforts to improve social and economic conditions throughout the world',[62] which was loosely connected to world peace. However, it soon becomes clear from Candau's rhetoric, that organisational expansion and influence, and not functionalism, are his aim. Less and less attention is paid to functionalist links to peace while a greater effort is made to formulate an ideology to justify the expansion of that particular organisation. As the memory of the Second World War became less harsh, it seems that there was less pressure on Candau to talk of total solutions and of his organisation's contribution to them, but rather health is seen as important for its own sake: 'The fundamental aim is the attainment of all peoples of the highest possible level of health'.[63] An example of this trend is a report published under his direction in 1958 as the *First Ten Years of the* WHO. After a brief mention of the Second World War and health's role in peace, the rest of the five hundred and thirty nine pages are spent discussing individual organisational programmes. In 1960, in fact, Candau singles out the emergency relief in the Congo as the organisation's 'outstanding activity'. In short, organisational pragmatism which lionises organisational tasks became the core of its ideology.

The 1960s were designated the First Development Decade. One might have expected that organisational pragmatism would have led the WHO to change its focus toward more fashionable projects. Candau states that 'improvement of health must underlie any activity which aims at raising standards of living', which naturally means that health becomes the *'sine qua non* for achieving the aims of the Development Decade'.[64] One could hardly view this as 'functionalist'. Health is sought as a discrete objective within the more general framework of UN development objectives, rather than as part of a working strategy for peace.

A Functionalist Void: IBRD Thus far, we have looked at three specialised agencies the ILO which has maintained a continuous functionalist ideology; UNCTAD which has some elements of functionalist ideology; and the WHO which was originally functionalist but has recently retreated into a narrower role. The last specialised agency to be examined, the World Bank or International Bank for Reconstruction and Development (IBRD), has never really exhibited elements of functionalism.

The IBRD does not recognise any explicit links with a more general peace system even in its Articles of Agreement. Its purpose is clear: reconstruction and development. Soon after the war—because its resources were too small and because the United States' concern with European recovery were adequately covered by the Marshall Plan—the goal became only development. The Bank was to make loans not for welfare, but only for solid economic reasons. In 1949 ECOSOC debates, this policy came under attack but the Bank stood firmly behind its 'ideals' to make loans on only sound economic grounds rather than on 'social or relief grounds'.[65] Without being unduly harsh, one could fairly say that the Bank's two principles—'it wants its money well-used and it wants to be paid back'[66]—are essentially those of Western capital exporting nations.

One could conceivably consider the Bank Group as functionalist. Such an interpretation would be the following: the IBRD essentially arose to meet postwar needs and it expanded its activities naturally to deal with development problems.[67] Technical self-determination guided the shift from reconstruction to development, to the establishment of IDA (International Development Association), as well as toward the world bond market as the source of its sustenance. If one looks at functionalism as a very vague formula (need, response, modified need, modified response), this point of view is valid.[68] Such an interpretation, however, ignores all of the ideology of the Bank which is totally non-functionalist. An introductory paragraph appears in five consecutive issues of its *Policies and Operations:* 'Early in World War II the economic and financial experts of the Allied Nations began to devote their energies to planning, by appropriate international and domestic measures of production, employment, and the exchange of consumption goods which are the material foundation of the liberty and welfare of all people'.

In the strictest sense as a specialised agency, the Bank has no politics. However, the above statements and the Bank's lending criteria (generally described as 'profitable') make its real ideology clear: Western liberalism.[69] The man who was the President—not Director General—of the IBRD from 1949-1963 was Eugene Black. By training an American financial wizard, it is not surprising that he developed stringent economic criteria, and did not suddenly evince a fondness for state socialism. What is rather unusual, however, is to find the blunt political statements in his speeches which confirm that the Bank was, at least under his guidance, an element of Western diplomacy. Black's world is 'divided into the camp of freedom and the camp of Communism'.[70] It naturally follows that the World Bank is an element of economic diplomacy which 'to be successful, requires the acceptance of development aid as a more or less permanent feature of *Western* policy with a separate and distinct status of its own'.[71] The other organisations under discussion at least had purposes which could not be implemented except through cooperation, that is, they had no autonomous means to enforce their decisions. The Bank, however, does have such a weapon—money—and can use it to demand capitalist ideological purity. The Bank's annual reports are striking for their lack of functionalist ideology. Development is important for development's sake. The reports are balance sheets which discuss particular projects in particular situations with no larger vision. In the first few years, one finds an opening section entitled the 'role of the Bank' which is soon replaced by a simple financial summary, 'The Bank's Year in Review'. Even in the first few years, however, in this more ideological section, no link is established between technical assistance and peace. In fact at one point, it is denied that any erosion of loyalties is possible by technical projects, which is exactly the familiar realist contention which Mitrany tried to overcome: 'The full realisation of the Bank's potentialities cannot be expected as long as economic and financial stability in large areas of the world continues to be threatened by political tensions and unrest'.[72] The very limited purpose and role of the Bank is 'to assist its member countries to draw maximum benefit from the development process'.[73] In such an ideology, it is indicators such as numbers of kilowatts or GNP, and no longer a larger purpose, which are important.

The birth of the International Development Association (IDA) in November 1960 has been considered as a relaxation of this mixture of the protestant ethic and capitalism. The staff itself explains: 'Some countries have already begun to draw close to the limit of debt they can prudently assume on conventional terms. It was an awareness of this problem which led to the founding of the International Development Association'.[74] The IDA constitution reflects a veritable functionalist credo: 'Mutual cooperation for constructive economic purposes, healthy development of the world economy, and balanced growth of international trade foster international relations conducive to the maintenance of peace'. IDA loans are made to the poorest of nations on easier credit than is available on the market. However, if one examines the needs of the World Bank, one realises that it was also the Bank and not only the poorer nations who needed the IDA. As debt servicing and political upheaval became more widespread, the Bank found itself rich but with few clients. The potential clientele of IDA, however, was limitless although its resources were completely inadequate. In addition, Bank investments were accruing an embarrassing interest balance which had to be used in face of the growing complaints from a more vociferous Third World. Black himself was never a supporter of easy credit policies. According to Andrew Shonfield, Black 'never liked the idea of "soft loans" but if they had to come he was going to make certain that he was the man who handled them'.[75]

Black himself comments on our functionalist concerns: 'It may seem to take a considerable feat of mental gymnastics to connect what I have been saying with the noble ends of world peace'.[76] The authors must agree with Black on this point. For by concentrating on 'economic development as if its only end were higher consumption and greater comfort',[77] the important questions of development and the ultimate logic of functionalism are completely avoided. In fact, it becomes almost anti-functionalist by assigning a subsidiary role to welfare: 'social services, they, too, are made *possible* by economic growth just as they are made *necessary* by economic growth'.[78] Therefore, for Black and the World Bank the aim of economic development is economic development for its own sake. Black's successors, George Woods and Robert McNamara, have also underlined these large differences with the idea of functionalism. Woods comments: 'Many of the most important factors affecting economic progress, such as social attitudes, population growth and forms of government, lie beyond the realm of financial institutions'.[79] McNamara demonstrates a kind of distorted functionalist logic by identifying the final aim of Mitrany's system, peace, as identical to the Bank's small functional task: *'Le Développement, c'est la Paix'.*[80]

It must be noted that the rhetoric of McNamara—while still embodying the essentials of Black's financial criteria—has begun to reflect some concerns of the 1970s. On 27 September 1971 before the Bank's Board of Governors, for instance, he said: 'Development has for too long been expressed simply in terms of growth and output. There is now emerging the awareness that the availability of work, the distribution of income, and the quality of life are equally important measures of development'. He has also changed programme emphases to eduction and agriculture, programmes which would never have been approved in the Black era. On balance, however, the strong anti-functionalist impact of Black—not to mention the influence of McNamara's background—remains a powerful force at the Bank's headquarters.

Regional Functionalism: ECE The Economic Commission for Europe (ECE) was established in 1947 and the first ten years of its existence coincided with a particularly high level of tension between the two principal groups of its members.

This tension resulted in the refusal of Socialist countries to participate in the greater part of ECE activities and, consequently, in the transformation of most of its subordinate bodies into purely Western groups.[81]

Gunnar Myrdal, who served as the Executive Secretary of ECE during it first ten years, refused to consider such a state of affairs as acceptable. In 1953 Myrdal, told delegates that . . . our Committees are gradually being transformed into purely Western bodies—perhaps I should more adequately say non-Eastern European bodies. This situation is, to say the least, awkward for all of you, and it is not tenable'.[82] In Myrdal's view this untenable situation could be mainly overcome as a result of fundamental changes in the East-West political processes which were not forthcoming. In the meantime, however, a number of 'business-like' activities carried out under the Commission's auspices could contribute to the improvement of intra-European relations and more generally to peace. Although Mydral never referred explicitly to any form of functionalist ideology when addressing the various Commission bodies, the implications of his warnings, advice and prescriptive criticisms addressed through the delegates to the European governments and the United States stemmed from a set of principles which are either part of, or very much akin to, the functionalist approach to international organisations.

First, he stressed that the ". . . Commission cannot be preserved merely as an empty structure with the sole purpose and function that it constitutes a reserve for the future. The Commission can exist only as long as active committees and working parties provide the indispensable under-structure . . . The Commission is a technical instrument which the United Nations, at considerable costs, have placed at the disposal of the governments in this region. It is an instrument for intergovernmental cooperation, and only on the condition that this instrument is usefully employed for its purposes by the governments in the region, can the United Nations' decision to create and maintain the Commission, and defray its costs, be justified'.[83] Stated differently, Myrdal was telling delegates that an organisation loses its *raison d'être* if it is emptied of its function and substance. Organisation maintenance cannot be an end in itself and the reification of institutions was condemned by Myrdal with a vigour equal to that of Mitrany.

The Executive Secretary chose to reiterate the second principle guiding his action at a most improbable time, in 1949, when the Cold War had resulted in a division of Europe reducing all-European transactions to their lowest level since the war. In his opening statement to the Commission's Annual Session, in 1949, Gunnar Myrdal stressed the need for ECE to become a real 'operational instrument for the reconstruction and development of the European economy', going beyond its function as a 'forum of economic discussion'.[84] This insistence on the need for concrete action, in order to overcome the divisions in the political sphere, was expressed during Myrdal's entire period in office. In addition, the greater the political obstacles, the stronger were the expressions of the Secretariat's determination to contribute to European peace by promoting functional cooperative activities.

Thirdly, Myrdal's refusal to assign other than a symbolic value to procedural questions was the necessary corollary to his general outlook concerning functional, 'business-like' cooperation. Speaking of voting, he said in 1955 that 'it is indicative of intergovernmental organisations that on more substantive issues voting has no . . . significance. No important political and economic problems can be solved in an intergovernmental organisation by a majority vote. A vote, if it is taken, must

185

remain a demonstration'.[85] On numerous other occasions as well, Myrdal seized every opportunity to set aside procedural questions, moving directly to the functional part of meetings organised under his auspices. Explaining to astonished diplomats and other national officials that he had no time to waste on trivial matters, he invited them to get down to 'business' as the Secretariat had defined it.

Lastly, Myrdal adhered to an essential functionalist principle concerning the need to have 'certain functions and, therefore, certain powers . . . collectively delegated' by governments participating in the work of international organisations: 'In every organisation which is not entirely futile the secretariat is awarded such functions and powers. There are, of course, great differences that are, as a matter of fact, not closely related to constitutional rules but more to practices as they develop and gradually acquire the character of common law. Favourable factors for the development of a wide area of delegations of functions in the secretariat are the presence in the particular case of a certain workable minimum of interest convergence between the governments in some well-defined issues, and also naturally the degree of confidence the secretariat has secured among the governments'.[86] Such transfers of functionally well-defined powers to centres operating outside, if not above, national governmental machineries are an essential part of any functionalist approach to international organisation. The ECE's first Executive Secretary obtained from member governments limited and temporary transfers of powers, even at times of high political tension. The exercise of these powers in an impartial manner even if it did not contribute directly to the lessening of tension, at least limited the extension of the areas of tension by making possible certain functional solutions of problems which would have otherwise been added to the long list of issues on which the East-West confrontation was developing during the early years of the Commission's existence.

Conclusion

We have thus examined the extent to which functionalist ideology has marked the professed ideology of the UN Secretaries General, the Directors General of several specialised agencies, and the first Executive Secretary of the ECE. Obviously, ideology is not the equivalent of reality, but it has been our fundamental assumption that it is certainly a strong indication of what bureaucracies think they are doing and hope to accomplish.

The UN and its specialised agencies were carefully kept from becoming supranational agencies. They were designed to be instruments taking their instructions from individual governments. Mitrany's functionalism, however, wanted to use non-controversial, non-political welfare programmes at the international level as a strategy for eroding gradually the basis of national loyalty and fear of supranational control. Mitrany's theory depended upon international civil servants who were convinced of his logic. Our analysis has shown that in their public statements key international civil servants are hesitant about committing themselves to functionalist propositions. The Secretaries General of the UN have never lost a desire to emphasise political actions so that ECOSOC has always been relegated to a second-class status. At the level of the specialised agencies, there were, however, varying degrees of functionalist orthodoxy—usually less rather than more. There was frequently an ambiguous attitude toward functionalist logic and sometimes an implied hostility. Another important factor was that institutions tended to lionise their own role: Functionally specific tasks became ends in themselves rather than a means to further integration. Instead of a minimum prescription for the erosion of state authority, organisational tasks became the institutions' overriding goals. In this context, it is possible that functionalism as a theory remains to be tested. Nevertheless, some international civil servants such as Gunnar Myrdal were convinced and practising functionalists. In his ten years at the head of ECE, he demonstrated more dramatically, if not more effectively than others, the value of a functionalist approach as a contribution to the building of a lasting peace system.

Notes and references

1 Egon Ranshofen-Wertheimer, *International Secretariat*, Washington, D.C., Dotation Carnegie, 1945, pp. 160-161.
2 Victor-Yves Ghébali, *La société des Nations et la Réforme Bruce, 1939-40*, Genève, Dotation Carnegie, 1970, and chapter above.
3 Ruth Russell, *A History of the United Nations*, Menosha, Wisconsin. Banta Co, 1958, p.421.
4 Francis Walters, *A History of the League of Nations*, London. Oxford, 1952, vol. 1.
5 Russell, *op.cit.*, p.957-958.
6 As an example, see *Preliminary Report*, Commission to study the Organisation of the Peace, New York, November 1940, p.11.
7 *Ibid.*, p.9.
8 *Ibid.*, p.13.
9 *1951 Annual Report of the Secretary General*, A/1844/add.1, p.7, (hereafter ARSG).
10 *1948* ARSG, A/565, p.xv-xvi.
11 *1946* ARSG, A/65, p.iii.
12 *Ibid.*, p.vi.
13 *1950* ARSG, A/1287, p.xiii.
14 Emphasis added, *1947* ARSG, A/315, p.viii.
15 *1951* ARSG, A/1844/add.1, p.7.
16 *1949* ARSG, A/930, p.xii.
17 *1952* ARSG, A/2141/add.1.
18 A/2404 and A/2663.
19 *1953* ARSG, A/2404, p.xii.
20 *1954* ARSG, A/2663, p.xiii.
21 *1953* ARSG, p.xii.
22 *1954* ARSG, p.xiii.
23 *1956* ARSG, A/2911 and A3137.
24 *1957* ARSG, A/3594/add.1, p.3.
25 *1958* ARSG, A/3844.
26 *1959* ARSG, A/4132/add.1, p.3.
27 *1960* ARSG, A/4390/add. 1, p.4.
28 *Ibid.*, p.8.
29 *1961* ARSG, A/4800/add.1, p.1.
30 *1962* ARSG, A/5201/add.1, p.3.
31 *Ibid.*, p.3.
32 *1966* ARSG, A/6301/add.1, p. 1.
33 *Ibid.*, p.2.
34 *1967* ARSG, A/6701/add.1, p.18 emphasis added.
35 *1968* ARSG, A/7201/add.1, p.10.

36 Ernst B. Haas, *Beyond The Nation State,* Stanford; Stanford University Press, 1964, p.169. The authors are very grateful for the work of Haas in this area. One reason this section is brief is that we assume most readers are familiar with Ch. 6-7, 'Organizational Ideology, 1919-1948, 1948-1963'.

37 *1950 Report of the Director General* p.3 (hereafter RDG).

38 *1951* RDG, p.2, emphasis added.

39 *1959* RDG, Part II, p.68.

40 'Appraisal of the ILO Program, 1959-1964'. *Official Bulletin,* XLIII, 1960, p.3.

41 *1969* RDG.

42 *Proceedings of* UNCTAD, vol.I, New York, United Nations Press, 1964, p.3.

43 Branislav Gosovic, UNCTAD: *Conflict and Compromise,* Leiden, A.W. Sijthoff, 1972, esp. pp. 3-27.

44 Raul Prebisch, *Towards a New Trade Policy for Development,* New York, United Nations Press, 1964, p.ix.

45 'Report of the Trade and Development Board', 1965, UNCTAD, A/6023/rev.1, p.5. (after "Report").

46 Raul Prebisch, *Towards a Global Strategy for Development,* New York: United Nations Press, 1968, p.12.

47 Raul Prebisch before GATT, 17 January 1967, TD/B/114, p.7.

48 Raul Prebisch, *Towards a Global Strategy for Development,* p.7.

49 Raul Prebisch, *Towards a New Trade Policy for Development,* p.125.

50 *"Report", p.5.*

51 Raul Prebisch, *Towards a New Trade Policy for Development,* p.122.

52 Raul Prebisch, 16 August 1967, TD/B/146.

53 U Thant in introduction to Prebisch, *Towards a New Trade Policy for Development,* p.vi.

54 Raul Prebisch, *Towards a Global Strategy for Development,* p.6.

55 Gosovic, *op.cit.,* p.265.

56 *First Ten Years of* WHO, Geneva, 1958, p. 38.

57 'Uniting the Nations for Health', Report to Commission for the Study and Organisation of the Peace, New York, 1947, p.23.

58 *1950 Annual Report of the Director General of* WHO, E/2020, p.2. (after ARW).

59 *Ibid.,* p.1.

60 *1949* ARW, E/1677. p.v.

61 *1952* ARW, E/2416, p.v.

62 *1953* ARW, E/2592, p.v.

63 *1958* ARW, E/3235, p.vi.

64 *1962* ARW, E/3752, p.v-vi.

65 Robert L. Garner, Vice-President of World Bank, *New York Times,* 26 April 1949, p.41.

66 James Morris, *The World Bank,* London, Faber and Faber, 1963, pp.64-65. While Morris himself does not use these words, he clearly refers to the Bank's 'Huddersfield' politics as essentially trying to bring the industrial revolution with all of its puritan values to the Third World.

67 In *'A Working Peace System',* London, Royal Institute of International Affairs, 1943, pp.36-40. Mitrany makes a reference to two hypothetical agencies which he calls 'International Investment Board' and 'International Development Commission'.

68 James Patrick Sewell, develops this thesis in *Functionalism and World Politics,* Princeton, Princeton University Press, 1966.

69 Morris quotes *Time Magazine* on p.185: 'Dollar for Dollar, the World Bank has proved itself one of the most effective weapons in the Cold War'.

70 Eugene Black, *The Diplomacy of Economic Development*, Cambridge, Mass. Harvard University Press, 1960, p.14.
71 *Ibid*, pp.44-45, emphasis added.
72 *1947-1948 Annual Report of the World Bank*, E/1077, p.6. (after A R W B),
73 *1953-1954* A R W B, E/2668, p.1.
74 *'The World Bank and the Americas'*, January 1962, pamphlet, pp.99-100.
75 Andrew Shonfield, *The Attack on World Poverty*, New York, Prager, 1962, p.156.
76 Eugene Black, 'The Age of Economic Development', speech at Oxford, 3 March 1960, p.8
77 *Ibid.*, p.6.
78 Eugene Black, 'Tale of Two Continents', Ferdinand Phinizv Lectures at the University of Georgia, 12-13 April 1961, p.28, emphasis in original.
79 *1962-1963* A R W B, E/3836, p.6.
80 'Discours devant le Conseil des Gouverneurs', 30 September 1968, p.1.
81 For a cursory view of the ECE Secretariat during its first ten years, see: Jean, Siotis, 'The Secretariat of the United Nations Economic Commission for Europe and European Economic Integration: The First Ten Years, in *International Organisation*, Vol. 19(2), 1965, pp.177-202.
82 United Nations Document E/ECE/148, p.2
83 United Nations Document E/ECE/154, p.5
84 Opening statement of the Executive Secretary on May 9, 1949, (mimeographed).
85 Gunnar Myrdal, *Realities and Illusions in Regard to Intergovernmental Organisations*, L.T. Hobbouse Memorial Trust, Lecture, London, Oxford University Press, 1955, p.7.
86 *Ibid.*, pp.21-22.

Transnational Associations and their Functions

Anthony J N Judge and Kjell Skjelsbaek

The purpose of this chapter is to describe and discuss a particular set of actors in the global social system which, in an historical perspective, may be considered newcomers on the scene. They are frequently called international non-governmental organisations (INGOs)[1], and this term covers a wide variety of organisational units with many and different functions. Our objective is not to put INGOs into a comprehensive theoretical model, but to give a description of them and their relationships and activities using ideas and terms borrowed from the theory of functionalism. First of all we shall discuss the context and concept of INGOs. Then we shall present some data showing the growth and spread of the INGO system. The following section is a presentation of what INGOs typically do, and what functions they perform. On the basis of this we will then try to outline what we think are likely future trends, and we conclude this chapter with a number of policy recommendations, aimed at increasing the effectiveness of INGOs and improving their relationship with other kinds of actors in the international system.

The Context and Concept of INGOs

In this section we want to widen the range of types of organisation (rather than organisations) prior to isolating those entities that conventionally are termed INGOs. The suggestion therefore is that many statements made elsewhere in this text are also applicable to styles of organisation found outside these narrow limits.

The Concept of an Organisation. There are many factors which determine the manner in which different functions are associated with particular styles of organisation drawn from the wide range of possibilities of kinds of organisation. An attempt at isolating some different combinations is presented in Table 1, which in no way is intended to be definitive, but is really an indication of how some different styles of organisation may be distinguished. One example of how a need satisfied by a conventional organisation may be satisfied by a functional equivalent in the table is the case of a 'subscriptionship'. In one setting it may be necessary to have interaction between members via an 'organization', while in another the need for such interaction may be satisfied by a journal to which individuals can subscribe. Another example is the case of an 'agreement' which may be considered an hyperformal organisation. In one setting a written or even verbal agreement may satisfactorily regulate relations between members, in another an equivalent agreement may have to be administered by a secretariat via an organisation. Where

*This paper is identifiable as PRIO Publication 22-37, from the International Peace Research Institute, Oslo.

Table 1: Different forms of organisation

Form of organisation	Effort to achieve membership	Activity level of members	Formality	Ephemerality
Conventional	M/H	M	H	L
Ad hoc org.	M/H	H	M	H
Meeting series	M/H	M	H	M
One meeting in a series	H	H	H	H
Demonstration	H	H	L	H
Movement	H	M	L	L
Campaign	H	H	M	M
Invisible college	M	L	L	L
Beliefship	L	L	L	L
Spectatorship (sport)	H	L	L	H
Subscribership	L	L	L	M
Listenership	M	L	L	H
Consumership (material goods)	M	M/H	L	M/H
Employeeship	H	H	H	L
Information system	M	M	M	L
Agreement	L/H	H	L	L
Primary group	L/H	H	L	L

Key: High = H, medium = M, and low = L.

formal agreement is not possible, an 'organisation' may even perform the necessary mediating or negotiating functions between its members. A final example is the case of a meeting, and particularly large regular meetings, in a series. In terms of activity, this may be more significant than a small normally constituted organisation.

One consequence of focusing on conventional organisations only is that functional equivalents, particularly in non-Western cultures[2], are excluded from the analysis thus introducing cultural bias and jeopardising comparative studies. Another consequence is that even with a certain culture an 'organisational analysis' will exclude many styles of organisation performing functions which mesh with those of the organisations we are trying to isolate for closer scrutiny in this chapter, thus rendering the analysis incomplete. A complicating feature is that a conventional organisation may, for example, perform functions for a 'membership', but at the same time produce a periodical which serves as a focal point for a 'subscribership' which is not identical nor co-terminous with the membership. A further complicating feature derives from the dynamics of a social system in that the growth or decay of a particular organisation form may be accompanied by transference of functions to another organisation form, for instance due to change in technology. The ability to accomplish this transference may be hindered by inertial features, such as vested interests identified with particular patterns of organisation.

Finally, it is useful to consider what may be termed 'potential' organisation, namely the facility with which a network of interacting bodies can gel out appropriate organisation forms and combinations of members in response to each new detected need. Such organisations come into existence when required but otherwise only exist potentially—their potential existence obviates the need for a permanent organisation in the domain in question.[3]

International vs. national. There is a series of problems connected with this dimension. Some organisations may have members from one or two nations, but financial support from one only.[4] Their *activities* may be geared towards the international system as such, towards the domestic situation in a specified set of countries or towards one single country regardless of the structure of the *membership* and/or financial contributions. In addition there is a difficulty connected with the distinction between manifest and latent functions. Activities of typically national NGOs to solve national problems—for instance a strike organised by a trade union—may very well have unintended repercussions in other nations thus affecting inter-nation relationships. Any cutting point is therefore bound to be arbitrary (see Table 2). The conventional requirements are that an INGO must have members and financial support from at least three different countries and the intention to cover operations in as many.

There is a further problem for many organisations in that the nationality of members, funding and activity or office location may be considered of little significance to the members—the organisation is not territorially-oriented. In such cases the term 'transnational' is more appropriate.[5]

The distinction between universal and regional organisations should be mentioned in this connection. About 70 per cent of all conventional INGOs are in principle open to persons and organisations from all countries, but only a fraction of these are in fact truly universal in their membership. Some of the regional organisations limit their field of operation to a certain continent, for example, Africa, or to some other geographical area, for instance the Mediterranean. Others recruit members only from those nations that are members of a certain inter-governmental organisation, for instance the European Communities.

Table 2: National/International Dimension

This dimension can in fact be applied to three distinct features of an organisation, namely its representativeness, activities, or fields of interest.

1   Universal organisation with countries from all continents as members. A distinction can be made between such organisations which permit representatives from states and territories, and organisations which only permit territories to be represented via states. A distinction can also be made between universal organisations which have major offices in one continent, and those which have major offices in all continents.
2   Political bloc organisations (e.g. Atlantic bodies)
3   Bi-continental organisations (e.g. Afro-Asian)
4   Continental organisations (e.g. Asian)
5   Sub-continental organisations (e.g. Scandinavian)

6 Bi-lateral organisations

7 Organisations with the majority (e.g. 75%) of its members, or officers, or funds from one country. There are two subtypes, those with their most important activities in the one country only, and those with much activity in other countries.

8 National organisations specifically interested in world affairs and international institutions, or with action programmes and offices in foreign countries.

9 International organisations under the control or domination of one person or family (e.g. multinational business enterprises or empires controlled by Onassis, Getty, Baron Empain, Du Pont family, etc.; Avery Brundage and the International Olympic Committee).

10 Groupings of INGOs with their headquarters in one country or city. (Federation of International Associations established in Belgium; Federation of Semi-official and Private International Institutions established in Geneva.)

11 National NGOs recognised as 'international' by receiving consultative status with UN (ECOSOC) or its agencies
All India Women's Conference
American Foreign Insurance Association
Japan Atomic Industrial Forum, Inc.
National Association of Manufacturers of the USA

12 Activities in a particular country directed by international boards.
Jungfraujoch Scientific Station
Zoological Station of Naples
International Auschwitz Committee
International Action Committee to Safeguard the Monuments of Nubia.

13 INGOs in which the base country and its nationals remain of pre-eminent importance.
Royal Commonwealth Society
Royal Overseas League.

14 National NGOs having a role recognized by and with respect to an international convention.
International Committee of the Red Cross (with respect to the Geneva Conventions)

15 International organisations which support, develop or commemorate the projects of one individual
International Grotius Foundation for the Propagation of the Law of Nations
Krishnamurti Foundation
International Heinrich Schütz Society
Hubbard Association of Scientologists International

16 National or subnational NGOs studying or facilitating transnational processes in general (as opposed to activities in a number of particular foreign countries) e.g. international relations and peace research institutes.

Nongovernmental vs. governmental. The concept of a 'nongovernmental' organisation is an extremely difficult one to handle satisfactorily. The definition at the international level derives from a compromise wording in the early days of the United Nations.[6]

Table 3 shows some of the many borderline areas (points 2-13) which are treated as 'nongovernmental'. The current crisis in INGO-UN relations[7] is in part due to the fact that the narrow Western concept of an NGO is not re-examined. (There is also a suspicion that the prefix 'non-' may translate badly into some non-Indo-European language and culture settings and give the sense of 'anti-', or at least a 'non-kosher' connotation.) More or less successful imitations exist as functional equivalents in non-Western societies, but frequently with a strong governmental component making them 'mixed' or 'intersect' organisations.[8] The government or party influenced 'NGOs' in socialist countries tend to be viewed as political front organisations by the West, whereas the socialist countries tend to view Western 'NGOs' as fronts for secret service activities. A more sophisticated typology is required.

Table 3: Governmental/Nongovernmental Dimension

1 *Conventional intergovernmental bodies*
   Administration of an intergovernmental agreement
   Ministerial level organisation
   Joint military command
   Technical agency
2 *Semi-formal contact mechanisms between top government officials*
   Corps diplomatique
   Inter-Parliamentary Union
   Ententes cordiales
   Bilderberg meetings (Prince Berhnard), Encuentros Siglo XX
3 INGOs *with government agencies or government-run bodies as members*
   International Air Transport Association
   International Secretariat for Volunteer Service
   International Criminal Police Organisation (INTERPOL)/International Union
      of Official Travel Organisations
4 INGOs *with major government involvement*
   INGOs with governments as members (e.g. International Union for the
      Conservation of Nature and Natural Resources, International Institute of
      Administrative Sciences, International Council of Scientific Unions)
   Intersect or Mixed organisations
   Government technical people in INGOs (in unofficial capacities)
   INGOs administered by officials on government payrolls
   INGOs receiving office space or facilities from governments
   INGOs funded principally by governments or IGOs.
5 *Staff associations of intergovernmental agencies*
   Individual staff associations of the UN, UNESCO, EEC, etc.
   Federation of International Civil Servants Associations (which groups about 30
      of the above associations)
6 INGOs *with a strong involvement in a given party line whose status may change*
   dramatically if that party achieves or loses political power
   INGOs specifically aligned with a political party
   'Peoples' organisations' in the Marxist sense
   International political parties
   International organisations of political parties
   Front organisations
7 *(International)* NGOs *with a commitment to change governments*

International revolutionary organisations (e.g. Organisation of Afro-Asian Latin American Peoples Solidarity)

Liberation movements(*)

Assembly of Captive European Nations

8 *National government agencies with 'nongovernmental' international programmes*

National governmental agencies with international programmes

Secret Services (e.g. CIA, KGB)

9 *Government-controlled enterprises*

Inter-governmental (profit-making) enterprises (e.g. Eurofima and Eurochemic)

Multinational enterprises with governmental shareholders

Mutual Assistance of the Latin-American Government Oil Companies (ARPEL)

10 *Nongovernmental organisations having a role recognised by and with respect to an intergovernmental convention*

International Committee of the Red Cross (with respect to the Geneva Convention)

11 Transnational bodies to which state-recognised churches report (e.g. Vatican)

12 *International Educational Institutes*

College of Europe (Bruges)

Institut Universitaire Européen (Florence)

University of the United Nations (proposed)

13 *Orders of Chivalry* (**)

Sovereign Military Order of Malta

Order of Knights Templar

(*) Recognised and heard by the UN Security Council meeting in Addis Ababa in 1972

(**) For a treatment as organisations, see: Gunnar Boalt et.al. *The European Orders of Chivalry (a sociological perspective).* Stockholm, Norstedt, 1971, 151 p.

Non-profit vs. Profit. Within the UN context, which originated the term NGO, there is no specific restriction on recognition of nongovernmental organisations which themselves have profit making objectives. To date, however, of the 350 organisations in consultative status with ECOSOC, more have such objectives—although some, as for example the various trade associations, are attempting more to facilitate profit making on the part of their members.[9] Many aspects of nonprofit status are indicated in Table 4.

Tax Law may further confuse the issue by recognising some nonprofit bodies as having 'charitable status' or as being 'benevolent' or 'philanthropic'. This varies very much from country to country.

Table 4: Profit/Nonprofit Dimension

1 All resources received as untied donations, subsidies, or grants

2 Some resources received in exchange for services at cost (e.g. consultancy or sale of publications)

3 Some resources received as a profit on services performed (e.g. consultancy or sale of publications)

4 All resources received as a profit on services performed, but profits are used to

develop the organisation and are never redistributed to shareholders (e.g. not-non-profit research institutes such as the Battele Memorial Institute)

5   Government-controlled and possibly subsidised (i.e. where profit is not the major criteria, e.g. nationalised enterprises, possibly with international operations)

6   Intergovernmental business enterprises created by intergovernmental agreement (e.g. European Company for the Chemical Processing of Irradiated Fuels, European Company for the Financing of Railway Rolling Stock)

7   Nonprofit corporations created or sustained by profit corporations and receiving direct subsidies from the 'parent' body (e.g. Esso European Research Laboratory (Research functions only), ITT Europe (administrative functions only), certain corporation-created foundations)

8   Organisations which in themselves are non-profit, but from which members derive financial profit by the regulatory and exclusive features arising from membership (e.g. trade unions, and certain professional bodies; trade associations and chambers of commerce)

9   Profit-making enterprises in the conventional sense

10 Joint business ventures and consortia (in which it is the members and not the temporary linking body which makes the profit)

11 Corporations forced by size and social forces to recognize that profit-making is not an adequate criterion for decision on long-term survival.

12 Business enterprises in the socialist-country style, where profit *per se* is not a favoured objective although increasingly introduced for purposes of evaluation and incentive

13 Consortia and consultative groups of agencies and corporations prepared to invest in developing countries (e.g. under the aegis of the World Bank)

14 Illegal enterprises which may in themselves be nonprofit to facilitate profit-making by members (international cartels, trusts and combines, and possibly 'organised crime')

15 Cooperatives run for profit although 'non-profit' in that the economic benefits are distributed back to members as users.

Voluntary vs. Nongovernmental. 'Voluntary' is as subject to confusion as 'nongovernmental'. Many INGOs have 'voluntary bodies' as members, and may even have programmes administered by 'volunteers'. But on the other hand, many differ from profit-making bodies only in the lack of a profit-objective, and would oppose the label 'voluntary'.[10] There is a tendency to treat 'voluntary agencies' as a special class of INGOs with programmes for developing countries.

Legal Status. INGOs are fictional entities in terms of international law. They are international 'outlaws'.[11] This is true of both profit and nonprofit organizations. No international convention exists to supply either with legal status. In both cases they are treated as national organisations in the country where they are headquartered[12] and as 'foreign' organisations in other countries.

This situation has had a marked negative influence on the thinking of scholars unwilling to recognise any body not accorded existence by law. Even at the national level, however, many organisations remain unincorporated for a variety of reasons—one of which may be the illegality of their activities.

Organised crime is an important feature of the social system, at least through the

196

influence of the 'nationwide cartel and confederation', 'the single loosely-knit conspiracy' operating in the United States, and most probably through other related international crime syndicates, about which information is unobtainable*. In some respects organised crime resembles a set of normal profit-making enterprises, although illegal; in others, the underlying 'family structure' (as with the Tong secret societies) is significant; or, as a totality, it may be a network of loosely-knit structures, possibly with a central arbitrating 'commission'. International organised crime is almost entirely ignored in analyses of governmental and business systems due to its 'abnormalities', but aside from this falling into a catchall category of INGOs it may through its functions as a network of pressure groups or established structures and properties bear a strong resemblance to the legitimate network of associations (as well as infiltrating some, such as unions and trade associations). Such organisations may perform some positive functions.[13]

Salience. Organisations may be distinguished by their visibility to the public eye. There appears to be a tendency to study the most visible.[14]

The following range should however be considered:
(a) secret societies (e.g. Freemasons), organised crime (e.g. Mafia), secret services (e.g. CIA), and liberation movements.
(b) deliberately not publicised for political reasons (e.g. Bilderberg Group), for reasons of profit (e.g. certain trade association-cum-cartels).
(c) known but closed to the 'nonqualified' public (e.g. certain professional association) or bodies with deliberately high entrance fees (e.g. exclusive with international reciprocity of membership).
(d) known and open to the interested.
(e) deliberately publicised (e.g. certain mass movements and proselytising organisations).

Duration. There is a marked tendency in sociology and political science to focus on 'permanent' organisations—particularly since they are reliable generators of comparable data for diachronic studies. Organisations are, of course, not permanent and in the case of business enterprises the average life may be as low as five years in the US. Less easily documented is the organisation associated with a single meeting—which may extend over five years with international meetings of 10 000 people—but which nevertheless may substitute for an ad hoc organisation with a regular meeting series.

Of increasing importance are temporary bodies specially incorporated for a specific task and generally grouping a number of permanent bodies. The most ambitious examples of these are the International Geophysical Year and the International Quiet Sun Year[15], which grouped a wide range of bodies. The boundary between such activities and international 'programmes' launched, for example, by the United Nations, may be unclear. Such bodies as the United Nations Development Programme gelled out of other UN programmes as an 'organisation' only halfway through the first UN Development Decade which became its major concern. Programmes and meetings may act as functional substitutes for conventional organisations.

* 'Our knowledge of the structure which makes 'organised crime' organised is somewhat comparable to the knowledge of Standard Oil which could be gleaned from interviews with gasoline station attendants.'

It is a moot point as to what degree of impermanence should be considered a cut off point. The informal temporary alliances between delegations with respect to an agenda point at an international conference can be of great significance during the hours they last. It is in this time period that much 'organisation' is created, modified and dissolved. A process oriented perspective would attempt to isolate any relative invariance as being significant.

Levels of Coordination. There is a prevailing assumption, particularly in UN circles, that every international NGO has national association members or branches. There is also a tendency to assume that the secretariat or executive committee has no constitutional limitation on its control over a national affiliate[16]. The reality of the situation is that there are many combinations of membership and degrees of control. Of particular significance is the emergence of international NGOs (e.g. the Council for International Organisations of Medical Sciences). In some cases, the member international NGOs may themselves have international NGOs as members (e.g. the International Council of Scientific Unions) and the latter type may in turn be member of several general conferences of International NGOs (e.g. the Conference of Nongovernmental Organisations in Consultative Status with ECOSOC). This phenomena may repeat itself at the national level (e.g. the American Council of Learned Societies) to give a complex multi-level structure separating the ultimate member from the highest level of coordination. This structuring and the potential of this mechanism has not been subject to academic scrutiny.

Cross-modality.[17] A given organisation's programme may be restricted to a mix of one or two concerns—typically:
— problem focus, i.e. where solutions to real world problems is of major concern
— discipline focus, i.e. where development of methodology, skills or theory is primary
— profession focus, i.e. where job security, status, remuneration, or possibly ethics, is primary.
More sophisticated organisations are faced with the interaction between these concerns and their integration within a viable and socially responsible strategy. The extent of this cross-modal integration could be an important means of highlighting particularly significant bodies. Other possible modes of importance might include: policy-making, programme management, education and public information. Lack of cross-modal coordination tends to give rise to 'spastic', autonomous effects in the social system.

Multidisciplinarity. Organisations may also be usefully distinguished by the range of disciplines which they attempt to work with or relate to. Many international organisations are concerned to interrelate different relevant perspectives expressed through member or sub-sections activity. To the extent that such activity is coordinated through complex multilevel structures, the integrative potential of the top most layer is high. There do, however, appear to be certain parallels between behaviour with respect to geographical and functional territory which merit study to avoid a repetition in a new domain of the existing territorial conflict.[44]

Participativeness. The participativeness of an organisation is especially important in the case of nongovernmental organisations. Potential members or supporters experiencing an organisation as non-participative will tend to allocate their resources to more participative groups. NGO activity as a whole may in some respect be considered a participative alternative to governmental activity—although there is a definite bureaucratisation of NGO activity which suggests that youth and volunteer movements represent a still more participative wave. There is need for measures of degree of participativeness, for example:

— Decisions are reached through the unanimous sense of the meeting, or in face-to-face groups.
— Decisions are by majority vote with every facility for the expression of minority views.
— Decisions are made by an in-group and then approved by an assembly in a democratic vote following appropriate speeches by the leaders.
— Decisions are made by an in-group and then presented in appropriate speeches by leaders.
— Decisions are made by a charismatic leader or dictator.

Autonomy. It is a truism that no organisation exists in splendid isolation. However, the extent of organisational inter-dependence is not well recognised. This may extend to a point where the boundaries between organisations or their sub-sections are fixed arbitrarily for legal, fiscal or funding convenience but do not constitute a meaningful boundary in the working activity of most of those involved. Organisations may be conceived as embedded in a network to a degree in some cases that the links in the network between organisations are of greater importance than the nodes, i.e. the organisations themselves.[18]

Conventional INGOs. The above paragraphs indicate the range and complexity of nongovernmental organisations in society. The UN system faced with this complexity in 1946 introduced, in Article 71 of its Charter a negative definition of NGO which in fact established no clear cut off points on any of the above dimensions. UN practice has, however, resulted in recognition as NGO of Western-style 'permanent organisations' with an 'established headquarters', a constitution and, where possible, members in a 'substantial number' of countries.

This definition has tended to disguise sociological reality, although it is convenient for some practical administrative purposes. Clearly it only discloses a small proportion of the activity which would be detected with a more comprehensive acceptance of styles of social organisation. The legalistic definition appears to result in embarrassment over such categories of organisation as churches (e.g. the Roman Catholic Church), youth movements, 'people organisations' (e.g. in the style of the Peoples Republic of China) and liberation movements. A new attitude and terminology is required. Perhaps 'transnational association networks' would be better—although to it should be added such adjectives as dynamic, evolving, adaptive, participative, and the like.

In the remainder of this article attention will be confined to conventional INGOs as recognised in the *Yearbook of International Organisations*. This means (i) permanent bodies with offices, officers and a constitution, (ii) not created by intergovernmental agreement, (iii) members, officers, and funds from at least 3 countries (iv) no redistribution of profits to members, (v) non-secret, (vi) democratic officers election procedure, (vii) autonomous, excluding subgroups of

199

organisations, (viii) currently active, (ix) excluding: (non-democratic) religious orders, educational or training institutions or social and entertainment clubs. This leaves us with a total of 2281 INGOs in 1970, 288 of which were European Common Market or EFTA business and professional groups.[19] (The latter group of organisations is not included in the statistical presentations which follow, leaving us with a net total of 1993. The overwhelming majority of these are European Common Market organisations. There are two reasons for not including them in the statistics. First, to the extent that the European Community is an emerging federation, these INGOs are losing some of their international character. Second, some of them are mere subcommittees of other European INGOs in which nations other than the six EEC countries also are represented.)

Some Illustrations. The 2281 organisations make up a very heterogeneous group. Among them are the International Air Transport Association (IATA), the International Federation of Kennel Clubs, the International Society for Plant Geography and Ecology, the World Council of Churches (WCC), the International Commission of Rules for the Approval of Electrical Equipment (CEE), and the International Olympic Committee (IOC). In addition, there are international trade unions, international political organisations, for instance the Socialist International,

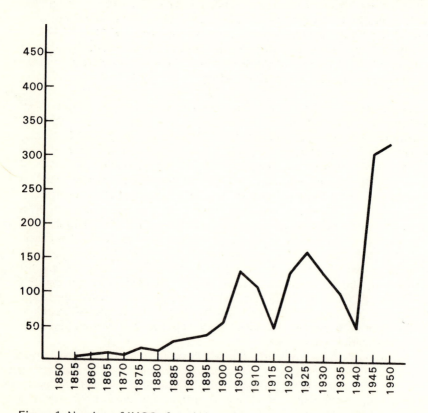

Figure 1. Number of INGOs founded per five-year period, 1850-1954

and a large number of professional, commercial, agricultural and cultural organisations. Other INGOs deal with problems of health, peace, documentation and finance. There seems to be almost no limit to the number of activities that can be and will be organised internationally.

The Growth and Spread of the INGO System

We have selected a few tables based on the data collected and published by the Union of International Associations (UIA), an INGO situated in Brussels. A more detailed presentation and discussion of these and related tables can be found elsewhere.[20]

Growth in Numbers and Memberships. Figure 1 shows the number of INGOs founded per five-year period since 1850. Before 1895 the number never exceeded fifty, but in the subsequent period lasting to the onset of the First World War there was a sharp increase. The war killed the boom, but after 1919 the world witnessed a resurgence of INGOs which lasted until a new political catastrophy emerged in the thirties. Since 1945 there has been an impressive and steady growth of organisations. Table 5 shows the number of active INGOs since 1954. It has practically doubled in the course of those sixteen years, which means that the mean annual increase has been somewhere between 4 per cent and 5 per cent. (EEC and EFTA INGOs are excluded from this as well as from the other tables.) The mean number of countries represented in each organisation has also increased considerably. It was 21·0 in 1951 and 25·7 in 1966, a growth of 22 per cent in fifteen years. These figures partly reflect the large number of new nations, of course, but it nevertheless means that INGOs generally have become more representative.

National Representations across Regions. In spite of the growth of the mean number of national representations, representativeness still remains one of the key problems in the INGO system, as this is illustrated in Table 6.[21] The Northwestern region has more than half of all the national representations in INGOs. The figure

Table 5: Active INGOs, 1954-1970

Year	Number of INGO's	Percentage increase
1954	1,012	—
1956	975	−3.7
1958	1,060	8.8
1960	1,255	18.4
1962	1,324	5.5
1964	1,470	11.0
1966	1,685	14.6
1968	1,899	12.7
1970	1,993	4.9

SOURCE: *Yearbook of International Organisations* (13th ed.; Brussels: Union of International Associations, 1955-1971).

Table 6: National representations in INGOs, 1951-1966

Region	Percentage by year					
	1951	1956	1960	1962	1964	1966
Northwest	66.2	63.5	58.3	57.8	54.5	53.5
Latin America	15.5	17.2	16.4	15.9	16.5	16.6
Arab world	3.5	5.4	4.8	5.2	5.2	5.3
Western Asia	6.6	6.7	8.5	7.4	7.7	8.3
Socialist Asia	.1	.4	.3	.3	.5	.5
Eastern Europe	7.9	6.6	7.5	7.7	8.0	7.9
Black Africa	.2	.3	3.5	4.8	6.7	6.8
Other	0	0	.9	1.0	.9	1.1
Sum	100.0	100.1	100.2	100.1	100.0	100.1
N*	12,249	20,027	24,144	28,827	34,486	36,341
Number of NGOs	583	897	—	—	1,458	1,416
Missing data	240	76	—	—	12	269
North America	8.0	5.2	4.6	4.6	4.5	4.3
Northern Europe	12.2	11.3	10.2	10.0	9.3	9.4
EEC group	20.9	20.0	18.9	18.4	17.0	16.4

*Number of individual representation

The regions in Table 6 are defined as follows:

Northwest:	North America and Western Europe, plus Australia, Cyprus, Israel, Japan, New Zealand, & The Republic of South Africa. This division obviously refers to political, not geographical, position.
Latin America:	all countries in the Western Hemisphere except the United States and Canada
Arab World:	all members of the League of Arab States plus Iran and the Arab ministates
Non-Communist Asia:	all other Asian states not ruled by Communist parties
Communist Asia:	the Democratic People's Republic of Korea (North Korea), the Democratic Republic of Vietnam (North Vietnam), the Mongolian People's Republic, and the People's Republic of China (Communist China)
Eastern Europe:	all socialist states of Europe
Black Africa:	All non-Arab countries in Africa not under colonial rule or ruled by white elites in 1969.
Other:	all other nation-states and territories

drops considerably from 1951 to 1966, but this is in large part due to the increasing number of nations in some of the other regions. The number of nations now seems to have reached its saturation point, and we therefore expect less reduction of the Northwestern bias in the future unless there is a conscious attempt to change this.

On the basis of other data regarding the site of headquarters, the nationality of INGO officers and the like, it is safe to conclude that the higher the level in the organisational structure at which involvement takes place, the larger is the percentage of Northwest representation. Moreover, the higher the organisational level, the more slowly the percentage of Northwest representation diminishes. Thus the INGO system is to a large extent, but certainly not exclusively, a Northwest dominated system.

The Structure and Functions of INGOs

Because INGOs are so varied in size and composition and operate in so many different issue areas, it is difficult to summarise their features in a few words. We shall first try to describe what immediately meets the eye, the upper part of the iceberg, and then examine the submerged problem of their latent functions and importance for other types of social factor. Finally we shall discuss the role of INGOs in relation to certain problem areas.

Membership Composition. The composition of the membership of INGOs varies tremendously from organisation to organisation. It may consist of individuals, national organisations, governmental agencies or their officers, national branches, business enterprises, international regional groupings of organisations, international universal organisations, or any mixture of these. There are presently approximately a hundred INGOs which partly or exclusively have other INGOs as members. Needless to say, the size of the membership also varies appreciably. The International Committee of Food Science and Technology consists of 28 individuals while the International Co-operative Alliance is made up of more than 600 000 cooperative societies whose membership totals 224 000 000 people. Only three nations can boast of a larger population. Other populous INGOs are: The League of Red Cross Societies with 214 million individual members in 110 countries, the World Federation of Trade Unions with 138 million individuals in fifty countries, and the World Federation of Democratic Youth, with 101 million members in 115 countries.

Activities of INGOs. One of the most important objectives of almost any INGO is to coordinate the activities of its members whether they are individuals or organisations in one form or another. Most international secretariats have little formal regulatory power, so the coordination usually takes the form of suggestions, exchange of views and information, and bargaining during organisational meetings. Exchange of information is also an important function in itself. An organisation frequently serves as a clearing-house between its members for the sector in which the INGO has competence. Some of them publish reference works, others compile bibliographical and documentation material. Scientific INGOs frequently administer the exchange of scientific data. A large proportion of all INGOs have their own periodicals which keep their members and other persons concerned informed about the state of affairs between their general conferences. On an average, such general meetings are held every second year while the executive boards meet more frequently, usually once or twice a year.

A few INGOs not only try to coordinate and encourage research among their members, but are also actively engaged in research projects themselves. Direct

INGO involvement in projects has certain advantages when the research includes cross-national comparisons. A related pair of functions is education and training. A large number of INGOs organise exchanges of scholars and students. An important part of the programme of the World Crafts Council, for instance, is to exchange apprentice and artists. INGOs also frequently provide opportunities for "on the job training" in connection with development aid programmes. Some of these programmes include education and training of the local population.

With respect to development aid, it is too often forgotten that national and international private nonprofit organisations and volunteers make a very substantial contribution to development. The Development Assistance Committee of the Organisation for Economic Cooperation and Development estimated that aid resources handled by nonprofit bodies exceed US $1 billion annually of which at least $700 million ($840 million in 1970) is raised from private resources (excluding foundations and missionary societies). For a comparison of aid flows to developing countries see Table 7. In 1968, some 25 000 people from developed countries were working as volunteers in the low-income countries. This figure had increased five-fold in six years and was then equivalent to nearly a quarter of all technical assistance personnel serving abroad under official programmes.[22]

Table 7: Selection of Data on Channels of Aid Disbursement ($US) to Developing Countries(*)

1   Official development assistance to LDCs and multilateral agencies
    $6315.3 million (1968) $6808.0 million (1970)
2   Bilateral technical assistance grants to LDCs
    $1527.9 million (1968), $1511.0 million (1970)
3   Gross disbursements by multilateral agencies in LDCs
    $1581 million (1968) $2091.0 million (1970)
4   Total net flow of multilateral finance to developing countries
    $877 million (1967) $1512.0 million (1970)
5   Gross disbursements by UN Institutions (excluding IBRD, IDA, IFC) to LDCs
    $346 million (1968) $415.0 million (1970)
6   Total aid resources raised by nongovernmental nonprofit bodies from private sources[1]
    $840 million (1970)

(*)   Organisation for Economic Cooperation and Development, Development Assistance Committee: 'Development Assistance; efforts and policies of the members of the DAC': Paris, OECD, 1971.

[1]   Excluding purely missionary activities. (The tentative estimates for earlier years are: $620 million (1969), $560 million (1968)). This figure does not include nongovernmental aid to intergovernmental bodies, e.g. up to 30% of UNICEF's budget.

A limited number of organisations have specialised in training courses for diplomats and other civil servants dealing with international politics. Finally it should be stressed that INGOs educate a large section of the general public through their branches. This is done in study groups, at meetings, and conferences, and in a number of other ways, as is well known.

The establishment and revision of technical standards is another activity of some INGOs. The need for standardisation of technical equipment and measurement has been one of the driving forces behind the growth of international organisation over the past hundred years and it has the side-effect of easing transnational communication in other areas. A related activity is the elaboration of professional and ethical codes and norms of operation. The World Medical Association, for example, is concerned with the ethics of medical doctors.

INGOs have often been described as international pressure groups, and this is perhaps the part of their activity that the political scientist will be most interested in. INGOs may focus on many different kinds of targets in order to promote their interest. Sometimes they try to influence national governments, but our impression is that this is practically always done through members in the respective countries. On the other hand, intergovernmental organisations (IGOs) are usually approached directly (sometimes on invitation) but there are instances in which INGOs have tried to influence the decision of an IGO by asking their national branches to exert influence on the respective governments. This latter approach seems more practical when an INGO tries to influence the content of an intergovernmental convention. Multinational business enterprises constitute another target of the political activities of some INGOs. They are of particular concern to international trade unions and consumer organisations, but other INGOs with a general interest in peace and development have also become aware of the mounting power of international business.[23] Finally, many INGOs try to influence the mass media. This is, of course, the case for most of those who seek mass support, but several limited membership organisations also wish to have their message distributed to a larger audience or to draw attention to specific problems. This may be done, for instance, in connection with the visit of a secretary general or a president to a national branch or local group.

Related to the pressure group activities is the consultative function many INGOs are performing, particularly *vis-à-vis* the United Nations, some of its specialised agencies, the Council of Europe and the OAS. About twenty per cent of all INGOs are formally given consultative status with one or more of these IGOs. Some of the problems involved in this relationship will be discussed below. INGOs often serve as channels of information complementary to those of conventional diplomacy. Many organisations have good contacts and recruit members from the 'grass roots' level, and they are less subject to short-term political considerations. This information may, of course, be used both positively and negatively.

In addition to serving as information channels, INGOs also serve as recruitment channels. In response to a questionnaire, about five per cent of the secretary generals who had made up their plans for future employment, said that they expected to serve in IGOs. Others will be involved to a varying extent in international programmes, sometimes serving in developing countries. Experience from INGOs, is supposedly, useful for national civil servants who, to a smaller or greater extent, become involved in international cooperation on the governmental level.

Parallel to the recruitment function is the participation function of INGOs.[24] They make it possible for persons other than diplomats and high ranking civil servants to participate in international affairs (in the broadest sense of that term). It is true that a stable leadership in member organisations of INGOs often monopolises the international contacts so that it should be possible to increase the degree of participation by such means as greater rotation of personnel in delegations to conferences.

Although social clubs (perhaps unwisely) are excluded from inventories of INGOs, there still remains a number of organisations that has value expression as one of their most important functions. Value expression is also a significant by-product of the activities of many others. An example of an organisation in which comradeship is particularly evident, is the International Association of Skål Clubs. An explicit objective of many INGOs is to increase international understanding. This is done in a number of ways, of which increased participation is one of the more important ones. Other means such as information dissemination and exchange programmes have been discussed above. Some INGOs are mainly protective, that is, they try to defend the interests of their members. The protective element may be strong in INGOs made up of minority groups (the Celtic League) or exile organisations.

Another INGO activity which deserves mention is the continuing attempt to integrate and formulate member concerns both for their own internal purposes and for third parties. This process goes on in all kinds of organisations, but one should pay special attention to it on the international level because, in addition to all ordinary causes of disagreement, there may be differences of opinion on the basis of loyalty to different nation states. For a number of reasons nongovernmental organisations are often able to respond quickly to new needs created by changes in the environment (breakthroughs in technology, natural disasters, etc.) or by changes of policies or quality of services provided by government and business, either prior to an awareness of the need in government or business, or after their programmes have terminated or deteriorated. INGOs can therefore perform the function of 'lookout' institutions for society. In this manner INGOs can serve as functional equivalents or substitutes for other actors.

Finally we want to mention that some INGOs see it as their duty to make relevant and interpret international programmes to national members or special constituencies. This is one way support for international programmes is mobilized. The above presentation of INGO activities and goals is by no means exhaustive although we think we have covered most of the essential features.

INGOs, their actual and potential impact. International nongovernmental organisations mean different things to different people. They are therefore called by different names and there is a lack of awareness of them as a class, as a whole. In this section we shall discuss the relevance of INGOs first to different classes of actors, and second, to different problem areas.

INGOs, functional for whom and in which way? At the present time, and partly due to the lack of an elaborated interorganisational conceptual framework, too few INGOs perceive themselves as part of a network of actors (other than in the metaphysical sense used when referring to the 'international community'). This network of organisations is constantly changing and evolving as different parts of it perceive and respond to new problems. Sub-networks of INGOs (perhaps in combination with non-INGOs) with a special interest in common come into existence for a period of joint action and are implicitly mandated to meet the challenge. A given INGO may be participating, terminating or commencing participation in any number of such partial networks.[25]

The lack of a network perception leads INGOs to be less functional for each other than they could be. There are, nevertheless, groups of international nongovernmental organisations that cooperate rather effectively with each other, particularly when they have a strong interest in the same relatively limited problem area such as care for the handicapped and training of social workers. INGOs with very different objectives also sometimes cooperate in order to promote the interests of INGOs as a class and to improve their status in the international system. This seems to be one of the main functions of the conferences of INGOs in consultative status with ECOSOC and UNESCO.

The functions of INGOs for their members are manifold, but to a large extent these have already been covered above. To the IGOs, the INGOs are of importance in three respects. Firstly, INGOs provide pools of competence on which IGOs can draw in the execution of specialised projects. This is recognised in the consultative relationship. INGO information may be more detailed over longer periods of time or information, which does not enter governmental channels for political reasons, may be collected by INGOs which are thus able to detect problems long before there is any trace of them in the ordinary information channels of IGOs. A good example is the whole environment issue, of which aspects have been for many years the major concern of the following:
— International Union for Conservation of Nature and Natural Resources (founded 1948)
— European Federation for the Protection of Waters (1956)
— International Association on Water Pollution Research (1962)
— International Association against Noise (1959)
— International Union of Air Pollution Prevention Associations (1964)
and others.

The United Nations is taking action on this issue following the UN Human Environment Conference.

Secondly, INGOs may carry out projects for IGOs under contract or carry on programmes which would otherwise have to be performed by IGOs. (Unfortunately, the current tendency is for an IGO to assess an INGO in terms of whether it contributes to the IGOs programmes rather than in terms of its effectiveness in tackling the problems the IGO and INGO have in common; in short, the INGOs are seen as satellites of the IGO). Thirdly, INGOs represent an extremely useful channel by which IGOs can influence special sectors of the public to support IGO programmes, for example, to create the political will to support development programmes. This leads some IGO officials to treat and assess INGOs as a new media to disseminate the current IGO message. A fourth unrecognized function of interest to IGOs with social development programmes, is the extent to which increase in INGO activity in itself is a form of social development—to the extent that social development may be interpreted as the complexification of the organisation of a society in terms of number, variety and interlinkages.

The way in which INGOs are relevant for national governments depends not only on the nature of the INGOs involved, but also on the kind of national government. As in the case of IGOs, INGOs can provide the governmental sector with specialized opinion and technical information, and this will be particularly welcome when the government concerned does not have adequate expertise in a particular area. Furthermore, INGOs may channel funds, technical and other forms of assistance to governments, and this may be especially important when other national governments are, for political reasons, debarred from assisting.

What are the functions of INGOs *vis-à-vis* multinational business enterprises? We have already mentioned that there are international consumer associations, and we expect these to play an increasingly important role in line with the growing consciousness of consumers in many countries. They may serve as effective checks on these international manufacturing and service organisations that up to now have had the opportunity to 'divide and rule' with respect to their scattered markets and sites of operation. International trade unions provide another kind of check on international business, although, according to some observers, they are not as effective as they could be. A difficult problem is, for instance, the tendency of multinational enterprises to exploit wage differences between countries in such a way that workers in high-pay and low-pay countries may find it difficult to formulate a common policy. In addition, several other INGOs which cannot be classified as trade unions and consumer organisations, are relevant for multinational business. Together they represent large segments of actual or potential markets and thereby provide channels of information about products, advertising, and buyers' reaction to this. (The international motor organisations wittingly or unwittingly performs these functions *vis-à-vis* the international automobile industry).

The INGOs themselves constitute an important market and have a significant effect on the tourism industry through the many widely dispersed international meetings to which they give rise.[26] Their presence in a country, or that of IGO offices for that matter, is not a drain on the host country, as used to be thought, but a minor source of foreign currency. The economic side-effects of the presence of many international bodies may, however, be extremely important in terms of, for example, use of the country's airline, hotel accommodation of incoming visitors, tendency to organise meetings in cities with many similar institutions, use of local services (printing, etc.). In small cities like Geneva and Brussels with relatively large numbers of foreign personnel, their internationalizing impact on the society may be quite significant. Brussels is unique as a host to major headquarters or regional offices of INGOs, and multinational corporations.

To the extent that multinational corporations take a significant interest in their social and environmental context and the social consequences of their activities, INGOs can provide an appropriate channel for application of the resources (skills, communications channels, contacts, funding, etc.) of multinationals to social problems.[27] This opportunity may prove increasingly significant for multinationals, given the growing business-career disillusionment of the young elites from which they attempt to recruit personnel for key positions.

A very important function of some INGOs is to be mechanisms for interaction and protection of competing businesses. The International Air Transport Association (IATA) is a prominent representative of this category of INGOs, but there are many others. They work out standards, defend their common interests *vis-à-vis* governments, IGOs and the general public, and regulate competition. Multinational enterprises sometimes become members, directly, but the usual practice is for their subsidiaries to join. It is very interesting that some of these INGOs serve as arbitrators in conflicts between business enterprises on the national and international level. An example of such an organisation is the Inter-American Commercial Arbitration Commission. In addition many of these organisations develop expertise and sponsor research that is utilised by their members, that is, business corporations. International professional organisations also possess specialised knowledge that is used in business. Furthermore, the professional organisations, together with the international trade unions, serve as vehicles for multinational employee concern. International nongovernmental organisations perform many functions that are very valuable to academics. We mentioned above their coordinating activities, research activities and information dissemination. The primary purpose of a large proportion of INGOs is simply to serve as communication channels between scholars. Furthermore, scientific INGOs provide academics with a channel through which they can make their research conclusions known to government, both on the national and on the international level. Finally, INGOs provide scholars with a means of formalising the many 'invisible colleges',[28] scientific milieux, and thus contribute to the universalisation of science.

Next we want to consider what INGOs do for underprivileged persons. The organisations working in this area seem to be very responsive to any form of discrimination, social injustice or physical deprivation. However, one side-effect of the very existence of these organisations, regardless of which issue area they are particularly concerned with, is to perpetuate a more or less elitist system insofar as they provide unequal status opportunities for those involved. If more thought was given to new forms of INGOs, this side-effect could possibly be counter-acted. Finally, INGOs contribute to the degree of pluralism in world society by providing isolated and special interest persons and specialists with a vehicle through which they can facilitate the information and furtherance of their activities. (A quick glance through any compilation of names of INGOs will convince the reader that some of the interests are quite off-beat.)

INGOs and World Problems. The importance of INGOs depends, of course, to a large extent on the degree to which they can contribute to the solution of grave world problems. There are, as we know, many of these, but the overriding one seems to be the absence of peace.

Like Galtung, we conceive of peace as the absence of violence, of which there are two sorts.[29] First, there is personal violence which becomes manifest when person A physically hurts person B (for instance, by shooting him during a battle). Second, there is structural violence which is analogous to exploitation and social injustice. This kind of violence usually occurs in a social structure which is set up in such a way that some people become rich (in terms of life expectancy, income, education, individual freedom and what not) and other people remain or become poor. This relationship may or may not be realised by the members of such a social structure. The net result of both kinds of violence is a reduced quality of life and/or shorter life expectancy due to untimely deaths.

INGOs can and do contribute to the reduction of violence in two different ways.[30] They can take direct action aimed at preventing war and reducing social injustice, and they can contribute to both ends by their mere existence without any deliberate efforts to promote peace. Given the two different kinds of violence, this leaves us with four distinct ways in which INGOs contribute to peace:

(i) They do many different things to prevent wars between nations. Indeed, 45 per cent of a highly representative sample of INGOs considered that 'to work for peace between all nations and peoples in the world' was one of their objectives. Among the different strategies are: peace research and education, political

209

action, exchange of persons and information and deliberate attacks on national loyalties of members and non-members.

(ii) Fifty-one per cent of the same sample stated that they worked 'for social and economic development in the world', and we have already discussed some of the ways in which this is done. An important trait in this picture is the transfer of know-how to developing countries. The problem here is that aid to development is often felt as an attempt to superimpose Western culture in non-Western societies. The scepticism against INGOs in some developing countries is probably sound and should be taken very seriously.

(iii) The very existence of a network of INGOs has an effect on the structure of nation states. Conflicts between nations or groups of nations frequently lead to the termination of most forms of interaction between them. This has at least two consequences. The opponents become less functionally dependent on each other, and their negative perceptions of each other become mutually reinforced. The setting is ideal for overt conflict behaviour (war).[31] It seems, however, that interaction through INGOs is less easily stopped than, for instance, trade and diplomatic relations. Although there are difficulties, INGOs relatively frequently penetrate the wall between the Warsaw Pact and NATO countries, they frequently include both Arab and Israeli members, and representatives of divided countries meet more often in INGO settings than one would expect by chance.[32] One reason for this is that INGOs constitute a multilateral form of interaction. It is often hard to withdraw from or resist becoming a member of an organisation in which adversaries are members because it is most likely that it includes quite a few 'friends' too. Another reason is that INGOs are nongovernmental. They do not get much public attention, and delegates to meetings and conferences do not have to participate in whatever official capacity they may have.

(iv) To what extent can the structure of the INGO network contribute to the reduction of structural violence on the world level? First of all, being represented in INGOs may be a coveted goal in itself, an indication of the prestige of status of a nation. Second, being represented in many INGOs makes it easier to obtain what is currently a highly regarded asset—specialised information. In addition, it may be easier to get funds for certain purposes and so on. Thus, to the extent that the distribution of the value 'INGO-membership' is less skewed than and uncorrelated with the distribution of other values in the international system, say GNP per capita, the INGO system contributes to the establishment of social justice between nations. Empirical investigations show that the number of INGO memberships is less unevenly distributed across nations than most indicators of social, economic and technological development, and the correlation between the number of representations and these indicators is positive and moderately high. Consequently, INGOs make a contribution to social justice through their activities although this is somewhat counteracted by their membership distribution.

Other problems. INGOs are also important to society in the process by which new values are generated by the emergence of new problems and in the process by which society debates which problems are of overriding importance. They also keep a watchful eye on other potentially significant problems. INGOs clamour for social recognition of the (often obscure) problems around which they were created. It is in this respect that they appear to perform a function for the psycho-social system analogous to aspects of population dynamics, which maintains the variety of a gene-pool and thus provides the best guarantee of racial survival. Efforts by any one organisation to coordinate other bodies to force them to subscribe to a particular value system, or to force them into any position of dependence for needed resources, information or recognition lead to a reduction in variety. These need to be carefully assessed for patterns of structural violence carried over with elitist-imperialist thinking habits.

Ignorance about INGOs and other Problems. In this section we shall first deal with the problems arising from the wide-spread ignorance about INGOs which is to the detriment not only of the nongovernmental organisations themselves, but also to those persons and institutions who are unable to benefit from the services INGOs provide. Then follows a discussion of some other problems of INGOs not directly related to ignorance about them.

Ignorance about INGOs and its consequences. The general neglect of INGOs takes many forms. Starting with the legal ignorance, we observe that INGOs are practically excluded from consideration in international law because of their lack of *de jure* status[33] despite the fact that they are well established *de facto*. Although apparently trivial, this lack of legal status is sufficient to convince wide segments of society, particularly governments, that INGOs do not exist—thus blinding governments to their social significance. In effect, INGOs are forced to function as international 'outlaws', and this weakens their ability to interact effectively with many official bodies. It also creates many kinds of practical problems in connection with taxation, recruitment, status of personnel, receipt and transfer of funds, and the like.

Secondly, there is scholarly ignorance. We have to admit that there is a regrettable tendency to exclude INGOs from 'systematic' analyses of the international system and from comparative studies of organisations.[34] This leads to over-simplified typologies of actors in the international system and possible forms of organisation, both of which in turn result in poor awareness of organizational ecology. Another consequence is insensitive predictions about the future of world society and the construction of unrealistic models for the same future. The same ignorance shows up in the poor education of students and briefing of government delegates and administrators as well as in the biased coverage of text books.[35] If INGOs are at all mentioned, the emphasis tends to be on isolated organisations or categories of organisations without recognising the many inter-organisational relationships in the INGO network and to the IGO network. In the case of applied research with policy implications, such as some peace research, there is, with a few notable exceptions, little awareness of the potentialities of the INGO system as an agent for change. In many countries there is a tendency not to make use of national NGOs in governmental programmes and thus to avoid using the international contacts provided by the related INGO system. This leads to inefficient use and development of available organisational resources.

Many IGOs give some kind of official recognition to INGOs, but the recognition is extended only to a small proportion of the international nongovernmental organisations and usually on a bilateral basis. For administrative purposes IGOs tend to ignore the network of INGOs as a phenomenon of the social system they

Table 8: Map of interconnected problems around the relationship between inter-governmental agencies and international associations (NGOs).

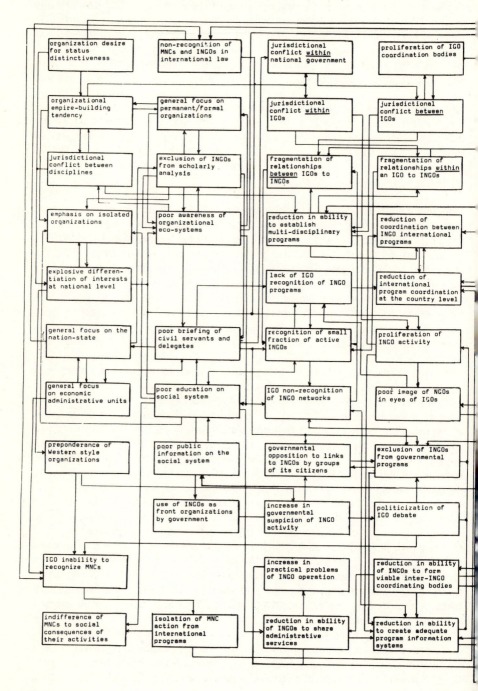

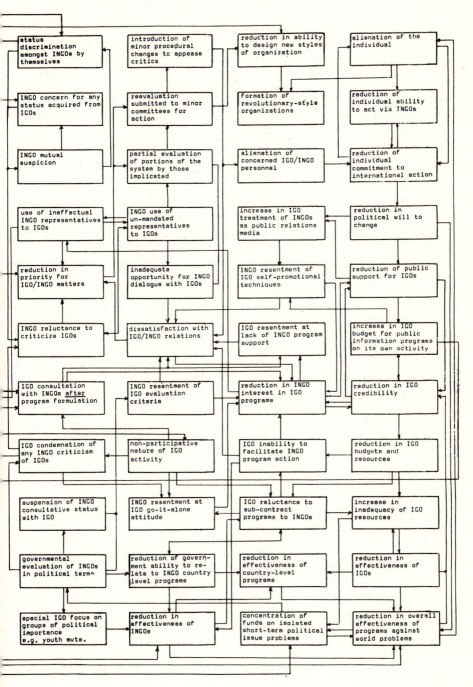

are trying to develop and instead treat a select group of INGOs as an administrative problem. In particular IGOs are short-sighted in their desire to monopolize competence in certain areas thus placing an unnecessary strain on their own administration and budget instead of seeking to delegate programme activity to the competent part of the INGO network where resources and support may be more readily available. Indeed, the fundamental problem for IGOs is to define an area of competence for INGOs without destroying their sense of commitment and thus depriving society of valuable organisational resources. However, the tendency of IGOs to give a shallow recognition to a small proportion of the INGOs leads to a kind of divide and rule strategy which means that the INGO system is fragmentized and polarized around a few IGO agencies. At the same time, IGOs perceive INGOs as satellites and query the relevance of many aspects of their programmes which do not directly reflect or support the current short-term political interests of the intergovernmental agency. We have tried to summarise our arguments in Table 8.

Other Problems of INGOs. It is often difficult for INGOs to stimulate interest on the part of members via regional and national branches, particularly interest in international activity. There seems to be a tendency for some leaders on the national level to monopolize international contacts, or to fail to relate international cooperation to the activities and problems of rank and file members. As a corollary, it is difficult to persuade national organisations to allocate significant resources to international activity. The focus of action tends to be at the national level.

Another problem some INGOs struggle with is the incompatibility of national members. In different social systems functional equivalents of national organisations may have different relationships to governments particularly with regard to the degree of governmental control, funding and staffing. National sections in different countries may perform ranges of functions that only partially overlap such that the non-overlapping features tend to result in suspicion and incompatibilities which probably lead some governments to hesitate in facilitating interaction between their national organisations and the equivalent INGOs. In particular, in some non-Western cultures there may be difficulty in locating organisational forms natural to that culture which could relate to a given INGO.[36] There may be resentment of any imposition of a new Western style organisation, and a lack of any socio-anthropological skill to match very different styles of organisations, or to create or adapt an INGO appropriate to them. Most INGOs require the same basic administrative services and facilities, but because of their restricted budgets, they are forced to use minimum facilities, which are often inadequate and insufficient. Because of great sensitivity to their independence and autonomy of their programme, they are reluctant to pool services and facilities in order to increase the efficiency of their administrative operations. This is partly due to an inability to distinguish between the objectives of the organisation and the facilities and professional skills required to achieve them.

Because of a combination of factors, INGOs individually or in small groups tend to think of themselves as operating in an international vacuum. They are often surprised to find other organisations with similar programmes or whose programmes are in some way affected by their own. There is, at present, no method to determine and set up the most appropriate inter-organisational contacts. Because of a narrow conception of socio-economic development in which 'social' is restricted to factors contributing to 'economic' growth, IGOs, and particularly the UN system, accept isolated INGOs as instrumental to development without being able to respond to the network of INGOs as a feature in itself, a new stage of psycho-social development. Consequently IGOs do not seek to improve the functioning of the INGO network independent of immediate governmental concerns, thus relegating INGOs to a form of 'third world' status *vis-à-vis* governmental and business organisations.

In conclusion, the nature of the problems to which INGOs are exposed places them in a vicious circle, in that the problems force them into a state of progressively greater inefficiency, preventing them from getting off the ground operationally. The inefficiency is seen as justifying the non-participative policies of intergovernmental organisations which in effect contribute directly to the inefficiency of the network. The IGOs are then, as in the case of UN development programmes, surprised to be faced with the seemingly unrelated problem of public apathy and lack of 'political will' for development.[37]

Probable Future Trends[38]

Increasingly rapid organisational creation, evolution, adaptation, and dissolution is to be expected with rapid membership turnover and constantly changing patterns of inter-organisational interaction, including splits and mergers. The rate at which people or organisational units link together in response to newly-perceived problems will increase. This will be facilitated by improvements in communication technology. Some information systems may even be deliberately designed to bring increasingly improbable combinations of bodies into the same organisation on very specific issues for very limited periods.[39]

New styles of INGO may arise as a result of contacts between the mixed government-voluntary sector organisations encountered in many socialist and Third World countries and the intersect organisations in the West. The influence of the position of the People's Republic of China in the debate on INGOs within the United Nations may prove to be particularly significant in this respect. Disillusionment with coordinating 'umbrella' and other inter-agency organisational mechanisms will lead to more sophisticated use of information systems to link organisations and by-pass the behavioural and 'territorial' problems of 'super-INGOs' to the point of substituting for many of the functions performed by them.

The difficulty for society to organise itself in advance in preparation for unknown problems which no existing official body is mandated to recognise, will lead to greater recognition of dependence on the network of nongovernmental bodies as 'lookout' and 'first-aid' institutions before the problem is politically respectable. It will be recognised that the network will 'generate' organisational forms appropriate to the problem. The option of channelling project funds through the most appropriate body under the circumstances, whether it be governmental business, academic, or nongovernmental will gain greater acceptance. The organisation of response to a problem will become much more complex as many interdependent channels in the network are used.

The effectiveness of INGOs will come under increasing criticism and new, more sensitive, criteria for evaluating their performance and significance will be developed. (One possibility is the development of a variety of organisational indicators, similar to corporation stock indicators, to show the utility of contribution through a particular nonprofit body.) The number of regional INGOs will increase. It is also probable that the number of INGOs formed from sub-national level NGOs will increase as the fragmentation of the nation-state becomes a social reality. The territorial basis of representation will become less significant. It will increasingly be recognized that INGOs and voluntary organisations constitute a participative, possibly part-time, career opportunity and a viable alternative to the frequently alienating and dehumanizing environments of the government and business sectors. This recognition by young people will be accompanied by a rejection of bureaucratic INGOs and the adaption in some cases of a new style of operation, which may have more of the features of movements and, possibly, networks of communes. This is also a central notion in Mitrany's thought.

Conclusions and Recommendations

The number of INGOs is growing, and they are expanding in terms of geographical representation and functional scope. Whilst the INGOs, directly or through their members, constitute an extremely useful group of actors in some respects, their full contribution to the global social processes can only be achieved if the development of the INGO network is stimulated along certain lines to correct for imbalance, side-effects and inadequate utilisation. A number of policy recommendations in this direction are listed below:

1—The degree of organisational interlinkage would seem to preclude simplistic analysis of organisations as isolated entities. Furthermore, the network of INGOs is constantly evolving in response to new insights, possibilities, and problems. It is therefore less the pattern at any one moment which should be the focus of concern and much more the pattern-forming potential of organisational subunits and active individuals.

2—To handle the problems associated with the catchall category of INGOs, the goal should be to map organisation in its broadest sense, namely as composed of relatively invarient entities. The entity is in fact a pattern of relationships, subject to change, but recognisably extended in time. The cut-off point, below which the duration of a pattern is considered too ephemeral, should be dependent upon data collection ability rather than preconceived models. This way of regarding the objects of attention in society helps to resolve the dichotomy between the individual and society and many other pseudo-problems resulting from the tendency, built into language, to regard entities as 'things' rather than systematically related sequences of events.[40]

This 'loose' approach can be achieved by handling the entities and relationships as networks which can be processed and represented using graph theory techniques[41]. In effect, a non-quantitative topological structure of the psycho-social system is built up, to which dynamic and quantitative significance can be added as and when appropriate data becomes available.

3—Greater effort should be made to map out transnational networks (possibly by a succession of overlapping surveys) so that organisations can see their direct and indirect relationships to one another—and also such that second and higher order patterns of dominance can be detected. (Interorganisational maps should have the same status and accessibility as road maps in order that people can navigate more effectively through the social system.)

4—The degree of possible functional substitution between different styles of organisation suggests that great care is required when establishing categories for the purposes of analysis, programme elaboration or legislation. There is in fact a need for greater understanding of organisational networks as ecosystems, such that the function of a significant, but seemingly insignificant, body in a communication web can be made apparent.

A greater tolerance of the variety of organisational species is required and of the manner in which particular types are more appropriate under given conditions. (It is perhaps appropriate to note that botanists and zoologists recognise around one million plants and animals respectively—whereas a sociologist might be said to recognize around one hundred types of collectivity.) A taxonomy and a new 'Origin of Species' is required to knot together this variety into an evolving psycho-social system.

5—Greater stress should be placed on the network of nongovernmental nonprofit bodies as a *social phenomenon* rather than as an *administrative or political problem* for government. The degree of organisation of a society is one measure of its social development. The number and variety of organisations or office-holders per capita is a measure of the participative opportunity or socializing potential of that society. Data on INGOs and their national counterparts could therefore constitute an important social indicator for development policy-making and should have a status equivalent to that of economic units of society. (As things stand, no systematic data collection on organisations between the national and local level is carried out.)[42]

6—Nongovernmental, nonprofit bodies pose a special problem for countries in the early stages of social development, since, as with the two-party system, they appear to constitute a threat to the stability of the government in power and are therefore the subject of suspicion if permitted to exist. Further study is required of the areas in which the different styles of INGOs can usefully function, at different stages of development, without constituting a rallying point for premature dissent. This should help to determine at what stage, and under what conditions, the (more suspect) link to an INGO becomes appropriate.

7—Besides the functions performed for their special constituencies, INGOs in a network perform functions for one another. Further study is required of the manner in which control information should be elaborated and circulated to govern the action of a network of organisations in the absence of any prime controller (due to the continuing emergence of new problems configurations) or any single permanent objective.

8—The degree of interconnectedness and direct or indirect interdependence of organisations suggests that, where two organisational systems have common objectives or concerns, it is short-sighted and possibly counter-productive for the first system to request the second for assistance in the accomplishment of its own system objectives—and to ignore or disassociate itself from the second when it pursues the same objectives in a different manner. Both systems should rather seek to improve their functioning as interdependent systems and ensure that their operations mesh effectively.

9—Any successful attempt by a particular organisation to mobilize all others in unquestioning support of its own programmes reduces the overall ability of the network of organisations to respond effectively to unforeseen problems. Recommendations to 'regroup', 'reduce proliferation', or 'increase coordination', should be assessed against the need for variety. The degree of fragmentation of organisational systems (whether governmental or nongovernmental) in part reflects the need for sufficient organisational frameworks through which active individuals can meaningfully participate in the social process. The interlocking complexity of the nongovernmental sector may be considered a major insurance against undetected manipulation of social processes by elite groups—provided such bodies have sufficient freedom of action to fulfill their responsibility.

10—Means are required to achieve an optimum degree of organisational coordination consistent with the arguments just advanced, such as:

(a) *Informal contact:* Provision of low-rent office and meeting facilities (or other shared administrative services) in one centre within major cities, brings a variety of organisations with potentially related concerns into fruitful informal contact. This increases their effectiveness, leads to working contacts where and when appropriate, provides the 'critical mass' required for mutual encouragement and outside recognition, and facilitates the conception and germination of new programmes. It also provides the facilitative base for newly-established bodies during their growth period. The creation of such focal points for the mobilization of untapped social forces should be viewed as a priority for city and national governments.

(b) *Information systems:* Bodies should be informed of each other's existence as soon as they are able to formulate a problem or interest in common. Prior to entering into some direct relationship potential partners need to be conceived of as 'members' of a 'potential association' from which particular groupings gel as required by the problem configuration, and into which they dissolve when their objective is achieved. Such a potential association could be given the necessary operational framework by substituting a form of information system or referral service for normally-constituted membership organisations—thus avoiding administrative and political problems of 'recognition' and proof of 'relevance'.

Provision of low-cost communication facilities (telephone, telex, datalink) between organisations in centres (see above) in different countries permits organisations to develop regional contacts more easily, to mesh their programmes more effectively with those of other bodies, to channel resources through the network more efficiently and rapidly in response to emergencies, and increases their ability to interact with their counterparts at the national level and with programmes in the field.

11—In order to reduce official hostility or indifference to INGOs in the future, steps should be taken to introduce material on nongovernmental action and its relation to social development into university curricula, diplomat training, and foreign service briefing sessions. Intergovernmental organisations, particularly the UN Specialised Agencies, could usefully focus in their public information and personnel training programmes on their relationships with INGOs.

12—Specific legislation concerning the status of INGOs with headquarters or branches in a given country (possibly on the Belgian model) should be recommended to States via intergovernmental assemblies. (This should take into account the apparently minor questions of status of 'alien' personnel, problems of double taxation, continuity of pension and social security rights for personnel moving between countries and organisations, which are the *sine qua non* of the effective professionalization of the INGO network.)

13—Steps should be taken to represent the case for an international convention

218

to give an international legal status to INGOs—with due consideration for their responsibilities *and* rights. As participants in the social process they have responsibilities for the well-being of individuals, other bodies, and society as a whole, in the spirit of the Universal Declaration of Human Rights—the principal responsibility is to make every effort to call attention to, or to counteract any errors of omission or commission in society which their special expertise enables them to detect. Organisations should have certain rights for their protection in the exercise of their responsibilities.

14—INGOs (and IGOs) must recognise the existence and need for a wide range of styles of organisation, that is, the 'significance' of an INGO should be rated on a combination of many measures rather than on membership or budget. Functional equivalents of Western-type organisations should be recognised in other cultures, and social systems. Allowances should be made for structural or constitutional incompatibilities between potential members. Research is needed on the problems of decision-making in multi-cultural organisations.

15—Regional IGOs should facilitate the formation of regional INGOs according to the styles of organisation in the region. IGO-INGO contact mechanisms at the regional level should be developed. In some issue areas super-INGOs of regional INGOs should be encouraged when appropriate. Efforts should also be made to increase the involvement of developing region INGOs or national bodies in multi-region INGOs. In particular communication links should be improved (see point 9), meetings should be rotated through developing region countries, or possibly travel expenses could be pooled so that everybody pays the same regardless of where he or she comes from.

16—It would be useful to consider the extent to which many INGOs and other bodies are 'non-territorial actors', that is, actors for which the geographical or national representation is of minor importance to their action.[43]. There is some possibility that such bodies may be sliding into a repetition of processes (structurally very similar to those encountered throughout the history of territorial conflict) with respect to what has been termed 'quasi-territory', namely the sort of functional domain which each body defines and stakes out as its special field of concern—a domain whose boundary line is constantly called into question by changing societal conditions[44]. The stress in the future may be less on the problems of national interest-coordination, which led to the formation of the United Nations, but increasingly on the problem of functional coordinations for which some equivalent global mechanism may eventually be evolved, possibly in part out of the existing INGO system, but certainly out of the three hundred to six hundred multinational corporations which it is expected will control much of the wealth of the Western world by the year 2000. Functional domains will be decreasingly fragmented by territorial preoccupations, but nation states will be increasingly fragmented by functional preoccupations. In this sense the problems of co-ordination would seem to be the common root concern of international relations and the policy sciences.

Notes and references

1   INGO is the accepted abbreviation in academic circles. Intergovernmental system documents refer to NGOs avoiding any definition of international or any clear distinction between national and international NGOs. The term is

usually restricted to nonprofit bodies, in which case the profit-making bodies are referred to as multinational corporations (MNCs) or business INGOs (BINGOs).

2 For example, in Arab countries or those with a Moslem culture, a common form or organisation for social development is the 'Waq' (mentioned in the Koran) which bears some resemblance to a Western religious fund or foundation. It is not known whether any of these are 'international'. Similarly, the family name and ancestral province association play an important role in and between countries with a Chinese population.

3 Each new issue inspires a new configuration of bodies. This has been discussed in connection with political party election machinery in Richard R. Fagan. *Politics and Communication*. Boston, Little, Brown, 1966 (Chapter on the 'Components of Communication Networks'). For a means of developing this technique, see: A.J.N. Judge, 'New types of social entity; the role of the potential association'. *International Associations* 23, 1971.

4 Many United States trade unions are 'international' in the title, e.g. International Longshoremen's Association.

5 There is a movement to restrict 'international' to 'intergovernmental' and to refer to INGOs as transnational associations; see: G.P. Speeckaert, Transnational ou International? *International Associations*, 24, 1972, 4, p. 225-232. It has also been suggested that the word transnational should be reserved for international organisations with individual members only. The term INGO would then apply to international organisations with national chapters, the structure of which is heavily influenced by the nation-state system, cf. Johan Galtung's forthcoming book on transnationalism and peace in the World Order Models series of the World Law Fund. At present about 50 per cent of the INGOs in the *Yearbook of International Associations* permit individual membership only via national chapters. In roughly 25 per cent of the cases individuals must be directly affiliated, and in the remaining 25 per cent of the organisations both types of affiliation are possible, cf. Kjell Skjelsbaek 'A Survey of International Nongovernmental Organisations,' unpublished paper, the International Peace Research Institute, Oslo, 1972.

6 'Any international organisation which is not established by intergovernmental agreement shall be considered as a nongovernmental organisation...' (UN ECOSOC Resolution 1296 (XLIV) June 1968). See discussion in G.P. Speeckaert, *ibid.*

7 A.J.N. Judge, 'Summary of the crisis in inter-organisational relationships at the international level' in *International Associations*, 24, 1972, 5, Also: 'The UN System's ivory tower strategy,' in *International Associations*, 23, 1971, 1, p. 24-48.

8 Kenneth E. Boulding. 'Management of "intersect" institutions,' in *Management in a Changing World* (Papers sponsored by the Conference Board (USA) to be published at the end of 1972).

9 The United Nations, even through its Agencies concerned with trade, cannot recognise the existence of multinational business enterprises as INGOs because of the political sensitivity of profit-making. The exception is FAO through its FAO/Industry Cooperative Programme on which multinationals are represented. This embarrassment is in sharp contrast with OECD which has a Business and Industry Advisory Committee.

10 For a broad definition of voluntary, see: David Horton Smith, *et. al.* 'Types of voluntary action; a definitional essay', in D.H. Smith (ed.) *Voluntary Action Research.* Lexington, Lexington Books, 1972. (See also: *Journal of Voluntary Action Research.*)

11 Those 'recognised' by the United Nations acquire a measure of legal significance. There have also been attempts to extend the interpretation of the status of private persons in international law to cover collectivities. See: Université Catholique du Louvain. *Premier colloque de Département des Droits de l'Homme (1969); les droits de l'homme et les personnes morales.* Bruxelles, Emils Bruylant, 1970.

12 Belgium is the only country to recognise and provide special legislation and facilities for INGOs (Law of 25 October 1919 expanded by Law of 6 December 1954) which is one reason why 490 INGOs have offices there. Efforts are being made by the European Economic Commission to define a 'European Corporation' to which international trade unions will have a specially recognised relationship.

13 President's Commission on Law Enforcement and Administration of Justice. *Task Force Report: Organised Crime.* Washington, US Government Printing Office, 1967. Note that profits to organised crime from gambling, loan sharking and narcotics (excluding infiltrated legitimate business and other operations) are probably in the region of $ 8 billion per year in the United States alone. One could perhaps also make the distinction between legality, in terms of laws and regulations, and legitimacy, in terms of moral codes. Some organisations and organisational activities may be legal, but not legitimate, and vice versa. Generally speaking, legal organisations are more visible than illegal ones.

14 Twenty-five per cent of the studies on international nongovernmental organisations listed in the International Political Science Bibliography over the past eight years are concerned with one organisation, the International Red Cross.

15 G.P. Speeckaert. 'Les associations momentanées d'organisations internationales.' *International Associations,* **23**, 1971, 4, p. 205-217.

16 G.M. Riegner. 'Consultative Status; recent developments and future prospects' (11th General Conference of Nongovernmental Organisations in Consultative Status with ECOSOC). Geneva, 1969, 11/GC/22, p. 2

17 'Cross-modal' is a term used in psychology, to refer to the ability of an individual to handle and integrate several modes of sensation (sight, sound, etc.). It seems equally applicable to the degree of integration of different modes of organisation action.

18 'The problem of the seventies will lie not so much within the organisation as between it and society. We shall have to look much more to the social and family life or organisations, at organisational marriage and divorce, at the children that organisations spawn. We shall begin to know organisations by the company they keep. The future, I think, will be social, political, inter-organisational.' Harold J. Leavitt, 'The Yesterday, Today, and Tomorrow of Organisations.' *European Business,* Spring 1971, **29**, p. 28-33.

19 United Nations, ECOSOC. Arrangements for consultation with non- governmental organisations. E/RES/1296 (XLIV), 25 June 1968. Text and commentary reprinted in *International Associations* 20, 9, 1968, p. 609-649.

20 *Yearbook of International Organisations* (1970-1971). Brussels, Union of International Associations, 1971, 1053 p.

21 Kjell Skjelsbaek. Development of the systems of international organisations; a diachronic study. *IPRA Papers on Peace Reserach: Proceedings of the Second International Peace Research Association General Conference.* Assen; Netherlands, Van Gocum, 1970.
Kjell Skjelsbaek. The growth of international nongovernmental organisations in the twentieth century. *International Organisation,* 25, 3, 1971, p. 420-442.

22 Lester B. Pearson. *Partners in Development; report on the Commission on International Development.* New York, Praeger, 1969, p. 185-189.

23 An example of the concern of trade unions is the action taken by the International Federation of Chemical and General Workers Union (ICF) in 1969. The ICF coordinated the confrontation with the French multinational glass manufacturing company, *Compagnie de Saint Gobain,* by unions in the Federal Republic of Germany, France, Italy and the United States. The confrontation dramatised a development which was taking place over a much wider front. See: Robert W. Cox, 'Labor and Transnational Relations', *International Organisation* XXV, No. 3 (1971), p. 556-557.

24 Anthony Jay suggests that the tendency of bureaucracies to frustrate the formation of natural working groups (ten-groups) leads to the enormous burgeoning of societies, professional associations, action committees and the like which provide the channel for the instinctively needed face-to-face purposeful group relationships. (Antony Jay: *Corporation Man.* London, Jonathan Cape, 1972, p. 58).

25 Donald Schon notes that the network of organisations is always out-of-phase with the reality of problems that people think are worth solving. The problem is to reduce this mismatch by increasing the response-time of the network. (Donald Schon: *Beyond the Stable State; public and private learning in a changing society.* London, Temple Smith, 1971).

26 Depending on assumptions annual non-travel expenditure by participants at international conferences in 1971 is estimated at US $ 0.25–3.0 billion. Travel expenditure is estimated at US $ 0.40–4.0 billion. (It has been estimated that one per cent of air travel arrivals are for international meetings.) Investment in conference facilities in 1966 was $ 0.8 billion ($ 8 billion required by 1980). The number of participants travelling annually to international-meetings is estimated at 2 million in 1971 (4-50 million in 1985). (Data at Union of International Associations. See also: *International Organisations and the Budgetary and Economic Aspects of their Congresses.* Brussels, UIA, 1971).

27 A group is currently forming in London to create an experimental INGO clearing body on which INGOs and MNCs would be represented. This would act as an interface to permit INGOs to benefit from MNC skills and to permit the latter to elaborate non-profit social programmes using INGO channels.

28 The term 'invisible college' is applied to the informal networks of scholars with an interest in a particular topic on which they exchange reprints, comments, etc. The network may be loose or very precisely defined but is vital to the research activity and professional standing of those concerned. (For their relationship to INGOs, see: Diana Crane. Transnational networks in basic science. *International Organisation,* 25, 1971, p.p. 585-601).

29   Johan Galtung. 'Violence, Peace and Peace Research', *Journal of Peace Research*, VI, No. 3 (1969).

30   Kjell Skjelsbaek. 'Peace and International Organisations', *Journal of Peace Research*, IX, No. 4 (1972).

31   Our reasoning here is parallel to that of David Mitrany as expressed in his book *A Working Peace System* (Chicago: Quardrangle Books, 1966). It should be noted, however, that Mitrany primarily thought of IGOs, but we feel that his functionalist propositions are equally applicable to INGOs.

32   Nils Petter Gleditsch: 'Interaction Patterns in the Middle East', *Cooperation and Conflict*, VI, No. 1 (1971), and Kjell Skjelsbaek, 'The Representation of Divided Countries in International Nongovernmental Organisations'. (Forthcoming)

33   Typically a volume of 580 pages on 'international organisations' may contain a 12 line reference excluding INGOs in the following terms,

'Des associations revêtant les formes d'une organisation internationale peuvent être créée par des personnes de droit privé ou de droit public non étatique . . . Mais, n'étant pas formées par les Etats, ce ne sont pas là des organisations internationales au sens strict des termes.'

(W.J. Ganshof van der Meersch. *Organisations Européennes.* Bruxelles, Emile Bruylant, 1966).

34   As an example, in justifying the exclusion of certain categories of organisations from an adequate data base on the global system, Michael Wallace and J. David Singer make the following point: 'First, our theoretical interests (and, we suspect, those of most of our colleagues) are more concerned with IGO's (intergovernmental organisations) than with nongovernmental organisations (NGOs) . . . One can hardly urge that the amount of NGO is likely to be important in accounting for many of the theoretically interesting phenomena which occurred in the system of the past century or so.' 'Intergovernmental organisations in the Global System, 1815-1960; A Quantitative Description' *International Organisation*, 24, 2, Spring 1970, p. 240) For some of the consequences of this attitude, see C.F. Alger, 'Research on Research; a decade of quantitative and field research on international organisations.' *International Organisation*, Summer 1970, p. 414-450. This study indicated that 66% of the studies were on the UN (28 bodies), 19% on the other IGO (201, possibly with the UN, 14% were on INGOs (2577), and 8% were on MNCs (2819). (Data on the numbers from the 1968-1969 edition of the *Yearbook of International Organisations*).

35   This general ignorance about INGOs is clearly reflected even in the deliberations of the ECOSOC subcommittee on NGOs, which, among other things, selects INGOs for consultative status.

36   For example, it proved impossible to create a national professional body in the USSR to work on public administration, stimulated by membership of the International Institute of Administrative Sciences, because public administration was not considered a science in the USSR.

37   In reviewing the results of the United Nations first Development Decade (1960-1970), the Secretary General of UNCTAD stressed that the highest priority should be placed on the persuasion of public opinion and the creation of political will to avoid a second Development Decade of even deeper frustration. The danger lies in the probability that the United Nations system

public information programme (together with those of the national United Nations Associations) will lead the informed public, many decision-makers, and UN officials to believe that the UN is doing all that can or need be done and has the attack on every world problem well-coordinated. This automatically devalues the activities of other bodies, reduces the allocation of resources and support to them, dampens initiative from the local and national level which is not channelled through governmental and UN channels, and effectively nullifies the type of constructive criticism which can lead to renewal of effort, new approaches, and galvanization of the political will necessary to the accomplishment of all internation (and *UN*) programme objectives.

38   See also: David Horton Smith. 'Future trends in voluntary action.' *International Associations.* **24**, 2, 1972, p. 166-169.

39   A.J.N. Judge. 'Wanted: New Types of Social Entity.' *International Associations*, 23, 3, 1971, p. 148-170. Also: 'Communication and International Organisations', *International Associations*, **22** 2, 1970, p. 67-69.

40   See argument, also appropriate to social system entities, in: David Bohn. *The Special Theory of Relativity.* New York, Benjamin, 1965, (Appendix on physics and perception).

41   See especially: Norman J. Schofield: 'A topological model of international relations' (Paper presented at a conference of the Peace Research Society, International, London, 1971—to be published in the Papers of the Society).

42   As an indication of the amount of internationally unrecognized organisation activity on which the more visible INGOs are based, David Horton Smith estimates for the USA that there are from 30 to 100 voluntary associations per 1000 population in towns with less than 10 000 (5 to 30 per 1000 for larger towns) giving approximately 5 million voluntary bodies for the USA as a whole. ('Estimation of the total number of voluntary associations in the United States'. Washington, D.C., Center for a Voluntary Society, 1970, unpublished paper; preliminary investigation shows that similar per capital figures hold in European countries). An indication of the amount of ad hoc linkage represented by the meetings of such bodies is given by a study for the Social Work Advisory Service (London). It was found that those with offices held an average of 23 inside meetings per year of more than 10 people, and an average of 5 outside meetings per year of which 50 per cent were for more than 200 people. (A study into the feasibility of establishing an administrative centre for a group of voluntary organisations. London, 1970, summarized in *International Associations*, 24, 1972, 3, p. 155-157).

43   Johan Galtung. 'Non-territorial actors and the problem of peace.' Oslo, Paper of the International Peace Research Institute, 1969.

44   'I have found in the corporation something that I can explain only in territorial terms even though it is not strictly territorial. It is a kind of territorial defense of role or job, and although it certainly operated within individuals, it is at its most powerful in groups: "my department's responsibility", "my salesmen's area", "my union's job" ... The result is something I can only call a quasi-territorial response, a defense of your means of livelihood calling upon territorial instincts but not precisely or exclusively territorial in its application'. (Antony Jay. *The Corporation Man,* op.cit. p. 132).

Functionalism and Multinational Companies
Michael Hodges

> An imbalance exists between the international industrial state and the national political state. Conflicts and tensions rather than areas of cooperation become emphasised. National governments and multinationals themselves will need to rethink their policies and operations in order to maximise cooperation but in addition and supremely what is now needed is negotiation on an international level.
>
> *Prospectus for the 1972 IBM Student Essay Prize Competition*

The quotation above illustrates the degree to which the emergence of the multinational company, and its potential conflict of interest with the nation-state, has become an item of conventional wisdom—a suitable case for essay treatment. Indeed, one of the most significant developments of the past twenty years is not the rise of the multinational company, which has a considerably longer pedigree, but the widespread acceptance of the notion of an international company, organising production and marketing across national frontiers. 'It's the Real Thing', the Coca-Cola commercial reminds us, and the symbol of that multinational company almost certainly commands wider public recognition than does the laurel-wreathed globe of the United Nations.

This is not to say that the multinational company is greeted with universal acclaim, but rather that it has been widely recognised as a new type of actor in the international system. If we accept Raymond Vernon's definition of a multinational company as 'a cluster of corporations of different nationalities that are joined together by a parent company through bonds of common ownership, that respond to a common strategy, and that draw on a common pool of financial and human resources',[1] then it would seem that the multinational corporation and its transnational activities are of some significance for functionalist theory. Given that the functionalist strategy is to 'overlay political divisions with a spreading web of international activities and agencies, in which and through which the interests and life of all the nations would be gradually integrated',[2] one would have expected that the role of multinational companies in creating interdependence would occupy some space in the literature of functionalism.

This does not, however, seem to be the case; functionalists have concentrated their attention on public international organisations such as the ILO or the economic development agencies of the UN,[3] rather than non-governmental organisations, and where NGOs have been considered these have generally been limited to non-profit bodies such as the International Air Transport Association or the World Federation of Trade Unions.[4] Jeffrey Harrod has suggested that the failure of Mitrany and later functionalists to accept multinational corporations as

225

worthy candidates for their theory was due to the Leninist assumption of an identity of interest between governments and corporations:

[Lenin's] argument that the corporation was an eventual arm of the State, if accepted, was fatal, in the functionalist's view, to any integrative potential. In contrast, the trade unions were always uncritically accepted.[5]

While Harrod's argument that Lenin's theory denied NGO status to corporations is somewhat overstated, it can be said that until the period following the Second World War the activities of multinational corporations were neither so geographically decentralised nor economically significant to enable them to be distinguished clearly from the policies of the governments of the nation-states in which the parent companies were located. Indeed, in one important review of international investment, published in 1937, the problems discussed were those of protecting overseas investors from government expropriation rather than protecting governments from undesirable investment.[6]

The source of the tension between multinational companies and national governments can only be understood if the growth and spread of multinational companies is seen to have taken place at the same time as the growth in the number of so-called sovereign states and the increasing importance of economic change and economic policy as the major function of their governments.[7] Although multinational companies in manufacturing (as opposed to resource-based companies which had perforce to be multinational in order to bridge the gap between their sources of raw material and their markets) began to develop at the end of the nineteenth century, they did so at a time when national governments attempted only the minimum of economic management. It is not therefore surprising that the transnational activities of these multinational companies were not considered to be significant: Frederick Mackenzie, the Servan-Schreiber of his day, addressed his warning of the 'American Invaders' not to the British government but to British manufacturers.[8]

One of the precursors of functionalism, Norman Angell, noted in 1909 that both capital and labour were becoming increasingly internationalised, and foresaw an incipient tension between the state system and the development of an international economy:

We have here, at present in merely embryonic form, a group of motives otherwise opposed, but meeting and agreeing on one point: the organisation of society on other than territorial and national divisions. When motives of such breadth as these give force to a tendency, it may be said that the very stars in their courses are working to the same end.[9]

The inability or unwillingness of international capital and labour to prevent the outbreak of the First World War, coupled with stagnation in international investment and the trend toward national economic self-determination in the depression which followed, were sufficient to cast doubt on the efficacy of the multinational corporation in developing transnational interdependence. The multinational corporation declined in economic significance as the contribution of the international sector to the growth in national GNP was reduced, while the intervention of national governments in their domestic economy increased.[10]

After 1950, however, the rate of international direct investment increased markedly, as the following table of foreign investment by US manufacturing companies indicates.

Book Value of Foreign Direct Investment by US Companies
in Manufacturing Subsidiaries, 1929-1969

Year	1929	1936	1940	1946	1950	1957	1964	1969
Book value in billions of dollars (=$000m.)	1·8	1·7	1·9	2·4	3·8	8·0	16·9	29·5

Source: US Department of Commerce

By 1966, the OECD estimated that the total value of foreign direct investment by companies originating in the advanced industrial countries amounted to $90 billion (thousand million), one-third of this in less developed countries. An increasing proportion of total investment was in manufacturing (40 per cent by 1966), reflecting a shift away from resource-based investment, and two-thirds of the total was controlled by companies whose headquarters were in the United States.[11] Raymond Vernon has calculated that multinational companies are responsible for between one-quarter and one-third of the output of goods in their 'home countries' and one-sixth of the output in countries that are foreign to the parent.[12] Still other estimates have put the value of overseas production accounted for by multinational companies at double the value of visible trade between the advanced industrial countries, and so on.[13]

The purpose of this dazzling array of estimates is to emphasise that multinational companies are becoming increasingly important as economic actors, and to make it quite plain that neither scholars nor governments possess a great deal of hard information about them; much of the hysteria inherent in the spectre of *le défi américain* is due to the fact that *les statistiques américaines* are far more comprehensive than those of any other country. The United Kingdom, for example, has only collected statistics on inward investments since 1958, and differentiated between domestic and foreign controlled business ventures for the first time in the 1963 census of industrial production. The activities of multinational companies have tended to evade the information-gathering capabilities of national governments in the same way that they evade national organs of economic management, and the result is that even the most scrupulous estimates of their economic significance suffer from the sin of exponentialism. Nevertheless, irrespective of whether the world economy of 1984 will be dominated by two hundred multinational companies or none at all, it is clear that students of international politics should pay some attention to the multinational company as an actor in the international system—if only because the value of the resources mobilised by some multinational companies approached the GNP of many nation-states and far outstrips the budgets of most public international organisations.[14]

The two most important implications of the multinational company so far as functionalism is concerned are: firstly, the degree to which multinational companies are themselves functional organisations, promoting international welfare and interdependence, however these may be defined: and secondly, the extent to

227

which the activities of multinational companies 'spill over', to use the functionalist term, into international integration.

The Multinational Company as a Functional Organisation

In recent years the argument has frequently been made that the multinational company possesses organisational capabilities which enable it to utilise resources more efficiently than purely national business enterprises, and that its role as a promoter of global economic growth and efficiency is frustrated by the division of the international system into increasingly obsolescent national economic units. Charles Kindleberger has contended that:

> ... The international corporation which scanned a world horizon would be more likely to improve the efficiency of goods and factor markets that function less than optimally because of distance, ignorance, and local monopoly.[15]

Leaving aside the questions of control of the multinational company, which will be considered in the next section of this chapter, it is important to examine the claims which have been made on behalf of the multinational company, and to assess whether it plays an indispensable role in the international system as a channel of capital, technology and managerial expertise. The discussion which follows will be limited to the role of manufacturing companies, rather than resource-based companies which have no option but to be multinational in order to unite their sources of raw materials and their markets.

Why do companies develop multinational operations? The reasons given are as diverse as the multinational companies themselves: defensive motives, such as a desire to surmount trade barriers by producing goods behind them, or to locate production facilities near markets or sources of raw materials, or simply to diversify markets in order to protect against cyclical movements; offensive motives, such as the need to sustain growth and profits despite governmental and competitive constraints in their home market, the opportunity to exploit lower costs of capital and/or labour, and the desire to penetrate a foreign market more effectively.[16] Perhaps the most persuasive general explanation, and one which has important implications for both those who argue that multinational corporations will dominate the world economy, and those who consider the multinational company to be a passing fashion, is the 'product cycle model' developed by Raymond Vernon.[17] According to this model, US companies developed new products and processes in response to their large, sophisticated and dynamic home market, which they then introduced abroad through exports. As overseas demand increased and competition intensified, the companies sought to retain their oligopolistic advantage by establishing foreign production facilities, using production techniques which had already been developed at home. After a time, development of competing products by local and other foreign firms erodes this oligopolistic advantage, and the multinational company is obliged to change the product, or differentiate it through increased advertising, or produce it at lower cost, or drop it altogether.

The implications of the product cycle thesis are important, since it hypothesises that the multinational company develops because it possesses a technological advantage which it wishes to exploit through maximum economies of scale, but that this advantage is a transitory one. The multinational company must continually innovate or make its production more efficient in order to survive the competition inspired by the success of its product, and must therefore possess an efficient management network and have access to a large pool of human and material resources in order to maintain its growth. Vernon found that the 187 most important US-owned multinational companies were of 'extraordinary size and profitability, committed to activities that involve the relatively heavy use of skilled manpower and of advertising outlays'.[18] The incentives for non-US companies to develop multinationally are even stronger, since they lack the large and dynamic home market which enables American companies to produce innovations, and need a substantial overseas market to attain economies of scale in production and marketing and to recoup research and development costs. It is significant in this context that Switzerland and the Netherlands have produced many important multinational companies—the Swiss pharmaceutical company F. Hoffman La Roche was founded in 1896 and within a decade was producing in the United States, United Kingdom, Germany and France.[19]

The advantages accruing to host economies from foreign investment by multi-national companies have been examined in some detail,[20] and it has been found that foreign investment in manufacturing industries makes a substantial contri-bution to the economic growth and efficiency of those countries in which subsidiaries of multinational companies operate. Foreign investment provides capital either from the parent company's own resources or from capital markets, where the size and profitability of the multinational company renders it an attractive risk, and the control network of the multinational company enables it to allocate this capital most profitably by raising it in the cheapest market and transferring it to areas of capital shortage. The multinational company has also tended to be more willing to locate its plants in depressed areas, both to win the approval of host governments and to take advantage of regional development grants, than have purely domestic companies, partly because it has a much more developed control network for managing geographically decentralised operations. The entry of a new manufacturing subsidiary can also have a beneficial effect on competition within the host economy, particularly where certain industries have a monopolistic or oligopolistic structure; in 1962 in France the entry of Firestone and Goodyear into the tyre market forced French tyre producers to reduce their prices and introduce product improvements.[21]

The most important contribution of the multinational company to the host economies in which its subsidiaries operate lies in the area of transfer of technology and managerial expertise. A.E. Safarian's study of foreign investment in Canada emphasised that 'access to the parents' stake of knowledge, as embodied in everything from its research and management skills to its production techniques and the product themselves, is at the heart of the process of direct investment. The emphasis so often given to the transfer of monetary capital . . . frequently pales by comparison.'[22] The oligopolistic nature of multinational companies indicates that the resources they control could not be easily obtained by other means: the Japanese experience demonstrates that other methods of technological transfer, such as licencing agreements, become less available where the proprietors of the technology see the applicant companies as potential competitors.[23] The result of this situation has been that the Japanese government has been obliged to permit more foreign investment in Japan, both to obtain the necessary foreign technology and to prevent retaliatory restrictions against overseas expansion by Japanese companies anxious to exploit their own technological advantages.[24]

229

As the soaring development costs of the Anglo-French Concorde project demonstrate, the development of an independent capability in the high technology field is an exercise which is beyond the resources of most national economies; yet it is precisely in the area of high technology that the greatest rates of economic growth are to be obtained. The establishment of a subsidiary of a multinational company offers the host economy access to the parent company's present and future technological resources, although the pace and extent of technological transfer lies within the discretion of the parent company. In order to develop a technologically advanced product, a company has to have access to large financial resources (whether public or private) and large markets in order to recoup research and development costs from sales of the finished product. It is for this reason that IBM, perhaps the archetypal multinational company, accounting for approximately 70 per cent of computer sales in the non-Communist world, manufactures in over a dozen countries and was able to devote $5 billion between 1964 and 1967 to develop and market its 360 range of computers—a sum which was ten times greater than the total sales of the largest British computer firm (ICT) during that period.[25]

The massive cost of technological innovation obliges companies to integrate their research, production and marketing on a worldwide basis in order to maintain their technologically-induced growth and profitability. As Christopher Layton has noted, a company has to possess not only the resources to develop technology, but also the ability to bring that technology swiftly into world markets:

> The company which is first or at least close second in the field makes the highest monopoly profits. Those which follow, say by buying the technology, only come into the market in time to see competition bring down prices and cut profit margins; by the time the market has stabilised, a new product may be ousting the old ... Time thus places a premium on internal innovation in a company, and on carrying out that innovation fast.[26]

The multinational company therefore is in a good position to maintain a competitive advantage, because it can develop, produce and market products on a global basis. The problem for host country governments is to weigh the advantages of access to technology—both in terms of the production of the finished article in the host country and the spin-off from such production in the form of supply of components to the subsidiary by domestic companies and imitation of the product by domestic competitors—against the disadvantages of technological dependence upon decisions taken by the parent-company outside the jurisdiction of the host government. Although such fears of dependence are frequently overemphasised, they are nevertheless well-founded. Advocates of the multinational company as an agent of international welfare argue that a company's overseas activities not only benefit the multinational company, by achieving maximum economies of scale in development, production and marketing of goods, but also make available to host countries technological and managerial skills at a lower cost than would be the case if these had to be generated by purely domestic companies.[27]

The crux of the relationship between multinational companies and national economies is that their respective interests may in some circumstances be complementary, but they are not identical. The multinational company's objective is to maximise its growth and profit by exploiting its competitive advantage to the full; the host government wishes to maximise national economic growth by gaining access to the technology possessed by the multinational company. This may lead to a situation where the multinational company is anxious to exploit obsolescent technology in less developed economies, and is reluctant to permit those economies to leap-frog by permitting them access to its 'state of the art' products—thus IBM has been criticised in India for perpetuating a time-lag between the development of new computer systems and their introduction to the Indian market.[28] Several advanced industrial countries, such as the United Kingdom and France, have used this argument as justification for creating national companies in 'commanding heights' industries—both ICL and CII, the British and French computer companies (which received extensive government support when they were created from an agglomeration of national companies), were seen as a means of forcing the multinational computer firms to make their most advanced products available in order to counteract the competition provided by the national companies.[29]

Multinational Companies and International Integration

There are two major obstacles to an assessment of the multinational company as an agent of international integration; the first is that in legal terms there is no such thing as a multinational company, only a cluster of companies registered under (and owing their identity to) various national laws, joined by links of common ownership and operating in accordance with a common management strategy; the second is that multinational companies vary considerably in the way in which they are organised and the managerial attitudes which govern their operations. Because companies are legal entities, and because there is as yet no international law of incorporation, both the parent company and its subsidiaries owe their personality and nationality to the national legal systems of the countries in which they are registered; unlike men, companies cannot be stateless. The subsidiary of a multinational company may be seen as an extension of the nationality of the parent company, as a foreign enclave in the host country's economy; alternatively, its links with the parent company may be almost invisible, and it is regarded as no different from the purely domestic companies operating in the host economy.

Management attitudes may reinforce either of these tendencies—Howard Perlmutter has characterised them as ethnocentric, where the subsidiary is subordinated to the parent company and nationals of the parent company's country of origin fill the most important positions, and polycentric, where the subsidiary is given more autonomy and links with the parent company are less salient.[30] Very few companies, however, have reached what Perlmutter calls the geocentric stage of development, where operations are planned on a global basis, promotion proceeds irrespective of nationality, and no fear or favour is shown in any country. Kindleberger considers that the truly international company would be conscious of the exchange risks it takes in any currency, including that of the parent country, and will equalise its profits throughout the world, discounting for risks at home as well as abroad.[31] As yet, the geocentric multinational company shows signs of developing only in the high technology field, where both markets and production are becoming increasingly decentralised.

Nevertheless, it is clear that there is a dichotomy between the national identities possessed by a multinational company and its transnational activities. Multinational companies have the capability to allocate resources across national frontiers, and are by definition institutionalised forms of transnational interdependence. The multinational company can increase economic interdependence not only by transferring goods through trade (as a purely domestic company can) but also by international rationalisation of production. A former chairman of General Motors, F.G. Donner, gave a graphic example of this interdependence of the production units of his company:

> If the South African assembly operation and its recently added manufacturing facilities are to function smoothly and efficiently, they must today receive a carefully controlled and coordinated flow of vehicle parts and components from West Germany, England, Canada, the United States and even Australia. These must reach General Motors South Africa in the right volume and at the right time to allow an orderly scheduling of assembly without accumulation of excessive inventories. This is a challenging assignment which must be made to work if the investment is to be a profitable one.[32]

In addition to increasing transnational interdependence by means of intra-company trade and specialisation of production, the multinational company has the capability to equalise factor costs and hence reduce sources of economic discrimination. Its ability to transfer capital across national frontiers, raising capital in the cheapest market and employing it in an area of capital scarcity improves capital formation and distribution, and might even tend to reduce international interest rate differentials. Equally, its ability to transfer technological and managerial expertise internationally would have a long term tendency to equalise levels of productivity. The key factor is the organisational nexus of the multinational corporation which enables it to allocate resources on a global basis far more quickly than national companies are able to do.

This organisational capability does not always have beneficial effects; as Richard N. Cooper has pointed out, 'most national economic policies rely for their effectiveness on the separation of markets . . . Increased economic interdependence, by joining national markets, erodes the effectiveness of these policies and hence threatens national autonomy in the determination and pursuit of economic objectives.'[33] The ability of multinational companies to transfer capital across frontiers not only reduces the effectiveness of monetary policy as a tool of national economic management, but also causes a marked acceleration in currency crises as these companies switch their currency holdings in order to protect themselves from a change in currency parities—foreign-owned subsidiaries whose parent company uses another currency for its accounting have far more reason to hedge against parity changes than a purely domestic company.[34] Another area of friction between national governments and multinational companies lies in the assessment of tax liabilities; because the subsidiaries of the multinational company are part of an integrated business enterprise, the allocation of profits among them involves an arbitrary element which the parent company can manipulate so that a high proportion of the profits accrue in a low-tax jurisdiction or are paid in a tax-exempt form such as royalty and service payments. To the extent that national governments perceive the activities of multinational companies as having a dysfunctional effect on their national economic policies, they have a choice of economic autarchy (foregoing the benefits of foreign investment) or attempting some measure of collaboration with other governments to control the multinational companies, such as Vernon's proposal for an international agreement on proportional allocation of the consolidated profit of the multinational company as a whole in order to assess its tax liability in the various countries where it operates.[35]

The multinational company may also provide a stimulus to further integration by other groups as a reaction to its activities. Because the production of the multinational company is geographically decentralised, there is an incentive for trade unions of the countries affected to conduct wage negotiations on a transnational basis: workers in high labour-cost areas have an incentive to aid the increase of wages in low labour-cost areas in order to prevent the multinational company from diverting production to those areas. The best example of transnational industrial action occurred in 1969, when the International Federation of Chemical and General Workers' Unions coordinated national union claims against the French-owned St. Gobain glass firm; twelve national unions contributed to a common strike fund and agreed not to work overtime in subsidiaries not on strike to prevent the company reallocating production. Strikes were organised in the US and Italian subsidiaries, and the management reached a settlement in both cases, implicitly accepting the argument of the American union that the losses sustained by the US subsidiary in 1967 and 1968 were irrelevant in view of the profits of the company as a whole.[36] The success of multinational companies in achieving growth and profitability also encourages hitherto national firms to seek out multinational links or to extend existing ones—such as the Agfa-Gevaert and Dunlop-Pirelli mergers and the proposal by the European Commission for a European Company statute to facilitate transnational industrial groupings.[37]

If multinational companies can sustain their growth and profitability (and there are signs that for US owned multinational companies there is a negative relationship between size and growth rate),[38] or at least maintain their current economic significance by shifting the balance of their activities geographically to offset international differences in the business cycle, then the incentive for existing national companies to go multinational will remain. If individuals employed by multinational companies believe that their wealth and well-being are associated with the growth of their employers, and that the restrictions imposed by a nation-state system inhibit the growth of multinational companies, then there may emerge a substantial transnational social grouping supporting international integration.[39] Support for integration will vary according to the extent that the multinational company adopts a non-discriminatory geocentric posture, with equal employment and promotion opportunities for individuals of all nationalities, but as yet there is little evidence that non-parent company nationals occupy strategic posts in multinational companies.[40] Quite apart from the employees of the multinational company, its products may have an effect in reducing international social and cultural differences—one thinks of coca-colonisation and the appeal of the Detroit-inspired sporty saloon car in this context. In short, the activities of the multinational company increase transnational interaction, and insofar as this fosters attitudes of mutual relevance and mutual responsiveness this will tend to promote fabourable conditions for social integration at the international level.

The extent to which the activities of the multinational company will spill over into political integration remains obscure. Although the multinational company has intensified what Karl Kaiser has called 'horizontal transnational interaction' because it operates simultaneously in several national economies in accordance with a common management strategy, the technological advances which make geographically decentralised business operations possible also have increased 'vertical interaction', to use Kaiser's phrase, within each nation-state.[41] It is now possible for national governments to intervene in almost every sphere of social activity, and to transmit information and form attitudes through the mass media; in a sense, both nationalism and transnationalism are creatures of technology. As Hymer and

Rowthorn point out, 'there is a conflict at a fundamental level between national planning by political units and international planning by corporations that will assume major proportions as direct investment grows.'[42] Since the multinational company requires a stable political environment if it is to function effectively, a disparity between the power of economic organisations and political ones is not necessarily in its interest.

Multinational companies may well come to consider that the disadvantages of effective political control over their activities (the loss of the capability to play one government off against another in order to gain maximum benefits from their global operations), are outweighed by the advantages of a more stable and predictable environment for their activities. Such a change in the attitudes of multinational companies—going beyond their frequent claim that they are 'good citizens' of the countries in which they operate to an assumption of the responsibilities of global citizenship—is of crucial importance in rendering international economic policy agreements effective. Just as instruments of national economic control require voluntary compliance by the majority of economic actors to be effective, so *a fortiori* do international agreements on matters such as monetary and fiscal policy, abuse of market power and allocation of tax liabilities depend upon the development by multinational companies of allegiance to the world community. As yet such an allegiance does not seem to have emerged—multinational companies remain firmly linked to their country of origin and, *in extremis*, look to their home government for protection.

What are the incentives for national governments to acknowledge the limits of their economic autonomy and establish international procedures for the control of multinational companies? The developing countries have long been conscious of their vulnerability to transnational economic activity, but there are indications that even the industrialised countries which have produced multinational companies are becoming acutely aware that multinational companies cannot be assumed to have an identity of interest with their home governments. The attempts made by both the British and United States governments in recent years to reduce their balance of payments deficits and strengthen their respective reserve currencies have been faced with the obstacle of American and British owned multinational companies counteracting these policies in order to defend their economic interests. There is a growing acceptance on the part of national governments that economic autarchy is more of a liability than an asset in promoting economic welfare, and that it is not sufficient to look to groups such as international trade unions, or countervailing 'national' multinational companies to control transnational economic activity.

Multilateral agreements on some of the major problems caused by the emergence of the multinational company are necessary and even feasible, but they are not sufficient in themselves. As Robert Cox has noted, there is a danger of a functional division between the rich and the poor:

> Nationalism ... is the ideology of revolution on behalf of the weak and poor; transnationalism is the ideology of the dynamic rich ... Historically, the geographically based power of the state has been the only power capable of counterbalancing unequal forces in the interests of welfare.[43]

The tension between the objectives of the nation-state and those of the multinational company can therefore only be resolved by imaginative institution-building at the international level. What is needed is a global institution which can make authoritative decisions on the allocation of resources, whose jurisdiction encompasses the activities of multinational companies, and which is capable of attracting the loyalty of both the dynamic rich and the powerless poor.

Such an institution, perhaps a federal world government, is an improbable feat of social architecture at this stage; for this reason the functionalist strategy of 'federalism by instalments', of defining common problems and proceeding to tackle them on the basis of converging group interests, would seem to be the most fruitful method of ensuring that the benefits and burdens of transnational economic activity are equitably distributed. Although the IBM slogan 'world peace through world trade' contains an element of hyperbole, it does indicate that the emergence of the multinational company presents a new opportunity for action at the international level in the interests of global welfare. Whether or not this opportunity will be exploited remains uncertain, but it is important that it be recognised, and it might perhaps be appropriate to end with the words of a writer who is by no means an advocate of international capitalism:

We are never completely contemporaneous with our present. History advances in disguise; it appears on stage wearing the mask of the preceding scene, and we tend to lose the meaning of the play. Each time the curtain rises, continuity has to be re-established. The blame, of course, is not history's, but lies in our vision, encumbered with memories and images learned in the past, even when the present is a revolution.[44]

Notes and references

1 Raymond Vernon, 'Multinational Business and National Economic Goals', *International Organisation.* 25 (3) (Summer 1971), p.694.
2 David Mitrany, *A Working Peace System.* London, Royal Institute of International Affairs, 1943, p.14.
3 Ernst Haas, *Beyond the Nation-State.* Stanford University Press, 1964; James Sewell, *Functionalism and World Politics.* Princeton University Press, 1966.
4 Kjell Skjelsbaek, 'The Growth of International Nongovernmental Organisation in the Twentieth Century', *International Organisation,* 25, (3) (Summer 1971), p. 421.
5 Jeffrey Harrod, 'Non-Governmental Organisations and the Third World', *Year Book of World Affairs 1970,* pp. 174-5.
6 Royal Institute of International Affairs: *The Problem of International Investment,* London:Cass, 1937.
7 Edward L. Morse: 'Transnational Economic Processes', *International Organisation,* 25 (3) (Summer 1971), pp.375-77.
8 Frederick A. Mackenzie: *The American Invaders,* London: Grant Richards, 1902, Unlike *Le défi américain,* Mackenzie's book was not a best seller and achieved notoriety only after 1945.
9 Norman Angell: *Europe's Optical Illusion,* London: Simpkin Marshall, 1909 p.119.
10 Simon Kuznets: *Modern Economic Growth: Rate, Structure and Spread* (Studies in Comparative Economics, No. 7) New Haven, Conn.: Yale University Press, 1966, pp.295, 321.
11 Sidney E. Rolfe and Walter Damm: *The Multinational Company in the World Economy,* New York: Praeger, 1970, pp.7-8.
12 Raymond Vernon: *Multinational Enterprise and National Security* (Adelphi

Papers no. 74) London: Institute for Strategic Studies, 1971, p.4.

13　Judd Polk: 'The New World Economy', *Columbia Journal of World Business*, January-February 1968.

14　In 1969 the total world sales of International Business Machines (IBM) were $7·2 billion (thousand million), the budget of the UN was $155 million, of the European Communities $3·9 billion, and the Gross National Product of Greece was $8·4 billion.

15　Charles P. Kindleberger: *American Business Abroad*, Yale University Press, 1969, p.189.

16　Michael Z. Brooke and H. Lee Remmers: *The Strategy of Multinational Enterprise*, London: Longman, 1970 pp.225-42.

17　Raymond Vernon: *Sovereignty at Bay: The Multinational Spread of US Enterprises*, London: Longman, 1971,pp. 65-77.

18　*Ibid*. p. 12.

19　Sidney E. Rolfe: *The Multinational Corporation* (Headline Series no. 199) New York: Foreign Policy Association, 1970 p.20.

20　See J.H. Dunning, *American Investment in British Manufacturing Industry*, London: Allen and Unwin, 1958; D.T. Brash, *American Investment in Australian Industry*, Canberra: Australian National University Press, 1966; A.S. Safarian: *Foreign Ownership of Canadian Industry*, New York: McGraw-Hill, 1966.

21　Jack N. Behrman: *National Interests and the Multinational Enterprise*, Englewood Cliffs, N.J.: Prentice-Hall, 1970 p.21.

22　Quoted in *Ibid*. p.17.

23　Thus in 1972 the Japanese electronics firm Sony unsuccessfully attempted to gain a licence from AEG-Telefunken of Germany to manufacture colour television sets using the European PAL system. See *The Sunday Times*, 6 August 1972, p.52.

24　Noritake Kobayashi, 'Foreign Investment in Japan', in I.A. Litvak and C.J. Maule (eds.): *Foreign Investment: The Experience of Host Countries*, New York: Praeger, 1970 p.153.

25　T.A. Wise: 'IBM's $5,000,000,000 Gamble', *Fortune*, September 1966, p. 118.

26　Christopher Layton: *European Advanced Technology*, London: PEP and Allen & Unwin, 1969, p. 19.

27　James Brian Quinn, 'Technology Transfer by Multinational Companies', *Harvard Business Review*, vol. 47 no. 6 (Nov.-Dec. 1969) pp. 147-161.

28　See Louis Turner, *Multinationals and the Developing World*, London: Allen Lane, 1973.

29　Economist Intelligence Unit, *The Growth and Spread of Multinational Companies*, London 1969.

30　Howard V. Perlmutter: 'L'entreprise internationale: trois conceptions', *Revue économique et sociale*, **23** (2), (May 1965), pp.151-66.

31　Kindleberger, *op.cit.*, p.183.

32　Quoted in Brooke and Remmers, *op.cit.*, p.71.

33　Richard N. Cooper, 'Economic Interdependence and Foreign Policy in the Seventies', *World Politics*, **24** (2), (January 1972), p. 164.

34　Joseph O. Vogel, 'The Real Culprit in International Money Crises', *Business Horizons*, **15** (2), (April 1972), pp.41-46.

35　Vernon. *op.cit.*, pp.274-277.

36 Hans Günter, 'The Future of Transnational Industrial Relations', in Hans Günter (ed.) *Transnational Industrial Relations,* London: Macmillan, 1972, p. 435.

37 Dietrich Maltzahn, 'Industrial Policy in the E E C', in *Industry and the Common Market,* London: Federal Trust, 1971 pp.66-78.

38 Stephen Hymer and Robert Rowthorn, 'International Corporations and International Oligopoly', in C.P. Kindleberger (ed.): *The International* Corporation, Cambridge, Mass.: M I T Press, 1970, p.70.

39 Bernard Mennis and Karl P. Sauvant, *Multinational Corporations and the Prospects for Regional Integration*, Paper prepared for the 1971 Anspach Conference, University of Pennsylvania, mimeo.

40 Kenneth Simmonds. 'Multinational? Well not quite', *Columbia Journal of World Business,* 1 (4), (Fall 1966), pp. 115-122.

41 Karl Kaiser, 'Transnational Politics: Toward a Theory of Multinational Politics', *International Organisation*, 25 (4), (Autumn 1971), pp.790-817.

42 Hymer and Rowthorn, *op.cit.*, p.90.

43 Robert W. Cox, 'Labor and Transnational Relations', *International Organization*, 25 (3), (Summer 1971), pp. 583, 584.

44 Régis Debray, *Revolution in the Revolution*? Harmondsworth; Middlesex: Penguin Books, 1968, p.19.

Functionalism and the Resolution of Conflict

John W Burton

The growth of functionalism has been observed most in international relations because international functional organisations, governmental and non-governmental, now comprise a significant part of the structural framework of world society. Mitrany[1], Haas[2], Sewell[3] and others have analysed functionalism and suggested that it is offering a practical alternative to more traditional notions of world government under a central political authority, and to power relations such as collective security and alliance structures. Most human and institutional activities cut across state boundaries, and are, indeed, universal. The functionalist looks at international relations as though there were one world society in respect of those concerns that are universal, such as air-traffic control, telecommunications and the like.

However, there appears to be no school of thought that directs attention to the growth of functionalism in decision-making within the state: political decision-making by a central authority seems to be generally accepted as being dominant at the domestic level, even by international functionalists. This concentration on functionalism as a development in the international system seems to carry the suggestion that structural trends and decision-making processes in the inter-state environment are different from those within the state. Whether this is so or not is important from the functionalists' point of view. Functionalists have a prescriptive, as well as an analytical interest, in the growth of international organisations. They see it as an alternative to the international system dominated by state authorities. Functionalists urge the encouragement of growth in these webs of human interaction, believing that it is possible to extend harmonious transactions in common and specific areas of interest, to relationships that are more political and less neatly organised. This prescriptive and optimistic view of functionalism is likely to be valid only if it is as inexorable at the domestic, as it is claimed to be at the inter-state level. The reason is that there is growing evidence that the failure of collective security schemes and alliance structures, and the reason for international conflict, can be traced to decision-making within the state[4]. If international conflict is essentially a spill-over of domestic politics, then this international functionalist alternative would not be successful in reducing it: no amount of functional cooperation at the inter-state level alone would eliminate the sources of conflict.

There is also an analytical reason why it is important to determine whether or not functionalism is essentially an inter-state phenomenon. We are dealing with the political organisation of social systems. Unless functionalism offers an alternative to political decision-making in certain specific fields at the domestic level, it is unlikely to develop and to provide an alternative form of organisation at the international level. Before it can be argued that health is best arranged internationally on a

238

functional basis, it needs to be demonstrated that this is also the case at the domestic level. Alternatively, if experience shows that health at the international level is best arranged within a functional framework, it should follow that it is best arranged in this way at the domestic level.

Many scholars concerned with international studies, including functionalists it would seem, refuse to entertain the view that there is a world society comprising different system levels, of which the inter-state is one. The traditional view is that there is a qualitative difference between world *society* and domestic *communities*. They point to the monopoly of power in the latter, and also to the additional complexities in the wider set of world relationships. But this is an untenable position—fortunately for the functionalists. There is no effective monopoly of power in any state where the legitimacy of authority is not universally recognised, and few states can claim a wholly legitimised status. Furthermore, if increased complexity were to make a qualitative difference, there could be no transference from one level of behaviour to another: psychology, sociology or political sociology would have no links. It has been academically and institutionally convenient to separate domestic politics and international politics; but this is an artificial and misleading distinction. In all cases of social organisation, no matter what size, we are dealing with the legitimised status of authority, role behaviour, decision-making, the nature of institutions, and the problems of change and adjustment. All these are matters involved in an analysis of any system, no matter where the boundaries are drawn.

Just as there are certain system properties common to all social organisations, so also there are organisational properties common to all: the problems of organisation and conflict that are experienced at the inter-state, inter-communal and state level are found also at industrial and other social levels. In addition, there is a constant spill-over from one level to another as when conflict in a depressed industry leads to measures that affect inter-state relations, and as when racial conflict within a state attracts external attention. In so far as functionalism is useful as a means of preventing or resolving conflict at any one level, it is likely to be useful at other levels: only in so far as functionalism is useful at lower levels of interaction, is it likely to be effective at others. Indeed, the functionalist argument is not a strong or persuasive one unless put forward in the context of a total world society that includes domestic relationships. It cannot be applicable and effective in reducing the political content of decision-making at any one level unless applicable at all levels that have a bearing on that level.

One reason why functionalists have concentrated on the inter-state level, and have gone along with traditional separations of domestic and inter-state politics, despite the logic of their position, is that the development of functionalism since the Second World War has been conspicuous, even dramatic, in the international field of governmental and non-governmental specialised institutions, but has been less conspicuous in the domestic field. Here, however, it is no less remarkable; it is less conspicuous because the institutional forms of democratic government disguise the functional nature of national administrations. It is the purpose of this chapter to examine the notion of functionalism in relation to domestic politics, and in relation to the handling of domestic conflicts that are likely to spill over into world society generally.

In doing this one is being descriptive and prescriptive. Functionalism at the domestic level is already advanced, and demonstrating that this is so is being merely descriptive, though perhaps drawing attention to circumstances that are not always recognised. On the other hand, one is being prescriptive in suggesting that in certain circumstances, in which intervention happens to be possible, advantage can be taken of functionalism as a means of preventing and resolving some types of conflict, especially communal conflicts, that spill over into the international field.

Functionalism in Domestic Politics

Functionalism is decision-making within a specialised area by persons skilled in that area, whose self-esteem and loyalties relate to their specialisation. A shift toward functionalism, and away from political decision-making, is already apparent in most developed societies. There are many areas of decision-making that have been made a-political in this way, just because governments find them politically too dangerous to touch. For example, in many states control of mass media and state instrumentalities such as TV and radio, is in the hands of appointed commissions. Their independence is formally guaranteed by terms of reference, and less formally, but more effectively, by public resistance to any governmental interferences. In some countries, once funds have been allocated to a University Grants Commission, further interference by governments is difficult.

One reason for this trend is that even societies that are not divided on some clearcut basis of religion or ideology, comprise peoples whose values ensure different groupings on different issues. Governments are thus in danger of alienating some of their own supporters when they take decisions on matters of general interest. In the Western party parliamentary system it is convenient for government and opposition to have 'free' votes on matters of divorce, capital punishment and the like about which supporters of all parties have their own personal viewpoints. The more politically developed a society and the higher the level of consensus politics, the greater are the number of issues that are a-political in a party framework. Leaving decision-making to appointed commissions or 'experts' is frequently a means of avoiding responsibility for decision-making at a political level. Where there are clear-cut communal divisions the need is even greater. The allocation of government built houses in a state divided ethnically or by religion is more conveniently carried out by commissioners who recommend the guide rules and are responsible for decisions based on them.

There is another class of governmental functional institutions which are created, not to avoid political embarrassment, but because day-to-day decision-making at the political level would be impractical. This is not a surprising development even in the most committed of private enterprise systems. Governments are being forced into formal responsibility for monopoly services, such as telephone and postal services; there are increasing demands for government control of welfare services such as health and education so as to ensure an equitable distribution; there are increasing technological reasons for government control of some services, such as railways and road building that are not attractive to private enterprise but may be regarded as socially essential and, perhaps, 'a strategic requirement'; there are increasing needs for research and advisory services which are designed to promote the long-term interests and development of the total community. There is a formal Ministerial responsibility for each of these, but little or no effective administrative control or management.

The process has gone further than at first appears to be the case. There are departments of agriculture, commerce and others which in practice operate as functional institutions. Many thousands of persons are employed in functional capacities with little supervision from a political level. There are services being performed, by relevantly skilled persons, and decisions taken, affecting the rest of the community. This involves something which is more than a mere delegation of authority: the department providing the services has an on-going behaviour of its own, not dependent upon political decision-making. Governments come and go, and there may be no effective government for periods of time, yet these organisations still function. Furthermore, most recommendations made for decision at the political level, give the political head little decision-making latitude. The temporary political head is formally, but not effectively, responsible.

Even in the allocation of resources between departments there is limited decision-making latitude: budgets are increased or decreased by small margins, and this, usually, on the advice of treasury officials who have the specialist function of determining the economic and financial trends of the economy. They in turn operate in an environment in which demands for instrumental needs and services are clearly expressed. Obvious anomolies, glaring social injustices and pressing developmental needs are not open to much question, and are likely to be dealt with administratively.

In effect, the parliamentary and governmental system is becoming a symbol of democracy rather than an important decision-making institution. The sudden elimination of decision-making at the political level through some major accident would not immediately affect the daily lives of the community. On the other hand, the break-down of functional services, would lead to chaos and hardship. More accurately, functionalism does not merely offer an alternative, it is inexorably altering political systems. Just as kings have become symbols, without decision-making roles, so will the political institutions of government. Indeed there are aspects of the parliamentary process in Western type democracies, and probably in others, which can be regarded as a game being played out in virtual isolation from the rest of the community. The annual ceremony on the steps of the residence of the British Chancellor of the Exchequer, in which he holds up his despatch case, is likely to continue even though his budget papers are presented to him in the House before he reads them, as the Crown reads its Parliamentary opening speech. There are aspects of social and economic relations which have a momentum and direction of their own, governments being passive and helpless by-standers. A recent settlement of a coal strike in Britain was decided against government policy and in favour of the miners after a recommendation made by a commission appointed by the government.*

Functionalist Theory

The size and complexity of modern industrial societies, planned or free-enterprise, are such that an increasing level of functionalism is inevitable. This is already creating a situation in which the location of political authority is difficult to determine. While the elected members of the Parliament at Westminster meet and debate government policy, representatives of trade unions and industry discuss wage and incomes policy, pensions policy, social service policies, the economic

*In the winter of 1972-3.

growth target and other matters of political moment. Their failure to reach agreement forces elected political authorities to take stop-gap action pending their agreement. In form authority is traditional state authority, in practice it is a functionalist process.

This becomes clear when we attempt to model political decision-making in the complex modern state. The models that have been put forward[5] seem to be applicable to particular institutions, such as a hospital, a factory or an army, but not to state decision-making. State decision-making is the end result of the processes that take place within and among all institutions, public and private. It is not one that can be traced or predicted by reference to input-output, cybernetic and other abstract models. All that can be said of the outcome, or can be predicted, is that it is likely to be one that reflects the dominant shared values, and the level of knowledge of the members of all the particular institutions concerned. However, there is not always a high level of shared values or widespread knowledge of political affairs. This means that modern societies, tending more and more toward functionalist structures, could move toward a Fascist state in which employers and employees in particular industries formed corporations and battled for a larger share of the national cake, at the expense of all consumers, including themselves; or, taking the other extreme, they could move toward an ideal form of a consensus society in which each member received according to his needs[6]. Functionalism is essentially a neutral concept in terms of values: it can be integrative or disintegrative. In domestic relations it will tend to be disintegrative in the absence of a high level of shared values. But in a condition in which there is a high level of shared values, almost all political systems work effectively: in its absence all are likely to experience instability. Functionalism is an organisational conception: it cannot be treated as solely an international one. If functional institutions can create a conflictual or integrative society domestically, they can no less promote such a society internationally. In either case there would probably be a spill-over into the wider world environment that would promote conflict or extended cooperation. Under stress conditions of any kind, the former is more likely. This is the issue which functionalists, in both their analytical and prescriptive roles, must face. Has functionalism particular features that overcome problems inherent in conditions in which shared values are at a low level, and does it promote shared values? What is its legitimacy status?

The effectiveness of each functional institution in producing expected results is an over-riding consideration in determining its legitimacy. Bureaucracy is associated in the public mind with inefficiency, failure to take responsibility and to adapt procedures to fit cases, lack of imagination and inattention to human needs. It is possible that a highly efficient administration does not attract the usual criticisms of bureaucracies: if needs and services are being provided effectively, the resistances to bureaucracy do not occur. Considering the powerful role of public administration in developed states, the fear and criticisms of bureaucracy are small. Advisory services to agriculturists and the management of utilities receive as much praise as criticism. The reason is, probably, the high and growing degree of efficiency of administrative elites. Bureaucracy is most criticised at local government levels and in less developed states.

International functional institutions do not yet have tasks, roles and responsibilities that attract the most skilled administrators and specialists in particular fields—except on short-term assignments. There is growing evidence of administrative inefficiencies and extravagant procedures. Large organisations like F A O, U N E S C O, the regional agencies of the Economic and Social Council are, for many different reasons, seriously inefficient as institutions. As functionalism at this level increases, so will reactions against international bureaucracy, at least until efficiency increases. While elimination of politics from functional decision-making overcomes many sources of tension, mal-administration and injustice, functional institutions like all institutions have within them their own sources of inefficiency. However, this is a criticism of management and a problem of organisation, and not directly a criticism of functionalism as such. The problem is that the growth of functionalism has been more rapid at the domestic and international levels, especially since the Second World War, than growth in the knowledge of decision-making, in organisational theory and in training.

Functionalism implies that the values of specialists, seeking to achieve their functional purposes efficiently, are compatible with the values of the consumers of their specialised activities. By confining decision-making to relevant technical considerations, non-rational behaviour, that is decision-making seeking personal, party or other sectional gains, is reduced if not eliminated. Thus the political decision-making of top management is confined to the allocation of resources between production, selling, investment and other competing claims on resources. Political decision-making at any systems level would be, in a system dominated by functional institutions, confined to its limited field, that is the allocation of resources among functional institutions operating at that particular systems level. The political decision-making of state authorities would be confined to the allocation of resources between different services, police, defence, education, health and others. Political decision-making at the inter-state level, ideally, would similarly be confined.

In neither the domestic nor the international case is there necessarily any decrease in the legitimacy of the authority involved. On the contrary, legitimacy is directly related to a particular activity by a particular authority: it becomes specific and probably measurable in terms of levels of satisfaction with services provided. One of the great problems of modern government is that authorities that are legitimised, in the sense that they have electoral support, are in a position to act in a non-legitimised way in respect of particular matters. Those over whom authority is exercised have a set of values, and are prepared to tolerate some unfavourable decisions rather than destroy more basic values. In the United Kingdom currently, people do not appear to accept the Common Market; but to prevent entry it would be necessary to destroy the parliamentary institutions and processes of electoral change of government. Functionalism is a means of taking general politics out of specific decision-making, a means of preventing decisions that are best made by relevantly skilled persons, being affected by the spill-over of party political pressures or rivalries. The legitimacy of functionalism is directly in relation to the services provided: there is unlikely to be tolerance of unacceptable decisions or behaviour, there being no wider political and institutional values to preserve. In a functionalist system, a post office or railway has to earn its legitimised status by performance: complaints by consumers must be on the basis of the service provided, and not on any basis of political, religious or other affiliation.

Furthermore, the legitimised status of a functionalist institution has to be achieved directly: there is no buffer between the institution and consumers as there is in a parliamentary system in which criticisms are by implication criticisms of the government and defended by the government. Attacks on financial policy are attacks on government, and treasury officials are thus protected from academic and other criticisms which could otherwise be made directly against the treasury, and particular persons in that department who might be known to be guided by particular financial opinions and theories. Functional institutions have no such protection. In this sense the legitimacy status of functional institutions is likely to be higher than would be the case within a Western type political system.

While particular decision-making in respect of a specific function is probably highly legitimised, the overall result of all functional decisions could render the total process wholly unacceptable. Whether at the national or international level, each functional institution could be efficient and satisfy those involved both as producers and consumers, yet create an overall situation in which all producers and consumers were in conflict with each other and with the system. This, indeed, is the result in a state organised along corporation lines. The car producer—worker and manager—seeks a higher share of the national cake, so do those engaged in the electrical appliance industry, in postal communications, in education and all others. While it is possible for everyone to gain in one field, everyone can lose in all others. What determines the political outcome of functionalism?

There is no fixed sum of satisfactions in a functionalist society: gains by those engaged in one functional enterprise do not necessarily lead to equivalent losses spread throughout the remainder of the political system. While this does tend to occur in monopoly capitalism in which production is restricted to the point at which increased prices maximise profits, it does not follow that functional institutions would respond to market conditions in the same way. A corporate state system is not a functionalist one: it is a variation on a free-enterprise one in which competition has been eliminated. Its origins, historically, are in conditions of economic depression, unemployment and decreased demand. It represents a defensive tactic by private enterprise seeking to maintain the value of capital. A closer analogy would be a set of conditions in which there were pressure on scarce labour and capital resources to satisfy demands, such as tends to occur in socialist systems. Furthermore, there appear to be tendencies in professional services, which form an important part of functional organisations, to push production to the limits of technical possibilities: health, education, space travel and communications. The limits are imposed only by resource scarcity.

Here we are forced back to the political issue: who determines the limits? who is responsible for the authoritative allocation of resources? Members of a functional enterprise have interests outside that enterprise. In practice they enact a great variety of roles and have a great variety of interests and values: the car producer is also concerned with local government services, education, housing, health, communications and others. His interests in his main role are constrained by his interests in his others. Trade unions, each struggling to improve incomes and conditions, are prepared to accept policies designed to prevent the inflation that in some circumstances their actions can create. There are shared values that tend to act as an invisible political decision-maker. It is to these that authorities respond in a parliamentary system, thus disguising or hiding from view the decision-making process that underlies developed political systems.

Furthermore, interests and values are not identical. The modern welfare state, and most federal structures, are based on a political philosophy that places values higher than interests: in them there is an accepted re-allocation of resources by grant systems or one-way non-reciprocated transactions. Many functional services are an outcome of this process. Not all are sponsored and decided by central or local authorities, and many of those that are have their origins within private activities. Probation and social services, education, health services and transport are but some examples. Resource allocation among these is a complex process that historically precedes official decision-making and goes much deeper into social interactions than formal processes of allocations of resources would suggest.

What is becoming clear is that functionalism is a condition that emerges in a highly complex and developed political system, in which there is a high level of over-lapping role behaviour creating shared values, in which there are administrative skills and awareness of interrelationships between different functional institutions, in which the complexity of political demands and tasks are beyond the decision-making capacity of any central authorities, in which interests and value systems extend well beyond the immediate requirements of survival. In such a political system, shared values are a consequence of a high degree of participation by the enactment of many roles by many members of society. Functionalism can provide opportunities for role enactment, and therefore can promote shared values; but on the other hand, it cannot emerge before there are the interactions associated with an advanced stage of social organisation. Attempts deliberately to form societies without formal political decision-making have not been notably successful. One essential of functionalism is a complexity of shared roles, and experimental, small scale societies have not had this. Like an intricate structure or a solid, society is held together, not by a central control, but by inter-connections of parts. Without this it is a pile of sand. Few national societies in our contemporary world measure up to these requirements. They are sometimes traditional, authoritarian and highly centralised, and this probably through necessity. Their stage of political and social development, relating to their economic development, limits interests and values to a degree that prevents integrative behaviour. Where does this leave functionalism as an international phenomenon?

Here we are led to stand traditional thinking on its head. For the most part, the nation-state, especially the multi-national state, is fragile and lacks cohesion. Its internal conflicts spill over into the wider environment because of cross national sympathies and identities. On the other hand, world society has many of these features of complexity and shared interests. States enact a wide variety of roles, and the state system is but one within the total world society. The very great number of governmental and non-governmental functional institutions that exist are a direct result of common interests and shared values. There is more cohesion in the world society of states, institutions and transactions than there is within most states. World society has many of the features of the reciprocating and un-reciprocated behaviour of a community, and many states have few.

Furthermore, a spill-back element from world society to the nation state is part of reality: membership of international functional institutions requires the development of national functional institutions in the same specialisation. The values and resource allocations of world society are thus transmitted to national societies: health, education, communications, agreed practices in commerce, standards of administration, are promoted. Developed and undeveloped states alike are now penetrated by world society. The narrower notion of state authorities was relevant only when values were predominantly confined within the boundaries of the state, and could therefore be subjected to the control of state authorities. In the modern world society state authorities are limited in their ability to control ethnic, ideological, scientific and other such trans-national linkages. The role of the state is no longer to protect and to defend certain interests once labelled 'national interests'. It is to assist in the process of adjustment to change that is an increasingly demanding one in the modern complex and rapidly altering world society. In this role the state is probably more active than it ever was, but its activities are more in relation to functional or instrumental services than in relation to values and their allocation. In short, there are developing within world society and within mature political systems 'overlapping webs of associations' related to specific purposes that cut across national boundaries and party politics, and enable societies and communities to live peacefully in conditions of continually changing affiliations, objectives and values.

Functionalism and the Resolution of Conflict

The main contribution that functionalism makes to the prevention and resolution of conflict between and within states is as a result of the spill-back process from international society. This is a long term process. Has functionalism a place in the immediate handling of conflict once it has occurred?

There are circumstances in which there are opportunities to encourage altered sets of relationships and changed institutions, as in a period of reconstruction after a break down of authority within a state, and after conflict between states. Examples are in the relationships between the communities in Cyprus and Northern Ireland, and between Israel, the Palestinians and the Arab States. In some cases the advantages of functionalism are more direct than in others. In Cyprus and Northern Ireland, for example, the issues seem to relate to majority—minority relationships, and one remedy is to find means of avoiding the problems of majority—minority decision-making. The role of functionalism is less obvious in the Middle East, though in this conflict the security and economic interests of all the parties involved can be attained ultimately only by functional cooperation in the allocation and employment of resources. Following the above analysis, three questions appear to be relevant in each instance. To what extent can functionalism be applied to a disintegrated society? What is the infrastructure or stage of development in each case? What further exposure to world society is possible?

There are two aspects of functionalism that are relevant to conflict within the state, as, for example, communal conflict. First, there are institutional developments that take place during conflict, and especially during long periods of stalemate, which inevitably influence possible outcomes: conventions regarding separate policing, as occurred in Cyprus and Northern Ireland, separate *ad hoc* administrations, and tacit cooperation between separate administrations, such as has taken place in Cyprus in relation to postal services, electricity and water supplies. At the same time education and other cultural activities tend to remain separate. Resolution of conflict must be based on these functional institutions for the reason that many vested interests and political roles become established during conflict, and talks between representatives that ignore these and seek some imaginative constitutional settlement are likely to be defeated by them. Part of a resolution is to allow such developments to continue, and in due course to consolidate them in a formal agreement. In Cyprus, as events proved, it was a mistake to attempt an overall constitutional settlement, and to try to alter a structure and relationships that had developed over years of stalemate. This live and let live process could lead to wasteful and inefficient functional processes; nevertheless, in due course the same felt needs that have led to separate development and limited functionalist cooperation are likely to induce other forms of functional cooperation and a larger degree of integration. This is the process by which federations emerge; separate states, going their own way (even to the extent of different rail gauges in Australia!) gradually feel needs for closer cooperation in a particular matter, forcing closer cooperation in others. Karl Deutsch has frequently observed that integration develops out of independence. The constitutional process is the making of a record of functional practices as they develop; and federal powers are thus differentiated, not by deliberate and logical decision, but by practice. A constitutional arrangement suggested by a third party, or arrived at by negotiation, is unlikely to satisfy all those involved in the very many functional arrangements that are affected.

Second, a functional approach would counsel against the allocation of political functions and political roles where there exists the possibility that functional institutions can adequately provide the services and the decisions required. The Cyprus Constitution, which finally was rejected by the Greek majority and led to further conflict, was a complex pattern of political functions and allocation of roles, imposed by external states, to ensure effective participation by the minority Turkish community, and protection of their political and social rights. The protection of the minority by constitutional means was itself a source of subsequent conflict. Communal conflicts relate to political power, and in this sense are to a large degree the direct consequence of power rivalries at an elite level. Prestige and the symbols of power are personally important. What is required in the resolution of a communal conflict is a structure that places operational power outside any formal political framework. Ideally there should be no political framework for the conduct of instrumental services: commerce, housing, communications, development, tourism and even educational standards and health are specialist functions. Decisions regarding them are best taken outside party or community politics. Proportions of community representation and role allocation are then not relevant. Majority voting, and definitions of democracy in terms of majorities, which have been a feature both in Cyprus and Northern Ireland, are quite irrelevant in a functional system. The Western party political system provides a structure that is calculated to encourage elitist rivalries, to maintain the ascendency role of majorities, and to aggravate if not to promote community conflict. Looking down the list of functions of the government of Northern Ireland, one wonders whether the conflict was about the division of a cake of given size and discrimination in its division, or the maintenance by the majority of an ascendency position, and in particular, the preservation of positions of political power by a small political elite. If Northern Ireland were an independent state, and if its government were required to take decisions regarding the allocation of resources between, for example, defence and social services, political conflict could be expected, as there always is during processes of authoritative allocation of resources. But the conflict would, in this case, not be on a communal basis as much as on a basis of privilege, and under-privilege, cutting across cultural boundaries.

It is interesting to note that in Northern Ireland, where there has been an opportunity to avoid party political decision-making except that which takes place at Westminster, the attempt is to reconstitute a local parliament on a party basis. In

September 1972 a conference took place of party political representatives. The selection of elected representatives, and the exclusion of community leaders, prejudiced the outcome: a parliamentary system with built-in safeguards for the minority was the agreed conclusion. This was shifting back to a status quo structure. On this basis Northern Ireland will suffer the fate of Cyprus. The identification of 'democracy' with party parliamentary systems, the notion of majority rule and, law and order under majority rule, are powerful influences in Western conventional wisdom. That they have within them structural pre-dispositions towards conflict, particularly in societies comprising several communities, is not a thought reflected in public policies. Perhaps the reason is that no alternatives seem possible: functionalism is still a novel notion. But more importantly, there appears to be a fundamental problem of change. Even though functionalism was widely acknowledged to be a viable and acceptable alternative, how is the political elite to be persuaded? The answer is probably that it cannot be: there can be no change in basic institutions in the short term except by violence, in order to make further resistance to change too expensive.

The practical test of any structural means of resolving conflict is, therefore, whether it has built in it some process of structural change. Constitutional amendments consolidate. Protections and guarantees within a political system that rests on majority control frustrate all parties and perpetuate conflict. Functionalism does have a built-in tendency to erode political decision-making, while not immediately requiring any structural changes. In fact, both in Cyprus and Northern Ireland this has been happening. The administration has carried on in Northern Ireland with a minimum of political supervision. Whatever political institutions are created, they will not again have the dominating influence they had, nor allow personal politics to control events. In Cyprus, the peace-keeping role of the UN has, over many years, enabled functional customs to grow, and the type of settlement being discussed provides for elements of cultural independence, and elements of functional cooperation, generally, within the framework established during conflict.

So far we have been concerned with conflicts within the state. Conflict between states is different only in that different systems levels are involved. However, the different system levels in practice are significant. Greek and Turkish Cypriots both seek to maintain ethnic and cultural identity, both for their own sakes and for reasons of security. Each community is, however, penetrated by the other and shares some common functional services. In the Middle East case the inter-penetration can be prevented effectively, and separate identity can be maintained as a policy and in practice at least for the years ahead. Zionism can survive, at least until the penetration of Jewish society occasioned by occupation of Arab territory and dependence on Arab labour has its effect. The level of transactions and shared values in the wider Jewish-Arab relationship is not such as to make functionalism a relevant solution. Nor do the separate infra-structures provide an adequate foundation on which to build cross-national transactions. Tourism is a weak link. Functionalism has a limited application in the provision of super-ordinate goals such as irrigation, nuclear power supplies and rehabitation of displaced persons, and such activities as those dependant upon a high level of cooperation between the rival authorities.

The conclusion must be drawn that while functionalism is a long term process by which shared values are created, it is relevant to the resolution of conflict only in those circumstances in which there are already shared values arising out of a high level of overlapping role behaviour. In such circumstances it can be promoted as a means of avoiding majority-minority decision-making, and the communal problems that occur as a result of it. Northern Ireland, Cyprus, East and West Germany, North and South Korea are examples where it could have an application.

It may be that the higher the level of functionalism within a state, the less frequent or likely is involvement in inter-state tensions and conflict by that state. We are going through a phase in political science in which we are being made aware of the great number of variables that influence political life. Empirical experience is that there are usually one or two variables of great significance—as when it was discovered that time taken to obtain petrol was the only significant one of scores of variables examined to find out why some service stations were profitable while others were not. In conflict studies attention is now focusing on legitimisation of authority and levels of structural violence, other variables such as participation, discrimination, aggressive behaviour and others being sub-variables. When political analysis passes through this phase, and by empirical means determines the relative significance of variables in such a way as to reduce those which operationally demand attention, so too will political theory dwell on some basic notions of human organisation. In the meantime political practice points the way. Functionalism will continue to be resisted by those whom it makes redundant—but for good or ill its supremacy nationally and internationally is a matter of time.

Notes and references

1 David Mitrany, *A Working Peace System*, Chicago: Quadrangle Books, 1966.
2 Ernst B. Hass, *Beyond the Nation State*, Stanford, California: Stanford University Press, 1964.
3 J.P. Sewell, *Functionalism and World Politics*, Princeton, N.J: Princeton University Press, 1966.
4 James N. Rosenau (ed.), *International Aspects of Civil Strife*, Princeton, N.J: Princeton University Press, 1964.
5 Richard C. Snyder, H.W. Bruck and Burton Sapin (eds.), *Foreign Policy Decision Making*, New York: The Free Press of Glencoe, 1962.
6 See the anarchist literature, for example, Peter Kropotkin.

Functionalism and International Economic Relations
James Mayall

The functionalist argument represents one of the few recent attempts in the academic study of international relations to design a political theory for the contemporary world. Like most political theories its object is, in the last analysis, normative: it is concerned with how the world could be better arranged than at present. Although several versions of the argument can be found in the literature, the core of the idea remains, as Professor Mitrany formulated it, an enfilading attack on the problem of international cooperation which is achieved by shifting the focus of diplomacy from divisive political issues to non-controversial technical problems in which states share a common interest.[1] As with Marxist analysis, the ultimate viability of the functionalist approach rests on a necessary assumption that the economic sub-structure of society ultimately determines its political character, or at least can be made to do so. Only on such an assumption, for example, could Mitrany conclude that 'economic unification would build up the foundation for political agreement even if it did not make it superfluous'.[2] I do not share this assumption; but it is not my purpose here to question its validity: for even if it is shown that the implied distinction between economics and politics is fallacious, or that it is the political order which determines the economic, it may still be the case that, in the contemporary world, international economic cooperation fulfills a 'need' in the sense that states could not manage without it; and that the system of economic cooperation contributes, therefore, even if only indirectly, to the maintenance of international welfare and security.

This, at any rate, is my initial assumption and the present essay is addressed to the two questions contained within it. Since from the mid-nineteenth century, most states have been involved, willy-nilly, in the international economy, the consequences of this involvement and the development, in the light of experience, of ideas for its management, must be central to any analysis. The first section attempts, therefore, to place functionalist theory as it applies to international economic relations, within its historical and intellectual context. The argument is then developed with reference to the Bretton Woods system, the network of post-Second World War economic institutions, which represents the first concerted attempt to establish, by diplomatic means, a system of international economic management.[3] The final section considers, in a functionalist perspective, recent developments in international trade and payments and their implications for the future.

The Laissez-faire Origins of Functionalist Thought

At the heart of most discussions about functionalism are two inter-related propositions: first that international harmony (if and when it is achieved) will be a

250

by-product of the growth of a 'genuine' international community; second that its emergence will be brought about by the growing inter-penetration and inter-dependence of national societies which will gradually render obsolescent—and indeed on one view have already done so—the nation-state framework of political organisation. Views as to what the new world will look like differ sharply, some seeing in the EEC and other regional organisations, a precursor of the new order, while others, like Professor Mitrany himself, see in the proliferation of regional organisations merely the old world writ large, and look, therefore, for an entirely new system of international organisation which will reduce, and eventually eliminate, the significance of political boundaries. But in a real sense such controversies are, at this stage, premature, partly because none of us have been there, more importantly because they confuse the issue. Where functionalism differs from the mainstream of Western political thought—although not, of course, from Hegel or Marx—is in presenting an argument about change rather than about human nature or a Platonic ideal. In the latter kind of argument it is the ideal, or the assumed immutability of human characteristics, which provide the basis for reflections on the nature of social and political organisation. A theory of change, on the other hand, can only appeal to history: to direct the future it is necessary to have interpreted correctly the process of social and political change in the past.

Whether acknowledged or not the intellectual lineage of functionalist thinking on international economic relations may be traced to the 'classical' liberal economic philosophers of the ninetheenth century who held, in opposition to the earlier Mercantalist theory, that trade was fundamentally contrary to war, that whereas political rivalry inflamed the passions, trade pacified. This was essentially a rationalist doctrine under which, as Raymond Aron has pointed out, 'a universal republic of exchanges' was assumed to exist.[4] 'Conquer the whole world', Bentham wrote, 'it is impossible you should increase your trade one half penny.'[5] But if the liberal economists exposed the irrationality of the Mercantalist proposition that power rested on a fixed stock of precious metals (and that commerce was thus no more than a functional equivalent or alternative to war) they were on weaker ground in dealing with the irrelevance of political boundaries. Since these manifestly exist, and since there was little evidence—then as now—to suggest that political antagonisms are, in fact, dissolved by commerce, it is necessary to introduce the concept of *community* if the 'peace argument for trade' is to be salvaged as an operational hypothesis.

It is not my intention to define precisely the concept of community; nor would a definition be particularly helpful. But if we are to understand the limits as well as the possibilities of international economic cooperation, two features of this development should be stressed. First, the idea of community is implicit in all liberal thought; but, secondly, it was weakened from the start by a mechanistic interpretation which bore little resemblance to any real society.

Whether or not the increasing economic inter-dependence of the modern world is leading towards the end state of a genuine international community, is a matter for debate. What is of immediate interest here is that in reacting to social and economic change, and in attempting to direct it creatively, there has been amongst Western economists and political thinkers, an almost universal nostalgia for the world before 1914. Even so *engagé* a writer as Professor Myrdal refers to the pre-First World War international system as 'like Athens in the days of Pericles, in many respects a model civilisation', vulnerable because it excluded from its benefits

251

the majority of mankind and because its mechanisms are no longer appropriate to arrest the trend towards greater world inequality, but encapsulating, nonetheless, an ideal.[6]

Such nostalgia should not surprise us, for the ideal is, in many respects, attractive. It takes shape in the idea of the free citizen living in a secure world in which political power is not abused and the individual is free to develop his talents. Political boundaries may exist, but the damage which they cause to individual welfare (and by extension to national and international welfare also) can be substantially reduced, on the liberal argument, providing that governments themselves agree to implement the laws of *positive* economics. Thus the classical economists prescribed a set of policies which derived from a philosophical commitment to individual freedom and an idealised conception of the market. The system was to be underpinned by universal rules and a self-denying ordinance by governments against interference in economic affairs at home and abroad.

Despite its social Darwinian implications, this *laissez-faire* model of the international economy rested on the prior assumption of a mechanistic harmony of interests. So long as governments refrained from active intervention in the market the law of comparative advantage would, in the long run, optimise welfare for all. Meanwhile, although individuals and even groups would unavoidably suffer as a result of the re-allocation of resources through the market, this need have no affect on political relations between states, all of which accepted the automatic operation of the gold standard as the foundation of the system.[7] Reduced to its essentials the attraction of classical economics for functionalist theory is clear: on the one hand the system required a code of international behaviour in commercial and monetary affairs, the observance of which constitutes *prima facie* evidence for the existence of an international community; on the other hand a vital and potentially explosive area of international life is removed from the political arena.

There is, of course, a difficulty. The case for international organisation, and its justification, is often held to rest on the identification of a 'felt and present need'. To argue, with Professor Mitrany, that this formula constitutes, in the present historical context, an imperative which is both non-ideological and non-territorial[8], is, perhaps, to beg the question. But what is clear is that 'needs' present themselves here and now and are not to be put off by a glib reference to the long-run benevolence of the market. The acceptance of the welfare principle, in theory by all governments, and in practice by a few, cannot be accommodated within the classical theory since it plainly involves government intervention. Within the domestic context, at least in the Western democracies, governments have attempted to soften the impact of the market in the interests of public welfare on a pragmatic rather than a theoretical basis. For functionalists, the problem has always been how to extend this principle (which is both an expression of community and emanates from it) from the national to the international level. The question is how?

They have generally responded to the problem with a characteristic blend of realism and idealism. This can be partly explained by the fact that the approach is heir both to classical liberal theory, with its distrust of political power, and of the social democratic tradition, which has tried to mitigate both the inefficiences and the inequalities of the *laissez-faire* system while retaining its respect for individual freedom. Where the functionalist theory may justifiably claim to be realistic, if not original, is in rejecting the *'positivist'* claims of classical economics. After all the gold standard, as the central mechanism of an allegedly a-political trade and payments system was in its wide (although never universal) appeal, a cultural not a natural phenomenon, and its operation depended upon British commercial and political supremacy. In fact, as Karl Polanyi effectively argues, far from describing a law of nature, economic liberalism was a response to specific historical circumstances in a few countries[9], just as the subsequent resurgence of economic nationalism was in part a response to an 'unnatural' (and unprecedented) dependence on foreign trade. But the world wide expansion of European power and ideas, even though they contained their own nationalistic backlash, nonetheless created for the first time a world economy on which the welfare of whole populations depended, and increasingly as time went on, the fate of governments hinged. The Great Depression proved the point conclusively. By 1945 management of economic inter-dependence was clearly 'a felt and present need' which demanded a system of functional cooperation.

So far so good. But here the argument often falters because it continues, in the tradition of the classical theory, to discount the importance of political boundaries. Once the problem has been identified as international, it follows, in functional terms, that it can only be handled successfully at the international level. This view, while true in part, is also dangerously unhistorical. During the last third of the nineteenth century there was little apparent conflict between the process of national integration in the industrial world and a continuous development towards international economic integration.[10] From the First World War, however, a tension developed within the two lines of development: in reaction first to the war and then to the great depression, most states 'built up an armoury of national policies to defend their economic welfare and stability from adverse influences of outside events'.[11] While experience of these 'beggar your neighbour policies' persuaded most governments that they were cumulatively disastrous, and, therefore, of the need for an effective institutional framework for international monetary and commercial relations, it was doubtful, even in 1945, whether economic relations could be successfully de-politicised. Experience since then suggests that these doubts were well-founded.

The reason for the stubborn refusal of the state to recede into the background in the economic sphere has more to do with the process of national integration, and with the expanding role of national governments in economic management and the social services, than with the venality of politicians, or the much quoted absence of political will. Political will cannot exist in a vacuum; indeed it would be most irrational of governments to surrender effective control over their international transactions to an international body, so long as they retain responsibility for the welfare of their own citizens, and—in the Western democracies at least—governments are more likely to be dismissed for economic mis-management than for anything else. It is true that inter-dependence in the industrial world has now reached a point where governments are often dangerously vulnerable to market movements over which they have no control.[12] But while this is an argument for closer cooperation between them, it suggests a need for a more sensitive understanding of the political implications of economic developments, rather than the transfer of responsibility for economic relations to a technical (and by implication a-political) agency.

A more serious proposal is to transfer responsibility for economic policy, incontestably a political matter, to a higher political authority on the grounds that the nation state can no longer discharge this function. Without debating this argument it is worth repeating that if it is advanced in support of regional integration then the problem of international cooperation and discord is merely taken to a higher (and possibly more dangerous) level; alternatively, if it is applied at the global level, however logical the argument may appear, it is bound to encounter immediate problems of psychological credibility. In short, there is no more evidence to support the functionalist contention that the state can be expected to wither away piece-meal as it recognises the needs of international society one by one, than there was for Marx's more sweeping view that, once its historical task had been accomplished, the state would simply disappear.

To accept that the state will continue to dominate international politics is neither to deny the significance of trans-national society for state behaviour, or to discount the contention that global problems require international cooperation. But it does introduce a note of caution about arguing from a domestic analogy about the needs of world society. If the state, and hence the criterion of national interests, are dissolved, how and to whom do these needs present themselves? There can be only two answers to such a question: either an organisation must be created with real powers, for example to re-distribute world income, in which case policies, however technical their basis, are likely to be the subject of intense political, even ideological, concern to interested parties; or we are back in the world of classical theory where 'needs' are already present 'in the nature of things'.

This is not merely an ambiguity implicit in academic theorising: it sometimes confuses the real objectives of the international economic organisations themselves. When, for example, the Final act of the 1964 UNCTAD called for 'remunerative, equitable and stable prices for primary commodities' the developing countries interpreted the phrase as a mandate for the establishment of international commodity agreements which would guarantee them increased foreign exchange earnings. On the other side, the industrial states argued that the phrase simply meant market clearing prices.[13] The developing states hoped that by devising a mechanism which would re-distribute wealth on the basis of an economic formula they could escape the unpredictable political largesse of the major powers. As the major aid donors, the industrial states opposed the concept of concealed transfers. Both sides, in other words, sought to invoke economic theory to settle an inescapably political point. But beyond such special pleading there is a more basic controversy over the form that functional cooperation should take. Once one moves away from the provision and coordination of specific international services, as for example, in the work of the Universal Postal Union, to policy areas such as commercial and monetary affairs, in which specificity is clearly more difficult to establish, the problem of cooperation becomes more complex. In such cases, where an acknowledged need for coordination in no way precludes sharply conflicting policies, should the objective be to establish a framework, universal in application, but, so far as possible, politically neutral, within which economic growth and social transformation will proceed 'naturally'? Or does the nature and urgency of the problem demand a more creative and purposive approach, in which case from where are both goals and authority to be derived? It is to this problem as it has presented itself within the existing structure of international economic institutions that we must now turn.

The Bretton Woods Framework

In a politically de-centralised international political system the difficulty of achieving agreement on this last question has almost inevitably led to an emphasis on cooperation to maintain a common framework of minimal rules, that is to passive rather than to active functionalism. This is true of all three institutions (IMF, IBRD and GATT) which were designed after the Second World War to deal respectively with international finance, investment and trade. But it applies with special force in the trade and monetary fields with which this argument is primarily concerned.[14]

The architects of the post-war economic institutions originally conceived a role for them which was considerably more interventionist than they turned out to be in practice. The emasculation of the principle of international control was the outcome of a conflict of interests between the United States and the rest of the world.[15] While for the United States the establishment of a liberal trade and payments system had been elevated to the front rank of American war aims from the Atlantic Charter on, Britain and the European powers were not prepared to surrender sovereignty over economic affairs without an effective guarantee that the United States would maintain a policy of full employment and thus save the industrial world from a replay of the great depression. In Britain, for example, there were important sections within both major political parties, who favoured a foreign economic policy directed fairly exclusively towards the Commonwealth; the Beveridge Report, by laying the foundations of the welfare state, had also ensured that the state would remain heavily involved in the management of the national economy. But such attitudes fed in turn into American fears of European financial irresponsibility and reinforced their determination to hold out for a system of universal multilateralism based solidly on the discipline of the market.

In the monetary field, American fears that they might be required to provide the rest of the world with unlimited and unrequited credit, restricted the role which they were prepared to allow the IMF in the management of international monetary relations. It was chiefly in anticipation of such political pressures on both sides of the Atlantic that Keynes and White, the main negotiators on each side, had striven to achieve a politically neutral and technically authoritative monetary system at the outset, which would overcome the problem of political boundaries, as it were, by decree.[16] But in negotiation neutrality is difficult to achieve: both men were national representatives and their proposals inevitably reflected national pre-occupations. In retrospect it may be argued, of course, that Keynes's plan would have suited the United States well.[17] It would after all have established an international currency, provided within fairly generous limits, automatic credit access and, beyond these limits, imposed equivalent sanctions on surplus as on deficit states, ideas which are not far removed from current United States views of international monetary reform.[18] But, at the time, the surrender of national control which appeared to be necessary to comply with these proposals would have rendered them unacceptable to American opinion and to Congress. Thus the Articles of Agreement of the IMF, as they finally emerged, bound member states to the principles of multilateralism and free convertibility, and made provision for short term relief for states in balance of payments difficulties; but it failed to establish a genuinely international mechanism for the management of the world economy—the function that had once been performed (at least in theory) by the gold standard.

Two aspects of this failure are of interest: first a national currency—the United States dollar—remained, *faute de mieux*, at the centre of the system; secondly the authority of the new institution, and the funds available from it, were inadequate to support the chosen system of fixed exchange rates. What emerged, therefore, was a system under which the major currencies were vulnerable to periodic crises, which in the end could only be resolved by a change in exchanges rates, a solution which (despite the bias of the system against such action) was open to all except the United States. The partial breakdown of the international monetary system in 1971 reflected this structural imbalance: one of the main questions currently under debate is *how* the United States should move from its position of *primus inter pares* in the post-Second World War system to being a mere state among states. What preoccupied governments between 1945-1960, however, was not the long-run problem of monetary stability, with which the IMF was supposedly intended to cope, but how to dismantle the apparatus of national economic protection and control built up during the war while acknowledging their primary and on-going responsibility for employment and social welfare. For this practical task the theory of liberal multilateralism was largely irrelevant. When the major European states returned to convertibility in 1958, the ground-work had been prepared not by the IMF, but within the European Payments Union and the OEEC, the institutions which had been established (with United States backing and support) to preside over European reconstruction under the Marshall Plan. While the commitment to the broad principles of universal multilateralism and free convertibility survived, the experience of reconstruction reinforced regional loyalties at the expense of universal ones.

A parallel development occurred in the trade field. The commitment to multilateralism in the Havana Charter, which was to have established the ITO[19], was so hedged about with qualifications and escape clauses, in particular to safeguard full employment policies, that in the end it was never even submitted to Congress for ratification. But it survived in a restricted form in the GATT, under which the *Contracting Parties* bound themselves to liberalise trade by the abolition of quotas, the reduction of tariffs and the binding of discriminatory preferences at their existing levels (the 'no new preference' rule). The last of these objectives represented the main concession which the United States was able to secure in return for what were, at the time, in effect, unilateral concessions on the tariff front: so long as it lasted the post-war dollar shortage meant that governments had no alternative to maintaining wide ranging physical controls over imports. But, as with money, the real obstacles to trade—this network of quota restrictions—were primarily overcome within OEEC, that is at the regional rather than at the universal level.

The tension between regional and universal levels of functional cooperation was, from the start, more marked in commercial than in monetary relations. While departures from multilateralism in international payments could always be defended as 'bowing to necessity' to protect the balance of payments, the GATT had to accommodate an exception to the rule of non-discrimination which was backed by an extensive (and authoritative) economic theory. In accordance with the views of Professor Viner and others on the theoretical basis for the establishment of Customs Union[20], Article XXIV of the GATT permitted Contracting Parties to discriminate in their trade relations provided their intention was to establish a full fledged Customs Union or Free Trade Area.

The practical implications of this major exception to the 'no new preference rule' have a direct bearing on the long-run viability of an international commercial system based on the principle of free trade, or, as the GATT system is in fact based, on progressive liberalisation. In theory a Customs Union is consistent with the optimisation of wealth (and presumably welfare) if and when the resulting growth of trade with the outside world is greater than the trade lost by suppliers who cannot compete over the new external tariff, the creation of which accompanies the dismantling of internal barriers to trade. But who is to say—and at what point in its history—that this is the case with any particular Customs Union? In practice, of course, optimisation, in the sense it is understood by economists, is not the sole or even the most important criterion on which a decision to establish a Customs Union is likely to be taken. If European experience is any guide, the evidence suggests the creation of a union is merely one sign amongst many that a group of states have decided (without going so far as federation) to change the political relationships between them.

Two consequences follow from the inclusion of the Customs Union and Free Trade Area provisions in the GATT. The first concerns the general structure of the international trading system. Since at any time various groups of states may decide to integrate economically, there is an inherent contradiction between the goals of non-discrimination and free trade, on which the system is allegedly based, and how it operates in practice. I shall return later to the implications of this contradiction in the current controversy over trading blocs: the point to note here is that the only way a Customs Union can mitigate the damage which its creation will cause to the established interests of third party suppliers (at least in the short-run) is to enter into special arrangements with them. Thus, as EEC experience has repeatedly demonstrated, the concept of special circumstances under which the MFN principle may legitimately be breached, must (and for legitimate political reasons also) seriously weaken the central principle itself.

The second consequence concerns the *actual* effect of the EEC on the operation of the GATT system. Despite the proliferation of regional economic arrangements, particularly amongst developing countries, it is—and for fairly obvious reasons—only the European experience which has so far posed a major challenge to the universal system. The outcome of this challenge however remains ambiguous. On the one hand a decision to establish a common market between six European states reinforced and extended the regional focus in matters of trade liberalisation; we have already noted that the main work on the dismantling of quota restrictions took place within the OEEC rather than GATT; the difficulty of evolving a common commercial policy on which the Six could negotiate with the outside world further restricted the scope for liberalisation at the global level. On the other hand, when in the early 1960s, an EEC commercial policy was finally worked out, the importance of GATT became apparent both as a forum within which the EEC could negotiate with the United States and its other major trading partners, and as the basis in law on which such a negotiation could be based. The Kennedy Round of negotiations (1964-67) was a practical demonstration by the major trading powers that, beyond their regional commitments, they accepted the desirability of promoting economic interdependence between them. Although the impact of tariff reductions on the growth of international trade is ultimately uncertain, so long as most states operate on the assumption of its desirability, the case for passive functionalism (i.e. the maintainance of a universal code of commercial behaviour) is clearly strong. This is not to suggest that the GATT system represents an irreversible, let alone ideal, stage of international economic integration—indeed I shall argue in the opposite sense in the final section of this essay—but merely to note that the economic strength of the EEC has intensified, rather than reduced, the problems of reconciling conflicting national or bloc interests with the facts of interdependence. Until such a time as a new code can be worked out the symbolic importance of GATT should not be underestimated.

The argument may be taken a stage further with regard to the international monetary system. When, after the return to convertibility by the major currencies in 1958, itself a response to the very rapid increase in world trade, it was considered necessary to expand the resources available to states in balance of payments difficulties, the means chosen—the General Agreement to Borrow (GAB)—was worked out by the so-called Group of Ten, not within the IMF, and the same group also retained ultimate authority for the activation of the Agreement.[21] Similarly the scheme for the creation of Special Drawing Rights (SDR's) in the late 1960s was conceived by the major trading powers acting in private, although its day to day administration is handled by the IMF. The reluctance of the major powers to work solely within the framework of the Fund suggests that, despite the sensitivity of national economies to international trade and money flows, they still resist any transfer of responsibility for economic policy as such. But it is significant that they have never pushed their distrust of the Organisation to the point of establishing a rival institution. In practice a system of decision-making by an inner caucus and formal ratification by the IMF is possible because the politico-economic philosophy (i.e. liberal multilateralism) enshrined in the IMF articles of agreement, is essentially the same as that professed by the ruling establishment in all the major trading states. It is not the same as that professed by the ruling establishment of any of the states with centrally planned economies. So, to the problem of reconciling national and bloc interests which will continue to exist so long as political boundaries retain their current importance, we must add the problem of ideology. If the tension between inter-dependence and national control is held to explain and justify international cooperation at the universal level, the coexistence of rival economic systems inevitably calls in question the possibility of a genuinely universal system.

This formulation confronts us with the second question raised at the beginning of this paper, namely whether international economic cooperation contributes to the establishment of a broader system of international security and welfare? At the time when the Bretton Woods system was devised, more immediate concerns inhibited speculation about the post-war collapse of the alliance between the Soviet Union and the Western Powers. But while it may be true that the discussions took place on a rather vague 'one world' assumption about the future, there is no evidence to suggest that the technical problems of integrating capitalist and communist states within a single international economy were considered in any detail. What is clear, as we have already noted, is that the United States regarded the re-establishment of a system of multilateral economic liberalism as an essential ingredient of a stable post-war international order. It is also clear that with the onset of the Cold War, the Soviet Union and its allies viewed the network of economic institutions with the same hostility with which they regarded NATO and the West in general. On this perspective the contribution of international economic cooperation to international security ultimately becomes a function of Western alliance politics. To put the same point less provocatively the framework of international economic institutions acted as one of the supports of a relatively homogenous international system which includes the Western powers, and in effect most of the Third World, but which from its inception has excluded by definition the Communist states.[22]

But if, from the Western point of view, a managed system of economic liberalism was essential to international welfare and security, the notion that it was, in fact, possible (and desirable) to distinguish between security and economic interests, was an integral, if paradoxical, component of the same philosophy. Thus, as leader of the Western alliance, the United States was strongly in favour of West European integration, and endorsed the method chosen by the Six for pursuing this objective. At the same time, if the EEC experiment was successful, then it would inevitably emerge as a powerful economic rival to the United States. By the early 1960s the prospect of a Community, enlarged to include Britain, directly confronted the United States with this dilemma. The Kennedy administration responded to this challenge with the conception of a 'Grand Design', under which the costs, if not the final responsibilities, of protecting the 'free world' (always defined to incorporate the Third World as well as Western Europe) would be more equitably shared between a reconstructed Europe and North America.[23] But just as the system of liberal multilateralism had been regarded by the Americans as an essential long-term objective of post-war reconstruction, though one which must be kept functionally separate from the defensive arrangements of the Western powers, so now they attempted to resolve the contradiction implicit in United States policy not by a formal marriage of economic and defence policy but by taking parallel initiatives in both areas at the same time.

The Trade Expansion Act rested on three implicit assumptions. The first was that the British application to join the EEC would succeed, and that consequently it would be both possible, and in the interests of all the major powers, to move rapidly towards the creation of free trade in industrial products.[24] Secondly, it was assumed that in order to secure the support of both agricultural exporters (amongst which the United States itself was the most important) and developing countries it would be necessary to include within the final settlement provision for the liberalisation of agricultural trade (so far GATT's most notorious failure) and concessions, which would be negotiated multilaterally but on a non-reciprocal basis, to meet the special interests of the Third World. Finally, it was assumed that although progress towards a *détente* with the Soviet bloc might spill over into relatively freer economic relations between East and West, there was no significant prospect of re-integrating the Socialist states within the world economy, or of reforming world economic institutions to include them. Thus, while on one level, the Kennedy Round demonstrated the flexibility of GATT in adapting to changed circumstances—for example the change-over from the laborious item by item method of negotiation to the exchange of linear tariff cuts across the board—at a deeper level the revival of GATT did little or nothing to meet the basic functionalist objective of transcending territory and ideology. On the contrary the negotiations took place on the one hand on the basis of a contractual agreement between states about tariff regimes, which are in the last analysis territorially defined, and on the other on an implicit understanding that socialist and market modes of economic organisation could not practicably be integrated within a single system.

The Ghost in the Machine

The outcome of the Kennedy Round was ambiguous in several respects. This was largely because the underlying assumptions were belied by events. President de Gaulle's veto on Britain's application for EEC membership reduced to 'two unpropitious categories of products, aircraft and margarine', the items for which the Trade Expansion Act had empowered the US executive to negotiate a total abolition of tariffs.[25] Moreover the difficulty of reconciling the interests of the major trading states—primarily those of the United States and the EEC but also Britain's and Japan's—left little time over for the developing countries, whose special interests should have been covered by the 'non-reciprocity' provision.[26] Despite a limited agreement on cereals the problem of agricultural protectionism proved as intractable as it had done in all previous GATT negotiations. Even so, the final settlement was impressive by previous GATT standards. [27] Indeed it was so impressive that when it was all over most observers concluded that once the Kennedy Round concessions had been implemented it would not be worth—on a straight cost-benefit basis—mounting a further multilateral assault on tariff protection. Yet it was also apparent that the promised land, free trade regained, was not in sight. It followed that the GATT (and indeed the entire structure of economic institutions) could not withdraw to their proper role, a kind of multilateralised night watchman, but must seek new lands to conquer. The dissatisfaction of the developing states with the international economic system, the scarcely suppressed dispute over agriculture and the growing debate about the parallel problem of non-tariff barriers, mapped out the field if they did nothing to suggest the strategies required. There was, it seemed, a ghost in the liberal multilateral machine. Or to put the same point in functionalist language, instead of a 'felt and present need' which could no longer be met except at the international level, there was a confusing and conflicting variety of needs and loyalties which threatened the operational philosophy of the existing framework of cooperation.

The problem of exorcising this ghost has dominated public debate about international economic relations in the five years since the Kennedy Round negotiations ended. Instead of a community of 'free states' sharing the same values and economic organisation and committed to 'burden sharing' arrangements for their defence, there has arisen the spectre of a new mercantalism, a potentially hostile confrontation, not between economically nationalist states but between five new major trading blocs which have gradually taken shape over the last twenty-five years.

Whether this view of contemporary developments contributes very much to our understanding of the problems involved is perhaps doubtful since only the EEC, and possibly COMECON, can properly be called blocs, while relations between the Communist states and the rest of the world raise different kinds of issues to those arising in economic relations between other industrial states. But like other simplifications, the five bloc model nonetheless attempts to formulate a response to a series of more complex and elusive changes in the international economy. It cannot simply be discounted.[28]

Two causes are generally identified as responsible for the current *malaise*. The first is the extended crisis of the United States balance of payments, in particular the steady decline after 1964 of the surplus on the American balance of trade, which in 1971 went into deficit for the first time since the beginning of the century.[29] It was this practical demonstration of the failing competitive position of the United States in world markets that finally exposed the artificiality of the distinction between trade and money in international economic organisation. The

1971 dollar crisis was essentially of American choosing. If, as the United States evidently believed, the ultimate option of devaluation was not open to them, as it was to their allies, the same end could only be achieved by an upward re-alignment of parities by their main trading partners. On 15 August 1971 the President suspended the dollar's convertibility into gold and imposed a 10 per cent import surcharge with the openly declared objective of forcing the other western powers to meet American demands.[30] It was, President Nixon implicitly argued, the stubborn refusal of the other industrial powers to put the interests of the system as a whole above narrow national concerns, that forced the United States to take unilateral action.

The second cause of friction concerns the post Kennedy Round emergence of previously concealed protection. Two conceptually related but separate problems are involved: one is the external impact of the EEC agricultural policy, the other the maintenance of various non tariff barriers to trade by all industrial states. The GATT system rested on the assumption of equality amongst contracting parties, as well as on the principles of reciprocity and non-discrimination. The fact that all states maintained tariff regimes lent practical credibility to this otherwise legal fiction: states could negotiate reductions in tariffs on the basis of reciprocity without the intrusion of major political obstacles caused by inequalities of power or differences in administrative and social practice. As the tariffs came down the failure of the system to embrace the agricultural sector, and the existence of non-tariff barriers even in the liberated industrial sector, rose in importance.[31] Whether or not the liberalisation formula can, in principle, be applied to agriculture (or extended over the broad field of non-tariff protection) the central political role of the Common Agricultural Policy with the EEC makes it unlikely that there will be any significant liberalisation in the immediate future.

From the United States point of view it is the agricultural problem which presents the greatest threat to the international economic system, including its institutional structure. Whatever the political rationale for the common agricultural policy (which has already led to EEC surpluses rivalling those of the United States) it hits directly at the United States balance of trade, and hence—in the American view—at the ability of the United States to underwrite the international monetary system. President Nixon's massive wheat deal with the USSR has no doubt alleviated the problem, but while this contract clearly has important political implications, it is unlikely to have any direct impact on the United States balance of payments, and in any case does not cover coarse grains which are those most affected by European agricultural protection. The trade deficit is, of course, economically a relatively insignificant part of the United States payments problem; but it is critical politically because it is the export interests, including the agricultural interest, that have traditionally supported American liberalism in foreign economic policy.[32]

It is this interaction between trade and money which has seriously weakened the Bretton Woods structure over the past five years. Yet beyond the endless debates about agricultural protectionism, disparate government purchasing policies and the like, there is a more fundamental and intractable problem. Put crudely the question which now confronts those involved in international economic organisation is whether they merely need a re-dedication to the basic objective of liberal multilateralism combined with the devising of new techniques to bring concealed forms of protectionism within the scope of further liberalisation; or whether some

261

more basic re-formulation is required of the rules of the system, and of the principles which underlie them?

In so far as an answer has been attempted, it has generally taken the form of re-dedication and pragmatic reform. Writing in the aftermath of the Kennedy Round, for example, Professor Curzon suggested that the movement towards a rationally organised international economy had to be maintained by progressive liberalisation. In his view, 'in the absence of any positive move forward, it is highly likely that back-sliding will take place, given the *perpetuum mobile* of human affairs. And the backsliding once started, could be all the greater because of the impressive degree of trade liberalisation that has been achieved in the past two decades.'[33] Essentially the same view was taken, more recently, by the OECD High Level Group on Trade and Related Problems.[34] Within the OECD, the American response to the challenge of the new mercantalism has characteristically been the most uncompromising and the closest to orthodox neo-classical economic theory. The argument may be summarised as follows: if it is accepted that the system of liberal multilateralism has made a significant contribution to the rapid, and unprecedented growth of world trade over the past twenty-five years, then this is because (and to the extent) that it has allowed the principle of comparative advantage to operate, at least in the industrial sector. Moreover, since both on the evidence, and in its original formulation, comparative advantage should be regarded as a positive rather than a normative principle, there is no good reason 'why countries whose comparative advantage is strong in agriculture should not have the same right to exploit that advantage as those countries whose comparative advantage lies in manufactures'.[35] But while the Americans are alone in pushing the doctrine to its logical conclusion against the majority view that governments base their agricultural policies 'not only on economic but also on social and political considerations'[36], it is significant that the other OECD states have also endorsed the view that 'the efforts of liberalisation should be pursued in all fields—tariffs, quotas and other non-tariff barriers—and cover trade in both agriculture and industrial products'.[37]

There are strong grounds, perhaps, for arguing that this is the only practicable approach available to the complex of problems now facing international organisations. If so, it is no doubt partly because the institutions themselves have not altogether avoided a 'natural' tendency towards bureaucratic conservatism; they were created to resolve a problem—the management of international economic interdependence—defined in a particular way, and it can be argued that they are now hamstrung in recognising and controlling a new situation by continuing commitment to an outworn definition. This argument has attractions, for it focusses on the weakest point of the liberal multilateralist philosophy, its timeless and positivist pretensions.

But since it is the policies of governments rather than of international institutions which have weakened the Bretton Woods structure, it is also unfair. A more compelling reason for reaffirming the commitment to the principles of the existing system (and the action programme implied thereby) is that it *actually* corresponds over a wide area not only to past experience but to the present needs of the major trading powers. Like other general views of the world the one embedded in economic liberalism reflected particular, and relatively localised, social-pre-occupations and interests[38]: but the pattern of inter-dependence which has evolved under its impact since the mid-nineteenth century, and more particularly the vastly increased inter-penetration of the economies of the major powers since 1945, cannot be reversed, and is in practice inseparable from the adjustment and coordination procedures which have been developed both within the Bretton Woods system and outside it on an *ad hoc* basis.

These procedures, international surveillance, the maintenance of relatively fixed exchange rates, safeguard provisions to prevent market disruption and so on, are no doubt both crude and subject to frequent evasion; but equally there is no doubt that they represent a major advance on the chaotic situation which prevailed throughout the inter-war period. Thus, while United States dominance of the international monetary system caused a growing (and so far unresolved) tension amongst the major powers once the dollar shortage disappeared and Europe and Japan emerged as effective competitors of the United States in world markets, official criticism of the monetary framework established at Bretton Woods has been 'directed less at the rules laid down at the time than at the use that has been made of them'.[39] In fact, while the international adjustment mechanism has proved increasingly inadequate in dealing with vast speculative movements of short-term capital, what is interesting, politically, is how resilient the underlying rationale of the system has proved. Since 1968, indeed, no state (not excluding France) has been prepared to challenge the system individually because of the restraints created by their own stake in its survival.[40] Because public power remains national, while the ready accessability and movement of capital has encouraged the rapid growth of international production, mostly in private hands, governments increasingly find themselves in the same boat, forced by their own impotence into defensive cooperation. Here, then, at least in the negative sense, the functionalist argument appears to be born out by experience. While there are deep rooted disputes, reflecting different national interests and aspirations, not about the need but about the direction of international monetary reform, the degree of economic inter-dependence already achieved under the multilateralist rationale has in effect created a system of no escape.

A similar, if less compelling, argument may be advanced with respect to international trade; similar because there are strong *a priori* grounds for accepting that the rapid post-war growth of international trade has been closely associated with the regime of liberalisation and that it has made a significant contribution to material welfare; less compelling in that while states are faced with a recurrent payments crisis it remains a relatively straightforward matter to impose physical controls on trade. Even leaving aside those states which are not contracting parties to the GATT, and which together account for perhaps 20 per cent of world trade, it is no secret that most of the remainder have from time to time been in breach of their obligations under the agreement. Nevertheless, the GATT system has had the great (and acknowledged) merit of establishing a framework—based on a theoretically universal code of international behaviour—within which multilateral negotiations can take place. Since negotiations depend on the mutual acceptance of some objectives, even if others are disputed, the existence of GATT represents a real advance on the inter-war situation when no such framework existed. Moreover, while in principle the autarchic option remains open, apart from the traditional dangers of reciprocal action by other states, in practice the growth of international production and transnational economic integration increasingly frustrates the objectives to which such a policy would be directed.

The Priority of the Framework

But if the acceptance of the need for international economic cooperation has been thus ensured by developments beyond the control of national governments, on what basis are they to cooperate in the future? So far I have argued that whatever the deficiencies of the Bretton Woods structure it represented an important innovation in establishing a framework of interaction which allowed states to retain essential control of national economic policy while openly acknowledging their inter-dependence. Even if this achievement is viewed as an effort of conservation rather than integration, at the very least it broke with the traditional, and traditionally arid, argument about state sovereignty. From a political point of view it is clearly the survival and strengthening of the framework which is more important than the original underlying doctrine. The realisation that this is so is clearly reflected in the re-affirmation of the multilateralist philosophy contained in the 1972 OECD report, and in frequent statements by official spokesmen from all the major Western powers. Yet while such protestations might seem, at first sight, to support the truth of a classic functionalist proposition, that form follows function, note that *in fact* the argument is generally presented in terms of the continuing relevance of the underlying principles. It may be that, with the help of internationally agreed codes for the regulation of non-tariff barriers and so on, further progress towards the goal of liberalisation will prove feasible.[41] But there is also some evidence to support another view, namely, that notwithstanding the interdependence of modern states, the framework itself is under threat precisely because, at certain critical points, the underlying philosophy is deficient. To the extent that this is so, the question is no longer merely technical: it is not just a matter of finding new methods better adapted to the problems of the 1970s and beyond but also designed to secure the same objectives as tariff negotiations did in the 1950s and 1960s; it is the basic objectives of the system, the rules behind the rule book, which must be critically re-examined.

We enter here on dangerous and uncharted waters. No solution seems self-evident; since the existence of the fundamental as distinct from the technical problem is scarcely admitted, public debate on what lies on these farther shores of economic liberalism has also hardly begun. The best that can be done here, therefore, is to conclude with a brief sketch of the kind of arguments which may be advanced, from a functionalist perspective, in support of the case for such a reappraisal.

Consider first the nature of economic relations amongst the Western powers. It seems intrinsically unlikely that the neo-mercantilist developments within the major trading states and the EEC can be easily reversed. The process of integrating large market areas in the industrial world and of differentiating between them is already far advanced, and in the period ahead it may well be difficult for those states remaining wholly or partially outside one or other of these major areas, such as Canada, Australia and New Zealand, to avoid seeking special treatment from one or other of them. Any reform of the international commercial system will ultimately be settled by the resolution of a series of problems, which are not multilateral in the sense that the term has so far been understood within GATT, but which chiefly arise in relations between the United States, Japan and the EEC. A global reassertion of free trade principles, theoretically the alternative solution to the threatened mercantalist confrontation, is unlikely because consolidation is a major political objective of the EEC, if not of the United States and Japan. In this context it is worth recalling that whatever the merits of the economic arguments advanced in support of the Customs Union exception to the most favoured nation principle, the necessary pre-requisite for such a union is a change in the political relationship between member states, even, as some of the more optimistic neo-functionalists tend to argue, an implicit shift of political boundaries. It is, of course, the ambiguity of the EEC status within the international community in this respect which sharpens external hostility to some Community policies, in particular the Common Agricultural Policy (CAP). But if the Community is accepted as a legitimate participant in the international economic system (and not viewed merely as a regional organisation whose objectives conflict with those of the global system) the CAP ceases to be an irrational protectionist device aimed malevolently at third country suppliers and must be accepted for what it is, namely a political deal between France and Germany of critical importance to the present functioning of the Community system. This is not to say that a new system, less damaging to third party interests, may not at some stage emerge, but that if and when it does, it will result not from an agreement to allow the law of comparative advantage to operate—the current United States position—but from changes in the internal political balance within the EEC on the one hand and from an explicit political settlement with the outside world on the other.

If EEC experience provides any guidance for the future of wider international economic negotiations—and there is no obvious reason why it should not—there is no avoiding a process of pragmatic diplomatic bargaining in which the trade-off may not necessarily take place within one economic sector or even be confined specifically to economic relations at all. In such a world an admittedly vague formula such as 'mutual advantage' favoured by the Eastern bloc, may be preferable to the unreal positivism of the liberal position. It is impossible to be precise about the form that such a negotiation might take; but it is likely that rather than agreeing in advance on some desirable common goal of foreign economic policy, as has been the case in the past with tariff negotiations, the major industrial powers would need to base their negotiations on a reconciliation of various domestic policies, for example the price support systems which all industrial states operate in the agricultural sector.

There are, of course, dangers in what can only be seen as a movement away from the principle of the separation of functional areas which underlies the existing framework of Western economic cooperation.[42] To begin with, the difficulties of achieving intra-bloc agreement within the EEC means that in practice the room for manoeuvre in bargaining with the outside world is very limited. It may reasonably be argued therefore that if the principle of specific reciprocity is abandoned internationally, as in an implicit way it has been abandoned within the EEC, it will be even more difficult than at present to maintain a wider commitment to international coordination. After all, the great merit of the system of liberal multilateralism under which trade and money, let alone such non-economic matters as security, were regarded at the same time as mutually reinforcing yet strictly separate, was its passive character: governments only had to agree on what not to do, an obviously easier proposition than agreeing on positive programmes of intervention and management. The danger of explicitly acknowledging the strategic interaction between economic and non-economic aspects of international relations was clearly demonstrated in August 1971 by President Nixon's action linking the removal of the United States import surcharge to 'progress' (i.e. concessions to the American position) in international negotiations over money and security (meaning the re-alignment of parities of the major currencies *vis-à-vis* the Dollar and a reduction in the cost of United States overseas troop deployment).

But while the dangers must be admitted so must the lack of plausible alternatives. It is the growing inter-dependence of industrial economies generally which has created the possibility of the kind of strategic interaction which Mr Nixon exploited. What was objectionable about his approach was not so much that it called in question the international movement towards freer trade—which had always been hedged around with practical qualifications—but that he acted unilaterally. By doing so he departed from the tradition of coordination which had been gradually developed since the Second World War as the only way of reconciling the conflicting requirements of national economic policies and a stable international economy. But if the economic and political conditions which governments face have really changed in ways which make it difficult for them to practice multilateralism, as originally conceived, can the tradition be restored merely by reconfirming the viability, and continuing relevance, of liberal economic theory? The difference between a system of liberal multilateralism in which any departure from a codified set of rules must be justified by reference to special circumstances, and a system within which the need for flexibility is itself codified as part of the institutional framework, is one of emphasis rather than of basic incompatibility.

It is, for example, difficult to imagine any of the major powers retreating from interdependence into economic isolation even if it was in their power to do so. For this reason alone the continued maintenance of a multilateral framework based on restrictionist principles seems improbable. But it is not so implausible to envisage international coordination to control the extent and scope of inter-dependence. The difference is, therefore, important if only because, under a reformed system, the framework of cooperation would be openly acknowledged as being more important than the allegedly 'rational' laws on which it was originally based. The distinction between the two kinds of system also seems likely to become progressively more important as the kinds of problems calling for international action—inflation and regional policy are two topical examples—will require detailed knowledge of specific social and political conditions rather than merely further doses of liberalisation.

A related argument arises in connection with economic relations between the industrialised and developing worlds. Neo-classical economics assumes that a régime of liberalisation with regard to monetary and trade flows will, *in the long run*, optimise the welfare of all. It was essentially this argument which led the United States to press for a prohibition of the creation of new preferencial systems after the Second World War. But the system which in fact emerged was much less stringent. Since politicians in rich and poor states alike, are primarily concerned with the *short run*, the existing preferential arrangements were frozen, left to wither away under the impact of inflation and non-discriminatory tariff cuts, but not abandoned. And exceptions were made to the general rule of non-discriminatory liberalisation, first to meet the theoretical cogency of the 'infant-industry argument', and then as a practical response to the chronic shortage of foreign exchange in most poor states. In practice, indeed, the infant-industry clause of the GATT has seldom, if ever, been invoked; instead the balance of payments constraint has explained (whether it has justified it is another matter) the import substitution and control policies adopted throughout the Third World.

But if the neo-classical orthodoxy has been frequently breached to allow developing states to remain within the Bretton Woods framework, it has for many years been clear that the existing system does not satisfy their aspirations; and that, from their point of view, it can do little to correct the prevailing asymmetry in the international economy and its institutional structure. This dissatisfaction has been voiced and given institutional expression in three sessions of the UNCTAD and in Part IV of the GATT (the Trade and Development Chapter) which was added to the original text in November 1964. Thus, at least in terms of political rhetoric, there is wide support, even within the industrialised world, for the proposition that the institutional system, despite its overall passive character, should be so arranged as to provide positive assistance for Third World development through both the removal of obstacles to trade in commodities of particular significance to developing countries and by facilitating a transfer of resources from rich to poor. Yet, while 'progress' in certain limited sectors has been achieved, for example by the establishment of the IMF Compensatory Financing Scheme[43], the 'gap' continues to widen and their dissatisfaction grows. On both sides the failure of the international economic system to meet the needs of the Third World is blamed on an absence of political will; on neither is there a willingness to confront the deficiencies of the underlying philosophy.[44]

It is again the mechanistic character of this philosophy which seems at fault. The issue is symbolised by the debate which continued throughout the 1960s about the creation of a generalised preference scheme. GATT negotiations on the basis of the MFN principle left most poor states without significant bargaining power. They mostly restricted imports for other reasons so that tariff concessions had relatively little impact while their own traditional exports were characteristically concentrated within a fairly narrow range. Whenever they attempted to diversify into semi- or simple manufactures they came into competition with declining (or at any rate politically sensitive) industries in the industrialised world. It was in response to this situation that the principle of nonreciprocity for developing states was written into the GATT, and that the notion of a generalised preference scheme to be granted by all industrialised states to the manufactures of all developing states was finally accepted in principle by the second UNCTAD in 1968.

I am not here concerned with whether or not these concessions could, or could not, make an important contribution to Third World development, but with their implications for the institutional management of an ordered world economy. Agreement, in principle, on the generalised preference scheme was only possible because in 1967 the United States finally reversed its traditional blanket opposition to all forms of preference. But progress towards the implementation of an effective scheme has so far been insignificant mainly because the United States has insisted, for reasons of economic doctrine, that the scheme should be applied on a non-discriminatory but also non-reciprocal basis by all the industrialised states to all the developing states. Implementation has also been hindered by the fact that those states already enjoying preferential treatment (for example from the EEC and Britain) are reluctant to give this up without some form of guarantee that they would not be worse off than before. American enthusiasm for the scheme—never strong in the first place—virtually evaporated once it became clear that there was no firm basis on which it could be made genuinely non-discriminatory and universal;

and their distaste has been strengthened by the proliferation of special arrangements between the EEC and third countries. Thus a largely doctrinal dispute over the issue of discrimination between the United States and her major trading partners has been added to the conflict over agriculture. Meanwhile the Third World continues to be alienated from the existing institutional framework for international economic cooperation, a development which is only limited by the fact that they have nowhere else to go.

Two closely related but separate issues are involved. First, the proposition that any special treatment for poor states must be on a nondiscriminatory and non-reciprocal basis derives from the theory that while politics and history can be blamed for the present asymetry of the world economy, economic arguments can, *in fact*, be separated from the historical and political context in which they arise. On this view, the correction of the asymmetry is something due to poor states as of right; after which presumably international economic relations will revert to a system based on non-discrimination and the positive laws of comparative advantage. But, in practice, as the French-speaking African states associated with the EEC are plainly aware, in any transactional system the admission that a state has non-reciprocal rights of participation is tantamount to admitting in advance that its interests are likely to be overlooked. This is not to say that the present system under which some developing states grant reverse tariff and trade preferences to some industrialised states, is the only imaginable, or the most sensible form that reciprocity might take; it is to suggest that whatever the shape of a reformed international economic framework, it will have to embrace the concept of obligation as well as the idea of rights. Granted that dependence on the markets of the industrialised world may frustrate the attempts of Third World governments to fashion their own destiny (just as the scale and autonomy of international market operations frustrates the attempts of rich governments to control their national economies) nevertheless the continued existence of legally sovereign and equal states remains of primary significance. Post-Second World War experience, for example, surely undermines the liberal and functionalist argument that the problem of poverty in the international economic system can be catered for by a system of progressive taxation derived by analogy from the system operating in some of the Western democracies. However desirable the idea might seem in terms of some generalised conception of Third World needs, there are no plausible grounds for believing that it is likely to be instituted in the foreseeable future.

Secondly, the insistence that poor states should be granted special treatment on a non-discriminatory and non-reciprocal basis, that is purely on economic grounds alone, automatically invalidates the broader political considerations which have led to the re-emergence of discriminatory trading patterns and special relationships. It is worth noting, therefore, that, although they contravene GATT's no new preference rule, many of the preferential agreements linking the states on the periphery of Western Europe with the EEC, have paradoxically been negotiated to soften the trade diversion, which both GATT and the economic theory would consider justified. In other words the purpose of such arrangements is to preserve not only an economic but a political relationship which existed at the time of Union. It is, of course, true that the arrangements linking the EEC with third party states in Southern Europe, the Mediterranean and Africa, constitute a potential threat to other states, for example those in Latin America. But if it is accepted that there is nothing intrinsically more rational about the EEC's own arrangements than those governing its policy towards third countries, it follows that the resolution of such conflicts of interest can only be handled within the context of a multilateral political negotiation in which the legitimacy of special relationships is not called into question merely by reference to an economic formula.

Finally, the changing context of East-West relations also supports the argument in favour of a recasting of the international economic structure and its underlying philosophy to reflect current political realities and aspirations. From the perspective of a continuing (if limited) *détente*, it no longer matters whether liberal multilateralism is regarded as a potentially universal system derived from positive economics or as part of the ideological infra-structure of the Western Alliance: the question now is how two systems whose opposing economic philosophies have entered deeply into their economic organisation and life can be contained within a single institutional structure that will work to their mutual advantage, and thus help to uphold a broader framework of East-West security. Partly because the relative level of East-West trade is still so low,[46] and partly because the system of central planning is designed to prevent such an outcome, market forces alone cannot be relied on to bring about a reintegration of the world economy. Indeed two developments could well deepen the present economic divide, despite the fact that the diplomatic climate is, perhaps, more favourable than at any time since 1945 for an attempt to normalise political relations. One is the ruling by the EEC that from the beginning of 1973 all Trade Agreements should be negotiated by the Commission, and not by individual member states; the other is the intensification of East European integration under COMECON's Complex Plan. At first sight it might seem an unwelcome paradox if at a time when the conventional distinction between economics and politics is breaking down in relations within the capitalist world, it should be institutionalised in relations between East and West.

Although the Soviet Union and her East European allies have placed considerable emphasis on economic cooperation in their approach to the European Security Conference, it is difficult to formulate with precision the kind of institutional arrangements which might have some chance of being acted on. Their appeal to both East and West would presumably have to be based on a kind of ideological neutrality which, while offering the advantages of increasing interdependence, would threaten neither system. The difficulties inherent in this formulation are compounded by the fact that liberalisation has different implications for states with centrally planned economies than for the rest of the world. I have argued that in economic relations between capitalist states, the process of bloc formation, the growth of international production and the significant reduction of tariff restrictions on trade in manufactures have brought states close to the limits of the system based on the philosophy of economic liberalism: in future they may conceivably, for example, need to cooperate more closely on curtailing and controlling their inter-dependence rather than promoting it. The situation is clearly different for the East where all have an interest in acquiring the freest possible access for their goods in Western markets and to Western capital to finance further industrialisation, but where in other respects the interests of the Soviet Union and the East European states, particularly those in which the economic reform movement has gone furthest, do not necessarily run parallel.

The Soviet attitude to international trade has always been ambiguous; trade has been sanctioned, even actively sought, as a means of 'catching up' with the West, but always providing it could be controlled to prevent any long term dependence on external sources of supply. While it is arguable that the maintenance of the Soviet social and political system is now even more dependent than in the past on Western credit to make good both the recurring failures of Soviet agriculture and the relative backwardness of Soviet advanced technology (and certainly Soviet trade negotiators favour long-term contracts as a means of managing trade between centrally planned and market economies) there remains a sense in which autarchy is an option for the Soviet Union, as it is for the United States, but not for the trade orientated states of Western or Eastern Europe. It is partly for this reason, of course, that the economic integration of Eastern Europe has been, since the late 1950s, as much a Soviet political objective as an economic one. But for those East European states whose economies have been traditionally orientated towards the West, both trade and integration have a different significance: for them integration is at least partly the price that must be paid to secure a degree of freedom in domestic economic policy, and their right to deal as states, on as liberal a basis as possible, with their Western European neighbours.

The Soviet and East European attitudes towards West European integration are thus subtly different. Although for several years after its formation, the Soviet authorities denounced the EEC as a glorified capitalist cartel, the present régime has publically declared its willingness to reach an accommodation with the Community on economic relations, and there is little doubt that they would welcome such an agreement as part of a wider set of arrangements endorsing the *status quo* in Europe. But for the East European states a political solution of this kind would only be welcomed in so far as it improved their prospects of expanding and diversifying their economic relations with the West. For these states, therefore, the operational distinction between economic and political relations, which is breaking down in the West, remains of fundamental importance.

It is in this context that the slow move towards multilateralism within COMECON on the one hand and the increased flexibility within GATT with regard to East-West trade on the other may offer some way forward. One reason why East European states have mixed feelings about multilateral trade within the bloc is that if they accumulate each others currencies rather than balancing accounts bilaterally on an annual basis, they do not at present know what real resources these holdings will command at some future date. If the decision to multilateralise payments completely within COMECON by 1980 is to be implemented, it presumably means that some solution to the problem of arbitrary pricing will by then be forthcoming. And on this assumption the reservations which certain East European states have towards integration may be allayed to the extent that they will have greater confidence than at present that intra-bloc trade will be based on the principle of mutual advantage. At the same time, the probable expansion of the global quota system under which Poland was extended full MFN status within GATT, to Hungary and Rumania, both of which are currently negotiating for membership, may provide Western states with an acceptable equivalent to free market access, the absence of which has hitherto been the main ground on which they have continued to discriminate against imports from the Eastern area. Liberalisation in this respect is of crucial importance to East European states since their ability to purchase from the West is still very closely governed by their ability to earn foreign exchange.

It is at this point that the East-West problem echoes, in some respects, the North-South problem. Most East European states are as worried about the structure of their trade with the industrialised West as with its volume; but the bulk of their exports continue to fall within the traditional sector of primary and agricultural products. Since demand for many commodities of this kind is relatively inelastic, while others may be threatened by certain EEC policies, primarily the common agricultural policy, the practical question which they have to face is the kind of *quid pro quo* which they could offer in a reformed institutional structure; this would need to give some substance to the concept of mutual advantage in relations between different economic systems. Certain explicit pre-conditions to any future arrangement are apparent. The East European states would have to abandon their opposition to dealing with the EEC, and they would also need to reiterate, either individually or collectively, their willingness to negotiate on a pragmatic basis the counterparts to be offered in exchange for full MFN status in Western markets. In the present political climate such changes seem both feasible, and indeed, may even come about anyway. But beyond this there would clearly need to be an implicit shift of the underlying assumptions about the role of economic cooperation in upholding a broader system of international welfare and security. If it is perhaps not unrealistic to hope that one result of the European Security Conference will be the final and formal abandonment of what remains of the Western strategic embargo, another might be a clear, even if implicit, indication that economic experimentation in Eastern Europe will not be regarded by the Soviet Union as evidence of a capitalist subversion whenever it strays beyond a line determined in Moscow.

Conclusion

The argument in this paper has rested on three assumptions. First, that the functionalist approach cannot in practice, and does not in theory, transcend political ideology; secondly, that it is in fact derived from a tradition of economic liberalism, which like the opposing doctrine of Marxism, attempts first to subordinate politics to an underlying mechanistic explanation of society, and then to make political arrangements which will support the operation of this mechanism; and finally that these arrangements no longer fit either the political or economic realities of the Western world (and its Southern dependencies) or the broader requirements of security between East and West. The conclusion to which I am led, namely the need for a more explicit acknowledgment of the political issues involved in the three broad sectors of the contemporary international economy, is in the nature of a salvage operation. If it is accepted that there is no general philosophy which can provide the normative underpinning of rules for an institutional system of economic cooperation, in the way that economic liberalism underpinned the Bretton Woods system, then at least let us preserve the minimal rule of international cooperation and the habits of coordination, which have been built up over the past twenty-five years, as an aid to containing future conflicts and more hopefully as a means of conducting public debate about more purposive positive action.

Here, two possible lines of development, already touched on earlier in this paper, suggest themselves. The first concerns both the objectives and the techniques appropriate to international economic negotiations: if the major trading states are indeed reaching the limits of what can be achieved by liberalisation, the focus of international negotiation will increasingly need to shift to the issues of harmonisation and standardisation. Many of the problems arising from the existence of non-tariff barriers will only be solved, if they are solvable at all, by a shift of this kind. The reason is simply that, as with many quality controls, they were imposed in the first place for reasons of public welfare which remain relevant; their protectionist effect was often incidental and unintended, but is not easily rectified. Since, moreover, there is no common denominator, such as the tariff provided in the past, by reference to which a multilateral negotiation of non-tariff barriers could be organised, it is doubtful whether there is a real future for set piece negotiations of the Kennedy Round variety.

On this view, what is now required is a standing body within which the new commercial rule book can be drawn up, and a complaints procedure evolved, on a case law basis. Such an organisation would almost inevitably serve a double function: it would provide a forum in which conflicting interests could be reconciled and it would give some institutional meaning to the declared commitment of the major powers to continued inter-dependence. In such a body, for example, the agricultural support policies of all the industrial states might be considered in terms both of their political role and their economic effects on other states: the problems of harmonisation would, of course, still be difficult, but the basis for a negotiation might emerge, which will clearly not be the case so long as the political and social obstacles to liberalised agricultural trade are regarded by the United States as an unfortunate, irrational and temporary departure from GATT obligations.

There is no reason, of course, why, if they were accepted in principle, these proposals could not be accommodated within a modified Bretton Woods structure. This is indeed an advantage. It is often said that the Bretton Woods system is dead. But it is plainly not dead in the sense that the unmanaged *laissez-faire* system was dead by 1945: then the architects of the new order were confronted by something much closer to a *tabula rasa* than we are likely to experience in the foreseeable future. But reforms in the institutional structure of the international economic system would solve only half the problem: hopefully they might improve the process whereby national governments and multinational economic authorities such as the EEC can adjust to their economic interdependence; but they would have no direct bearing on the inter-locking of political, security and economic relations which increasingly undermines the ability of governments to deal with problems by treating them solely within a specific functional context.

There are at present a whole series of international negotiations either in progress or pending, the results of any one of which will affect what is possible in all the others. There is a certain parallelism here between the problems arising in relations between the United States and Western Europe and those which arise in relations between the two halves of Europe itself. If one looks not at the historical justice (or otherwise) of the American pressure for increased burden sharing within the Atlantic Alliance, but at the political context in which this pressure is being applied, it may be argued that the European ability to respond is contingent, in the trade field, on finding substantive concessions which do not at the same time under-mine the political consolidation of the Communities, and in the defence field, on an improvement in European security which would allow a reduction of the American presence in Western Europe to a point where governments could more readily contemplate assuming a larger share of the financial burden than at present. In other words there is a sense in which economic cooperation with the United States would be easier if improvements in European security had been negotiated first.

In East-West relations, however, it is clear that improved economic relations are either a precondition, or at least must accompany, any further normalisation of political relations. In other words it is no longer obvious that the issues involved in the forthcoming trade and monetary negotiations and in the European Security Conference can easily be separated. Yet there are two practical difficulties. The first is that, even if the basic interaction between these issues is acknowledged, they are likely to come to a head at different times, as the result of a different organisational and diplomatic dynamic, and be pursued according to different timetables. But secondly, even if there was a willingness to cooperate in devising an overall strategy within which the inter-relationships could be accommodated, the institutional machinery for doing so does not at present exist. In this context, then, the traditional functionalist argument must be stood on its head: far from isolating each problem as it arises in a specific functional area, in the present historical context, the need is for over-arching arrangements which will allow for a more coherent and self-conscious handling of the inter-dependence between functional areas.

At a time when much current speculation is concerned with the possible dangers of economic confrontation for the political relations of the major powers, such a conclusion may, perhaps, claim to be realistic, even if there seems little immediate likelihood of the kind of institutional developments which it would seem to imply. In the last analysis, it remains, nonetheless, a holding operation. A system of functional cooperation in which states agree in advance to handle peacefully their conflicts as well as their common pre-occupations, would clearly contribute to a system of general welfare. But only by a more widespread acceptance of the need for a philosophy which subordinates the economic or political order to the moral order will the ghost finally be exorcised. Meanwhile any system of international security must remain both tenuous and liable to decay, a matter for relief not for self congratulation.

Notes and references

1 David Mitrany, 'The Functional Approach to World Organization', *International Affairs*, July 1948, p. 359.

2 David Mitrany, *A Working Peace System*, Chicago, Quadrangle Books, 1966 p. 97.

3 Only two of the international economic institutions, the International Monetary Fund (IMF) and the International Bank for Reconstruction and Development (IBRD), were established at the Bretton Woods Conference in 1944. In this essay, however, I have used the phrase to include also the General Agreement on Tariffs and Trade (GATT); although GATT was an offshoot of the abortive International Trade Organisation (ITO), the Charter of which was drafted at the Havana Conference, its purpose is to establish and protect a liberalised, non-discriminatory trading system, ultimately the same function as that performed by the multilateral payments system, which was formally established by the IMF. The three institutions are thus complementary.

4 Raymond Aron, *Peace and War*, London, Weidenfeld and Nicholson, 1966, pp. 245-52.

5 J. Bentham, *Principles of International Law (1843)*, Quoted in *Peace and War*, *ibid.*, p. 248.

6 Gunnar Myrdal, *An International Economy: Problems and Prospects*, London, Routledge and Kegan Paul, 1956, p. 1.

7 In theory the international gold standard provided a direct link between domestic and international transactions. Interstate debts which were not covered by credits were settled in gold. Since the amount of currency in circulation was closely related to the amount of gold in a country's national reserves, settlement had an automatic impact on the level of economic activity. Defecit states lost gold, contracted money supply and credit thus choking off imports and forcing prices down. The fall in prices in turn led to a rise in exports, the accumulation of gold, an increase in the money supply and credit, and so on. The process was held to work in the same way, but in reverse, for surplus states.

8 David Mitrany, 'The Functional Approach in Historical Perspective', *International Affairs*, July 1971, p. 538.

9 Karl Polanyi, *The Great Transformation: Origins of Our Time*, London, Victor Gollancz, 1945.

10 Myrdal, *An International Economy, op. cit.*, p. 32.

11 *Ibid.*

12 See Susan Strange, 'The Dollar Crisis', in *International Affairs*, April 1972, p. 198.

13 The Resolution on Commodity Agreements reflected the uneasy compromise that was reached between the two sides. While on the one hand it called for 'secure remunerative equitable and stable prices for primary commodities, especially those exported by developing countries, having due regard for the import purchasing power of the commodities exported', it also referred, as did the Final Act itself, to the interests of consumers in importing countries. United Nations, *Proceedings of the UNCTAD, Volume I, Final Act and Report*, Part II, section II paragraph 58 (a) and Annex A II 1 pp. 26-27.

14 For a functionalist analysis of the IBRD see J.P. Sewell, *Functionalism and World Politics*, Princeton, Princeton University Press, 1966.

15 In the first instance the conflict was primarily between Britain and the United States. On Anglo-American finance and trade negotiations in this period see Richard N. Gardener, *Sterling Dollar Diplomacy*, London, Oxford University Press, 1956.

16 *Sterling Dollar Diplomacy, ibid.*, pp. 80-81.

17 Keynes' plan for a Clearing Union would have provided an institution capable of creating a new international currency, BANCOR, which would have ended the role of gold as the central medium of international settlement. Within generous limits deficit countries would have enjoyed automatic access to the new currency, the intention being that the supply of international money should be related to the needs of trade in the way that domestic money supply is geared to the requirements of the national economy. Discipline within the system was to be maintained by the operation of automatic sanctions which would apply to debtor and creditor states once their overdraft facility or credit balance exceeded half their quota. For the text see, *Proposal for an International Clearing Union*, Cmd. 6437, London, 1943. The United States plan for a Stabilisation Fund was less ambitious and bore a closer relationship to the IMF as it finally emerged. A modified version, which with a few changes was adopted in the constitution of the IMF, was contained in the *Joint*

Statement by Experts on the Establishment of an International Monetary Fund Cmd. 6519, London 1944.

18 See the statement made before the Boards of Governors of the IMF and IBRD on 30 September 1971 by John Connally, Secretary of the Treasury and US Governor of the Fund. United States, *Department of State Bulletin*, 25 October 1971, pp. 452-57. For more detailed background on current US views on the need for international economic reform see *United States International Economic Policy in an Inter-Dependent World*, Washington D.C., July 1971, Volume I, Parts I and II.

19 International Trade Organisation.

20 Joseph Viner, *The Customs Union Issue*, New York, Stevens, 1950.

21 For background on the General Agreement to Borrow (GAB) see J. Keith Horsefield, *The International Monetary System 1945-55: Twenty Years of International Monetary Cooperation, Vol. I: Chronicle*, Washington, DC, IMF 1969, pp. 510-12.

22 This statement requires qualification, Czechoslovakia joined the IMF and GATT before the Communist take-over in 1948, and has remained a largely dormant member of both organisations since. Poland and Yugoslavia acceded to GATT during the Kennedy. Round. Hungary and Rumania have more recently held exploratory negotiations with a view to their accession. On these later developments see below.

23 For an analysis of the Kennedy Round Negotiations see Ernest H. Preeg, *Traders and Diplomats*, Washington, D.C., The Brookings Institution, 1970.

24 In addition to the basic tariff cutting authority which permitted the United States Executive to negotiate a 50 per cent across the board cut for all tariff positions, The Trade Expansion Act contained authority to eliminate tariffs completely on product groups where the United States and the EEC together accounted for at least 80 per cent of world exports. For background to the US decision to extend the act in this way, and on foreign reactions to the industrial free trade proposals, see *Traders and Diplomats, ibid.*, pp. 48-52.

25 It is indeed arguable that United States pressure for industrial free trade under the 80 per cent formula, which with an enlarged EEC would have placed the United States in a strong net export position, itself made a minor contribution to President de Gaulle's decision to veto British entry. *Traders and Diplomats, ibid.*, p. 52.

26 In the Resolution adopted by the Ministerial Meeting of GATT on 21 May 1963 it was stated that 'every effort shall be made to reduce barriers to exports of the less developed countries, but that the developed countries cannot expect to receive reciprocity from the less developed countries'. The meeting laid down the principles and procedures under which the Kennedy Round negotiations were to be held. GATT *Press Release*, No. 794, 29 May 1963.

27 The average Kennedy Round reduction was between 36-39 per cent by all major industrial states. Tariff reduction, however, was uneven: the largest reductions were achieved in industries typified by advanced technology, product innovation and large, often international, firms, for example, the machinery, transportation equipment and chemical sectors. Only modest cuts were achieved in the textile sector, which remained the most prominent major industry enjoying a high level of protection against imports.

28 See William Diebold, Jr., 'The Economic System at Stake', in *Foreign Affairs*, October 1972, pp. 173-74.

29 Organisation for Economic Cooperation and Development, *Policy Perspectives for International Trade and Economic Relations: Report by the High Level Group on Trade and Related Problems* (Paris, OECD, 1972), pp. 31-32. For a useful comparative statistical summary of the United States balance of payments and those of its major trading partners, see tables 11 and 12 (pp. 150-151) of the same report.

30 For the text of President Nixon's announcement see United States, *Department of State Bulletin*, 6 September 1971, pp. 253-56.

31 Non-tariff barriers occur in a variety of guises. Apart from classic forms of protection, e.g. quantative restrictions and 'voluntary export restrictions', there are studies at present in progress within GATT and the OECD on government procurement, customs valuation procedures, standards, licencing, export subsidies, import documentation including Consular formalities and packaging and labelling. Cf. *Policy Perspectives for International Trade and Economic Relations, op. cit.,* pp. 59-62.

32 On the impact of protectionism on US trade policy see Harold B. Malmgrem, 'Coming Trade Wars?' in *Foreign Policy*, Winter 1970-71, pp. 115-43.

33 Gerard and Victoria Curzon, *After the Kennedy Round: What Trade Policies Now?*, London, The Atlantic Trade Study, 1968 p. 48.

34 *Policy Perspectives for International Trade and Economic Relations, op. cit.*

35 *Policy Perspectives for International Trade and Economic Relations, ibid.,* p. 115. The quotation is taken from the commentary on the Report by the United States Representative, Mr Eberle. Although he signed the Report, Mr Eberle expressed his disappointment with its treatment of both agriculture and the proliferation of discriminatory trading agreements by the European Communities.

36 *Ibid.,* p. 67.

37 *Ibid.,* General Conclusions, paragraph 347, p. 110.

38 *The Great Transformation, op. cit.,* Chapter I.

39 *Policy Perspectives for International Trade and Economic Relations, op. cit.,* p. 24.

40 E. Morse, 'The Confidence Problem and International Monetary Crises', (Mimeographed) see *Economics and Politics in International Studies: Report of the International Political Economy Summer Conference*, July 1972, London, Chatham House, 1972, pp. 7-8.

41 For a discussion on the possibilities for multilateral negotiations on non-tariff barriers see H.B. Malmgren, 'Modes of Negotiating in the 1970s', in *United States International Economic Policy in an Interdependent World*, Vol. II, pp. 493-514.

42 Cf. J.P. Sewell, 'Functional Agencies', in Cyril E. Black and Richard A Falk (eds), *The Future of the International Legal Order* IV Princeton, Princeton University Press, 1972 pp. 482-3.

43 *The International Monetary System*, 1945-55, Vol. I. Chronicle, pp. 531-6 and 612-3.

44 For example, see the conclusion on this subject by the OECD High Level Trade Group: 'The Responsibility of the industrialised countries in this field is great and will continue to grow in the future. They should prepare themselves to

make much greater efforts in this field than they have been willing to do so far, and to treat this as a priority requirement. In working out their external economic policies, the developed countries should take this urgent problem fully into account'. *Policy Perspectives for International Trade and Economic Relations.* p. 111.

45 *Policy Perspectives for International Trade & Economic Relations,* p. 92; for a summary of the debate prior to the 1972 UNCTAD see David Wall, 'Problems with Preferences', *International Affairs,* January 1971, pp. 87-99.

46 In 1970, the share of the Centrally Planned economies in world export trade was 10.6%, in world import trade 10.5%. The comparable figures for Western Europe were 44.4% and 42.1% respectively. *Policy Perspectives for International Trade and Economic Relations, op. cit.,* p. 140. See also C.F.G. Ransom, 'West European Integration and East-West Economic Relations', in *International Organization and the Changing European System* (Report of the Second Conference sponsored by the European Centre of the Carnegie Endowment for International Peace, 1972) pp. 43-64.

The Limits of Functionalist Endeavour : the Experiences of South-East Asia

Michael Leifer

In his seminal approach to the problems of world order,[1] Professor Mitrany indicated his approval of 'the functional alternative' applied on a less than universal scale. The utility of such 'administrative devolution' was admitted if promoted outside the context of a 'sectional union' which in close form was alleged to be merely a rationalised nationalism. In the case of South-east Asia, a region which possesses greater conventional than actual coherence, functionalist endeavour has been attempted both within the framework and under the aegis of universal organisation and also to some extent on a more exclusive basis. The experience and achievement of such endeavour has been limited, however, and understandably so given the factors sustaining the fragmentation of a region characterised by some as the Balkans of the Orient.

With the exception of Thailand, all of the states of South-east Asia—from Burma to the Philippines—have been subject to direct colonial domination. Their acquisition of international status dates only from after the termination of the Second World War. In partial consequence, their political leaderships cherish jealously individual national sovereignty and have not demonstrated, in any sense, a propensity to render the state-form superfluous or to facilitate any slicing off of sovereignty to any supranational seat of authority. In addition, the states of South-east Asia have been beset by a variety of mutual differences and antagonisms whose sources lie in both pre-colonial and modern experience. Intensely aware of conflicts of state interest and of the reality that geographic propinquity does not necessarily make for international harmony, the political leaders of South-east Asian countries have shown themselves to be extremely cautious in the extent to which they have been willing to commit themselves to regional cooperative enterprise.

Apart from the predilections and apprehensions of the political beneficiaries and successors of colonialism, a common feature of the states of South-east Asia is for popular horizons and cognitive patterns to be circumscribed by primordial or sub-national considerations. While such a common condition might appear appropriate for some as a context in which to attempt to channel loyalties beyond the idea of nation-state, the overriding emphasis of governmental action is directed to the goal of political integration and the consolidation of the territorial entity which succeeded to colonial rule. In consequence the prospects for functionalism, which in principle gravitates against such a goal, is somewhat bleak. Indeed, that small measure of success in functionalist endeavour which has been attained has been possible only where it has operated well within the conventional context of the state system and where it has appeared to assist that particularistic practice which Professor Mitrany had hoped would be overcome through the application of the functional alternative.

278

In so far as functionalism may be understood to mean international cooperation in piecemeal or special purpose enterprise of an ostensibly non-political kind, this chapter will not seek to evaluate that aspect of regional association which has been expressed in unequivocal political form.[2] Rather, it is hoped to assess those more specific forms of cooperative endeavour which, although falling within the scope of regional association, fit more closely the criteria of Professor Mitrany's conception.

Functionalism is not an activity which emerges simply in response to some objective notion of common need. If such were the case, South-east Asia might well be a suitable *milieu* for its active promotion. Functionalist activity tends rather to be the product of a convergence of perceived interests underpinned by suitable political and economic circumstances. In the case of South-east Asia, convergence of perceived interests has been minimal and the majority of enterprises which possess a functionalist component have represented in practice a deliberate attempt to secure an exclusive form of political advantage. In this respect, it is possible to write of pseudo-functionalism, that is, where the functionalist argument serves as the ostensible reason for promoting the enterprise in question.

During 1950, the President of the Philippines, Elpidio Quirino, sought to sponsor an anti-communist alliance among Asian states. Motivated by the success of communist revolution in China and distressed by a failure to interest the United States in the idea of a Pacific Pact, he managed to secure the attendance of a number of Asian and Australian political leaders at the hill resort of Baguio, near Manila, in May 1950. But in order to attract the participation of important Asian states, such as India and Indonesia, whose attitude to Cold War enterprise was well defined, the Philippine President found himself obliged to exclude South Korea and Taiwan who had been involved in the original sponsorship of a conference. Thus, the underlying purpose of the gathering was compromised at the outset. In addition, it became necessary to represent the meeting as a forum for the promotion of economic and cultural cooperation. In the event, the functionalist facade was not sufficient to engender any sense of genuine rapport among the participants at Baguio. The occasion was marked instead by the passage of pious and vacuous resolutions and by a failure to agree on any practical proposal for economic cooperation. Functionalism, in so far as it possessed any relevance to the conference, served solely as an implausible cover to facilitate its convening.

At Bandung in Indonesia in April 1955, there occurred a somewhat different type of gathering with a constituency also beyond that of South-east Asia. This was the Asian-African Conference which was intended to promote the international standing of the host country, assist the China policy of India and also demonstrate Afro-Asian solidarity. A more honest occasion than Baguio, the Bandung Conference also did little more than produce fine sounding declarations. There was no response from among the delegates to suggestions for a technical cooperation council for mutual assistance, while no progress was made in promoting intra-regional trade.

One of the issues which divided delegates to the Bandung Conference was membership of the South-east Asia Treaty Organisation (SEATO), established in Manila in September 1954. For a country like the Philippines which had sponsored the ill-fated Baguio Conference, the advent of SEATO was a welcome addition to its provision for national security. But by the end of the decade there arose increasing doubts about the efficacy of the organisation and especially the degree of commitment to its purposes by the extra-regional powers. Such doubts were

279

strengthened with the onset of crisis in Laos at the beginning of the 1960s. Concurrently, two members of SEATO, Thailand and the Philippines, together with Malaya which was in close defence association with a SEATO member, sought to sponsor a regional association in part to satisfy personal ambitions of national leaders but also to promote common political interests. It was perhaps unfortunate that their preliminary initiative took the proposed form of a South-east Asia Friendship and Economic Treaty, represented in acronym as SEAFET. This expression, together with the alliance associations of the sponsors of the treaty, suggested to the non-aligned countries of South-east Asia, including Indonesia and Cambodia, that an indigenous alternative to SEATO was in the making. In addition, the Soviet Union, the Chinese People's Republic and North Vietnam all denounced the undertaking.

Both Malaya and the Philippines persisted in the joint enterprise but changed the name of the proposed association. In July 1961 they sponsored, with Thai support, the Association of South-east Asia (ASA). This body was represented as a vehicle for economic, social and cultural cooperation. However, in spite of the declared non-political objectives of the association, it failed to attract members in addition to its three founders. The non-aligned states of the region had no desire to compromise their status and also had little inclination to incurr the antagonism of Peking and Hanoi over a suspect venture. Even the exclusion by its sponsors of South Vietnam did not make the association an attractive prospect.

ASA represents another example of pseudo-functionalism in that the prospect of non-political forms of inter-state cooperation was held out as a bait to promote a regional association of undoubted political significance. In the event, the actual functional enterprise of ASA between its three members was little more than nominal. Apart from the inauguration of an express train service between Kuala Lumpur and Bangkok, already in rail communication, the various joint projects announced never went beyond the stage of consultation. Various governmental, official and expert committees were established to assist in consultation but no progress was made towards the establishment of a common secretariat for the association. ASA did not promote any real measure of economic integration between states whose economies, as with others in South-east Asia, did not stand in any complementary relationship.

However, before ASA had any real opportunity to demonstrate either success or failure over time, it was disrupted by the onset of Indonesian Confrontation against Malaysia and the claim by the Philippines to Sabah (North Borneo). During the three and a half year period of confrontation in which the Philippines was aligned diplomatically with Indonesia in order to advance its territorial claim, ASA rested in a state of suspended animation. With its termination, the foreign ministers of ASA met once more in formal session only to adjourn *sine die*. In effect, ASA was to be subsumed within a new regional grouping called the Association of South-east Asian Nations (ASEAN) which was established in August 1967. Indonesia and Singapore joined the new association in addition to the three founder members of ASA.

ASEAN, although undoubtedly limited in its achievements, has emerged as much less of a pseudo-functionalist body than its regional predecessors. Its initial purpose was political. Indeed, its founding document made reference to the temporary nature of foreign military bases in South-east Asia. ASEAN represented an institutional means whereby a politically transformed Indonesia might find scope for a measure of regional leadership without displaying the urge for dominance suggested by the rhetoric and bellicose conduct of the Sukarno era. In essence, however, ASEAN has operated in a manner somewhat similar to ASA before that body was seized with internal discord. Although the members of ASEAN jointly pay attention to matters of regional security and have committed themselves in principle to the goal of neutralisation for South-east Asia, the energies of its membership have been directed in the main to limited functional enterprise.

The members of ASEAN, however, have not sought to force the pace of regional cooperation. They have come to recognise that their divergent conceptions of security interest plus competitive economic policies do not permit any rapid move in this direction. To this end, ASEAN, which is regarded as a useful if modest vehicle for diplomatic consultation and possible harmonisation of goals has a pragmatic cast about its activities. In its degree of institutionalisation it does not represent a dramatic advance over the limited achievement of ASA. For example, it does not possess a common secretariat. On the other hand there is an awareness of the value of functional cooperation if only because this is the only kind of cooperation that is really practical. To this end permanent sub-committees do exist in national capitals to oversee functional projects in food production and supply, civilian transport, communications and civil air traffic, shipping, commerce and industry.

Bureaucratic arrangements do not of themselves make for meaningful cooperation and ASEAN has yet to achieve the condition of embryonic form of regional functionalism. In essence, it is a diplomatic forum within which common interests can be identified and cooperation planned on that basis. At this point in time, the visible achievement is minimal. Nonetheless, the members of the association do not show any signs of wishing to dismember or replace it. On the contrary, it has come to represent a symbolic assertion of local autonomy in a region which has been long subject to the influence of external powers.

A more authentic example of regional functionalism, albeit with a wider geographic compass, from Iran to the West Pacific, is demonstrated in the workings of the United Nations Economic Commission for Asia and the Far East (ECAFE) established in March 1947 which has its permanent headquarters in Bangkok. At its initial formation ECAFE did not assume a functionalist role. It began activities as an instrument for post-war economic reconstruction. As such it received a mandate from the Economic and Social Council to make or sponsor studies of economic and technical problems and also to collect, evaluate and disseminate economic information. It has been pointed out that there was an early realisation that ECAFE was not likely to assume an important role in the channelling of external economic assistance because prospective donors preferred bilateral arrangements.[3] Also, because of great power and UN Secretariat obstruction, it had considerable difficulty in assuming an administrative role in the UN technical assistance programme. It was not until the 1960s with the designation of the ECAFE secretariat as executive agency for the UN special fund for the Lower Mekong Project that the Commission began to take an operational responsibility of any kind.

ECAFE serves as an all embracing organisation which sponsors activities of a functional kind. But in the main because of limited access to funds and the greater willingness of governments to promote economic development through bilateral associations with external powers, it has been restricted in its activities to the investigation and collection of data, the provision of advisory services and assisting states in the promotion of regional cooperation.

In the realm of functional endeavour, it has two well-established undertakings in hand. First, it oversees the Asian Highway Project. The Commission assists in providing surveys and specifications for routes, bridges and road signs. Its main role, however, is advisory, including the organisation of motor rallies. The project itself does not point up the special merits of functionalism. It has been explained: 'The Asian Highway did not raise serious political difficulties as much of the project is part of the national road development plans to be executed by the governments concerned.[4] Indeed, the example and the experience of the Asian Highway Project, which has been seriously interrupted by war in Indochina, underpins an earlier argument that interstate cooperation of a functionalist kind is most likely to occur when it serves the particular and separate interests of the participating states.

Such an axiom has been borne out in the experience of what has been the most notable achievement of ECAFE and the most significant example of functionalist endeavour in South-east Asia. As far back as 1952 a preliminary report had been prepared on the prospects of controlling and utilising the waters of the lower reaches of the river Mekong and its tributaries which run through Thailand, Laos, Cambodia and South Vietnam. But it was not until 1957 that a project under ECAFE auspices assumed tangible form. In effect, the Committee for the Coordination of Investigations of the Lower Mekong Basin was established by the governments of the riparian states. It works, however, in close conjunction with the secretariat of ECAFE. The actual financing of the project had been on a multilateral basis with over $200 million in funds being received from twenty-six external donors as well as from UN agencies and private foundations. A notable feature of the progress of the project, which has experienced numerous difficulties because of the political condition of Indochina, is the extent to which the riparian states have demonstrated a continuing willingness to cooperate despite recurrent strains in their mutual relations. Indeed, the Committee proceeded with its task with full membership even when diplomatic relations were ruptured between some of the participant states. However, there has been no evidence that the degree of interstate cooperation inspired by the project has been able to prevent a deterioration in inter-state relations arising out of political differences.

A special feature of the Mekong Project has been that the prospect of advantage for participating states has been approximately equal. This is reflected in the distribution of the specific programmes within the overall project which takes the form of ten for the main stream and sixteen in the tributaries divided equally between the four riparian states. This somewhat fortuitous circumstance has been unique within South-east Asia and the extent of functionalist endeavour, although significant and meritorious, does not show any sign of servicing as a means of transforming the nature of inter-state relationships which in Indochina in particular are beset by great strains.

The habit of cooperation of a functionalist kind has been demonstrated in other ways in South-east Asia, in great part through ECAFE,[5] and since the mid-1960s a number of standing ministerial conferences have been established to discuss matters of common regional interest. For example, there is the South-east Asian Agricultural Development Conference and also the South-east Asian Ministerial Conferences on Development and on Education. However, in the main, such gatherings do little more than exchange informed views, while the annual meeting of finance ministers serves more than anything else as a means of channelling economic assistance from Japan.

The needs of the state in South-east Asia as perceived by the various governments do not suggest much prospect of the extensive adoption of functional techniques of cooperation. Besides a plenitude of political differences, the nature of the economies of the region are such that, with the exception of Singapore, they have a minimal complementary relationship. They are concerned in the main to provide for import substitution in industrial development and, where it does not yet already exist, self-sufficiency in rice production. That measure of specificity from which complementary interest might facilitate substantive functional activity has yet to be attained within South-east Asia.

Professor Mitrany conceived of the functional approach as a way of limiting authority to specific activity and hopefully in the process to break away from the traditional link between authority and defined territory. Only in the example of the Mekong Project has there been any resemblance to such a process within South-east Asia. The states of the region in common with others elsewhere whose political and economic situation is similar are not prepared to contemplate the functional approach in any genuine sense unless there is a clear prospect of tangible advantage of a kind which in practice will work against the very process which Professor Mitrany has sought to encourage and promote.

Notes and references

1 David Mitrany, *A Working Peace System*, Chicago, Illinois: Quadrangle Books 1966.
2 For such an evaluation, see Michael Leifer, *Dilemmas of Statehood in South-east Asia*, Singapore, 1971. Chapter 9.
3 L.P. Singh, *The Politics of Economic Cooperation in Asia: A Study of Asian International Organisations*, Columbia, University of Missouri, 1966. p. 57.
4 *Ibid*, p. 126.
5 Regional projects related to ECAFE include:
   (a) Committee for the Coordination of Investigations of the Lower Mekong Basin.
   (b) Asian Institute for Economic Development and Planning.
   (c) Asian Highway Coordinating Committee.
   (d) Asian Industrial Development Council.
   (e) Committee for Coordination of Joint Prospecting for Mineral Resources in Asian Offshore Areas.
   (f) Typhoon Committee (in Manila—in association with World Meteorological Organisation)
   (g) ECAFE Trade Promotion Centre.
   (h) Asian Coconut Community (Djakarta)
   (i) Asian Statistical Institute (in Tokyo)
   (j) Trans-Asian Railway Project.
   (k) Asian Centre for Development Administration.

Bibliography*

The bibliography has been prepared according to the following criteria:
1 We have concentrated on functionalism insofar as it relates to problems of international organisation and world society.
2 We have especially tried to include references from Eastern European and third world writers, since their work is not likely to be very familiar to readers.
3 We have selected references in the hope of securing a reasonable balance between theory, description and prescription as well as between organisations and regions.
4 We have been rather less liberal with the 'structural-functional' literature and with that on international trade, development and technical assistance programmes.
5 We have included a few standard works on anarchism and cooperatives.
6 In general, we have excluded documents of International Governmental and Nongovernmental Organisations.
7 In compiling this bibliography the following journals were scanned for articles and reviews: *International Organisation, International Conciliation, International Affairs, World Politics, American Political Science Review, Political Studies, Journal of Common Market Studies.*

ADAM, H.T. *Les Organismes Internationaux Spécialisés: Contribution à la Théorie Générale des Etablissements Internationaux* Paris: Librairie Générale de Droit et de Jurisprudence, 1965.
ADLER-KARLSSON, GUNNAR *Functional Socialism: A Swedish Theory for Democratic Socialization* Stockholm: Bokforlaget Prisma, 1967.
AGOSTON, ISTVAN *Le Marché Commun Communiste: Principes et Pratiques du COMECON* Genève: Librairie Droz, 1964.
DE AGUIAR, PINTO 'Fundementos, Objetivos e Bases do Mercado Regional Latino-Americano', *Livraria Progresso*, 1959.
AHMED, L.N. 'The Organisation and Methods of the United Nations' Administrative Committee on Coordination', *International Review of Administrative Sciences*, **24**, (3), 1958.
AKI, KOICHI 'A Model of International Cooperation over Mekong', *Asian Affairs*, **4**, (1), 1959.
AKZIN, BENJAMIN *New States and International Organisations: A Report Prepared on Behalf of the International Political Science Association* Paris: UNESCO, 1955.

*The editors wish to acknowledge the considerable assistance of S.F. Condit in the preparation of this bibliography.

ALBRECHT-CARRIÉ, R. *The Unity of Europe, A Historical Survey*, London: Secker and Warburg, 1966.

ALCOCK, ANTHONY *History of the International Labour Organisation* London: Macmillan, 1971.

ALEXANDER, LEWIS H. *The Law of the Sea: International Rules and Organisation for the Sea: Proceedings of the Third Annual Conference of the Law of the Sea Institute June 24-27, 1968* Columbus: Ohio University Press, 1969.

ALEXANDER, YONAH *International Technical Assistance Experts: A Case Study of the UN Experience* New York: Frederick A. Praeger, 1966.

ALEXANDROWICZ, CHARLES, H. *World Economic Agencies, Law and Practice* New York: Frederick A. Praeger, 1962.

ALGER, CHADWICK 'Comparison of Intranational and International Politics', *American Political Science Review,* 57, (2) 1963.

ALLEN, CHARLES E. 'World Health and World Politics', *International Organisation,* 4, (1), 1950.

ALLEN, ROBERT L. 'United Nations Technical Assistance: Soviet and East European Participation', *International Organisation,* 11 (4), 1957.

ALMOND, GABRIEL A. 'Comparative Political Systems', *Journal of Politics,* 18, (3), 1956.

ALMOND, GABRIEL A. 'A Developmental Approach to Political Systems', *World Politics,* 17, (1), 1964.

ALMOND, GABRIEL A. and COLEMAN JOHN S. *The Politics of the Developing Areas* Princeton, New Jersey: Princeton University Press, 1960.

ALMOND, GABRIEL A. and POWELL, G. BINGHAM *Comparative Politics* Boston: Little Brown and Co., 1966.

ALVAREZ, A. *L'Organisation Internationale, Précedents de la Société des Nations* Paris; Editions Internationales, 1931.

ANDERSON, CHARLES W. *Politics and Economic Change in Latin America* Princeton, New Jersey: Van Nostrand, 1967.

ANDERSON, STANLEY V. *The Nordic Council; A Study of Scandinavian Regionalism* Seattle: University of Washington Press, 1967.

ANDREN, NILS 'The Nordic Cultural Commission 1947-1957', *The Norseman,* 15, (6), 1957.

ANDREN, NILS 'Nordic Integration', *Cooperation and Conflict,* No.1, 1967.

ANGELL, NORMAN *Europe's Optical Illusion* London: Simpkin Marshall, 1909.

ANGELL, NORMAN *The Great Illusion: A Study of the Relations of Military Power in Nations to their Economic and Social Advantage* London: Heinemann, 1910.

ANGELL, NORMAN 'The Mirage of the Map', *International Conciliation,* April 1912.

ANGELL, NORMAN *The Foundations of International Polity* London: Heineman, 1914.

ANGELL, NORMAN *From Chaos to Control* London: Allen & Unwin, 1933.

ANGELL, NORMAN *The Great Illusion—Now* Harmondsworth: Penguin Books, 1939.

ANGELL, ROBERT C. 'An Analysis of Trends in International Organisation', *Peace Research Society (International) Papers,* 3, 1965.

ANGELL, ROBERT C. 'The Growth of Transnational Participation', *Journal of Social Issues,* 23, (1), 1967.

ANGELL, ROBERT C. *Peace on the March* Princeton, New Jersey: D. Van Nostrand, 1969.

ANGUS, N.C. 'United Nations and Public Administration', *New Zealand Journal of Public Administration*, **22**, (1), 1959.

ANITCHKOW, MICHAEL *War and Labor* Westminster: Archibald Constable and Co., 1900.

APREMONT, B. 'Difficultés et Progrès de l'Intégration Economique au Sein du Comecon'. *Politique Etrangère*, 26th Year, No. 3, 1961.

ARAGAO, JOSÉ MARIA 'La Teoria Económica y el proceso de Integración de America Latina'. *Revista de la Integración*, No.2, 1968.

ARMAND, L. and DRANCOURT, M. *Le Pari Européen.* Paris: Fayard, 1968.

ARNOLD, GUY *Economic Cooperation in the Commonwealth.* New York: Pergamon Press, 1968.

ARON, RAYMOND *The Industrial Society: Three Essays on Ideology and Development.* New York: Frederick A. Praeger, 1967.

ARON, RAYMOND, (ed.) *World Technology and Human Destiny.* Ann Arbor: University of Michigan, 1967.

ARSIĆ, DRAGINJA 'Role of SEV in Economic Cooperation in the "Socialist Camp".' *Review of International Affairs*, Vol. **11**, No. 252, 1960.

ARSIĆ, DRAGINJA 'First Results of Changes in the Structure and Method of COMECON.' *Review of International Affairs*, Vol. **14**, No. 311, 1963.

ARSIĆ, DRAGINJA 'Certain Problems of Economic Development and Cooperation within the COMECON'. *International Problems*, 8th Year, 1967.

ASCHER, CHARLES S. 'The Development of UNESCO's Program'. *International Organisation*, Vol. 4, No.1, 1950.

ASCHER, CHARLES S. *Program Making in UNESCO, A Study in the Processes of International Administration.* Chicago: Public Administration, 1951.

ASCHER, CHARLES S. 'Current Problems in the World Health Organisation's Program'. *International Organisation*, **6**, (1), 1952.

ASHER, ROBERT E. 'Economic Cooperation under UN Auspices'. *International Organisation*, **12**, (3), 1958.

ASHER, ROBERT E. 'International Agencies and Economic Development: An Overview'. *International Organisation*, **22**, (1), 1968.

ASHER, ROBERT E. et al. *The United Nations and Economic and Social Cooperation.* Washington D.C.; The Brookings Institution, 1957.

ASHER, ROBERT E. et al. *The United Nations and Promotion of the General Welfare.* Washington D.C.; The Brookings Institution, 1957.

ATLANTIC COUNCIL 'Non-Military Functions of NATO'. *Atlantic Community Quarterly*, **3**, (4), 1966.

AUBREY, HENRY G. *Atlantic Economic Cooperation.* New York: Frederic A. Praeger, 1967.

AUFRICHT, HANS *The International Monetary Fund: Legal Aspects, Structure, Functions, 1945-1964.* New York: Frederick A. Praeger, 1964.

AUGUSTOWSKI, ZBIGNIEW 'Ukland Ogolny o Clach: Handlu (GATT) a interesey Polski'. *Sprawy Miedzynarodowe*, 14, (3), 1961.

AXLINE, W. ANDREW *European Community Law and Organisational Development.* Dobbs Ferry, New York: Oceana Publications, 1968.

BAADE, FRITZ *Dynamische Weltwirtschaft.* München: List Verlag, 1969.

BABIC, LJUBOMIR 'Cooperation with International Economic Organisations for Industrial Development'. *Review of International Affairs*, **18**, 406, 1967.

BAILEY, LIBERTY H. *Universal Service: The Hope of Humanity*. New York: Sturgis and Walton, 1918.

BAILEY, SIDNEY D. *The Secretariat of the United Nations*. London: Pall Mall, 1964.

BAILEY, STANLEY H. 'Some Problems of Article XXIV of the Covenant'. *American Political Science Review*, **25**, (2), 1931.

BAILEY, STANLEY H. *The Framework of International Society*. London: Longmans, 1932.

BAILEY, STANLEY H. 'International Economic Cooperation at the Cross-Roads'. *American Political Science Review*, **28**, (5), 1934.

BAILEY, STANLEY H. *The Anti-Drug Campaign: An Experiment in International Control*. London: P.S. King and Son, Ltd., 1936.

BAKKEN, HENRY *Basic Concepts, Principles and Practices of Cooperation*. Madison, Wisconsin: Mimir Publishers Inc., 1963.

BALAKRISHNA, R. and SINGH, D. BRIGHT 'The ECAFE and the Economic Reconstruction of South-East Asia'. *The Indian Yearbook of International Affairs*, **3**, 1954.

BALASSA, BELA *The Theory of Economic Integration*. Homewood, Illinois: Richard D. Irwin, Inc., 1961.

BALASSA, BELA *Economic Development and Integration*. Mexico City: Centro de Estudios Monetarios Latinoamericanos, 1965.

BALDWIN, SIMEON E. 'The International Congresses and Conferences of the Last Century as Forces Working Toward the Solidarity of the World'. *American Journal of International Law*, **1**, 1907.

BALL, GEORGE W. 'COSMOCORP: The Importance of Being Stateless'. *Atlantic Community Quarterly*, **6**, (2), 1968.

BALOGH, THOMAS 'The Strategy and Tactics of Technical Assistance'. *Public Administration*, **37**, 1959.

BANKS, MICHAEL 'Systems Analysis and the Study of Regions'. *International Studies Quarterly*, **13**, (4), 1969.

BARBOUR, K.M. 'A New Approach to the Nile Waters Problem'. *International Affairs (London)*, **33**, (3), 1957.

BARKER, SIR ERNEST *The Development of Public Services in Western Europe, 1660-1930*. London: Oxford University Press, 1944.

BARKUN, MICHAEL *Law Without Sanctions: Order in Primitive Society and the World Community*. New Haven: Yale University Press, 1968.

BARNARD, C.I. *The Functions of the Executive*. Cambridge: Harvard University Press, 1938

BARNES, G.N. *History of the International Labour Office*. London: Williams, 1926.

BARRACLOUGH, GEOFFREY *European Unity in Thought and Action*. Oxford: Basil Blackwell, 1964.

BARRERA, MARIO and HAAS, ERNST B. 'The Operationalisation of Some Variables Related to Regional Integration: A Research Note'. *International Organisation*, **23**, (1), 1969.

BARTOŠ, MILAN 'Position and Function of the UNO Secretary General: Proposals for the Reorganization of the UNO Secretariat'. *Review of International Affairs*, **11**, (253), 1960.

287

BASCH, ANTONIN 'The Colombo Plan: A Case of Regional Economic Co-operation'. *International Organisation*, 9, (1), 1955.

BASU, R.K. 'Regional Cooperation in Technical Assistance'. *India Quarterly*, 14, (4), 1958.

BAUMANN, CAROL E. (ed.) *Western Europe: What Path to Integration?* Boston: D.C. Heath and Co., 1967.

BAXTER, R.R. *The Law of International Waterways.* Cambridge: Harvard University Press, 1964.

BEARD, CHARLES A. *The Idea of National Interest: An Analytical Study of American Foreign Policy.* New York: Macmillan and Co. Inc., 1934.

BEARD, WILLIAM 'Technology and Political Boundaries'. *American Political Science Review*, 25, (3), 1931.

BECK, ROBERT H. et. al. *The Changing Structure of Europe: Economic, Social and Political Trends.*, Minneapolis: University of Minnesota Press, 1970.

BECKEL, GRAHAM *Workshops for the World: The United Nations Family of Agencies.* (rev. ed.) London: Abelard-Schuman, 1962.

BEDJAOUI, MOHAMMED *International Civil Service.* London: Stevens and Sons, 1958.

BEELER, A.B. *International Labor Organisation, 1953-55: Changes in its Structure, Functions and Policy.* unpublished Ph.D., Cornell University, 1955-56.

BEER, FRANCIS O. *Integration and Disintegration in NATO: Process of Alliance Cohesion and Prospects for Atlantic Community.* Columbus: Ohio State University Press, 1969.

BEEVER, R. COLIN *European Unity and the Trade Union Movements.* Leyden: Sijthoff, 1960.

BELL, DANIEL *The End of Ideology: On the Exhausting of Political Ideas in the Fifties.* New York: Collier Books, 1961.

BELLQUIST, ERIC C. 'Inter-Scandinavian Cooperation'. *Annals of the American Academy of Political and Social Science*, CLXVIII, 1933.

BENHAM, FREDERIC *The Colombo Plan and Other Essays.* London: Royal Institute of International Affairs, 1956.

BENJAMIN, PETER 'The Work of the Economic Commission for Europe in the Field of International Commercial Arbitration'. *The International and Comparative Law Quarterly*, 7, Part 1, 1958.

BENN, ANTHONY WEDGWOOD *The New Politics: A Socialist Reconnaissance.* London: Fabian Tract 402, 1970.

BENOIT, EMILE *Europe at Sixes and Sevens.* New York: Columbia University Press, 1961.

BENVENISTE, GUY and MORAN, WILLIAM E. JR., *African Development; A Test for International Cooperation.* Menlo Park, Calif.; Stanford Research Institute, 1960.

BERENSTEIN, ALEXANDRE *Les Organisations ouvrières—leurs compétences et leurs rôles dans la Société des Nations et notamment dans l'Organisation Internationale du Travail.* Paris: Pedove, 1936.

BERENSTEIN, ALEXANDRE 'The Influence of International Labour Conventions in Swiss Legislation'. *International Labour Review*, 77, (6), 1958.

BERGTHUN, O.L. and NIELSEN, T.T. 'COMECON and EEC: A Comparative Analysis' *Res Publica*, 10, (3), 1968.

BERKHUUS, A. *The Sanitary Conferences.* Ciba Symposia 5, (7), 1943.

BERKOV, ROBERT *The World Health Organisation: A Study in Decentralised International Administration.* Genève: Librairie E. Droz; Paris: Librairie Minard; 1957.

BERNSTEIN, EDUARD (tr. by **S. HARVEY**) *Evolutionary Socialism.* New York: B.W. Huebsch, 1909.

BERNSTEIN, EDWARD M. 'The International Monetary Fund'. *International Organisation*, **22**, (1), 1968.

BERTHET, E. 'L'Organisation mondiale de la santé'. *Etudes*, April 1962.

BIEMILLER, CARL L. 'Tomorrow's Seas: The Problems and Promises of Man's Newest Frontier'. *Vista*, **3**, (2), 1967.

BIEMILLER, CARL L. 'Tomorrow's Seas—Part II: The UN Searches for New Sources of Food'. *Vista*, **3**. (3), 1967.

BIRCH, A.H. 'Approaches to the Study of Federations'. *Political Studies*, XIV (1) February, 1966.

BISHOP, A.S. and MUNRO, ROBERT D. 'The UN Regional Economic Commissions and Environmental Problems'. *International Organisation*, **26**, (2), 1972.

BLACK, EUGENE R. *Diplomacy of Economic Development.* Cambridge: Harvard University Press, 1960.

BLAKESLEE, GEORGE H. 'The Establishment of the Far Eastern Commission'. *International Organisation*, **5**, (3), 1951.

BLANKENSTEIN, H. VAN *L'Organisation d'Hygiène de la Société des Nations.* Paris: J. Muusses-Purmeraud, 1934.

BLAU, PETER M. and SCOTT, W. RICHARD *Formal Organisations.* London: Routledge and Kegan Paul, 1963.

BLEICHER, SAMUEL A. 'UN v. IBRD: A Dilemma of Functionalism'. *International Organisation*, **24**, (1), 1970.

BLOCH, HENRY S. 'Regional Development Financing'. *International Organisation.* **22**, (1), 1968.

BLOCH, ROGER and LEFÉVRE, JACQUELINE *La Fonction Publique Internationale et Européene.* Paris: Librairie Générale de Droit, 1963.

BLOET-HAMERLIJNCK, RITA P. 'The Development of Air Law and European Cooperation'. *International Relations* (London), **2**, (11), 1965.

BLOOMFIELD, LINCOLN P. 'Outer Space and International Cooperation'. *International Organisation*, **19**, (3), 1965.

BLOUGH, ROY *International Business.* New York: McGraw-Hill, 1966.

BLOUGH, ROY 'The World Bank Group'. *International Organisation*, **22**, (1), 1968.

BLUM, LÉON *Les Problèmes de la Paix.* Paris: Librairie Stock, 1931.

BOCK, EDWIN A. *Fifty Years of Technical Assistance; Some Administrative Experiences of US Voluntary Agencies.* Chicago: Public Administration Clearing House, 1954.

BOCK, KENNETH 'Evolution, Function and Change'. *American Sociological Review*, **28**, 1963.

BODENHEIMER, SUSANNE J. *Political Union: A Microcosm of European Politics, 1960-1966.* Leyden: Sijthoff, 1967.

BOGARDUS, E.S. *Principles of Cooperation.* Chicago: Cooperative League of the United States, 1952.

BOGARDUS, E.S. *Toward a World Community.* Los Angeles: University of Southern California Press, 1964.

BOISSON, HENRI *La Société des Nations et les Bureaux Internationaux des Unions Universelles Postales et télégraphiques*. Paris: Pedove, 1932.

BONSDORFF, GORAN VON 'Regional Cooperation in the Nordic Countries'. *Cooperation and Conflict*, 1, (2), 1966.

BORGEAUD, MARC-AUGUSTE *L'Union Internationale de Secours*. Paris: Sirey, 1932.

BOUGH, JAMES 'The Caribbean Commission'. *International Organisation*, 3, (4), 1949.

BOURNE, RANDOLPH S. (ed.) *Towards an Enduring Peace: A Symposium of Peace Proposals and Programs, 1914-1916*. New York: American Association for International Conciliation, 1916.

BOURQUIN, MAURICE *Dynamism and the Machinery of International Institutions*. Geneva: Geneva Research Centre, 1940.

BOWLE, JOHN *Politics and Opinion in the 19th Century*. London: Jonathan Cape, 1954.

BOZEMAN, ADDA B. *Politics and Culture in International History*. Princeton, New Jersey: Princeton University Press, 1960.

BRAILSFORD, H.N. *A League of Nations*. London: Macmillan and Co., 1917.

BRANBOVIC, S. 'Economic Cooperation of the Balkan Countries'. *Review of International Affairs*, 5, (111), 1954.

BRENNER, MICHAEL J. *Technocratic Politics and the Functionalist Theory of European Integration*. Ithaca: Cornell University Press, 1969.

BREWSTER, HAVELOCK and THOMAS, CLIVE Y. *The Dynamics of West Indian Economic Integration*. Jamaica: Institute of Social and Economic Research, University of the West Indies, 1967.

BRIDGEMAN, RAYMOND L. *World Organisation*. Boston: Ginn & Co., 1905.

BRIGGS, HERBERT *The International Law Commission*. Ithaca: Cornell University Press, 1965.

BRINTON, CLARENCE C. *From Many One: The Process of Political Integration, the Problem of World Government*. Cambridge: Harvard University Press, 1948.

BROAD, ROGER and JARRETT, ROBERT *Community Europe*. London: Oswald Wolff, 1967.

BROMBERGER, MERRY and SERGE *Jean Monnet and the United States of Europe*. New York: Coward-McCann, 1969.

BRONZ, GEORGE 'An International Trade Organisation: The Second Attempt'. *Harvard Law Review*, 69, (3), 1956.

BROWN, ROBERT T. *Transport and the Economic Integration of Latin America*. Washington D.C.: Brookings Institution, 1966.

BRUGMANS, HENRI *L'Idée Européenne, 1918-1965*. Bruxelles: De Temple, 1965.

BUCHAN, ALASTAIR, (ed.) *Europe's Futures, Europe's Choices. Models of Western Europe in the 1970's*. London: Chatto and Windus, 1969, for the Institute for Strategic Studies.

BUCKLEY, WALTER *Sociology and Modern Systems Theory*. Englewood Cliffs, New Jersey: Prentice-Hall Inc., 1967.

BUERGENTHAL, THOMAS *Law-Making in the International Civil Aviation Organisation*. Syracuse, New York: Syracuse University Press, 1969.

BURCHALL, H. 'The Politics of International Air Routes'. International Affairs (London). 14, (1), 1935.

BURKE, WILLIAM T. *Towards a Better Use of the Ocean.* New York: Humanities Press, 1969.

BURNHAM, JAMES *The Managerial Revolution.* London: Putman, 1943.

BURTON, JOHN W. 'Regionalism, Functionalism and the United Nations'. *Australian Outlook,* **15,** (1), 1961.

BURTON, JOHN W. *Peace Theory: Preconditions of Disarmament.* New York: Alfred A. Knopf, 1962.

BURTON, JOHN W. *International Relations: A General Theory.* Cambridge: Cambridge University Press, 1965.

BURTON, JOHN W. *Systems, States, Diplomacy and Rules.* Cambridge: Cambridge University Press, 1968.

BURTON, JOHN W. *Conflict and Communication.* London: Macmillan, 1969.

BUSEY, JAMES L. 'Central American Union: The Latest Attempt'. *The Western Political Quarterly,* **14,** (1), Part 1, 1961.

BUSTAMONTE, JOSE C. 'La política regional de transportes en función de la integración latinoamericana'. *Revista de la Intergración, No. 1, 1967.*

BUTLER, HAROLD, *The Lost Peace.* London: Faber & Faber, 1941.

BUTLER, J.R.M. *Origin and Functions of the League.* London: League of Nations Union, 1924.

BUXTON, CHARLES R. *The Alternative to War: A Programme for Statesmen.* London: Allen and Unwin, 1936.

CABLE, VINCENT 'The "Football War" and the Central American Common Market'. *International Affairs* (London), **45,** (4), 1969

CALMANN, JOHN *European Cooperation in Defence Technology.* London: Institute for Strategic Studies, 1967.

CAMPS, MIRIAM *European Unification in the Sixties.* New York: McGraw Hill, 1966.

CAMPS, MIRIAM *Britain and the European Community, 1955-1966.* London: Oxford University Press, 1967.

CANTORI, LOUIS J. and SPIEGAL, STEVEN L. *International Politics of Regions.* Englewood Cliffs, New Jersey: Prentice Hall, 1970.

CAPEK, M. *Cooperatives and the State.* Prague: Central Cooperative Council, 1960.

CAPORASO, JAMES A. *Functionalism, Spill-over and International Integration.* unpublished Ph.D., University of Pennsylvania, 1968.

CAPORASO, JAMES A. 'Encapsulated Integrative Patterns vs. Spill-over: The Cases of Transport Integration in the European Economic Community'. *International Studies Quarterly,* **14,** (4), 1970.

CAPORASO, JAMES A. *Functionalism and Regional Integration: A Logical and Empirical Assessment.* Beverly Hills, Calif: Sage Publications, Inc., 1972.

CAIRE, GUY 'Chances et difficultés d'avenir des organisations économiques régionales en milieu sous-developpé. Example: l'OAMACE'. *Développement et Civilisations,* **(16),** 1963.

CARLSTON, K.S. *Law and Organisation in World Society.* Urbana: University of Illinois Press, 1962.

Carnegie Endowment for International Peace: *Coordination of Economic and Social Activities.* New York: CEIP, United Nations Studies 2, 1948.

Carnegie Endowment for International Peace: *Consultation between the United Nations and Non-governmental Organisations: A Working Paper Transmitted by the Interim Committee.* New York: United Nations Studies **3**, 1949.

CARR, E.H. *Nationalism and After.* London: Macmillan, 1945.

CARR, E.H. and de MADARIAGA, S. *The Future of International Government.* London: National Peace Council, 1941

CARTER, APRIL *The Political Theory of Anarchism.* London: Routledge and Kegan Paul, 1971.

CARTER, HENRY *Towards World Recovery: Plans and Proposals for International Functional Cooperation.* London: National Peace Council, 1945.

CASADIO, FRANCO A. 'I dieci anni della Organizzazione meteorologica mondiale'. *La Comunità Internazionale.* **15**, (3), 1960.

CASTANOS, STELIOS 'Les nouveaux principes du fonctionnalisme dans la CECA'. *Revue Héllenique de Droit International,* 13th Year, (1-4), 1962.

CASTILLO, CARLOS M. *Growth and Integration in Central America.* New York: Frederick A. Praeger, 1966.

CATTELL, DAVID T. 'Multilateral Cooperation and Integration in Eastern Europe'. *The Western Political Quarterly,* **13**, (1), 1960.

CHAMBERLAIN, J.P. *The Regime of the International Rivers: Danube and Rhine.* New York: Columbia University Press, 1923.

CHAMBERLAIN, J., JESSUP, P., LANDE, A., LISSITZYN, O. *International Organisation.* New York: Carnegie Endowment for International Peace, 1955.

CHEEVER, DANIEL S. 'The Role of International Organisations in Ocean Development' *International Organisation,* **22**, (3), 1968.

CHEEVER, DANIEL and HAVILAND, H. FIELD, JR. *Organising for Peace: Integrational Organisation in World Affairs* Cambridge: Harvard University Press, 1944.

CHISHOLM, BROCK *Prescription for Survival.* New York: Columbia University Press, 1957.

CHISHOLM, A. *Labour's Magna Carta.* London: Green, 1925.

CIAMAGA, LUCJAN *'Les problèmes clés de la coopération économique des Etats socialistes'. Annuaire Polanais des Affaires Internationales,* 1963.

CIAMAGA, LUCJAN *Od Wapolpracy do Integracji; Zarys Organizacji i Dzialalmosci RWPG w Latch 1949-1964.* Warsaw: KiW, 1965.

CLARK, G. and SOHN, L. *World Peace Through World Law.* Cambridge: Mass. Harvard University Press, 1960; and 3rd ed. rev. 1966.

CLAUDE, INIS L., Jr. *National Minorities: An International Problem.* Cambridge: Harvard University Press, 1955.

CLAUDE, INIS L., Jr. 'Multilateralism—Diplomatic and Otherwise'. *International Organisation,* **12**, (1), 1958.

CLAUDE, INIS L., Jr. *Power and International Relations.* New York: Random House Inc., 1962.

CLAUDE, INIS L., Jr. *Swords into Plowshares: The Problems and Progress of International Organisation.* Revised edition. New York : Random House, 1964.

CLAUDE, INIS L., Jr. 'Collective Legitimization as a Political Function of the United Nations'. *International Organisation,* **20**, (3), 1966

CLAUDE, INIS L., Jr. *European Organisations in a Global Context.* Brussels: Université Libre de Bruxelles, 1966.

CLAWSON, MARION *Natural Resources and International Development.* Baltimore: The John Hopkins Press, 1964.

CLEMENTS, F.W. 'The World Health Organisation in Southern Asia and the Western Pacific'. *Pacific Affairs,* **25,** (4), 1952.

COBB, ROGER W and ELDER, CHARLES *International Community: A Regional and Global Study.* New York: Holt, Rinehart and Winston Inc., 1970.

COCHRANE, JAMES D. 'Central American Economic Integration: The Integrated Industries Scheme'. *Inter-American Economic Affairs,* **19,** (2), 1965

COCHRANE, JAMES D. *The Politics of Regional Integration: The Central American Case.* New Orleans, 1969.

CODDING, GEORGE A., Jr. *The International Telecommunication Unions: An Experiment in International Cooperation.* Leyden: E.J. Brill, 1952.

CODDING, GEORGE A., Jr. *The Universal Postal Union: Coordinator of the International Mails.* New York: New York University Press, 1964.

CODDING, GEORGE A., Jr. 'The Relationship of the League of Nations and the UN with the Independent Agencies: a Comparison'. *Annals of International Studies,* 1970.

COHEN, ALVIN 'ECLA and the Economic Development of Peru'. *Inter-American Economic Affairs,* **17,** (1), 1963.

COHEN, JEROME B. 'The Colombo Plan for Cooperative Economic Development'. *Middle East Journal,* **5,** (1), 1951.

COLE, G.D.H. *Guild Socialism Restated.* London: Leonard Parsons, 1920.

COLE, G.D.H. *Workshop Organisation.* Oxford: The Clarendon Press, 1923.

COLE, G.D.H. *The Intelligent Man's Guide through World Chaos.* London: Gollancz, 1932.

COLE, G.D.H. 'Planning International Trade'. *International Conciliation* (299), 1934.

COLE, G.D.H. *Fabian Socialism.* London: Allen and Unwin, 1943.

COLE, G.D.H. *A Century of Cooperation.* London: Allen and Unwin, 1944.

COLE, G.D.H. *A History of Socialist Thought.* (3 vols.). London: Macmillan and Co., 1953-56.

COLLIARD, CLAUDE-ALBERT *Institutions Internationales.* Paris: Librairie Dalloz, 1956.

COLLIER, DAVID S. and GLASER, KURT (eds.) *Western Integration and the Future of Eastern Europe.* Chicago: Henry Regnery, 1964.

COLOMBAT, F.H. *Commonwealth of Nations.* Stanford: Stanford University Press, 1943.

CONDLIFFE, J.B. 'Problems of Economic Reorganisation'. *International Conciliation,* (389), 1943.

CONFORTI, BENEDETTO *La Funzione dell'Accordo nel Sistema delle Nazioni Unite.* Padova CEDAM, 1968.

CONSTANT, S.C. et. al. *L'Europe du Charbon et de l'Acier.* Paris: Presses Universitaires, 1968.

CONSTANTIN, L.A. *The Development of Regulation of International Aviation. United States Particpation and Policy.* unpublished Ph.D., University of Texas, 1949-50.

CONWAY, H. McKINLEY, Jr. *Area Development Organisations.* Atlanta: Conway Research, 1966.

COOK, THOMAS I. 'Theoretical Foundations of World Government'. *Review of Politics,* **12,** (1), 1950.

COOMBES, DAVID *Towards a European Civil Service.* London: Chatham House and PEP, 1968.

COOMBES, DAVID *Politics and Bureaucracy in the European Community.* London: Allen and Unwin, 1970.

COOPER, RICHARD N. *The Economics of Interdependence: Economic Policy in the Atlantic* New York: McGraw—Hill, 1968.

COPLIN, WILLIAM D. *The Functions of International Law: An Introduction to the Role of International Law in the Contemporary World.* Chicago: Rand McNally and Co., 1966.

CORBETT, P.E. *Post-War Worlds.* New York: Institute of Pacific Relations, 1942.

CORDIER, ANDREW W. and FOOTE, WILDER (eds.) *The Quest for Peace: The Dag Hammarskjold Memorial Lectures.* New York: Columbia University Press, 1965.

CORKRAN, HERBERT, Jr. *From Formal to Informal Cooperation in the Caribbean.* Dallas: The Arnold Foundation, 1966.

CORKRAN, HERBERT, Jr. *Patterns of International Cooperation in the Caribbean, 1942-1969.* Dallas: Southern Methodist University Press, 1970.

COSER, LEWIS A. *The Functions of Social Conflict.* London: Routledge and Kegan Paul, 1956, 1968.

COSER, LEWIS A. *Continuity in the Study of Social Conflict.* New York: The Free Press, 1967.

COSGROVE, CAROL A. and TWITCHETT, KENNETH J. *The New International Actors: The United Nations and the European Economic Community.* London: Macmillan and Co., 1970.

COX, ROBERT W. 'Education for Development'. *International Organisation,* **22,** (1), 1968.

COX, ROBERT W. 'The Executive Head: An Essay on Leadership in International Organisation'. *International Organisation,* **23,** (2), 1969.

COX, ROBERT W. (ed). *The Politics of International Organisations: Studies in Multilateral Social and Economic Agencies.* New York: Frederick A. Praeger, 1969.

COX, ROBERT W. (ed.) *International Organisation: World Politics* London: Macmillan, 1969.

CRANSTON, MAURICE *What are Human Rights?* New York: Basic Books Inc., 1962.

CRIPPS, SIR STAFFORD *The Struggle for Peace.* London: Gollancz, 1936.

CRIVON, R. 'Multilateral Cultural Cooperation in Europe'. *European Yearbook,* **16,** 1959.

CURTIS, MICHAEL *Western European Integration.* New York: Harper and Row Publishers, 1965.

CURZON, GERARD *Multilateral Commercial Diplomacy: An Examination of the Impact of the General Agreement on Tariffs and Trade on National Commercial Policies and Techniques.* London: Michael Joseph, 1965.

DAHL, K.N. 'The Role of ILO Standards in the Global Integration Process'. *Journal of Peace Research,* , (4), 1968.

DAHL, ROBERT A. and LINDBOLM, CHARLES E. *Politics, Economics and Welfare.* New York: Harper and Bros. Inc., 1953.

DAHLBERG, KENNETH A. 'Regional Integration: The Neo-Functional Versus a Configurative Approach'. *International Organisation*, **24**, (1), 1970.

DAM, KENNETH W. *The GATT—Law and International Economic Organisation.* Chicago: University of Chicago Press, 1970.

DAVIES, DAVID A. 'The Role of the WMO in Environmental Issues'. *International Organisations*, **24**, (2), 1972.

DAVID, HARRIET E. (ed.) *Pioneers in World Order: An American Appraisal of the League of Nations.* New York: University of Columbia Press, 1945.

DAVIS, KINGSLEY 'The Myth of Functional Analysis as a Special Method in Sociology and Anthropology'. *American Sociological Review*, **24**, 1959.

DAVIS, KINGSLEY and MOORE, WILBERT E. 'Some Principles of Stratification'. *American Sociological Review*, **10**, (2), 1945.

DAWSON, RAYMOND H. and NICHOLSON, GEORGE E., Jr. 'NATO and the SHAPE Technical Center'. *International Organisation*, **21**, (3), 1967.

DELL, SIDNEY *Trade Blocs and Common Markets.* New York: Alfred A. Knopf, 1963.

DELL, SIDNEY 'UNCTAD: Retrospect and Prospect'. *Annual Review of United Nations Affairs 1964-1965*, 1966.

DENDIAS, MICHEL 'Les principaux services internationaux administratifs'. *Recueil des cours de l'Académie de droit international*, Tome 63, **1**, 1938.

DELPÉRÉE, ALBERT *Politique Social et Intégration Européenne.* Liège: Georges Thone, 1956.

DEMERATH, N.J. III and PETERSON, R.A. *System, Change and Conflict: A Reader on Contemporary Sociological Theory and the Debate over Functionalism.* New York: The Free Press, 1967.

DENTON, GEOFFREY *Planning in the EEC: The Medium-term Economic Policy Programme of the European Economic Community.* London: European Series (5), Chatham House, 1967.

DENTON, GEOFFREY, (ed.) *Economic Integration in Europe.* London: Weidenfeld and Nicolson, 1969.

DESCAMPS, E.E.F. *Les Offices Internationaux et leur Avenir.* Bruxelles; 1894.

DESPICHT, NIGEL S. *Policies for Transport in the Common Market: A Survey of the National Transport Policies of the Six Member States of the European Economic Community and of the Implementation of the Transport Provisions of the Treaty of Rome.* Sidcup: Lambarde Press, 1964.

DEUTSCH, KARL W. *Nationalism and Social Communication.* New York: John Wiley and Sons Inc., 1953.

DEUTSCH, KARL W. *Political Community at the International Level.* Garden City, New Jersey: Doubleday, 1954.

DEUTSCH, KARL W. 'Social Mobilization and Political Development'. *American Political Science Review*, **55**, (3), 1961.

DEUTSCH, KARL W. 'Towards Western European Integration: An Interim Assessment'. *Journal of International Affairs*, **16**, (1), 1962.

DEUTSCH, KARL W. 'Supranational Organisations in the 1960's'. *Journal of Common Market Studies*, **1**, (3), 1963.

DEUTSCH, KARL W. *The Nerves of Government: Models of Political Communication and Control.* New York: The Free Press, 1963.

DEUTSCH, KARL W. *Nationalism and Its Alternatives.* New York: Alfred A. Knopf, 1969.

DEUTSCH, KARL W. et al. *Political Community and the North Atlantic Area.* Princeton, N.J.: Princeton University Press, 1957.

DEUTSCH, KARL W. et al. *France, Germany and the Western Alliance: A Study of Elite Attitudes on European Integration and World Politics* New York: Charles Scribner's and Sons, 1967.

DEWAR, MARGARET 'Economic Cooperation in the Soviet Orbit'. *Yearbook of World Affairs*, **13**, 1959.

DIAB, MUHAMMAD A. *Inter-Arab Economic Cooperation, 1951-1960.* American University Economic Research Institute, Beirut, 1964.

DIAB, MUHAMMAD A. 'The Arab Common Market'. *Journal of Common Market Studies*, **4**, (3), 1966.

DIAMOND, WILLIAM *Development Banks.* Baltimore: The John Hopkins Press, 1957.

DIEBOLD, WILLIAM, H. Jr. *Trade and Payments in Western Europe: A Study in Economic Cooperation, 1947-1951.* New York: Harper and Row, 1952.

DIEBOLD, WILLIAM, H. Jr. *The Schuman Plan. A Study in Economic Cooperation, 1950-1958.* New York: Frederick A. Praeger Inc., 1958.

DI NARDI, GIUSEPPE 'I mezzi di intervenzione per la creazione di nuove attività'. *Rivista di Politica Economica*, 51st Year, 3rd Series, (2), 1961.

DJORDJENIK, MILINKO 'Economic Reforms in Eastern Europe and International Cooperation'. *Review of International Affairs*, **17**, (386), 1966.

DODD, NORRIS E. 'FAO Work and Aims in Asia'. *United Asia*, **3**, (2), 1950.

DODD, NORRIS E. 'A Summary of Activities of the Food and Agricultural Organisation in the Middle East'. *Middle East Journal*, **4**, (3), 1950.

DOIMI di DELUPIS, INGRID *The East African Community and the Common Market.* London, Longmans, Green and Co., 1970.

DUBOIS, CHARLES *Le droit des Gens et les Rapports des Grandes Puissances avec les autres Etats avant le Pacte de la SdN.* Paris: Plon, 1921.

DOLAN, PAUL 'The Nordic Council'. *Western Political Quarterly*, **12**, (2), 1959.

DOWSE, ROBERT E. 'A Functionalists Logic'. *World Politics*, **18**, (4), 1966.

DRAGOMANOVIC, VLADIMIR 'The Cairo Conference on the Problems of Economic Development', *Medjunarodni Problemi*, 14th English Issue, 1963.

DUFFY, NORMAN F. 'Organisational Growth and Goal Structure: The Case of the ILO'. *International Organisation*, **26**, (3), 1972.

DUNN, FREDERICK, S. *War and the Minds of Men.* New York: Harper and Row, 1950.

DUPLESSIX, E. *L'Organisation Internationale.* Paris: Larose et Tenin, 1909.

DURAS, VICTOR H. *Universal Peace by International Government.* New York: Broadway Publishing Co., 1908.

DURAS, VICTOR H. *La Paix par l'Organisation Internationale.* Paris: Giard, 1910.

DURKHEIM, EMILE *The Rules of Sociological Method.* Glencoe, Ill. The Free Press, 1938.

DURKHEIM, EMILE *The Division of Labour in Society.* New York: The Free Press, 1947.

DURKHEIM, EMILE *Socialism and Saint-Simon.* London: Routledge and Kegan Paul, 1959.

DUTCH, OSWALD *Economic Peace Aims,* London: Arnold, 1941.

EAGLETON, CLYDE *International Government.* New York: Ronald Press Co., 1948.

EARLE, EDWARD M. 'International Financial Control of Raw Materials'. *International Conciliation,* (226), 1927.

EATON, H.O. et. al. *Federation: The Coming Structure of World Government.* University of Oklahoma Press, 1944.

EDELMANN, ALEXANDER T. 'The TVA and Inter-Governmental Relations'. *American Political Science Review,* 37, (3),·1943

EDWARDS, STEWART (ed.) *Selected Writings of Pierre-Joseph Proudhon.* London: Macmillan and Co. Ltd., 1969.

EFIMENCO, N. MARBURY 'Categories of International Integration'. *India Quarterly,* 16, (3), 1960.

EFRON, RUBEN and NAVES, ALLEN S. 'The Common Market and Euratom Treaties: Supernationality and the Integration of Europe'. *The International and Comparative Law Quarterly,* 6, Part 4, 1957.

EGGER, ROWLAND *The Organisation of Peace at the Administrative Level.* New York: Committee to Study the Organisations of Peace, 1945.

EICHELBERGER, CLARK M. (ed.) *New Dimensions for the United Nations: The Problems of the Next Decade.* Dobbs Ferry, New York: Oceana Publications, 1966.

EIDE, ASBJORN and SCHON, AUGUST (eds.) *Nobel Symposium 7: International Protection of Human Rights.* New York: John Wiley and Sons, 1968.

EISENLOHR, L.E.S. *International Narcotics Control.* London: George Allen and Unwin, 1934

ELDER, R.E. *Economic Development: Special United Nations Fund for Economic Development (SUNFED).* New York: Woodrow Wilson Foundation, 1954.

ELLIOT, W.A. and others *International Control in the Non-Ferrous Metals.* New York; Macmillan, 1937.

ELSNER, HENRY Jr. *The Technocrats, Prophets of Automation.* Syracuse, N.Y.: Syracuse University Press, 1967.

EMELIANOFF, I. *Economic Theory of Cooperation.* Washington, 1948.

ENGLE, HAROLD E. 'A Critical Study of the Functional Approach to International Organisation'. unpublished Ph.D. dissertation, Department of Public Law and Government, Columbia University, 1957.

ETZIONI, AMITAI *A Comparative Analysis of Complex Organisations.* New York: The Free Press, 1961.

ETZIONI, AMITAI 'A Paradigm for the Study of Political Unification'. *World Politics,* 15, (1), 1962.

ETZIONI, AMITAI 'The Dialectics of Supranational Unification'. *American Political Science Review,* 56, (4), 1962.

ETZIONI, AMITAI *The Hard Way to Peace.* New York: Collier Books, 1962.

ETZIONI, AMITAI 'European Unification: A Strategy of Change'. *World Politics,* 16, (1), 1963.

ETZIONI, AMITAI 'The Epigenesis of Political Communities at the International Level'. *American Journal of Sociology,* 28, (3), 1963.

ETZIONI, AMITAI 'European Unification and Perspectives on Sovereignty'. *The Atlantic Community Quarterly,* 2, (1), 1964

ETZIONI, AMITAI *Political Unification: A Comparative Study of Leaders and Forces.* New York: Holt, Rinehart and Winston, 1965.

ETZIONI, AMITAI *The Active Society: A Theory of Societal and Political Processes.* New York: The Free Press, 1968.

EVANS, JOHN W. 'The General Agreement on Tariffs and Trade'. *International Organisation,* **22,** (1), 1968.

EVANS, LUTHER H. 'Some Management Problems of UNESCO. *International Organisation,* **17,** (1), 1963.

FAINSOD, MERLE *International Socialism and the War.* Cambridge: Harvard University Press, 1935.

FALK, RICHARD A. *Legal Order in a Violent World.* Princeton, N.J.: Princeton University Press, 1968.

FALK, RICHARD A. and HANREIDER, WOLFRAM, (eds.) *International Law and Organisation: An Introductory Reader.* Philadelphia: J.B. Lippincott Co., 1968.

FALK, RICHARD A. and MENDLOVITZ, SAUL H. (eds.) *The Strategy of World Order. Vol.1: Toward a Theory of War Prevention.* New York: World Law Fund, 1966.

FALK, RICHARD A. and MENDLOVITZ, SAUL H. (eds.) *The Strategy of World Order. Vol.II: International Law.* New York: World Law Fund, 1966.

FALK, RICHARD A. and MENDLOVITZ, SAUL H. (eds.) *The Strategy of World Order, Vol. III: The United Nations* New York: World Law Fund, 1966.

FALK, RICHARD A. and MENDLOVITZ, SAUL H. (eds.) *The Strategy of World Order, Vol. IV: Disarmament and Economic Development.* New York: World Law Fund, 1966.

FARNSWORTH, HELEN C. 'International Wheat Agreements and Problems, 1949-1956'. *The Quarterly Journal of Economics.* **70,** (2), 1956.

FAWCETT, J.E.S. *International Means of Conservation of National Resources.* London: The David Davies Memorial Institute, 1969.

FAWCETT, J.E.S. 'International Conservation: Questions of Method'. *International Affairs, (London),* **48,** (2), 1972.

FELD, WERNER 'National Economic Interest Groups and Policy Formation in the EEC'. *Political Science Quarterly,* **81,** (3), 1966.

FELD, WERNER *The European Common Market and the World.* Englewood Cliffs, N.J.: Prentice-Hall, Inc., 1967.

FELD, WERNER 'Political Aspects of Transnational Business Collaboration in the Common Market'. *International Organisation,* **24,** (2), 1970.

FELD, WERNER *Transnational Business Collaboration among Common Market Countries: Its Implications for Political Integration.* New York: Frederick A. Praeger, 1970.

FERNANDEZ-SHAW, FELIX *La Integración de Centroamérica.* Madrid: Ediciones Cultura Hispánica, 1965.

FILLITZ, FRANZ 'Die Entwicklung der Donauschiffahrt seit 1955'. *Der Donauraum,* 6th Year, (1), 1961.

FINER, HERMAN *The United Nations Economic and Social Council.* Boston: World Peace Foundation, 1946.

FISCHER, ANDRÉ *L'Organisation des Transports dans le Cadre de l'Europe des Six.* Leyden: A.W. Sijthoff, 1968.

FISCHLOWITZ, STANISLAU 'Política Social Internacional'. *Revista Braziliera de Política Internacional,* 4th Year, (13), 1961.

FISHER, ALLAN G.B. 'International Economic Collaboration and the Economic and Social Council'. *International Affairs*, (London), **21**, (4), 1945.

FISHER, WILLIAM E. 'An Analysis of the Deutsch Sociocausal Paradigm of Political Integration'. *International Organisation*, **23**, (2), 1969.

FITZGERALD, MARK J. *The Common Market's Labour Programs*. South Bend, Ind.: University of Notre Dame Press, 1966.

FLEISSIG, ANDREAS *Planeuropa: Die soziale und wirtschaftliche Zukunft Europas* München: Auncker und Humboldt, 1930.

FLEXNER, KURT F. 'The Creation of the European Payments Union: An Example in International Compromise'. *Political Science Quarterly*, **72**, (2), 1957.

FLUKER, ROBERT 'Regional Cooperation and Modernization of South-East Asia'. *Review of Politics*, **31**, (2), 1969.

FOLDI, T. (ed.) *Studies in International Economics*. Budapest: Institute of Economics, Hungarian Academy of Sciences, 1966.

FOLLETT, M.P. *Creative Experience*. New York. Longmans, Green and Co., 1924.

FOLLOWS, J.W. *Antecedents of the International Labour Organisation*. Oxford: The Clarendon Press, 1951.

FORD, HENRY J. 'Politics and Administration'. *Annals of the American Academy of Political and Social Science*, **16**, 1900.

FORD, HENRY J. 'Principles of Municipal Organisation'. *Annals of the American Academy of Political and Social Science*, 1904

FORD, HENRY J. *The Natural History of the State*. Princeton, N.J.: Princeton University Press, 1915.

FOX, ANNETTE B. 'President Truman's Fourth Point and the United Nations'. *International Conciliation*, (452), 1949.

FOX, ANNETTE B. *Freedom and Welfare in the Caribbean, A Colonial Dilemma*. New York: Harcourt Brace and Co., 1949.

FRANCK, THOMAS M. (ed.) *Why Federations Fail*. New York: New York University Press, 1968.

FRANGES, BOZIDAR 'Institutional Framework of Economic Cooperation'. *Review of International Affairs*, **15**, (335), 1964

FRANK, ISAIAH *The European Common Market, An Analysis of Commercial Policy*. New York: Frederick A. Praeger, 1961.

FRANKLIN, HARRY *Unholy Wedlock: The Failure of the Central African Federation*. London: George Allen and Unwin, 1963.

FREY-WOUTERS, A.E. *United Nations Children's Fund*. unpublished Ph.D., Columbia University, 1958.

FRIEDMANN, WOLFGANG *International Public Corporations as Agencies of Reconstruction*. London: World Unity Booklets No.2, 1946.

FRIEDMANN, WOLFGANG 'Limits of Functionalism in International Organisation'. *The Year Book of World Affairs*, 1956.

FRIEDMANN, WOLFGANG *Law in a Changing Society*. Berkeley: University of California Press, 1959.

FRIEDMANN, WOLFGANG *The Changing Structure of International Law*. New York: Columbia University Press, 1964.

FRIEDMANN, WOLFGANG G. and KALMANOFF, GEORGE (eds.) *Joint International Business Ventures*. New York: Columbia University Press, 1961.

FRIEDRICH, CARL J. *Trends of Federalism in Theory and Practice*. New York: Frederick A. Praeger, 1968.

FRIEDRICH, CARL J. (ed.) *Politische Dimensionen der europäischen Gemein-schaftsbildung*. Köln: Westdeutscher Verlag, 1968.

FRIEDRICH, CARL J. *Europe: An Emergent Nation*. New York, 1969.

FRISCH, RAGNAR 'A Multilateral Trade Clearing Agency'. *Review of International Affairs*, 14, (316), 1963.

FURNISS, EDGAR S. Jr 'Western Alliance Development and Technological Cooperation'. *International Studies Quarterly*, 11, (4), 1967.

GALBRAITH, JOHN K. *The New Industrial State*. Boston: Houghton Mifflin, 1967.

GALLOWAY, JONATHAN F. 'Worldwide Corporations and International Integration: The Case of Intelsat'. *International Organisation*, 24, (3), 1970.

GALTUNG, INGRID E. 'The Status of the Technical Assistance Expert: A Study of UN Experts in Latin America'. *Journal of Peace Research*. (4), 1966.

GALTUNG, JOHAN 'East-West Interaction Patterns'. *Journal of Peace Research*, (2), 1966.

GALTUNG, JOHAN 'A Structural Theory of Integration'. *Journal of Peace Research*, 5, 1968.

GALTUNG, JOHAN 'Non-territorial actors and the problem of peace'. International Peace Research Institute, Oslo, 1969.

GANGULI, B.N. *Integration of International Economic Relations*. London: Asia Publishing House, 1969.

GARCÍA-AMADOR, F.V. *The Exploitation and Conservation of the Resources of the Sea: A Study of Contemporary International Law*. Leyden: A.W. Sijthoff, 1959.

GARCÍA-AMADOR, F.V. *Instruments Relative to the Economic Integration of Latin America*. Dobbs Ferry, N.Y.: Oceana Publications, 1968.

GARCÍA-REYNOSO, PLÁCIDO 'Problemas de integracíon industrial latino-americana'. *Revista de Ciencas Sociales*, 4, (2), 1960.

GARDNER, RICHARD N. 'Cooperation in Outer Space'. *Foreign Affairs*, 41, (2), 1963.

GARDNER, RICHARD 'GATT and the United Nations Conference on Trade and Development'. *International Organisation*, 18, (4), 1964

GARDNER, RICHARD N. *In Pursuit of World Order: US Foreign Policy and International Organisations*. New York: Frederick A. Praeger, 1964.

GARDNER, RICHARD N. 'The United Nations Conference on Trade and Development'. *International Organisation*, 22, (1), 1968.

GARDNER, RICHARD N. 'The Role of the UN in Environmental Problems'. *International Organisation*, 26, (2), 1972.

GARDNER, RICHARD N. (ed.) *Blueprint for Peace: Being the Proposals of Prominent Americans to the White House Conference on International Cooperation*. New York: McGraw Hill, 1966.

GARRICK, DANIEL H. 'On the Economic Feasibility of a Middle Eastern Common Market'. *The Middle East Journal*, 14, (3), 1960.

GARRETSON, A.H., HAYTON, R.D. and OLMSTEAD, C.J. (eds.) *The Law of International Drainage Basins*. Dobbs Ferry, N.Y.: Oceana Publications, 1967.

GEHLEN, MICHAEL P. 'The Integrative Process in East Europe: A Theoretical Framework'. *Journal Of Politics*, 30, (1), 1968.

GEHRELS, FRANZ and JOHNSTON, BRUCE F. 'The Economic Gains of European Integration'. *The Journal of Political Economy,* **63,** (4), 1955.

GEMMAS, SCIPIONE *Il Diritto Internazionale del Lavoro.* Padova: Dott, Antonio Milani, 1938.

GERBET, P. *Les Organisations Internationales.* Paris: Presses Universitaires de France, 1958.

GHÉBALI, VICTOR-YVES *La Société des Nations et la Réforme Bruce, 1939-1940.* Genève; Dotation Carnegie pour la Paix Internationale, 1970.

GIACHETTI, CARLO 'La FAO e il Progresso Economico-sociale'. *Aggiornamenti Sociali,* 11th Year, (1), 1960.

GIDE, CHARLES *Consumers' Cooperative Societies.* London: Unwin, 1921.

GIDE, CHARLES *Communist and Cooperative Colonies* London: G. Harrap, 1930.

GIJSSELS, J. 'Le moyens d'action d'Euratom'. *International Review of Administrative Sciences,* **27,** (2), 1961.

GILCHRIST, HUNTINGDON 'Technical Assistance from the United Nations—As Seen in Pakistan.' *International Organisation,* **13,** (4), 1959.

GILPIN, ROBERT *American Scientists and Nuclear Weapons Policy.* Princeton N.J.: Princeton University Press, 1962.

GILSON, RICHARD P. 'The South Pacific Commission'. *World Affairs Interpreter,* **21,** (2), 1950.

GINSBURGS, GEORGE 'Soviet Atomic Energy Agreements'. *International Organisation,* **15,** (1), 1961.

GLADDEN, E.N. 'The East African Common Services Organisation'. *Parliamentary Affairs,* **16,** (4), 1963.

GLASER, EDWIN 'International Cooperation for the Exploitation for Peaceful Purposes of the Natural Resources of the Sea-Bed and the Ocean Floor and the Subsoil Thereof'. *Revue Roumaine d'Etudes Internationales,* (3-4), 1968.

GLICK, PHILIP M. *The Administration of Technical Assistance: Growth in the Americas.* Chicago: University of Chicago Press, 1957.

GLIGORIĆ, SAUKA 'Prospects of Cooperation with Comecon Countries'. *Review of International Affairs,* **17,** (386), 1966.

GLOS, ERNEST *International Rivers: A Policy-Oriented Perspective.* Singapore: University of Malaya, 1961

von GOECKINGK, JOHANNA *United Nations Technical Assistance Board: A Case Study in International Administration.* New York: Woodrow Wilson Foundation, 1955.

GOLDSCHMIDT, B. 'Le problème du contrôle international de l'utilisation de l'énergie atomique'. *Revue de Défense Nationale,* **24,** 1968.

GOLDSEN, J.M. *Outer Space in World Politics* New York: Frederick A. Praeger, 1963.

GOODMAN, NEVILLE M. *International Health Organisations and Their Work.* London: J. and A. Churchill, 1952.

GOODNOW, FRANK *Politics and Administration.* New York: Macmillan, 1900.

GOODRICH, LELAND M. 'New Trends in Narcotics Control'. *International Conciliation,* (530), 1960.

GOODSPEED, STEPHEN S. *The Nature and Function of International Organisation.* New York: Oxford University Press, 1967.

GOORMAGHTIGH, JOHN 'European Integration'. *International Conciliation,* (488), 1953

GOORMAGHTIGH, JOHN 'European Coal and Steel Community'. *International Organisation,* (503), 1955.

GOORMAGHTIGH, JOHN 'Some Thoughts on Economic Policies and International Organisations'. *Acta Oeconomica,* **7,** (2), 1971.

GORDENKER, LEON *United Nations Secretary-General and the Maintenance of Peace.* London: Columbia University Press, 1967.

GORDON, LINCOLN 'Myth and Reality in European Integration'. *The Yale Review,* **55,** (1), 1955.

GORDON, LINCOLN 'The Organisation for European Economic Cooperation'. *International Organisation,* **10,** (1), 1956.

GORGÉ, CAMILLE *L'Union Internationale de Secours. Ses Origines, son But, ses Moyens, son Avenir.* Genève: Union Internationale de Secours, 1938.

GOSOVÍC, BRANISLAV 'UNCTAD: North-South Encounter'. *International Conciliation,* (568), 1968.

GOSOVÍC, BRANISLAV *UNCTAD: Conflict and Compromise.* Leyden: A.W. Sijthoff, 1972.

GRAUBARD, STEPHEN (ed.) *A New Europe?* Boston: Houghton-Mifflin, 1964.

GREAVES, H.G.R. *The League Committees and World Order. A Study of the Permanent Expert Committees of the League of Nations as an Instrument of International Government.* London: Oxford University Press, 1931.

GREEN, ANDREW W. 'Mitrany Re-read with the Help of Haas and Sewell'. *Journal of Common Market Studies,* **8,** (1), 1969.

GREEN, J.R. *The United Nations and Human Rights.* Washington D.C.: The Brookings Institute, 1956.

GREEN, REGINALD H. 'Multi-purpose Economic Institutions in Africa'. *Journal of Modern Africa Studies.* June, 1963.

GREEN, REGINALD H. and KRISHNA, K.G.V. *Economic Cooperation in Africa: Retrospect and Prospect.* London: Oxford University Press, 1967.

GREGG, ROBERT W. *The United Nations and the Limitation of Opium Production.* unpublished Ph.D, Cornell University, 1955-56.

GREGG, ROBERT W. 'The Economic and Social Council: Politics of Membership'. *Western Political Quarterly,* **16,** (1), 1963.

GREGG, ROBERT W. 'The UN Regional Economic Commissions and Integration in the Under-Developed Regions'. *International Organisation,* **20,** (2), 1966.

GREGG, ROBERT W. (ed.) *International Organisation in the Western Hemisphere.* Syracuse: Syracuse University Press, 1968.

GREGG, ROBERT W. and BARKUN, MICHAEL, (ed.) *The United Nations System and its Functions: Selected Readings* Princeton, N.J.: D. Van Nostrand, 1968.

GRÉGOIRE, ROGER *National Administration and International Organisations.* Brussels: UNESCO, n.d.

GREER, GUY *The Ruhr-Lorraine Industrial Problem, A Study of the Economic Inter-dependence of the Two Regions and their Relation to the Reparation Question.* London: Macmillan, 1925.

GROOM, A.J.R. *Peacekeeping.* Bethlehem: Lehigh University, International Relations Monograph No. 4, 1973.

GROOM, A.J.R. and TAYLOR, PAUL (rapporteurs) *Functionalism: Final Report of the Bellagio Conference.* New York: Carnegie Endowment for International Peace, 1971.

GRUHN, ISEBILL *Functionalism in Africa: Scientific and Technical Cooperation.* unpublished Ph.D., Berkeley: University of California, 1967.

GRZYBOWSKI, KAZIMIERZ *The Socialist Commonwealth of Nations: Organisations and Institutions.* New Haven: Yale University Press, 1964.

GSOVSKI, VLADIMIR, (ed.) *Economic Treaties and Agreements of the Soviet Bloc in Eastern Europe, 1945-51.* New York: Mid-European Studies Center, 1952

GUETZKOW, H. *Multiple Loyalties: Theoretical Approach to the Problem in International Organisation.* Princeton, N.J.: Publication (4), Centre for Research on World Political Institutions, Princeton University Press, 1955.

GULLION, EDMUND A. (ed.) *Uses of the Sea.* Englewood Cliffs, N.J.: Prentice-Hall, 1968.

GUPTA, SISI *India and Regional Integration in Asia.* Bombay: Asia Publishing House, 1964.

HAAS, ERNST B. 'Regionalism, Functionalism and International Organisation'. *World Politics,* **8,** (2), 1956.

HAAS, ERNST B. 'Persistant Theories in Atlantic and European Unity'. *World Politics,* **10,** (4), 1958.

HAAS, ERNST B. 'The Challenge of Regionalism'. *International Organisation,* **12,** (4), 1958.

HAAS, ERNST B. *The Uniting of Europe: Political, Social and Economic Forces, 1950-57.* Stanford: Stanford University Press, 1958.

HAAS, ERNST B. *Consensus Formation in the Council of Europe.* Berkeley: University of California Press, 1960.

HAAS, ERNST B. 'International Integration: The European and the Universal Process'. *International Organisation,* **15,** (3), 1961.

HAAS, ERNST B. *Beyond the Nation State: Functionalism and International Organisation.* Stanford: Stanford University Press, 1964.

HAAS, ERNST B. 'The Uniting of Europe and the Uniting of Latin America'. *Journal of Common Market Studies,* **5,** (4), 1967.

HAAS, ERNST B. *Tangle of Hopes, American Commitments and World Order.* Englewood Cliffs, N.J.: Prentice Hall, 1969.

HAAS, ERNST B. 'The Study of Regional Integration: Reflection on the Joy and Anguish of Pretheorizing'. *International Organisation,* **24,** (4), 1970.

HAAS, ERNST B. *Human Rights and International Action: A Case of Freedom of Association.* Stanford: Stanford University Press, 1970.

HAAS, ERNST B. and SCHMITTER, PHILIPPE C. 'Economics and Differential Patterns of Political Integration: Projections about Unity in Latin America'. *International Organisation,* **18,** (4), 1964.

HAAS, ERNST B. and SCHMITTER, PHILIPPE C. *The Politics of Economics in Latin American Regionalism: The Latin American Free Trade Association After Four Years of Operation.* Denver: University of Denver Press, 1965.

HAAS, ERNST B. and WHITING, A.S. *Dynamics of International Relations.* New York: McGraw Hill Book Co, 1956.

HAAS, MICHAEL 'A Functional Approach to International Organisation'. *Journal of Politics,* **27,** (3), 1965.

HAGRAS, K.M. *United Nations Conference on Trade and Development: A Case Study in United Nations Diplomacy.* New York: Frederick A. Praeger, 1965.

HAINES, C. GROVE, (ed.) *European Integration.* Baltimore: John Hopkins Press, 1957.

HAIRE, MASON, (ed.) *Modern Organisation Theory.* New York: John Wiley and Sons, Inc., 1959.

HALLSTEIN, WALTER *United Europe: Challenge and Opportunity.* Cambridge: Harvard University Press, 1962.

HALLSTEIN, WALTER 'NATO and the European Economic Community'. *Orbis,* **6,** (4), 1963.

HALLSTEIN, WALTER *L'Unité de l'Action Européenne.* Lausanne: Centre de Recherches Européennes, 1965.

HALLSTEIN, WALTER *Europe in the Making.* London: George Allen and Unwin, 1972.

HALLSTEIN, WALTER and SCHLOCHAUER, JÜRGEN, (eds.) *Zur Integration Europas.* Karlsruhe: Müller, 1965.

HALM, GEORGE N. *International Monetary Cooperation.* Chapel Hill: University of North Carolina Press, 1945.

HAMBRIDGE, GOVE *The Story of FAO.* New York: Van Nostrand, 1955.

HAMMARSKJOLD, DAG 'The International Civil Service'. *Current Notes on International Affairs,* **32,** (6), 1961.

HAMMARSKJOLD, DAG 'The International Civil Service in Law and Fact'. Oxford: The Clarendon Press, Oxford, 1961.

HAMMARSKJOLD, DAG 'Two differing Concepts of United Nations Assayed: Introduction to the Annual Report of the Secretary General on the Work of the Organisation, 16 June 1960–15 July 1961'. *International Organisation,* **15,** (4), 1961.

HANREIDER, J. WILLIAM 'International Organisations and International Systems'. *Journal of Conflict Resolution,* **10,** (3), 1966.

HANSEN, ROGER D. *Central American: Regional Integration and Economic Development.* Washington D.C.: National Planning Association, 1967.

HANSEN, ROGER D. 'Regional Integration: Reflections on a Decade of Theoretical Efforts'. *World Politics,* **21,** (2), 1969.

HANSON, SIMON G. 'The International Coffee Agreement'. *Inter-American Economic Affairs,* **17,** (2), 1963.

HARNWELL, GAYLORD P. 'Science, Technology and the Atlantic Community'. *Orbis,* **2,** (2), 1958.

HARRIS, SEYMOUR *The European Recovery Program.* Cambridge: Harvard University Press, 1948.

HARSANYI, JOHN C. 'Rational Choice Models of Political Behavior vs. Functionalist and Conformist Theories'. *World Politics,* **21,** (4), 1969.

HARTSHORE, R. 'The Functional Approach in Political Geography'. *Annals of the Association of American Geographers,* (40), 1950.

HARROD, JEFFREY 'Non-Governmental Organisations and the Third World'. *Year Book of World Affairs,* **24,** 1970.

HASKEL, BARBARA G. 'External Events and Internal Appraisals: A Note on the Proposed Nordic Common Market'. *International Organisation,* **23,** (3), 1969.

HAYTER, TERESA *Aid as Imperialism.* London: Penguin Books, 1971.

HAYWARD, J.E.S. 'From Functional Regionalism to Functional Representation in France: The Battle of Brittany'. *Political Studies,* **17,** (1), 1967.

HAZLEWOOD, ARTHUR 'The East African Common Market: Importance and

Effects'. *Bulletin of the Oxford University Institute of Economics and Statistics,* **28,** (1), 1966.

HAZELWOOD, ARTHUR (ed.) *African Integration and Disintegration: Case Studies in Economic and Political Union.* New York: Oxford University Press, 1968.

HEDTOFT, HANS 'The Nordic Council'. *American-Scandinavian Review,* **42,** (1), 1954

HEILPERIN, MICHAEL A. 'La coopération économique internationale et la securité collective.' *Recueil des cours de l'Académie de droit international,* Tome 68, **2,** 1939.

HENDERSON, WILLIAM O. *The Zollverein.* Chicago: Quadrangle Books, 1959.

HENRY, PAUL-MARC 'The United Nations and the Problem of African Development'. *International Organisation,* **16,** (2), 1962.

HERMANN, SANDRA R. *Eleven against War: Studies in International Thought, 1898-1921* Stanford: Hoover Institution Press, 1969.

HERRIOT, EDUARD *The United States of Europe.* London: G. Harrap, 1930.

HERSHEY, AMOS S. *The Essentials of International Public Law and Organisation.* Rev. ed., New York: Macmillan, 1927.

HERZ, JOHN H. *International Politics in the Atomic Age.* New York: Columbia University Press, 1959.

HERZ, JOHN H. 'The Territorial State Revisited: Reflections on the Future of the Nation-State.' *Polity,* **1,** (1), 1968.

HEWES, AMY 'Functional Representation in the International Labour Organisation'. *American Political Science Review,* **22,** (2), 1928.

HEXNER, ERVIN P. *International Steel Cartel.* Chapel Hill: University of North Carolina Press, 1946.

HEXNER, ERVIN P. 'The Executive Board of the International Monetary Fund: A Decision-Making Instrument'. *International Organisation,* **18,** (1), 1964

HEYMANN, HANS *Plan for Permanent Peace.* London: George Allen and Unwin, 1942

HILL, MARTIN *The Economic and Financial Organisation of the League of Nations: A Survey of Twenty Years' Experience.* Washington: Carnegie Endowment for International Peace, 1946.

HILL, NORMAN L. *International Administration.* New York: McGraw Hill, 1931.

HILL, NORMAN L. *The Economic and Financial Organisation of the League of Nations.* Washington D.C.: Carnegie Endowment for International Peace, 1946.

HIRSCH, ABRAHAM M. 'Utilisation of International Rivers in the Middle East'. *American Journal of International Law,* **50,** (1), 1956.

HIRSCH, ABRAHAM M. 'From the Indus to the Jordan: Characteristics of Middle East International River Disputes'. *Political Science Quarterly,* **71,** (2), 1956.

HIRSCHMAN, ALBERT O. *Journeys toward Progress: Studies of Economic Policy-Making in Latin America.* New York: Twentieth Century Fund, 1963.

HIRSCHMAN, ALBERT O. *Development Projects Observed.* Washington D.C.: Brookings Institute, 1967.

HOAG, MALCOLM W. 'The Economic Problems of Alliance'. *The Journal of Political Economy,* **65,** (6), 1957.

HOBSON, ASHER *The International Institute of Agriculture.* Berkeley: University of California Press, 1931.

HOBSON, JOHN A. *Towards International Government.* London: Allen and Unwin, 1915.

HOBSON, JOHN A. *Problems of a New World.* London: Allen and Unwin, 1921.

HOBSON, W. *World Health and History.* Bristol: John Wright, 1963.

HODGES, MICHAEL, (ed.) *European Integration.* Harmondsworth: Penguin Books, 1972.

HODGETT, J.E. *Administering the Atom for Peace.* New York: Atherton Press, 1964.

HOE, Y.C. *The Programme of Technical Cooperation between China and the League of Nations.* Honolulu: Institute of Pacific Relations, mimeo, 1933.

HOFFMAN, PAUL G. *Peace Can be Won.* New York: Doubleday, 1951.

HOFFMAN, PAUL G. *World Without Want.* New York: Harper and Row, 1962.

HOFFMAN, PAUL G. *The United Nations Development Programme: A Note on the Range and Results of its Activities.* Detroit: Economic Club of Detroit, 1968.

HOFFMANN, STANLEY *Organisations internationales et Pouvoirs politiques des Etats.* Paris: Colin, 1954.

HOFFMANN, STANLEY 'The Role of International Organisation: Limits and Possibilities'. *International Organisation,* **10**, (3), 1956.

HOFFMANN, STANLEY 'Obstinate or Obsolete? The Fate of the Nation-State and the Case of Western Europe'. *Daedalus,* **95**, (3), 1966.

HOFFMANN, STANLEY (ed.) *Conditions of World Order.* Boston: Houghton Mifflin, 1968.

HOGAN, WILLARD N. *Representative Government and European Integration.* Lincoln, Nebraska: University of Nebraska Press, 1967.

HOLBORN, LOUISE W. *The International Refugee Organisation: A Specialised Agency of the United Nations. Its History and Work, 1946-52.* London: Oxford University Press, 1956.

HOLT, STEPHEN *The Common Market: The Conflict of Theory and Practice.* London: Hamish Hamilton, 1967.

HOMAN, J. LINTHORST 'Europese sector-integratie'. *International Spectator,* 19th Year, (5), 1965.

HONDELINK, E.R. 'Transport Problems in Europe'. *International Affairs* (London), **21**, (4), 1945.

HORIE, S. *The International Monetary Fund.* New York: St. Martin's, 1964.

HOROWITZ, DAVID (ed.) *Corporations and the Cold War.* New York: Monthly Review Press, 1969.

HORSEFIELD, J. KEITH, (ed.) *The International Monetary Fund, 1945-1965.* (3 vols). Washington: International Monetary Fund, 1969.

HUBBARD, URSULA P. 'The Cooperation of the United States with the League of Nations and with the International Labour Organisation'. *International Conciliation,* (274), 1931.

HUBBARD, URSULA P. 'The Cooperation of the United States with the League of Nations, 1931-1936'. *International Conciliation,* (329), 1937.

HUBENY, M. 'The Underdeveloped Countries and the Economic Commission for Europe'. *Review of International Affairs,* **12**, (266), 1961.

HUDSON, MANLEY O. *Current International Cooperation.* Calcutta: University Press, 1927.

HUDSON, MANLEY O. *Progress in International Organisation.* Stanford: Stanford University Press, 1932.

HUELIN, DAVID 'A Free Trade Area in South America'. *The World Today:* **16,** (2), 1960.

l'HUILLIER, JACQUES A. *Théorie et pratique de la coopération économique internationale.* Paris: M.T. Génin, 1957.

HUTCHINSON, T.W. *A Review of Economic Doctrines, 1870-1929.* Oxford: Clarendon Press, 1953.

HUTH, ARNO G. 'Communications and Economic Development'. *International Conciliation,* (477), 1952.

HUTH, ARNO G. 'Cooperative Radio Agreements'. *International Organisation,* **6,** (3), 1952.

HUTT, C.W. *International Hygiene.* London: Methuen, 1927.

HUXLEY, JULIAN *'UNESCO, Its Purpose and Its Philosophy'.* UNESCO *document C/6,* September 15, 1946.

IBRAMULLAH, MOHAMMAD 'The Commonwealth Economic Committee and its Work'. *Pakistan Horizon,* **16,** (1), 1963.

IKONNIKOV, I. 'CMEA's Role in Cooperation between the Socialist Countries'. *International Affairs* (Moscow), (4), 1969.

INLOW, BURKE *'Natural Law: A Functional Interpretation'. American Political Science Review* **41,** (5), 1947.

INNIS, HAROLD A. (ed.) *The Cod-Fisheries: The History of an International Economy.* New Haven: Yale University Press, 1940.

JACKSON, SIR ROBERT G.A. *The Case for an International Development Authority.* Syracuse: Syracuse University Press, 1959.

JACOB, PHILIP and TOSCANO, JAMES (ed.) *The Integration of Political Communities.* Philadelphia: J.B. Lippincott Co, 1964.

JACOB, PHILIP and ATHERTON, ALEXINE L. *The Dynamics of International Organisation. The Making of World Order.* Homewood, Ill.: The Dorsey Press, 1965.

JACOBSON, HAROLD K. 'Labor, the UN and the Cold War'. *International Organisation,* **11,** (1), 1957.

JACOBSON, HAROLD K. 'The USSR and ILO'. *International Organisation,* **14,** (3), 1960.

JACOBSON, HAROLD K. *The USSR and the UN's Economic and Social Activities.* Indiana: University of Notre Dame Press, 1963.

JACOBSON, HAROLD K. and STEIN, ERIC *Diplomats, Scientists and Politicians.* Ann Arbor: University of Michigan Press, 1966.

JACOBSON, P. *International Monetary Problems.* Washington D.C., International Monetary Fund, 1964.

JAMES, A.M. 'The UN Economic Commission for Asia and the Far East'. *The Year Book of World Affairs,* 1959.

JAMES, ROBERT R. *Standardization and Common Production of Weapons in NATO.* London: Institute for Strategic Studies, 1967.

JAMES, WILLIAM *Pragmatism.* New York: Longmans, 1907.

JARRETT, HENRY (ed.) *Science and Resources: Prospects and Implications of Technological Advance.* Baltimore: The John Hopkins Press, 1959.

JARVIS, C.E. *International Efforts to Promote Social Security.* unpublished Ph.D., University of Pennsylvania, 1956-7.

JASTER, ROBERT A. 'CEMA's Influence on Soviet Policies in Eastern Europe'. *World Politics,* **14,** (3), 1962.

JENKS, C. WILFRED 'The International Labour Organisation and Peaceful Change'. *New Commonwealth Quarterly,* **4,** (4), 1939.

JENKS, C. WILFRED 'Co-ordination: A New Problem of International Organisation. A Preliminary Survey of the Law and Practice of International Relationships'. *Académie de Droit International, Recueil des Cours,* **77,** 1950

JENKS, C. WILFRED 'An International Regime for Antarctica'. *International Affairs (London),* **32,** (4), 1956.

JENKS, C. WILFRED *The International Protection of Trade Union Freedom.* London: Stevens and Sons, Ltd., 1957.

JENKS, C. WILFRED *Human Rights and International Labour Standards.* London: Stevens and Sons, Ltd. 1960.

JENKS, C. WILFRED *The Proper Law of International Organisation.* Dobbs Ferry, N.Y.: Oceana Publications, Inc., 1962.

JENKS, C. WILFRED *Law, Freedom and Welfare.* London: Stevens and Son, 1963.

JENKS, C. WILFRED 'One Process of Law in International Organisations'. *International Organisation,* **19,** (2), 1965.

JENKS, C. WILFRED 'Work, Leisure and Social Security as Human Rights in the World Community'. *Journal of the International Commission of Jurists,* **9,** (1), Part II, 1968.

JENKS, C. WILFRED *The World Beyond the Charter in Historical Perspective: A Tentative Synthesis of Four Stages in World Organisation.* London: George Allen and Unwin, 1969.

JENKS, C. WILFRED *A New World of Law? A Study of the Creative Imagination in International Law.* London: Longmans, 1969.

JENKS, C. WILFRED *Social Justice in the Law of Nations: The ILO Impact after Fifty Years.* London: Oxford University Press, 1970.

JENNINGS, W. IVOR *A Federation for Western Europe.* New York: Macmillan and Co., 1940.

JESSUP, PHILIP C. *Transnational Law.* New Haven: Yale University Press, 1956.

JESSUP, PHILIP C. *The Use of International Law.* Ann Arbor: University of Michigan Law School, 1959.

JESSUP, PHILIP C. and TAUBENFELD, HOWARD J. 'Outer Space, Antarctica and the United Nations'. *International Organisation,* **13,** (3), 1959.

JESSUP, PHILIP C. and TAUBENFELD, HOWARD *Controls for Outer Space and the Antarctic Analogy.* New York: Columbia University Press, 1959.

JOHANSSON, A. *International Cooperation and Peace.* Chicago: Cooperative League of the United States, 1959.

JOHNSON, BRIAN 'The United Nations' Institutional Response to Stockholm: A Case Study in the International Politics of Institutional Change'. *International Organisation,* **26,** (2), 1972.

JOHNSON, D.H.N. 'IMCO, The First Four Years (1959-1962)'. *The International And Comparative Law Quarterly,* **12,** Part 4, 4th Series, 1963.

JOHNSON, RALPH W. 'The Danube Since 1948'. *Yearbook of World Affairs,* **17,** 1963.

JOHNSTON, ERIC 'Arab-Israeli Tensions and the Jordon Valley'. *World Affairs,* **117,** (2), 1954

JOHNSTON, GEORGE A. *International Social Progress.* New York: The Macmillan Co., 1924.

JOHNSTON, GEORGE A. *The International Labour Organisation: Its Work for Social and Economic Progress.* London: Europa Publications, 1970.

JOLL, JAMES *The Second International.* London: Weidenfeld and Nicolson, 1955.

JOLL, JAMES *The Anarchists.* London: Eyre and Spottiswoode, 1964.

JONES, JOSEPH M. The United Nations at Work: Developing Land, Forests, Oceans . . . and *People.* London: Pergamon Press, 1965.

JORDAN, ROBERT S. *The NATO International Staff Secretariat 1952-1957. A Study in International Administration.* London: Oxford University Press, 1967.

JORDAN, ROBERT S. (ed.) *International Administration: Its Evolution and Contemporary Applications.* London: Oxford University Press, 1971.

JORDAN, ROBERT S. (ed.) *Multinational Cooperation: Economic, Social and Scientific Development.* New York: Oxford University Press, 1972.

JOUCLA, GÉRARD *La Coopération Internationale dans les Industries Aéronautiques Européennes.* Paris: Librairie Générale de Droit et de Jurisprudence, 1971.

JOYCE, JAMES A. (ed.) *World Organisation: Federal or Functional?* London: L.A. Watts and Co., Ltd., 1945.

JOYCE, JAMES A. *World of Promise: A Guide to the United Nations Decade of Development.* Dobbs Ferry, N.Y.: Oceana Publications, 1965.

KAARLEHTO, PAAVO 'On the Economic Nature of Cooperation'. *Acta Agriculturae Scandinavica,* 1956.

KAHNERT, F. et. al. *Economic Integration among Developing Countries.* Paris: Development Centre of the OECD, 1969.

KAISER, KARL *EWG und Freihandelszone.* Leyden: A.W. Sijthoff, 1963.

KAISER, KARL 'The Interaction of Regional Subsystems'. *World Politics,* October 1968.

KAISER, KARL 'Transnational Politics: Toward a Theory of Multinational Politics'. *International Organisation,* XXV, (4), Autumn, 1971.

KÄMMERER, LUDWIG 'Der Integrationsgedanke und das europäische Post und Fernmeldewesen'. *Archiv des Völkerrechts,* **10,** (2), 1962.

KANG, SHIN JOE, with BOECK, KLAUS *Economic Integration in Asia.* Hamburg: Weltarchiv Publishers, 1969.

KAPLAN, MORTON *Systems and Process in International Politics.* New York: John Wiley and Sons, Inc., 1957.

KAPLAN, MORTON, (ed.) *The Revolution in World Politics.* New York: John Wiley and Sons Inc., 1962.

KAPLAN, MORTON, (ed.) *New Approaches to International Relations.* New York: St. Martin's Press, 1968.

KAPLAN, MORTON A. and KATZENBACH, NICHOLAS DE B. *The Political Foundations of International Law.* New York: John Wiley and Sons, Inc., 1961.

KAREFA-SMITH, JOHN (ed.) *Africa: Progress through Cooperation.* New York: Dodd, Mead and Company, 1966.

KARNES, THOMAS L. *The Failure of Union: Central America, 1824-1960.* Chapel Hill: University of North Carolina Press, 1961.

KARP, B. *Development of the Philosophy of UNESCO.* unpublished Ph.D., University of Chicago, 1951-1952.

KASANSKY, PIERRE 'Théorie de l'administration internationale'. *Revue Générale de Droit International Public,* Tome 9, 1902.

KASER, MICHAEL *Comecon, Integration Problems of the Planned Economies.* London: Oxford University Press, 1965.

KASHEFI, R. (ed.) *Report on First Two Years of RCD*. Teheran: Regional Cooperation for Development, 1966.

KATZ, SHERMAN E. 'The Application of Science and Technology to Development'. *International Organisation,* **22,** (1), 1968.

KAUL, N.N. *India and the ILO.* New Delhi: Metropolitan Book Co., 1956.

KAY, DAVID A. and **SKOLNIKOFF, EUGENE B.** (ed.) 'International Institutions and the Environmental Crisis'. *International Organisation,* special issue, **26,** (2), 1972.

KEEN, F.N. *The Abolition of War.* London: The David Davies Memorial Institute of International Studies, 1955.

KEENLEYSIDE, HUGH L. *International Aid: A Summary with Special Reference to the Programme of the United Nations.* New York: James H. Heineman Inc., 1966.

KEENY, S.M. *Half the World's Children: A Diary of UNICEF at Work in Asia.* New York: Association Press, 1957.

KELMAN, HERBERT C. 'Patterns of Personal Involvement in the National System: A Social-Psychological Analysis of Political Legitimacy'. in Rosenau, J.N. (ed.) *International Politics and Foreign Policy.* New York: The Free Press, 1969.

KELSEN, HANS *Peace Through Law.* Chapel Hill: University of North Carolina Press, 1944.

KENNAN, GEORGE F. 'To Prevent a World Wasteland'. *Foreign Affairs,* **48,** (3), 1970.

KENNY, R.A. *A Sociological Analysis of the Conceptual Framework, Structure and Functioning of UNESCO.* unpublished Ph.D., St. John's University, 1955.

KENWORTHY, L.S. *Telling the UN Story: New Approaches to Teaching About the UN and its Related Agencies.* Dobbs Ferry, N.Y.: Oceana Publications, 1963.

KEOHANE, ROBERT O. and **NYE, JOSEPH S.** Jr. (ed.) *Transnational Relations and World Politics.* Cambridge: Harvard University Press, 1972.

KEYNES, JOHN MAYNARD *The Economic Consequences of the Peace.* London: Macmillan, 1919.

KEYNES, JOHN MAYNARD *The End of Laissez-Faire.* London: Hogarth, 1926.

KINDLEBERGER, CHARLES P. 'Economists in International Organisations'. *International Organisation,* **9,** (3), 1955.

KIRDAR, U. *The Structure of United Nations Economic Aid to Underdeveloped Countries.* The Hague: Martinus Nijhoff, 1966.

KITZINGER, UWE W. *The Challenge of the Common Market,* 4th Ed. Oxford: Blackwell, 1962.

KITZINGER, UWE W. *The Politics and Economics of European Integration: Britain, Europe and the United States,* expanded edition. New York: Frederick A. Praeger, 1963.

KITZINGER, UWE W. *Britain, Europe and Beyond: Essays in European Politics* Leyden: A.W. Sijthoff, 1964.

KITZINGER, UWE W. 'Regional and Functional Integration—Some Lessons of Brussels'. *Journal of Common Market Studies,* **3,** (2), 1965.

KLOMAN, ERASMUS H. Jr. 'African Unification Movements'. *International Organisation*, **16**, (2), 1962.

KNAUTCH, ARNOLD W. 'The Law of International Rivers and Seas'. *Pakistan Horizon*, **12**, (3), 1959.

KNOTT, JAMES E. Jr. *Freedom of Association: A Study of the Role of International Non-Governmental Organisations in the Development Process of Emerging Countries*. Brussels: Union of International Associations, 1962.

KNUDSON, JOHN I. *Methods of International Legislation with Special Reference to the League of Nations*. Genève: Librairie Droz, 1928.

KOHLER, HEINZ *Economic Integration in the Soviet Bloc: With an East German Case Study*. New York: Frederick A. Praeger, 1965.

KOJANEC, GIOVANNI 'Equilibre écologique et pollution de la mer: Donnée d'une règlementation internationale'. *La comunità internazionale*, July 1971, **26**, (3)

KOLOSA, JAN *International Intellectual Cooperation*. Warsaw: Wroclawskie Towarzistwo, 1970.

KORBONSKI, ANDRZEJ 'Theory and Practice of Regional Integration: The Case of Comecon'. *International Organisation*, **24**, (4), 1970.

KOTSCHNIG, WALTER M. 'The United Nations as an Instrument of Economic and Social Development'. *International Organisation*, **22**, (1), 1968.

KRAINS, HUBERT *L'Union Postale Universelle, Sa Fondation et son Développement*. Berne: 1908.

KRAMER, FRANCISCO V. *Integración económica centro-americana: Aspectos sociales y politicos*. Guatemala City: University of San Carlos, 1967.

KRAMER, HANS R. *Formen und Methoden der Internationalen wirtschaftlichen Integration*. Tübingen: Mohr, 1969.

KRAMER, MORTON A. et. al. 'International Health Security in the Modern World: The Sanitary Conventions and the World Health Organisation'. Washington D.C.: *Department of State Bulletin*, November 16, 1947.

KRAMISH, ARNOLD *The Peaceful Atom in Foreign Policy*. New York: Harper and Row, 1963.

KRAUS, HERBERT *Probleme des Europäischen Zusammenschlusses*. Würzburg: Holsner-Verlag, 1956.

KRAUSE, GUNTER B. *Der Internationale Fernmeldeverein*. Berlin: Alfred Metzner, 1960.

KRAUSE, LAWRENCE B. *The Common Market: Progress and Controversy*. Englewood Cliffs: Prentice Hall, 1968.

KRAUSE, LAWRENCE B. *European Economic Integration and the United States*. Washington D.C.: Brookings Institution, 1968.

KREHBIEL, EDWARD 'European Commission of the Danube: an Experiment in International Administration'. *International Conciliation*, (131), 1918.

KRILL DE CAPELLO, H.H. 'The Creation of the United Nations Educational, Scientific and Cultural Organisation'. *International Organisation*, **24**, (1), 1970.

KROPOTKIN, PETER *Mutual Aid*. Boston, Mass.: Extending Horizon Books, no date.

KROPOTKIN, PETER *The Conquest of Bread*. London: Allen Lane. The Penguin Press, 1972.

KUHL, WARREN *Seeking World Order: The United States and International Organisations to 1920*. Nashville, Tenn.: Vanderbilt University Press, 1969.

311

KULISIC, JOSIP 'Multilateral Assistance on Food'. *Review of International Affairs,* **19,** (446), 1968.

LACY, R.H. Jr. *Uniting Nationals in Support of the United Nations.* unpublished Ph.D., Harvard University, 1952.

LADOR-LEDERER, J.J. *International Non-Governmental Organisations and Economic Entities* Leyden: Sijthoff, 1963.

LADOR-LEDERER, J.J. *International Group Protection: Aims and Methods in Human Rights.* Leyden: A.W. Sijthoff, 1968.

LA FONTAINE, H. *Existing Elements of a Constitution of the United States of the World.* New York: American Association for International Conciliation, 1911.

LAMBERT, J.R. 'The European University: A European Communities Project'. *The World Today,* **18,** (2), 1962.

LAMBERT, P. *Studies in the Social Philosophy of Cooperation.* Manchester: Cooperation Union Ltd., 1963.

LAMBRINIDIS, JOHN S. *The Structure, Function and Law of a Free Trade Area: The European Free Trade Association.* London: Stevens and Sons Ltd., 1965.

LANDAU, MARTIN *Political Theory and Political Science.* New York: The Macmillan Company, 1972.

LANDAUER, CARL 'ERP, Planning and Controls'. *American Perspective,* **3,** (1), 1949.

LANDE, ADOLF 'The Single Convention on Narcotic Drugs, 1961'. *International Organisation,* **16,** (4), 1962.

LANDY, E.A. *The Effectiveness of International Supervisions: Thirty Years of ILO Experience.* London: Stevens and Sons, 1966.

LANGE, HALVARD 'Scandinavian Cooperation in International Affairs'. *International Affairs* (London), **30,** (3), 1954.

LANG, P.A. *Sociological Analysis of the Conceptual Framework and Operation of the Food and Agricultural Organisation.* unpublished Ph.D., St. John's University, 1957.

LANG, RIKARD 'Balkan Economists Cooperate'. *Review of International Affairs,* **5,** (101), 1954

LANGROD, GEORGES 'Observations sur le recrutement à la fonction publique internationale'. *Revue de Droit International,* 13th Year, (1-4), 1960.

LANGROD, GEORGES *The International Civil Service: Its Origins, Its Nature, Its Evolution.* Dobbs Ferry, New York: Oceana Publications, 1963.

LA PALOMBARA, JOSEPH, (ed.) *Bureaucracy and Political Development.* Princeton: Princeton University Press, 1963.

LASKI, HAROLD J. *Studies in the Problem of Sovereignty.* New Haven: Yale University Press, 1917.

LASKI, HAROLD J. *The Problem of Administrative Areas.* Northampton, Mass.: Smith College Studies in History, **4,** 1918.

LASSWELL, HAROLD D. *Politics: Who Gets What, When, How.* New York: McGraw Hill Book Co. Inc., 1936.

LASSWELL, HAROLD D. *The Decision Process: Seven Categories of Functional Analysis.* College Park: Bureau of Government Research, College of Business and Public Administration University of Maryland, 1956.

LASSWELL, HAROLD D. *World Politics and Personal Insecurity.* New York: The Free Press, 1965.

de LATTRE, JEAN-MICHEL 'Organisation africaine et malgache de coopération économique'. *Politique Etrangère*, 25th Year, (6), 1960.

LAVES, WALTER H.C. and THOMSON, CHARLES A. *UNESCO: Purpose, Progress, Prospects.* Bloomington: Indiana University Press, 1957.

LAVES, WALTER H.C. and WILCOX, FRANCIS O. 'Organising the Government for Participation in World Affairs'. *American Political Science Review*, 38, (5), 1944.

LAYTON, C. *European Advanced Technology: A Programme for Integration.* London: Allen and Unwin, 1969.

LEDERMANN, LASZLO *Les précurseurs de l'organisation internationale.* Neuchâtel: Editions de la Baconnière, 1945.

LE FOYER, LUCIEN 'L'union internationale de secours et l'Espagne'. *Revue politique et parlementaire*, 1939.

LEGUM, COLIN 'Economic Commission for Africa: Progress Report'. *The World Today*, 17, (7), 1961.

LEONARD, L. *International Regulations of Fisheries.* New York: Columbia University Press, 1944

LEPARVSKY, ALBERT 'International Development of River Resources'. *International Affairs* (London), 39, (4), 1963.

LEVI, WERNER *Fundementals of World Organisation.* Minneapolis: University of Minnesota Press, 1950.

LEVY, MARION J. Jr. *The Structure of Society.* Princeton: Princeton University Press, 1950.

LEVY, MARION J. Jr. *Modernization and the Structure of Societies: A Setting for International Affairs*, 2 vols. Princeton: Princeton University Press, 1966.

LEWIS, SULWYN *Towards International Cooperation.* Oxford: Pergamon Press, 1966.

LEYS, COLIN and ROBSON, PETER (ed..) *Federation in East Africa: Opportunities and Problems.* Chicago: University of Chicago Press, 1966

LICHTHEIM, GEORGE *The New Europe: Today—and Tomorrow.* New York: Frederick A. Praeger, 1963.

LIE, TRYGVE *In the Cause of Peace: Seven Years with the United Nations* New York: Macmillan and Co., 1954.

LIJPHART, AREND 'Tourist Traffic and Integration Potential'. *Journal of Common Market Studies*, 2, (3), 1964.

LILIENTHAL, DAVID E. *TVA, Democracy on the March.* New York: Harper and Row Publishers, 1944

LINDBERG, LEON N. *The Political Dynamics of European Economic Integration.* Stanford: Stanford University Press, 1963.

LINDBERG, LEON N. 'Decision Making and Integration in the European Community'. *International Organisation*, 19, (1), 1965.

LINDBERG, LEON N. 'Integration as a Source of Stress on the European Community System'. *International Organisation*, 20, (2), 1966.

LINDBERG, LEON N. 'Political 'Integration as a Multidimensional Phenomenon Requiring Multivariate Measurement'. *International Organisation*, 24, (4), 1970.

LINDBERG, LEON N. and SCEINGOLD, STUART A. *Europe's Would-Be Polity: Patterns of Change in the European Community.* Englewood Cliffs, N.J.: Prentice-Hall Inc., 1970.

313

LINDBERG, LEON N. and SCHEINGOLD, STUART A. *(eds.) Regional Integration.* Cambridge: Harvard University Press, 1971.

LINDGREN, RAYMOND E. 'International Cooperation in Scandinavia'. *Year Book of World Affairs,* 13, 1959.

LINDGREN, RAYMOND E. *Norway-Sweden: Union, Disunion and Scandinavian Integration.* Princeton: Princeton University Press, 1959.

LINSEL, H. 'Economic Development and International Integration'. *L'Egypte Contemporaine,* 58, (327), 1967.

LISKA, GEORGE *Europe Ascendent: The International Politics of Unification.* Washington D.C., John Hopkins Press, 1964.

LISTER, LOUIS *Europe's Coal and Steel Community, an Experiment in Economic Union.* New York: Twentieth Century Fund, 1960.

LITTLE, I.M.D. 'Regional International Companies as an Approach to Economic Integration'. *Journal of Common Market Studies,* 5, (2), 1966.

LITTLE, VIRGINIA 'Control of International Air Transport'. *International Organisation,* 3, (1), 1949.

LJUNGBERG, CARL 'International Civil Aviation Organisation and the Non-Governmental Organisations'. *International Associations,* 8, (11), 1956.

LOKANATHAN, P.S. 'Regional Economic Cooperation in Asia'. *India Quarterly,* 7, (1), 1951.

LONDON, KURT L. 'The "Socialist Commonwealth of Nations': Pattern for a Communist World Organisation'. *Orbis,* 3, (4), 1960.

LONG, OLIVIER, et. al. *International Cooperation at a Crossroad.* Geneva: Graduate Institute of International Studies, 1970.

LORWIN, LEWIS L. *Labor and Internationalism.* London: Macmillan, 1929.

LOVEDAY, ALEXANDER 'The Economic and Financial Activities of the League'. *International Affairs,* 17, (6), 1938.

LOVEDAY, ALEXANDER 'Suggestions for the Reform of the United Nations Economic and Social Machinery'. *International Organisation,* 7, (3), 1953.

LOVEDAY, ALEXANDER *Reflections on International Administration.* London: Oxford University Press, 1956.

LOWE, BOUTELLE E. *International Aspects of the Labor Problem.* New York: W.D. Gray, 1918.

LOWELL, A. LAWRENCE *Essays on Government.* New York: Houghton Mifflin, 1890.

LUARD, EVAN (ed.) *Evolution of International Organisations.* London: Thames and Hudson, 1966.

LUARD, EVAN (ed.) *The International Protection of Human Rights.* New York: Frederick A. Praeger, 1967.

LYONS, F.S.L. *Internationalism in Europe 1815-1914* Leyden: Sijthoff, 1963.

McCLOY, JOHN H. 'The Lesson of the World Bank'. *Foreign Affairs,* 27, (4), 1949.

McDOUGAL, MYRES S. and ASSOCIATES. *Studies in World Public Order.* New Haven: Yale University Press, 1960.

McGROVE, GAVIN 'Agricultural Integration in Western Europe'. *Planning,* 29, (470), 1963.

McKINLEY, CHARLES 'The Valley Authority and its Alternatives'. *American Political Science Review,* 44, (3), 1950.

McMAHON, J.F. 'The Legislative Techniques of the International Labour Organisation'. *British Yearbook of International Law,* **41,** 1965-1966.

McNULTY, A.B. and EISSEN, MARC ANDRÉ 'The European Commission of Human Rights: Procedure and Jurisprudence'. *Journal of the International Commision of Jurists,* **1,** (2), 1958.

McWHINNEY, EDWARD (ed.) *The Freedom of the Air.* Leyden: A.W. Sijthoff, 1968.

MABBOTT, J.D. *The State and the Citizen: An Introduction to Political Philosophy.* London: Hutchinson University Library, 1948, 1955.

MacDONALD, GORDON J. 'International Institutions for Environmental Management'. *International Organisation,* **26,** (2), 1972.

MacIVER, ROBERT M. *The Nations and the United Nations.* New York: Carnegie Endowment for International Peace, Manhattan Publishing Co., 1959.

MACKENZIE, FREDERICK A. *The American Invaders.* London: Grant Richards, 1902.

MAGEE, JAMES S. 'Structure and Substance: The Politics of Decentralization in the United Nations'. *Journal of Politics,* **27,** (3), 1965.

MAHAIM, ERNEST *Le droit international ouvrier.* Paris: Recueil Sirey, 1913.

DE LA MAHOTIÈRE, STUART *Towards One Europe.* Harmondsworth: Penguin Books, 1970.

MALESER, EMIL 'Activities of Danube Commission'. *Review of International Affairs,* **9,** (189), 1958.

MALINOWSKI, B. *A Scientific Theory of Culture.* Chapel Hill: University of North Carolina Press, 1944.

MALINOWSKI, W.R. 'Centralization and Decentralization in the United Nations Economic and Social Activities'. *International Organisation,* **16,** (3), 1962.

MALLERY, OTTO T. 'Typical Plans for Postwar World Peace'. *International Conciliation* (384), 1942.

MALLERY, OTTO T. *Economic Union and Durable Peace.* New York: Harper and Brothers, 1943.

MANCE, SIR H. OSBORNE *International Air Transport.* London: Oxford University Press, 1943.

MANCE, SIR H. OSBORNE *International River and Canal Transport.* London: Oxford University Press, 1944.

MANCE, SIR H. OSBORNE *International Road Transport, Postal, Electricity and Miscellaneous Questions.* London: Oxford University Press, 1947.

MANGER, WILLIAM (ed.) *The Alliance for Progress: A Critical Appraisal.* Washington: Public Affairs, Press, 1963.

MANGONE, GERARD J. *A Short History of International Organisation.* New York: McGraw Hill, 1954.

MANGONE, GERARD J. (ed.) *UN Administration of Economic and Social Programs.* New York: Columbia University Press, 1966.

MANNHEIM, KARL *Man and Society in an Age of Reconstruction.* London: Kegan Paul, Trench Trubner and Co., 1940.

MANUEL, FRANK E. (ed.) *Utopias and Utopian Thought.* Boston: Houghton-Mifflin, 1966.

MANZER, RONALD A. 'The United Nations Special Fund'. *International Organisation,* **18,** (4), 1964

MARCH, JAMES G. and SIMON, HERBERT A. *Organisations.* New York: John Wiley and Sons, 1967.

MARCHAL, ANDRÉ 'De quelques faux dogmes en matière d'organisation européenne'. *Revue Economique,* (5), 1960.

MARKS, EDWARD 'Internationally Assisted Migration: ICEM Rounds out Five Years of Resettlement'. *International Organisation,* 111, (3), 1957.

MARTIN, CURTIS W. 'The History and Theory of the Functional Approach to International Organisation'. unpublished Ph.D. dissertation, Department of Government, Harvard University, 1950.

MARTINDALE, DON (ed.) *Functionalism in the Social Sciences* Philadelphia; The American Academy of Political and Social Science, 1965.

MARTYN, HORNE *International Business: Organisation, Management and Social Impact of the Multinational Business Corporation.* New York: The Free Press, 1964.

MARX, DANIEL Jr. *International Shipping Cartels: A Study of Industrial Self-Regulation by Shipping Conferences.* Princeton N.J.: Princeton University Press, 1953.

MASON, H. *The European Coal and Steel Community—an Experiment in Supranationalism.* The Hague: Martinus Nijhoff, 1955.

MASTERS, RUTH D. 'International Organisation of European Rail Transport'. *International Conciliation,* (330), 1937.

MASTERS, RUTH D. *International Organisation in the Field of Public Health.* Washington: Carnegie Endowment for International Peace, 1947.

MATECKI, B.E. *Establishment of the International Finance Corporation and United States Policy: A Case Study in International Organisation.* New York: Frederick A. Praeger, 1957.

MATHIASEN, KARL 'Multilateral Technical Assistance'. *International Organisation,* 22, (1), 1968.

MAXIMOF, G.P. (ed.) *The Political Philosophy of Bakunin.* New York: The Free Press, 1953.

MAYNE, RICHARD J. *The Community of Europe.* New York: W.W. Norton and Co., 1963.

MEADE, J.E., LIESNER, H.H. and WELLS, S.J. *Case Studies in European Economic Union: The Mechanics of Integration.* New York: Oxford University Press, 1962.

VON MEHREN, ROBERT B. 'The International Atomic Energy Agency in World Politics'. *Journal of International Affairs,* 1959.

MENON, V.R.R. 'The Influence of International Labour Conventions on Indian Labour Legislation'. *International Labour Review,* 73, (6), 1956.

MERRIAM, CHARLES E. 'The National Resources Planning Board: A Chapter in American Planning Experience'. *American Political Science Review,* 38, (6), 1944.

MERRY, HENRY J. 'The European Coal and Steel Community—Operations of the High Authority'. *The Western Political Quarterly,* 8, (2), 1955.

MERTON, ROBERT K. *Social Theory and Social Structure.* Enlarged Edition. New York: The Free Press, 1968.

METCALF, H.C. and URWICK, L. (ed.) *Dynamic Administration: the Collected Works of Mary Parker Follett.* New York: Harper and Row, 1941.

MEYNAUD, JEAN and SIDJANSKI, DUSAN *L'Europe des affaires: Rôle et structure des groupes.* Paris; Payot, 1967.

MEYNAUD, JEAN and SIDJANSKI, DUSAN *Interest Groups in the EEC.* Montreal: Montreal University Press, 1969.

MEZERIK, A.G. (ed.) 'The International Atomic Energy Agency'. *International Review Service,* January, 1957.

MEZERIK, A.G. (ed.) 'Energy and the United Nations'. *International Review Service,* 6, (59), 1960.

MICHAELIS, ALFRED 'International Bank Activities in the Middle East' *Middle Eastern Affairs* 8, (5), 1957.

MICHEL, ALOYS A. *The Indus Rivers: A Study of the Effects of Partition.* New Haven: Yale University Press, 1967.

MILES, EDWARD 'Organisations and Integration in International Systems'. *International Studies Quarterly,* 12, (2), 1968.

MILLER, DAVID H. *The Drafting of the Covenant.* 2 vols. London: Putman, 1928.

MISIAK, MAREK 'Research Cooperation within CMEA'. *Polish Perspectives,* 11, (7), 1968.

MITCHELL, CHRISTOPHER 'The Role of Technocrats in Latin American Integration'. *Inter-American Economic Affairs,* 21, 1967.

MITRANY, DAVID *The Progress of International Government* New Haven: Yale University Press, 1933.

MITRANY, DAVID 'The Political Consequences of Economic Planning'. *Sociological Review,* 26, (4), 1934.

MITRANY, DAVID *The Road to Security.* London: National Peace Council, 1944.

MITRANY, DAVID 'Problem of International Administration'. *Public Administration,* 23, 1945.

MITRANY, DAVID 'A General Commentary'. in: *The United Nations Charter: The text and a Commentary.* London: National Peace Council, 1945.

MITRANY, DAVID 'The Growth of World Organisation'. *Commonwealth Review,* June 1946.

MITRANY, DAVID 'National Planning and International Conflict'. *Commonwealth Review,* July 1946.

MITRANY, DAVID 'Human Rights and International Organisation'. *India Quarterly,* 3, (2), 1947.

MITRANY, DAVID 'The Prospect of Functional Cooperation'. *The Eastern Economist,* 9, (9), 1947.

MITRANY, DAVID 'The International Consequences of National Planning'. *Yale Review,* 37, (7), 1947.

MITRANY, DAVID 'The Functional Approach to World Organisation', *International Affairs* 24, (3), 1948.

MITRANY, DAVID 'Reflections on UNESCO Exchange of Persons Programme'. *International Social Science Bulletin,* 2, (2), 1950.

MITRANY, DAVID 'Functional Federalism'. *Common Cause,* 4, (4), 1950.

MITRANY, DAVID *'The International Technical Assistance Programme; United Nations: Success or Failure'?* Proceedings of the Academy of Political Science, 25, (2), 1953.

MITRANY, DAVID 'A New Democratic Experiment: the Role of Non-Governmental Organisations'. *Review of International Cooperation,* 47, (5), 1954.

MITRANY, DAVID 'International Cooperation in Action'. *International Associations*, September, 1959.

MITRANY, DAVID 'The Prospect of Integration: Federal or Functional', *Journal of Common Market Studies*, 4, (2), 1965.

MITRANY, DAVID *A Working Peace System* Chicago, Illinois: Quadrangle Books, 1966.

MITRANY, DAVID 'The Functional Approach in Historical Perspective', *International Affairs* 47, (3), 1971.

MITRANY, DAVID and GARNETT, MAXWELL *World Unity and the Nations.* London: National Peace Council, no date.

MODELSKI, GEORGE *The Communist International System.* Princeton, N.J.: Center of International Studies, Princeton University, 1961.

MOLL, A.A. *The Pan American Sanitary Bureau: Its Origin, Development and Achievements, 1902-44.* Washington: Pan American Sanitary Bureau, 1948.

MONCONDUIT, FRANCOIS *La Commission européenne des Droits de l'Homme.* Leyden: A.W. Sijthoff, 1965.

MONNET, JEAN *Les Etats-Unis d'Europe Ont Commercé.* Paris: Robert Laffert, 1955.

MONNET, JEAN *Perspectives on Peace, 1910-1960.* New York: Frederick A. Praeger, 1960.

MONNET, JEAN *L'Europe et l'Organisation de la Paix.* Lausanne: Université de Lausanne, Centre de Recherches Européennes, 1964.

MONTGOMERY, ARTHUR 'From a Northern Customs Union to EFTA'. *Scandinavian Economic History Review*, 8, (1), 1960.

MONULIU, FORIN 'Perspectives d'une intégration économique latino-americaine'. *Tiers-Monde*, 4, (13-14), 1963.

MOORE, FREDERICK T. 'The World Bank and Its Economic Missions'. *The Review of Economics and Statistics*, 42, (1), 1960.

MORAWIECKI, W. 'Some Problems Connected with the Organs of International Organisations'. *International Organisation*, 19, (3), 1965.

MORDINOV, V. and MAIROV, B. 'The UN Economic Commission for Europe and European Economic Cooperation'. *International Affairs (Soviet)*, (7), 1955.

MORLOCK, GEORGE A. 'International Cooperation Relating to Narcotic Drugs'. *American Foreign Service Journal*, 26, (3), 1949.

MOROZOV, G.I. *International Organisation: Some Theoretical Problems.* Moscow: Mysl, 1969.

MORRIS, JAMES *The World Bank*: London: Faber and Faber, 1963.

MORSE, DAVID A. 'The International Labor Organisation in a Changing World'. *The Annals of the American Academy of Political and Social Science*, 310, 1957.

MORSE, DAVID A. *The Origin and Evolution of the ILO and its Role in the World Community.* Ithaca, N.Y.: New York State School of Industrial and Labor Relations, Cornell University, 1969.

MORSE, EDWARD L. 'Transnational Economic Processes'. *International Organisation*, 25, (3), 1971.

MORTISHED, R.J.P. *Problems of International Organisation.* London: Worker's Educational Association, Study Outlines No.12, 1944.

MOSHER, ARTHUR T. *Technical Cooperation in Latin American Agriculture.* Chicago: University of Chicago Press, 1957.

MOSKOWITZ, MOSES *Human Rights and World Politics.* Dobbs Ferry, N.Y.: Oceana Publications, 1958.

MOSKOWITZ, MOSES *The Politics and Dynamics of Human Rights.* Dobbs Ferry, N.Y.: Oceana Publications, 1968.

MOYNIER, G. *Les Bureaux Internationaux des Unions Universelles.* Genève: Cherbuliez, 1892.

MUDALIAR, SIR ARCOT 'World Health Problems'. *International Conciliation,* (491), 1953.

MUMFORD, LEWIS *Technics and Civilisation.* London: Routledge and Kegan Paul, 1967.

MUNCH, P. *Les Origines et l'Oeuvre de la Société des Nations.* 2 vols. Kopenhagen: Gyldendalske Boghandel, 1933-4.

MUSREY, ALFRED G. *An Arab Common Market: A Study in Inter-Arab Trade Relations, 1920-67.* New York: Frederick A. Praeger, 1969.

MYERS, DENYS P. 'Representation in Public International Organs'. *American Journal of International Law,* (8), 1914.

MYRDAL, ALVA et. al. *America's Role in International Social Welfare.* New York: Columbia University Press, 1953.

MYRDAL, GUNNAR 'Realities and Illusions in Regard to Intergovernmental Organisations'.. London School of Economics, London, 1955.

MYRDAL, GUNNAR *An International Economy, Problems and Prospects.* New York: Harper and Row, 1956.

MYRDAL, GUNNAR *Economic Theory and Underdeveloped Regions.* London: Duckworth, 1957.

MYRDAL, GUNNAR *Beyond the Welfare State: Economic Planning and Its International Implications.* New York: Bantam Books, 1960, 1967.

MYRDAL, GUNNAR 'An Economists Vision of a Sane World'. *Cahiers Economiques et Sociaux.* **5,** (4), 1967.

MYRDAL, GUNNAR 'Twenty Years of the United Nations Economic Commission for Europe'. *International Organisation,* **22,** (3), 1968.

NAGEL, HEINRICH 'The Nordic Council: Its Organs, Functions and Juridicial Nature'. *Annual Journal of the A.A.A.,* **26,** 1956.

NDEGWA, PHILIP *The Common Market and Development in East Africa.* Nairobi: East African Publishing House, 1968.

NEF, JOHN (ed.) *Towards World Community.* The Hague: W. Junk, 1968.

NELSON, ROBERT A. 'Scandinavian Airlines System Cooperation in the Air'. *Journal of Air Law and Commerce,* **20,** 1953.

NETTL, J.P. 'The Concept of System in Political Science'. *Political Studies,* (3), 1966.

NETTL, J.P. and ROBERTSON, ROLAND *International Systems and the Modernization of Societies: The Formation of National Goals and Attitudes.* London: Faber and Faber, 1968.

NEWMAN, PHILIP C. *Public Control of Business: An International Approach.* New York: Frederick A. Praeger, Inc., 1956.

NIEBUHR, REINHOLD 'The Theory and Practice of UNESCO'. *International Organisation,* **4,** (1), 1950.

NIEBURG, H.L. 'The International Atomic Energy Agency: A Critical Appraisal'. *Year Book of World Affairs,* **19,** 1965.

NIEHAUS, HEINRICH 'Effects of the European Common Market on Employment and Social Conditions in Agriculture'. *International Labour Review*, **77**, (4), 1958.

NIEMEYER, G. *Law Without Force: The Function of Politics in International Law.* Princeton: Princeton University Press, 1941.

NISBET, R.A. *The Sociological Tradition.* London: Heinemann, 1967.

NORTH, R.C., KOCH, H.E. and ZINNES, D.A. 'The Integrative Functions of Conflict'. *Journal of Conflict Resolution*, **4**, (4), 1960.

NYE, JOSEPH S. Jr. 'East African Economic Integration'. *Journal of Modern African Studies*, **1**, (4), 1963.

NYE, JOSEPH S. Jr. 'Patterns and Catalysts in Regional Integration'. *International Organisation*, **19**, (3), 1965.

NYE, JOSEPH S. Jr. *Pan-Africanism and East African Integration.* Cambridge: Harvard University Press, 1965.

NYE, JOSEPH S. Jr. 'Central American Regional Integration'. *International Conciliation*, (562), 1967.

NYE, JOSEPH S. Jr. 'Comparative Regional Integration: Concept and Measurement'. *International Organisation*, **22**, (4), 1968.

NYE, JOSEPH S. Jr. 'Comparing Common Markets: A Revised Neo-Functionalist Model'. *International Organisation*, **24**, (4), 1970.

NYE, JOSEPH S. Jr. *Peace in Parts.* Boston: Little, Brown and Co., 1971.

NYE, JOSEPH S. Jr. (ed.) *International Regionalism. Readings* Boston, Little Brown and Co., 1968.

ODA, SHIGERU *International Control of Sea Resources.* Leyden: A.W. Sijthoff, 1963.

OGBURN, WILLIAM F. (ed.) *Technology and International Relations.* Chicago: University of Chicago Press, 1949.

OHLIN, GORAN 'The Organisation for Economic Cooperation and Development'. *International Organisation*, (1), 1968.

OKECHUKWU, MEZU S. (ed.) *The Philosophy of Pan-Africanism: A Collection of Papers on the Theory and Practice of the African Unity Movement.* Washington D.C., 1965.

OKIGBO, P.N.C. *Africa and the Common Market.* London: Longmans, 1967.

OLSEN, MARVIN E. (ed.) *Power in Societies.* London: Collier-Macmillan, 1970.

OLSSON, BERTIL 'The Common Employment Market for the Northern Countries'. *International Labour Review*, **68**, (4-5), 1953.

ORANTES, ISAAC C. 'Functionalismo e integración centroamericana'. *Foro Internacional*, **9**, (2), 1969.

OSTERGAARD, G.N. and HALSEY, A.H. *Power in Cooperatives.* Oxford: Blackwell, 1965.

OUDEMANS, G. *The Draft European Patent Convention.* London: Stevens and Sons, Ltd., 1963.

OWEN, DAVID 'International Technical Aid to the Middle East: The United Nations Family'. *Middle Eastern Affairs*, **7**, (1), 1956.

PADELFORD, NORMAN J. 'Cooperation in the Central American Region: The Organisation of Central American States'. *International Organisation*, **11**, (1), 1957.

PADELFORD, NORMAN J. 'Regional Cooperation in Scandinavia'. *International Organisation*, **11**, (4), 1957.

PADELFORD, NORMAN J. 'Regional Cooperation in the South Pacific: Twelve Years of the South Pacific Commission'. *International Organisation*, **13**, (3), 1959.

PADELFORD, NORMAN J. 'Politics and the Future of ECOSOC'. *International Organisation*, **15**, (4), 1961.

PADLEY, WALTER *The Economic Problem of the Peace. A Plea for World Socialist Union.* London: Gollancz, 1944.

PADWA, DAVID 'The Curriculum of IMCO'. *International Organisation*, **14**, (4), 1960.

PALMER, MICHAEL, LAMBERT, JOHN et. al. *European Unity: A Survey of European Organisations.* London: George Allen and Unwin, 1968.

PAPI, GUISEPPI U. *The First Twenty Years of the Bank for International Settlements.* Rome: Bancaria, 1951.

PAPI, UGO 'Effects of Western European Integration Schemes'. *Review of International Affairs.* **13**, (287, 288, 289), 1962.

PAPINI, ROBERTO *Les relations entre l'UNESCO et les Organisations Non-Gouvernementales.* Brussels: Union of International Associations, 1967.

PARKINSON, F. 'European Integration: Obstacles and Prospects'. *The Year Book of World Affairs*, **13**, 1959.

PARKINSON, F. 'The Alliance for Progress'. *Year Book of World Affairs*, **18**, 1964.

PARMELEE, MAURICE *Geo-Economic Regionalism and World Federation.* New York: Exposition Press, 1950.

PARSONS, TALCOTT *The Structure of Social Action.* New York: McGraw-Hill, 1937.

PARSONS, TALCOTT *The Social System.* New York: The Free Press, 1951.

PARSONS, TALCOTT *Structure and Process in Modern Societies.* New York: The Free Press, 1960.

PARSONS, TALCOTT *Societies: Evolutionary and Comparative Perspectives* Englewood Cliffs, N.J.: Prentice-Hall, 1966.

PARSONS, TALCOTT and SHILS, EDWARD (ed.) *Toward a General Theory of Social Action.* New York: Harper Torchbook, 1962.

PARSONS, TALCOTT and SMELSER, NEIL J. *Economy and Society: A Study in the Integration of Economic and Social Theory.* London: Routledge and Kegan Paul Ltd., 1956.

PASTUHOV, VLADIMIR D. *Memorandum on the Composition Procedure and Functions of Committees of the League of Nations.* Washington: Carnegie Endowment for International Peace, 1943.

PATEL, H.M. 'International Economic Cooperation—A Survey of Foreign Assistance in Post-War Years'. *The Indian Year Book of World Affairs*, **4**, 1955.

PATERSON, WILLIAM F. 'The Limitations of the Functional Approach to European Integration—A British View'. *Australian Outlook*, **22**, (3), 1968.

PEARSON, LESTER 'International Economic Cooperation in a Changing World'. *Australian Outlook*, **23**, (2), **1969.**

PEARSON, LESTER *Peace in the Family of Man.* London: Oxford University Press, 1969.

PENA, MARINHO, ILMAR *O Funcionamento do Sistema Interamericano dentro do Sistema Mundial.* Rio de Janeiro: Livraria Freitas Bastos, 1959.

PENROSE, EDITH T. *The Large International Firm in Developing Countries.* London: Allen and Unwin, 1968.

PENROSE, ERNEST F. *Economic Planning for the Peace.* Princeton, N.J.: Princeton University Press, 1953.

PENTLAND, CHARLES C. *Integration Theory and European Integration: A Critical Analysis.* unpublished Ph.D., University of London, 1970.

PERETZ, DON 'Development of the Jordan Valley Waters'. *The Middle East Journal,* 9, (4), 1955.

PERLMUTTER, HOWARD 'The Tortuous Evolution of the Multinational Corporation'. *Columbia Journal of World Business,* 4, (1), 1969.

PERROUX, FRANCOIS *L'Europe sans Rivages* Paris: Presses Universitaires de France, 1954.

PERO, GIUSEPPE 'Cooperazione industriale per l'America Latina'. *Mondo Aperto.* 17, (1), 1963.

PETERSSON, HANS F. *Power and International Order: An Analytical Study of Four Schools of Thought and their Approaches to the War, the Peace and a Post-War System, 1914-1919.* Lund: C.W.K. Gleerup, 1964.

PFALTZGRAFF, ROBERT L. Jr. and DEGHAND, JAMES L. 'European Technological Collaboration: The Experience of the European Launcher Development Organisation (ELDO)'. *Journal of Common Market Studies,* 7, (1), 1968.

PHELAN, E.J. *Yes and Albert Thomas.* London: Cresset Press, 1936.

PHILIP, ANDRÉ 'Social Aspects of European Economic Cooperation'. *International Labour Review,* 76, (3), 1957.

PHILLIPS, WALTER A. *The Confederation of Europe.* London: Longmans, Green, 1920.

PIGNOCHET, ANNE *L'organisme le plus évolué du droit international, la Commission internationale de navigation aérienne.* Paris: Editions internationales, 1936.

PINCUS, JOSEPH *El Mercado Común Centroamericano.* Guatemala City: Oficina Regional para Asuntos de Centroamérica y Panama, 1963.

PIONTEK, EUGENIUSZ 'Growth of Competances of the Secretary General'. *International Affairs* (Polish), 12, (11-12), 1959.

PLAMENATZ, JOHN *The English Utilitarians.* Oxford: Basil Blackwell, 1949.

PLANO, JACK C. and RIGGS, ROBERT *Forging World Order. The Politics of International Organisation.* London: The Macmillan Company, Collier-Macmillan Ltd., 1967, 1969.

PLAZA, CARLOS 'Los recursos nationales en la integración latinoamericana'. *Revista de la Integración, (2), 1968.*

PLESSZ, NICHOLAS *Problems and Prospects of Economic Integration in West Africa.* Montreal: McGill University Press, 1968.

PLISCHKE, ELMER *Systems of Integrating the International Community.* Princeton, N.J.: D. Van Nostrand and Company, Inc., 1964.

POINSARD, LEON *Comment se prépare l'unité sociale du monde. Le droit international au xxe siècle, ses progrès et ses tendances.* Paris: Bureaux de la Science Sociale, 1907.

POISSON, E. *La République coopérative.* Paris: Grasset, 1920.

POLACH, JAROSLAV *Euratom: Its Background, Issues and Economic Implications.* Dobbs Ferry, N.Y.: Oceana Publications Inc., 1964.

POLITICAL AND ECONOMIC PLANNING: *Building Peace out of War: Studies in International Reconstruction.* London: Oxford University Press, 1944.

POLITICAL AND ECONOMIC PLANNING *European Organisations, 1959.* Fair Lawn, N.J.: Essential Books, 1959.

POOLE, BERNARD L. *The Caribbean Commission—Background of Cooperation in the West Indies.* Columbia: University of South Carolina, 1951.

POTTER, PITMAN B. 'The Future of the Consular Office'. *American Political Science Review.,* **20,** (2), 1926.

POTTER, PITMAN B. *This World of Nations.* New York: Macmillan, 1929.

POTTER, PITMAN B. 'The League of Nations and Other International Organisations. An Analysis of the Evolution and Position of the League in Cooperation among States'. *Geneva Special Studies,* **5,** (6), 1934.

POTTER, PITMAN B. 'Note on the Distinction between Political and Technical Questions'. *Political Science Quarterly,* 1935.

POTTER, PITMAN B. 'Développement de l'Organisation Internationale 1815-1914'. *Hague Receuil,* II, 1938.

POTTER, PITMAN B. *An Introduction to the Study of International Organisation.* New York: Appleton Century Crofts, 1948.

POTTER, PITMAN B. 'Relative Values of International Relations, Law and Organisations'. *American Journal of International Law,* **54,** (2), 1960.

PREBISCH, RAUL 'The Economic Development of Latin America and its Principal Problems'. *Economic Bulletin for Latin America,* **7,** (7), 1962

PREBISCH, RAUL *Towards a Dynamic Development Policy for Latin America.* New York: United Nations 1963

PREBISCH, RAUL *Towards a New Trade Policy for Development.* New York: United Nations Press, 1964.

PREBISCH, RAUL 'Before the Second Conference on Trade and Development'. *Inter-Parliamentary Bulletin,* **47,** (2), 1967.

PREBISCH, RAUL *Towards a Global Strategy for Development.* New York: United Nations Press, 1968.

PRICE, ARNOLD H. *The Evolution of the Zollverein.* Ann Arbor: University of Michigan Press, 1949.

PRICE, JOHN 'Industrial Committees of the ILO". *International Labour Review,* **65,** (1), 1952.

PRICE, JOHN *ILO: 50 Years On.* London: Fabian Society, 1969.

PRITCHETT, C. HERMAN *The Tennessee Valley Authority.* Chapel Hill: University of North Carolina; 1943.

PROCOPÉ, HJALMAR J. 'Economic Cooperation Between the Northern Countries and the Joint Delegation for its Promotion'. *Le Nord,* I, 1938.

PROCTOR, JESSE H. Jr. 'The Functional Approach to Political Union: Lessons from the Effort to Federate the British Caribbean Territories'. *International Organisation,* **10,** (1), 1956.

PUCHALA, DONALD J. *European Political Integration: Progress and Prospects.* New Haven: Political Science Research Library, Yale University, 1966.

PUCHALA, DONALD J. 'The Pattern of Contemporary Regional Integration'. *International Studies Quarterly,* **12,** (1), 1968.

PURCELL, V.W.W.S. 'The Economic Commission for Asia and the Far East'. *International Affairs,* (London), **24,** (2), 1948.

PURVES, CHESTER *The Internal Administration of an International Secretariat.* London: Royal Institute of International Affairs, 1945.

PYE, LUCIEN W. 'The Concept of Political Development'. *The Annals of the American Academy of Political And Social Sciences,* **358,** 1965.

PYE, LUCIEN W. *Aspects of Political Development.* Boston: Little, Brown and Co., 1966.

PYE, LUCIEN W. (ed.) *Communications and Political Development.* Princeton N.J.: Princeton University Press, 1963.

RADCLIFFE-BROWN, A.R. *Structure and Function in Primitive Society.* New York: The Free Press, 1952.

RADOVANOWITCH, V.M. *Le Danube et l'application du principe de la liberté de la navigation fluviale.* Genève, 1925.

RAES, JEAN 'Economic Integration of Nations: Panacea for World Peace'. *World Justice,* **9,** (3), 1968.

RAJH, SDENKO 'The EEC Crisis: Siginificance and Causes'. *Review of International Affairs,* **16,** (372), 1965.

RANSHOFEN-WESTHEIMER, EGON 'International Administration: Lessons from the Experience of the League of Nations'. *American Political Science Review,* **37,** (5), 1943.

RANSHOFEN-WESTHEIMER, EGON *The International Secretariat.* Washington DC: Carnegie Endowment for International Peace, 1945.

RANSHOFEN-WESTHEIMER, EGON 'The International Civil Service of the Future'. *International Conciliation,* (418), 1946.

RANSOME, P. (ed.) *Studies in Federal Planning.* London: Macmillan and Co., 1943.

RAO, V.K.R.V. 'An International Development Authority'. *India Quarterly,* **8,** (3), 1952

VON RAUCHAUPT, FR. W. 'Las organizaciones espaciales en Europa, en particular ELDO y ESRO'. *Revista de Politica Internacional,* **89,** 1967.

REDSLOB, R. *Théorie de la Société des Nations.* Paris: Rousseau, 1927.

REIF, HANS *Europäische Integration.* Köln: Westdeutscher Verlag, 1962.

REIFF, HENRY 'The United States and International Administrative Unions: Some Historical Aspects'. *International Conciliation,* (332), 1937.

REINSCH, PAUL S. *Public International Unions: Their Work and Organisation: A Study in International Administrative Law.* Boston: Ginn and Company, 1911.

REINTON, PER OLAV 'International Structure and International Integration'. *Journal of Peace Reserach.* (4), 1967.

REISMAN, WILLIAM M. 'The Role of the Economic Agencies in the Enforcement of International Judgements and Awards: A Functional Approach'. *International Organisation,* **19,** (3), 1965.

REITT, H. 'United States and International Administrative Unions'. *International Conciliation,* (332), 1937.

RENAULT, LOUIS 'Les Unions internationales: Leurs avantages et leurs inconvénients'. *Revue générale de droit international public,* Tome 3, 1896.

RENBORG, BERTIL A. *International Drug Control: A Study of International Organisation by and through the League of Nations.* Washington: Carnegie Endowment for International Peace, 1947.

RENS, JEF 'Latin America and the International Labour Organisation: Forty Years of Collaboration 1919-1959'. *International Labour Review*, **80**, (1), 1959.

REUTT, BOGUSLAW W. 'Planned Partnership in the CMEA'. *Polish Perspectives*, **12**, (5), 1969.

REUTER, P. *International Institutions* London: George Allen and Unwin, 1958.

REVELLE, ROGER 'International Cooperation in Food and Population'. *International Organisation*, **22**, (1), 1968.

REY, JEAN 'Etat présent des problémes européens'. *Chronique de Politique Etrangére*, **19**, (2), 1966.

REYNAUD, PAUL *Unite or Perish: A Dynamic Program for a United Europe.* New York: Simon and Schuster Inc., 1951.

RICHARDSON, C.B. *The United Nations and Arab Refugee Relief, 1948-1950: A Case Study of International Organisation and Administration.* unpublished Ph.D., Columbia University, 1950-51.

RIPKA, HUBERT *Small and Great Nations: The Conditions of a New International Organisation.* London: Czechoslovak Ministry of Foreign Affairs, 1944.

RISTELHUEBER, RENÉ 'The International Refugee Organisation'. *International Conciliation*, (470), 1951.

RIVKIN, ARNOLD 'An Economic Development Proposal for Africa: A New Multilateral Aid Organisation'. *International Organisation*, **12**, (3), 1958.

ROBBINS, LIONEL *Economic Planning and International Order.* London: Macmillan and Co., 1937.

ROBBINS, LIONEL *Economic Aspects of Federation.* London: Federal Tract No.2, Macmillan, 1941.

ROBERTSON, A.H. *European Institutions: Cooperation, Integration, Unification.* New York: Frederick A. Praeger Inc., 1959; rev. ed. 1966.

ROBERTSON, A.H. *Human Rights in Europe.* Dobbs Ferry, N.Y.: Oceana Publications, 1963

ROBINSON, JACOB *International Law and Organisation.* Leyden: A.W. Sijthoff, 1967.

RODGERS, RAYMOND S. *Facilitation Problems of International Association: The Legal, Fiscal and Administrative Facilities of International Non-Governmental Organisations.* Brussels: Union of International Associations, 1960.

ROHN, PETER H. *Relations between the Council of Europe and International Non-Governmental Organisations* Brussels: Union of International Associations, 1957.

ROLFE, SIDNEY E. and DAMM, WALTER (ed.) *The Multinational Corporation in the World Economy: Direct Investment in Perspective.* New York: Frederick A. Praeger, 1970.

ROLL, ERIC *The Combined Food Board: A Study in Wartime International Planning.* Stanford: Stanford University Press, 1956.

ROMMEN, HEINRICH 'Towards the Internationalisation of Human Rights'. *World Justice*, **1**, (2), 1959.

ROPKE, WILHEIM *International Order and Economic Integration.* Dordrecht, Holland: D. Reidel Publishing Co., 1960.

ROSBERG, CARL G., with SEGAL, AARON 'An East African Federation'. *International Conciliation*, (543), 1963.

ROSE, EDWARD 'The English Record of a Natural Sociology'. *American Sociological Review*, **25**, 1960.

ROSENAU, JAMES N. 'Foreign Policy as Adaptive Behaviour'. *Comparative Politics*, (2), 1970.

ROSENAU, JAMES N. *The Adaption of National Societies: A Theory of Political System Behavior and Transformation.* New York: McCaleb-Seiler, 1970.

ROSENAU, JAMES N. (ed.) *Linkage Politics: Essays on the Convergence of National and International Systems.* New York: The Free Press, 1969.

ROSS, L.R. *Historical Growth and Influence of the Specialized Agencies of the Economic and Social Council of the United Nation.* unpublished Ph.D.: Georgetown University, 1948.

ROSSELLO, P. *Forerunners of the International Bureau of Education.* London: Evans Brothers Ltd., 1944.

ROSTOW, WALT W. 'The Economic Commission for Europe'. *International Organisation*, 3, (2), 1949.

ROTHCHILD, DONALD (ed.) *Politics of Integration: An East African Documentary.* Nairobi: East African Publishing House, 1968.

ROZANSKI, HENRYK 'La Coopération économique des États socialistes et le rôle du Conseil d'Assistance Économique Mutuelle'. *Annuaire Polonaise des Affaires Internationales*, 1961.

ROZANSKI, HENRYK 'RWPG—problemy rozwoju miedzynarodowego podzialu pracy'. *Sprawy Miedzynarodowe*, 19th Year, (7), 1966.

RUBENSTEIN, ALVIN Z. 'Soviet Policy in ECAFE: A Case Study of Soviet Behaviour in International Economic Organisation'. *International Organisation*, 12, (4), 1958.

RUBENSTEIN, ALVIN Z. 'Soviet and American Policies in International Economic Organisations'. *International Organisations*, 18, (1), 1964.

DE RUSSETT, ALAN *Strengthening the Framework of Peace.* London: Royal Institute of International Affairs, 1950.

RUSSETT, BRUCE *International Regions and the International System.* Chicago: Rand McNally, 1967.

RUSSETT, BRUCE M. and SULLIVAN, JOHN D. 'Collective Goods and International Organisation'. *International Organisation*, 25, (4), Autumn 1971.

RUZIE, DAVID *Les fonctionnaires internationaux.* Paris: Librairie Armand Colin, 1970.

SABELLA, DOMENICO *L'Europa ed il Mezzogiorno.* Rome: Editoriale di Cultura e Documentazione, 1959.

ŠABIĆ, MUSTAFA 'Yugoslav -Rumanian Industrial Cooperation'. *Review of International Affairs*, 20, (460), 1969.

SALAH-BEY, ANISSE *L'Organisation Internationale du Travail et le Syndicalisme Mondial (1945-1960).* Paris: Librairie Medicis, 1963

SALAH-BEY, ANISSE *'L'Afrique et l'OIT—Evaluation Politique'.* Revue algérienne des Sciences juridiques, politiques et économiques, (1), 1964.

SALIBA, SAMIR N. *The Jordan River Dispute.* The Hague: Nijhoff, 1968.

SALTER, J.A. (Sir ARTHUR) *Allied Shipping Control: An Experiment in International Administration.* Oxford: Clarendon Press, 1921.

SALTER, Sir ARTHUR *Recovery—The Second Effort.* London: G. Bell and Sons, 1932.

SALTER, Sir ARTHUR *The Framework of an Ordered Society.* Cambridge: Cambridge University Press, 1933.

SALVERESEN, KAARE 'Cooperation in Social Affairs Between the Northern Countries of Europe'. *International Labour Review,* **73** (4), 1956.

SASEK, ALOIS The Danube: *Link of Central Europe.* Prague: Privately printed, 1936.

SASSEN, E.M.J.A. 'Euratom and the Question of Dependence, Independence or Inter-dependence'. *International Spectator,* 19th Year, (7), 1965.

SATHYAMURTHY, T.V. 'Problems of Central and Regional Coordination in Functional International Organisation'. *Midwest Journal of Political Science,* August, 1963.

SATHYAMURTHY, T.V. *The Politics of International Cooperation: Contrasting Conceptions of UNESCO.* Geneva: Librairie Droz, S.A., 1964

SATHYAMURTHY, T.V. 'Twenty Years of UNESCO: An Interpretation. *International Organisation,* **21,** (3), 1967.

SATHYAMURTHY, T.V. 'Functional International Cooperation: UNESCO'. *International Studies (New Delhi),* **8,** (3), 1967.

SATTERFIELD, M.H. 'TVA-State-Local Relationships'. *American Political Science Review,* **40,** (5), 1946.

SATTLER, ANDREAS *Das Prinzip der 'Funktionellen Integration' und die Einigung Europas.* Göttingen, Otto Schwarz, 1967.

SAUWENS, ANDRE 'Quelques aspects des politiques économiques sectorielles des communautés européennes'. *Chronique de Politique Etrangère,* **21,** (2), 1968.

SAYRE, FRANCIS B. *Experiments in International Administration.* New York: Harper and Bros., 1919.

SCELLE, GEORGES *L'Organisation internationale du Travail et le BIT.* Paris: Librairie des Sciences Sociales Marcel Rivière, 1930.

SCHAAF, C. HART 'The United Nations Economic Commission for Asia and the Far East'. *International Organisation,* **7,** (3), 1953.

SCHAAF, C. HART 'The Role of the Resident Representative of the UN Technical Assistant Board'. *International Organisation,* **14,** (4), 1960.

SCHAAF, C. HART and FIFIELD, RUSSELL H. *The Lower Mekong: Challenge to Cooperation in Southeast Asia.* Princeton N.J.; Van Nostrand, 1963.

SCHAPER, B.W. *Albert Thomas: Trente Ans de Réformisme Social.* Netherlands: Van Gorcum and Co., 1959.

SCHEINGOLD, STUART A. 'Domestic and International Consequences of Regional Integration'. *International Organisation,* **24,** (4), 1970.

SCHEINMAN, LAWRENCE 'Some Preliminary Notes on Bureaucractic Relationships in the European Economic Community'. *International Organisation,* **20,** (4), 1966.

SCHEINMAN, LAWRENCE 'Euratom: Nuclear Integration in Europe'. *International Conciliation,* (563), 1967.

SCHEINMAN, LAWRENCE and FELD, WERNER 'The European Economic Community and National Civil Servants of the Member States'. *International Organisation,* **26,** (1), 1972.

SCHENKMAN, JACOB *International Civil Aviation Organisation.* Paris: Librairie E. Droz, 1955.

SCHEVENELS, WALTER *Forty-five Years: International Federation of Trade Unions.* Brussels: Board of Trustees of IFTU, 1956.

SCHLOSS, HENRY H. *The Bank for International Settlements: An Experiment in Central Bank Cooperation.* Amsterdam: North Holland Publishing Co., 1958.

SCHMIDT, DANA A. 'Prospects for a Solution of the Jordan River Valley Dispute'. *Middle Eastern Affairs*, **6**, (1), 1955.

SCHMITTER, PHILIPPE C. 'Three Neo-Functional Hypotheses About International Integration'. *International Organisation*, **23**, (1), 1969.

SCHMITTER, PHILIPPE C. 'Further Notes on Operationalizing Some Variables Related to Regional Integration'. *International Organisation*, **23**, (2), 1969.

SCHMITTER, PHILIPPE C. 'La dinámica de contradicciones y la conducción de crisis en la integración centroamericana'. *Revista de la integración*, (5), 1969.

SCHMITTER, PHILIPPE C. 'A Revised Theory of Regional Integration'. *International Organisation*, **24**, (4), 1970.

SCHON, DONALD *Beyond the Stable State*. London: Temple Smith, 1971.

SCHOU, AUGUST *Histoire de l'Internationalisme*. Oslo: H. Aschehoug, 1963.

SCHUMACHER, E.F. 'The Struggle for a European Energy Policy'. *Journal of Common Market Studies*, **2**, (3), 1964.

SCHWARTZ, LEONARD E. *International Organisations and Space Cooperation*. Durham, N.C.: World Rule of Law Center, Duke University, 1963.

SCHWEBEL, STEPHEN M. (ed.) *The Effectiveness of International Decisions*. Dobbs Ferry, N.Y.: Oceana Publications, 1971

SCHWELB, EGON 'International Conventions on Human Rights'. *The International and Comparative Law Quarterly*, **9**, Part 4, 1960.

SCHWELB, EGON 'On The Operation of the European Convention on Human Rights'. *International Organisation*, **18**, (3), 1964.

SCOTT, F.R. 'The World's Civil Service'. *International Conciliation*, (496), 1954.

SEGAL, AARON 'The Integration of Developing Countries: Some Thoughts on East Africa and Central America'. *Journal of Common Market Studies*, **5**, (3), 1967.

SEGAL, AARON *The Politics of Caribbean Economic Integration*. Rio Piedras: Institute of Puerto Rico, 1968.

SEGAL, AARON 'Le integración en Africa: Problemas y perspectivas'. *Revista de la integración*, (5), 1969.

SELZNIC, P. *TVA and the Grass Roots*. Berkeley: University of California Press, 1949.

SEN, SUDHIR *United Nations in Economic Development: Need for a New Strategy*. Dobbs Ferry, N.Y.: Oceana Publications, 1969.

SENGHAAS-KNOBLOCH, EVA *Frieden durch Integration und Assoziation. Literaturbericht und Problemstudien*. Stuttgart: Klott, 1969.

SEWELL, JAMES P. *Functionalism and World Politics: A Study based on United Nations Programs Financing Economic Development*. Princeton N.J.: Princeton University Press, 1966.

SEWELL, W.R. DERRICK and WHITE, GILBERT F. 'The Lower Mekong'. *International Conciliation*, (558), 1966.

SHARP, WALTER R. The Specialized Agencies and the United Nations: Progress Report I'. *International Organisation*, **1**, (3), 1947.

SHARP, WALTER R. 'The New World Health Organisation'. *American Journal of International Law*, **41**, (3), 1947.

SHARP, WALTER R. 'The Specialized Agencies and the United Nations: Progress Report II'. *International Organisation*, **II**, (2), 1948.

SHARP, WALTER R. 'The Role of UNESCO: A Critical Evaluation'. *Proceedings of the Academy of Political Science*, **24**, (2), 1951.

SHARP, WALTER R. *International Technical Assistance: Programs and Organisations* Chicago: Public Administration Service, 1952.

SHARP, WALTER R. 'The Institutional Framework for Technical Assistance'. *International Organisation,* 7, (3), 1953.

SHARP, WALTER R. 'The United Nations System in Egypt: A Country Survey of Field Operations'. *International Organisation,* 10, (2), 1956.

SHARP, WALTER R. 'Trends in United Nations Administration'. *International Organisation,* 15, (3), 1961.

SHARP, WALTER R. 'The Administration of United Nations Operational Programs'. *International Organisation,* 199, (3), 1965.

SHARP, WALTER R. 'Decision-making in the Economic and Social Council'. *International Organisation,* 22, (4), 1968.

SHARP, WALTER R. *The United Nations Economic and Social Council* New York: Columbia University Press, 1969.

SHERIF, MUZAFER *Group Cooperation and Conflict.* London: Routledge and Kegan Paul, 1966.

SHERIF, MUZAFER and SHARING, CAROLYN W. (ed.) *Interdisciplinary Relationships in the Social Sciences.* Chicago: Aldine Publishing Co., 1969.

SHKUNAEV, V.G. *The International Labour Organisation, Past and Present.* Moscow: International Relations Publishing House, 1969.

SHOTWELL, JAMES T. *Labour as an International Problem.* London: Macmillan, 1920.

SHOTWELL, JAMES T. *The Origins of the International Labour Organisation.* 2 vols London: Humphrey Milford, 1934.

SHUSTER, GEORGE N. *UNESCO: Assessment and Promise.* New York: Harper and Row, 1963.

SIBTHORP, M.M. *Oceanic Pollution: A Survey and Some Suggestions for Control.* London: David Davies Memorial Institute, 1969.

SICAULT, GEORGES (ed.) *The Needs of Children.* New York: The Free Press, 1963.

SIDDIQUI, QAMAR SAEED 'European Integration and Economic Development in the Commonwealth'. *Pakistan Horizon,* 13, (4), 1960.

SIDJANSKI, DUSAN *Le Processus d'Intégration dans les Communautés Européennes.* The Hague: Martinus Nijhoff, 1963.

SIDJANSKI, DUSAN *Dimensiones institucionales de la integración latino-americana.* Buenos Aires: Instituto para la Integración de America Latina, 1967.

SINGER, J. DAVID *Financing International Organisations: The United Nations Budget Process.* The Hague: Martinus Nijhoff, 1961

SINGER, H.W. *International Development: Growth and Change.* New York: McGraw Hill, 1965.

SINGH, LALITA P. *The Politics of Economic Cooperation in Asia: A Study of Asian International Organisations.* Columbia, Miss.: University of Missouri Press, 1966.

SIOTIS, JEAN *Essai sur le secrétariat international.* Genève: Librairie Droz, 1963.

SIOTIS, JEAN 'Some Problems of European Secretariats'. *Journal of Common Market Studies,* 2, (3), 1964.

SIOTIS, JEAN 'The Secretariat of the United Nations Economic Commission for Europe and European Economic Integrations'. *International Organisation,* 19, (2), 1965.

329

SIOTIS, JEAN, 'ECE in the Emerging European System'. *International Conciliation*, (561), 1967.

SKJELSBAEK, KJELL 'The Growth of International Nongovernmental Organisation in the Twentieth Century'. *International Organisation*, **25**, (3), 1971.

SKOLNIKOFF, EUGENE B. 'Science and Technology'. *International Organisation*, **25**, (4), Autumn, 1971.

SKUBISZEWSKI, KRZYSZTOF 'Forms of Participation of International Organisations in the Law-Making Process'. *International Organisation*, **18**, (4), 1964.

SLOTEMAKER, L.H. *Freedom of Passage for International Air Services.* Leyden; A.W. Sijthoff, 1932.

SLY, JOHN F. 'The Genesis of the Universal Postal Union'. *International Conciliation*, (233), 1927.

SMELSER, NEIL *The Sociology of Economic Life.* Princeton, N.J.: Prentice-Hall Inc., 1963.

SMITH, DELHERT D. *International Telecommunication Control: International Law and the Ordering of Satellite and other Forms of International Broadcasting.* Leyden; A.W. Sijthoff, 1969.

SMITH, HERBERT A. *Economic Uses of International Rivers.* London: P.S. King and Son, 1931.

SMITH, HERBERT A. 'The Waters of the Jordan: a Problem of International Water Control'. *International Affairs* (London), **25**, (4), 1949.

SMITH, J. ERIC 'The Role of Special Purpose and Nongovernmental Organizations in the Environmental Crisis'. *International Organization*, **24**, (2), 1972.

SMUTS, JAN C. *The League of Nations: A Practical Suggestion.* London: Hodder and Stoughton, 1918.

SPATARU, AL and BOTA, LIVIU 'L'Organisation des Nations Unies et la Coopération Internationale pour l'Exploration et l'Utilisation pacifique de l'Espace extra-atmosphérique'. *Revue roumaine d'études internationales.* (3-4), 1968.

SPAULL, HEBE *The Agencies of the UN: A Survey of Economic and Social Achievements.* London: Allen & Unwin, 1967.

SPEECKHAERT, G.P. *International Institutions and International Organization, A Select Bibliography.* Brussels; Union of International Associations, 1956.

SPEECKHAERT, G.P. *1978 International Organizations since the Congress of Vienna.* Brussels; Union of International Associations, 1958.

SPEECKHAERT, G.P. *Select Bibliography on International Organisation (1885-1964).* Brussels: Union of International Associations, 1965.

SPEECKHAERT, G.P. 'On the Structure and Functioning of International Non-Governmental Organizations'. *International Associations* 18th Year, (3), 1966.

SPENCER, HERBERT *The Principles of Sociology.* 1, New York: Appleton-Century Crofts, 1897.

SPINA, E. 'Il Commonwealth e la integrazione europe'. *Ricerche Economiche*, March 1961.

SPINELLI, ALTIERO *The Eurocrats.* Baltimore: The John Hopkins Press, 1966.

SPRECKELSEN, HEINRICH VON *Die rechtlichen Beziehungen des Völkerbundes zu internationalen Unionen.* Münster: Helios-Verlag, 1929.

SPRINGER, HUGH W. 'Federation in the Caribbean: An Attempt that Failed'. *International Organization*, **16**, (4), 1962.

STAMENBOVIK, RADOS 'The Economic and Social Council and the Special UN Fund for European Development'. *Review of International Affairs*, 5, (103), 1954.

STANOVNIK, JANEZ 'Some Problems of Theory and Policy of Economic Development in the Light of the Cairo Declaration'. *Medunarodni Problemi* (4th English Issue), 1963.

STARKE, J.G. *An Introduction to the Science of Peace.* Leyden: A.W. Sijthoff, 1968.

STELLING-MICHAUD, S. *David Luhin, 1849-1919, un Pionnier de l'Organisation Internationale.* Berne, Lang, 1951.

STEPHEN, LESLIE *The English Utilitarians.* 3 vols. London: Duckworth and Co., 1900.

STEPHENS, GEORGE W. *The St. Lawrence Waterway Project.* Montreal: Louis Carrier, 1930.

STEPHENS, JEROME 'The Logic of Functional and Systems Analyses in Political Science'. *Midwest Journal of Political Science*, (13), 1969.

STEPHENS, JEROME 'An Appraisal of Some System Approaches in the Study of International Systems'. *International Studies Quarterly*, 16, (3), 1972.

STEVENS, GEORGIANA G. 'The Jordan River Valley'. *International Conciliation*, (506), 1956.

STIKKER, DIRK U. 'The Functional Approach to European Integration'. *Foreign Affairs*, 29, (3), 1951.

STOCKDALE, SIR FRANK 'The Work of the Caribbean Commission'. *International Affairs* (London), 23, (2), 1947.

STRESSINGER, JOHN G. The International Atomic Energy Agency: The First Phase'. *International Organization*, 13, (3), 1959.

STOSIC, BORKO *Les organisations non-gouvernementales et les Nations Unies.* Genève: Librairie Droz, S.A., 1964

STOWELL, ELLERY C. 'Plans for World Organization'. *Columbia University Quarterly*, (18), 1916.

STREETEN, PAUL *Economic Integration: Aspects and Problems.* enlarged edition. Leyden: A.W. Sijthoff, 1964.

DE ST. SIMON, H. *De la Réorganisation de la Société Européenne.* Paris: Les Presses Françaises, 1925.

SULLIVAN, WALTER 'The International Geophysical Year'. *International Conciliation*, (521), 1959.

SUTHERLAND BALDWIN, K.D.S. *The Niger Agricultural Project: An Experiment in African Development.* Oxford: Blackwell, 1957.

SWANWICK, H.M. *Builders of Peace Being Ten Years' History of the Union of Democratic Control.* London: The Swarthmore Press, 1924.

SWARBRICK, JAMES 'The Arid Zone—An International Task'. *Impact*, 4, (4), 1953.

SWEETSER, ARTHUR 'The First Ten Years of the League of Nations'. *International Conciliation*, (256), 1930.

SWEETSER, ARTHUR 'The Non-Political Achievements of the League'. *Foreign Affairs*, October 1940.

SWERLING, B.C. *International Control of Sugar, 1918-1941.* Stanford: Stanford University Press, 1949.

331

DE SYDOW, GUNNAR 'The Scandinavian Cooperation in the Field of Legislation after the Second World War'. *Unification of Law, Unidroit,* Rome, III, 1954

SZOBOLOCZY-SYLLABA, JANOS *Les Organisations Professionelles Francaises et le Marché Commun.* Paris: Colin, 1965.

SZAWLOWSKI, RICHARD 'L'évolution du COMECON, 1949-1963'. *Annuaire Francais de Droit International,* (9), 1963.

TAILLADES DE YULITA, LEONOR 'Influencia de la tecnología en las relaciones internacionales'. *Revista de Derecho Internacional y Ciencias Diplomáticas,* 8th year, (15-16), 1959.

TAUBENFELD, HOWARD J. 'A Treaty for Antarctica'. *International Conciliation,* (531), 1961.

TAUBENFELD, HOWARD J. 'The Antarctic Treaty of 1959'. *Disarmament and Arms Control,* 2, (2), 1964.

TAUBENFELD, HOWARD J. (ed) *Space and Society.* Dobbs Ferry, N.Y.: Oceana Publications, Inc., 1964.

TAUBENFELD, RITA F. and TAUBENFELD, HOWARD J. 'Some International Implications of Weather Modification Activities'. *International Organization,* 23, (3), 1969.

TAYLOR, PAUL 'The Concept of Community and the European Integration Process'. *Journal of Common Market Studies,* 7, (2), 1968.

TAYLOR, PAUL 'The Functionalist Approach to the Problem of International Order: A Defence'. *Political Studies,* 16, 1968.

TAYLOR, PAUL *International Cooperation Today.* London: Elek, 1971.

TEAD, ORDWAY 'The Importance of Administration in International Action'. *International Conciliation,* (407), 1945.

TEAF, HOWARD, M. Jr. and FRANCK, PETER G. (eds.) *Hands Across Frontiers: Case Studies in Technical Cooperation.* Ithaca: Cornell University Press, 1955.

TENNEY, ALVAN A. 'Theories of Social Organization and the Problem of International Peace'. *Political Science Quarterly,* (3), 1915.

TEW, BRIAN *International Monetary Cooperation.* New York: Longmans, 1952.

THAYER, FREDERICK C. 'International Air Transport: A Microsystem in Need of New Approaches', *International Organization,* 25, (4), Autumn, 1971.

THOMAS, ALBERT 'The League of Nations'. *Atlantic Monthly,* (122), 1918.

THOMAS, ALBERT *International Social Policy.* Geneva: International Labour Organization, 1948.

THOMAS, JEAN *UNESCO.* Paris: Gallimard, 1963.

THOMPSON, JAMES D. (ed.) *Approaches to Organizational Design.* Pittsburgh: University of Pittsburgh Press, 1966.

THOMPSON, MARGARET C. and others. *Political Integration: A Survey of Theories* Amsterdam: Europa Institut, University of Amsterdam, 1968.

THORBECKE, ERIC *The Tendency Towards Regionalism in International Trade 1928-1956.* The Hague: Martinus Nijhoff, 1960.

TICKNER, F.J. *Technical Cooperation.* London: Hutchinson University Library, 1965.

TINBERGEN, JAN *Shaping the World Economy: Suggestions for an International Economic Policy.* New York: The Twentieth Century Fund, 1962.

TINBERGEN, JAN *International Economic Integration.* 2nd rev. edition. New York: Elsevier, 1965.

TINBERGEN, JAN 'Wanted—a World Development Plan'. *International Organization*, **22**, (1), 1968.

TIPTON, JOHN B. *Participation of the United States in the International Labor Organization*. Urbana: Institute of Labor and Industrial Relations, University of Illinois, 1959.

TOMASEVITCH, J. *International Agreement on Conservation of Marine Resources.* Stanford: Food Research Institute, Stanford University, 1943.

TOMBS, LAWRENCE C. *International Organization in European Air Transport.* New York: Columbia University Press, 1936.

TOMLINSON, JOHN D. *The International Control of Radiocommunications.* Geneva: Imprimerie du Journal de Genève, 1938.

DE TRAZ, ROBERT *De l'Alliance des Rois à la Ligue des Peuples.* Paris: Grasset, 1936.

TREVELYAN, CHARLES *The Union of Democratic Control: Its History and Its Policy.* London: Simson and Co., 1919.

TRIBOLET, L.B. *The International Aspects of Electrical Communication in the Pacific Areas.* 1929.

TRIPP, BRENDA M.H. 'UNESCO in Perspective'. *International Conciliation*, (497), 1954.

TROCLET, LEON-ELI *Législation sociale internationale.* Bruxelles: Librairie Encyclopédique.

TROCLET, LEON-ELI 'Le Problème de la collaboration des partenaires sociaux et la politique sociale européenne'. *Chronique de Politique Etrangère*, **22**, (2), 1969.

TUNG, WILLIAM L. *International Organization under the United Nations System.* New York: Thomas A. Crowell, 1969.

TURNER, LOUIS *Invisible Empires: Multinational Companies and the Modern World.* London: Hamish Hamilton, 1970.

UNWIN, R. *Functions of a League of Nations.* London: League of Nations Society, 1971.

URQUHART, BRIAN *Hammarskjold.* New York: Alfred A. Knopf, 1972.

URQUIDI, VICTOR L. 'Integración latinoamericana y planeación. *Foro Internacional*, **7**, (1-2), 1966.

VAJDA, IMRE 'Problems and Prospects of an All-European Cooperation. *Review of International Affairs*, **17**, (390-391), 1966.

VALTICOS, NICOLAS 'Un système de contrôle international: La Mise en Oeuvre des Conventions Internationales du Travail'. *Recueil des Cours de l'Academie de Droit International*, **133**, (1), 1968.

VAN DUYN, ROEL *Message of a Wise Kabouter* London: Duckworth 1972.

VANEK, J. 'The Second Conference of the International Atomic Energy Agency in Vienna'. *Casopis pro Mezinárodni Právo*, **3**, (2), 1959.

VASAK, KAREL *La Commission interaméricaine des Droits de l'Homme.* Paris: Librairie Générale de Droit et de Jurisprudence, 1968.

VAN WAGENEN, RICHARD *Research in the International Organization Field: Some Notes on a Possible Focus.* Princeton, N.J.: Center for Research on World Political Institutions Publication (1), 1952.

VAN WAGENEN, RICHARD W. 'The Concept of Community and the Future of the United Nations'. *International Organisation,* **19,** (3), 1965.

VERNON, RAYMOND *Sovereignty at Bay: The Multilateral Spread of US Enterprise.* New York: Basic Books, 1971.

VICKERS, GEOFFREY *Towards a Sociology of Management.* London: Chapman and Hall, 1967.

VICKERS, GEOFFREY *Freedom in a Rocking Boat: Changing Values in an Unstable Society.* Harmondsworth: Penguin Books, 1970.

VONK, K. 'The Transport Sector: A Struggle for Balance and Mobility'. *International Spectator,* 19th Year, (7), 1964.

VON MEERHAEGHE, M.A.G. *International Economic Institutions.* London: Longmans, 1966.

WALLACE, B.B. and EDMINSTER, L.R. *International Control of Raw Materials.* Washington: Brookings Institution, 1930.

WALLACE, MICHAEL and SINGER, J. DAVID 'Intergovernmental Organization in the Global System 1815-1964: A Quantitative Description'. *International Organization,* **24,** (2), 1970.

WALTERS, F.P. *Administrative Problems of International Organization.* London: Oxford University Press, 1941.

WALTERS, F.P. *A History of the League of Nations* 2 vols. London: Oxford University Press, 1952.

WALTERS, ROBERT S. 'International Organisations and Political Communication: The Use of UNCTAD by Less Developed Countries'. *International Organization,* **25,** (4), Autumn 1971.

WALTZ, KENNETH *Man, the State and War.* New York: Columbia University Press, 1954, 1968.

WASSENBERGH, H.A. *Post War International Civil Aviation Policy and the Law of the Air.* The Hague: Martinus Nijhoff, 1962.

WATERS, MAURICE *The United Nations: International Organization and Administration.* New York: Macmillan, 1967.

WATKINS, JAMES T. (ed.) *General International Organization, A Source Book.* Princeton, N.J.: D. Van Nostrand, 1956.

WATKINS, W.P. *The International Cooperative Alliance, 1895-1970.* London: International Cooperative Alliance, 1970.

WATTS, R.L. *New Federations: Experiments in the Commonwealth.* Oxford: The Clarendon Press, 1966.

WEAVER, J.H. *The International Development Association: A New Approach to Foreign Aid.* New York: Frederick A. Praeger, 1965.

WEBER, MAX *Theory of Social and Economic Organization.* New York: The Free Press, 1947.

WEDGWOOD, RALPH L. *International Rail Transport.* London: Oxford University Press, 1946.

WEHBERG, H. *L'Idée de l'Organisation Internationale à l'Epoque des Conférences de la Haye.* Paris: Librairie Générale de Droit et de Jurisprudence, 1950.

WEIL, GORDON, L. *The European Convention on Human Rights.* Leyden: A.W. Sijthoff, 1963.

WELLS, H.G. *A Modern Utopia.* New York: Scribner's, 1905.

WELLS, H.G. *In the Fourth Year: Anticipations of a World Peace.* London: Chatto & Windus, 1918.

WELLS, H.G. *Men Like Gods.* London: Fisher Unwin, 1927.

WELLS, H.G. *The New World Order.* London: Secker & Warburg, 1940.

WELLS, SIDNEY 'The Developing Countries: GATT and UNCTAD'. *International Affairs.* (London), **45**, (1), 1969.

WEMELSFELDER, J. 'Benelux: An Experiment in Economic Integration'. *Economia Internazionale*, **8**, (3),1955.

WENDT, FRANTZ *The Nordic Council and Cooperation in Scandinavia.* Copenhagen: Munksgaard, 1959.

WESOLOWSKI, WLODZIMIERZ 'Some Notes on the Functional Theory of Stratification'. *The Polish Sociological Bulletin* (3-4), 1962.

WESSELY, KURT 'Donaustaaten und Westeuropäische Integration'. *Der Donauraum*, **7**, (2-3), 1962.

WHEARE, K.C. *Federal Government.* London: Oxford University Press, 1946.

WHITE, GILBERT F. 'National Executive Organization for Water Resources'. *American Political Science Review*, **44**, (3), 1950.

WHITE, JOHN 'The Asian Development Bank: A Question of Style'. *International Affairs* (London), **44**, (4), 1968.

WHITE, LYMAN C. and ZOCCA, MARIE R. *International Non-Governmental Organizations: Their Purposes, Methods and Accomplishments.* New Brunswick, N.J.: Rutgers University Press, 1951.

WIGHTMAN, DAVID *Economic Cooperation in Europe: A Study of the United Nations Commission for Europe.* New York: Frederick A. Praeger, 1956.

WIGHTMAN, DAVID 'East-West Cooperation and the United Nations Economic Commission for Europe'. *International Organization*, **11**, (1), 1957.

WIGHTMAN, DAVID *Toward Economic Cooperation in Asia: The United Nations Economic Commission for Asia and the Far East.* New Haven: Yale University Press, 1963.

WILBUR, MARGUERITE E. *The East India Company and the British Empire in the Far East.* New York: Richard R. Smith, 1945.

WILK, KURT 'International Organization and the International Chamber of Commerce.' *Political Science Quarterly*, **55**, June, 1940.

WILK, KURT 'International Administrative Regulation: The Case of Rubber'. *American Political Science Review*, **36**, (2), 1942.

WILLIAMS, PETER 'The Use of World Food Surpluses'. *The World Today*, **18**, (7), 1962.

WILLIAMS, ROGER *Politics and Technology.* London: Macmillan, 1971.

WILLIAMSON, F.H. 'The International Postal Service and the Universal Postal Union'. *Journal of the Royal Institute of International Affairs*, **9**, (1), 1930.

WILLOUGHBY, WILLIAM R. *The St. Lawrence Waterway: A Study in Politics and Diplomacy.* Madison: University of Wisconsin Press, 1961.

WILSON, FRANCIS G. 'The International Labour Organisation'. *International Conciliation*, (284), 1932

WILSON, FRANCIS G. *Labor in the League System: A Study on the International Labour Organization in Relation to International Administration.* Stanford: Stanford University Press, 1934.

WINSLOW, C-E. A. 'World Health Organization: Program and Accomplishments'.

International Organization, (437), 1948.

WINSLOW, C-E. A. 'International Cooperation in the Service of Health'. *Annals of the American Academy of Political and Social Science,* **273**, 1951.

WIONCZEK, MIGUEL S. (ed.) *Latin American Economic Integration: Experiences and Prospects.* New York: Frederick A. Praeger, 1966.

WIONCZEK, MIGUEL S. (ed.) *Economic Cooperation in Latin America, Africa and Asia: A Handbook of Documents.* Cambridge: MIT Press, 1969.

WOLF, FRANCIS *Le Métier de Fonctionnaire International.* Genève: Association du Foyer John Knox, 1967.

WOLFERS, ARNOLD *Discord and Collaboration.* Baltimore: John Hopkins Press, 1962.

WONG, W.Y. *Burma Malaria: A Case Study of UNICEF Administration.* unpublished Ph.D. New York University, 1958.

WOOD, ROBERT S. (ed.) *The Process of International Organization.* New York: Random House, 1971.

WOODBRIDGE, GEORGE (ed.) *The History of the United Nations Relief and Rehabilitation Administration.* New York: Columbia University Press, 1950.

WOODCOCK, GEORGE *Anarchism.* London: Penguin Press, 1963.

WOODROW WILSON FOUNDATION 'Economic Commission for Europe'. *United Nations News,* **2**, (8), August 1947.

WOOLF, LEONARD S. *International Government.* London: George Allen and Unwin, 1916

WOOLF, LEONARD S. and the FABIAN SOCIETY *International Government: Two Reports* New York: Brentano's, 1916.

WOOLF, LEONARD S. *The Framework of a Lasting Peace.* London: Allen and Unwin, 1917.

WOOLF, LEONARD S. *Socialism and Cooperation.* London: L. Parsons, 1921.

WOOLF, LEONARD S. *Imperialism and Civilisation.* London: Hogarth Press, 1928.

WOOLF, LEONARD S. *The Way of Peace.* London: Benn, 1928.

WOOLF, LEONARD S. (ed.) *The Intelligent Man's Way to Prevent War* London: Gollancz, 1933.

WOOLF, LEONARD S. *The International Post-War Settlement.* London: Fabian Publication, Research Series, (85), 1944.

WOOTTON, BARBARA *Socialism and Federation.* London: Federal Tract No. 6, Macmillan, 1941.

WOOTTON, BARBARA *Freedom under Planning.* London: George Allen and Unwin, 1946.

WRIGHT, C.P. *The St. Lawrence Deep Waterway: A Canadian Appraisal.* London: Macmillan, 1935.

WRIGHT, QUINCY (ed.) *The World Community.* Chicago: University of Chicago Press, 1948.

WRIGHT, QUINCY *Problems of Stability and Progress in International Relations.* Berkeley: University of California Press, 1954

WRIGHT, QUINCY 'International Organization and Peace'. *Western Political Quarterly,* **8**, (2), 1955.

WRIGHT, QUINCY *A Study of War.* abridged edition. Chicago: University of Chicago Press, 1964.

WRIGHT, WILLIAM C. 'Somebody Up There'. (ICAO). *Vista,* **3**, (6), 1968.

WSZELAKI, JAN 'Economic Developments in East-Central Europe'. *Orbis,* 4, (4), 1961

YALEM, RONALD J. *Regionalism and World Order.* Washington D.C.: Public Affairs Press, 1965.
YALEM, RONALD J. 'The Study of International Organization, 1920-1965; A Survey of the Literature'. *Background,* 10, (1), 1966.
YAMAMOTO, NOBORO 'Problems of Regional Economic Cooperation and "Common Market" in Asia'. *Asian Affairs,* 2, (3), 1957.
YEMELYANOV, U.S. 'Atomic Energy for Peace: The USSR and International Cooperation'. *Foreign Affairs,* 38, (3), 1960.
YEMIN, EDWARD *Legislative Powers in the United Nations and Specialized Agencies.* Leyden: A.W. Sijthoff, 1969.
YONDORF, WALTER 'Monnet and the Action Committee: The Formative Period of the European Communities'. *International Organization,* 19, (2), 1965.
YUDELMAN, MONTAGUE, with HOWARD, F. *Agricultural Development and Economic Integration in Latin America.* London: George Allen and Unwin, 1970.

ZARRAS, JEAN *Le contrôle de l'application des conventions internationales du travail.* Paris: Recueil Sirey, 1937.
ZDANOWICZ, JERZY 'Economic Reasons behind Integration Movement in Western Europe'. *International Affairs* (Polish), 13, (3), 1960.
ZELLENTIN, GERDA (ed.) *Formen der Willensbildung in den Europäischen Organisationen.* Frankfurt: Athenäum Verlag, 1965.
ZIMMERN, A.E. (SIR ALFRED) *Learning and Leadership.* London: Oxford University Press, 1928.
ZIMMERN, SIR ALFRED 'The Prospects of Democracy'. *Journal of Royal Institute of International Affairs,* 7, May 1928.
ZIMMERN, SIR ALFRED *The League of Nations and the Rule of Law 1918-35,* London: Macmillan, 1936.
ZIMMERMAN, ERICH W. *World Resources and Industries: a Functional Appraisal of the Availability of Agricultural and Industrial Materials.* London: Hamish Hamilton, 1951.
ZOBER, M. *The Universal Postal Union: A Case Study in International Organization.* unpublished Ph.D.; University of Pittsburgh, 1950.
ZOUREK, J. 'The Membership of the German Democratic Republic in the Universal Postal Union'. *Casopis pro Mezinárodní Pravo,* 3, (2), 1959.
ZURCHER, ARNOLD *The Struggle to Unite Europe:* 1940-1958. New York: New York University Press, 1958.
ZWALF, M. *European Transport: The Way to Unity.* London: Fabian Publications, 1946.

Les Congrès Internationaux de 1681 a 1899: Liste Complète. Bruxelles: Publication No. 14, Union des Associations Internationales, 1960.

Euratom and the Common Market, A Symposium. Moscow: Foreign Literature Publishing House, 1957.

The Future of East African High Commission Services: Report of the London Discussion, June, 1961. London: HMSO, Cmnd. 1433, 1961.

International Congresses 1900-1919. Brussels: Union of International Associations, 1964.

International Organizations. London: George Allen and Unwin, 1961.

International Political Communities: An Anthology. Garden City, N.Y.: Anchor Books, Doubleday and Co. Inc., 1966.

'UNO: Economic Commission for Europe'. *International Affairs* (Moscow), (4), 1969.

Les organisations internationales économiques, scientifiques et techniques des états socialistes. Moscow: Editions Ekonomika, 1966.

Ten Years of World Cooperation. Geneva: League of Nations Secretariat, 1930.

Towards a Better Use of the Oceans. Stockholm: SIPRI, 1968.

Biographical Notes on Contributors

John Burton was educated at the University of Sydney, (B.A.) and London University, (Ph.D. D.Sc.). He was Permanent Head, Department of External Affairs in Australia, 1945-50, and Australian High Commissioner in Ceylon, 1951. Currently, he is a Reader in International Relations at University College London. John Burton's publications include *The Alternative* (1954); *Peace Theory* (1962); *International Relations: A General Theory* (1965); *Systems, States, Diplomacy and Rules* (1968); *Conflict and Communication* (1969); *World Society*, (1972).

Victor-Yves Ghébali studied at Geneva and Grenoble Universities. His present position is Assistant at the European Centre, Carnegie Endowment for International Peace (Geneva). His publications include *La France en guerre et les organisations internationales, 1939-1945* (Paris, Mouton, 1970); *La Société des Nations et la Réforme Bruce, 1939-1940* (Genève, Centre européen de la Dotation Carnegie pour la paix internationale, 1970); Michel Virally, Pierre Gerbet, Jean Salmon, Victor-Yves Ghébali: *Les missions permanentes auprès des organisations internationales*, Tome 1, Bruxelles, Bruylant, 1971 ('Les delegations permanentes auprès de la Société des Nations'), Pierre Gerbet, Victor-Yves Ghébali and Marie-Renée Mounton: *La Société des Nations et l'organisation des Nations unies*, Paris, Editions Richelieu, 1973 ('La Société des Nations, 1931-1946'); *A Repertoire of League of Nations Documents, 1919-1946* (Dobbs Ferry, Oceana Publications, forthcoming.

A.J.R. Groom received his university education in Britain, the United States and Switzerland. He has been a Lecturer in International Relations at University College London since 1965 where he is also associated with the Centre for the Analysis of Conflict. He has edited *The Management of Britain's External Relations* with Robert Boardman, and his *British Thinking about Nuclear Weapons* will be published in 1974 by Frances Pinter. He has published articles in American, Austrian, British, Canadian, Swiss and Yugoslav journals as well as contributing to various symposia.

R.J. Harrison, formerly Senior Lecturer in Politics at Victoria University, Wellington, New Zealand, returned to Britain in 1967 to take up an appointment at Lancaster University where he is now Senior Lecturer. He was awarded a Ph.D. in 1964 by Ohio State University for his dissertation on the New Zealand Parliament. His forthcoming study of contemporary theories of international regional integration is to be published by Allen and Unwin in 1974.

Nina Heathcote read History at the University of Western Australia. She has worked mainly at the Australian National University (currently a Research Fellow) with extended visits to the United States (Research Associate at Carnegie Endowment for International Peace, New York, 1966), and more recently to the UK and Europe. Her early work centred on United Nations peace-keeping. Since 1965 her main interest has been on the politics of the European Community and theories of integration in Western Europe. She has written a number of articles, the two more significant of which are 'The Crisis of European Supranationality', 1966, and 'Agricultural Politics in the European Community', 1971. She co-authored (with A.L. Burns) *Peacekeeping by UN Forces from Suez to the Congo,* New York: Praeger, 1963.

Michael Hodges is Lecturer in Interdisciplinary Studies at the University of Kent, Canterbury, where he has developed an interdisciplinary course on European Integration for social science undergraduates. He read Law and History at St. John's College, Cambridge, and undertook graduate work in International Relations at the University of Pennsylvania. He edited *European Integration* (Harmondsworth, Penguin Books, 1972), has written on international business topics for the *Journal of Common Market Studies,* and is currently working on a study of the British Labour Government's policy toward multinational companies, 1964-70.

Anthony J.N. Judge has an academic background in Chemical Engineering (London) and Management (Capetown). Since 1962 he has been connected with the Union of International Associations in Brussels where he is now Assistant Secretary General. He has written a number of articles and reports on the interrelationship between the network of international organisations and the design of the information systems on which they depend. Currently he is working on the production of a Yearbook of World Problems as a sister volume to the Yearbook of International Organisations which is a standard reference book now produced from computer-held data by the U.I.A.

Michael Leifer is Reader in International Relations at the L.S.E. He has held posts at the Universities of Adelaide and Hull and during 1971 was Visiting Professor of Government and Asian Studies at Cornell University. His most recent writings include *Dilemmas of Statehood in Southeast Asia.* (Singapore and Vancouver, 1972), and (Ed.) *Constraints and Adjustments in British Foreign Policy,* London 1972.

James Mayall was educated at Cambridge and Princeton. He joined the Civil Service in 1961 and worked first for the Board of Trade and also for a time in the Diplomatic Service. He joined the staff of the L.S.E. in 1966 where his main research interests have been concerned with African international relations and political and economic relations between the industrialised and developing countries. From 1968-71 he was also Associate Editor of the Survey and Documents of International Affairs at Chatham House. His publications include *Africa: The Cold War and After,* (Elek, 1971); *British Foreign Policy 1970* (Ed. with D.C. Watt), (Temple Smith 1971); *British Foreign Policy 1971,* (Ed. with D.C. Watt) forthcoming.

Allan McKnight graduated from Sydney University with Honours in Law in 1938.

He entered the Australian Federal Public Service and soon became Private Secretary to the Attorney-General. After 5 years in the Navy, he held several important positions in the Australian Public Service, namely Legal Adviser in Quantas Empire Airways, Deputy Secretary of the Cabinet, Permanent Secretary to the Army, and Executive Member of the Australian Atomic Energy Commission. He then served 4 years as Inspector-General of the International Atomic Energy Agency before proceeding to the Science Policy Research Unit at the University of Sussex in 1968 where he wrote 'Atomic Safeguards', 'Nuclear Non-proliferation: IAEA and Euratom', 'Scientists Abroad', numerous articles and partook in the preparation of three research reports on 'Scientific and Technological Co-operation in Europe', 'Application of Science and Technology to Development', and 'Future Growth of Energy Demand'. He is presently Lecturer in Government at the Civil Service College and Fellow of the Science Policy Research Unit, University of Sussex.

David Mitrany (D.Sc., Ph.D. London.) was a student in Sociology at the L.S.E. in 1912. During both World Wars he undertook work for the Foreign Office. In the inter-war period he was on the editorial staff of the *Manchester Guardian* and the Assistant European Editor of the Carnegie Endowment's Economic and Social History of the First World War, before lecturing at Harvard and Yale. In 1933 he became Professor and later the first Permanent Member of the Institute for Advanced Study in Princeton. From 1944 until 1960 he was political consultant to the Board of Unilever, which was the first appointment of its kind. Professor Mitrany's *A Working Peace System*, (Chicago: Quadrangle Press, 1966), and his other essays on Functionalism have proved highly influential. Among his other works, *Marx Against the Peasant* (New York: Collier Macmillan, 1961), is well known, Professor Mitrany was among the first to recommend the adoption in Britain of the institution of an Ombudsman.

Charles Pentland, a Canadian, was born in Montreal and educated at the University of British Columbia and the London School of Economics, where he completed his Ph.D. in International Relations. His thesis—published by Faber and Faber, under the title *International Theory and European Integration*—is a critical analysis of integration theory in the light of recent European experience and of theoretical developments in the field of International Relations. Since 1969 he has been teaching International Relations in the Department of Political Studies, Queen's University, in Kingston, Canada. He has published articles on international organisation and Canadian foreign policy.

Jean Siotis. Since 1958 he has been successively Assistant, Instructor and Professor at the Graduate Institute of International Studies and, since 1960, Assistant and later Consultant with the Carnegie Endowment for International Peace. His main areas of specialisation are International Organisation and Theory of International Relations. He has published books and articles in both of these areas.

Kjell Skjelsbaek received his Magister of political science from the University of Oslo in 1970. He has been associated with the International Peace Research Institute, Oslo, since 1967, and became its executive director in 1973. He was a research fellow at the Center for International Affairs, Harvard University in 1970 and at the Mental Health Research Institute, the University of Michigan in 1971.

Paul Taylor received his University education at the University College of Wales, Aberystwyth, where he obtained the degrees of B.A. in Geography and International Politics, and M.Sc. (Econ). He worked as an Assistant Lecturer at the University of Liverpool 1962-1964, and as a Lecturer at the University of Hull, 1964-1966, and at the London School of Economics, 1966 to date. His published works include *International Cooperation Today* (Elek, 1971), and articles in *Political Studies, the Journal of Common Market Studies and Orbis*. His interests include European integration and international relations theory.

Thomas G. Weiss was educated at Harvard, Princeton and the Graduate Institute of International Studies. He is currently Assistant Director of the World Law Fund University Programme and has previously been associated with UNITAR and the ILO. He has published several papers .

Index